SLEEPY PRINCESS
IN THE DEMON CASTLE

13

Story & Art by
KAGIJI KUMANOMATA

NIGHTS

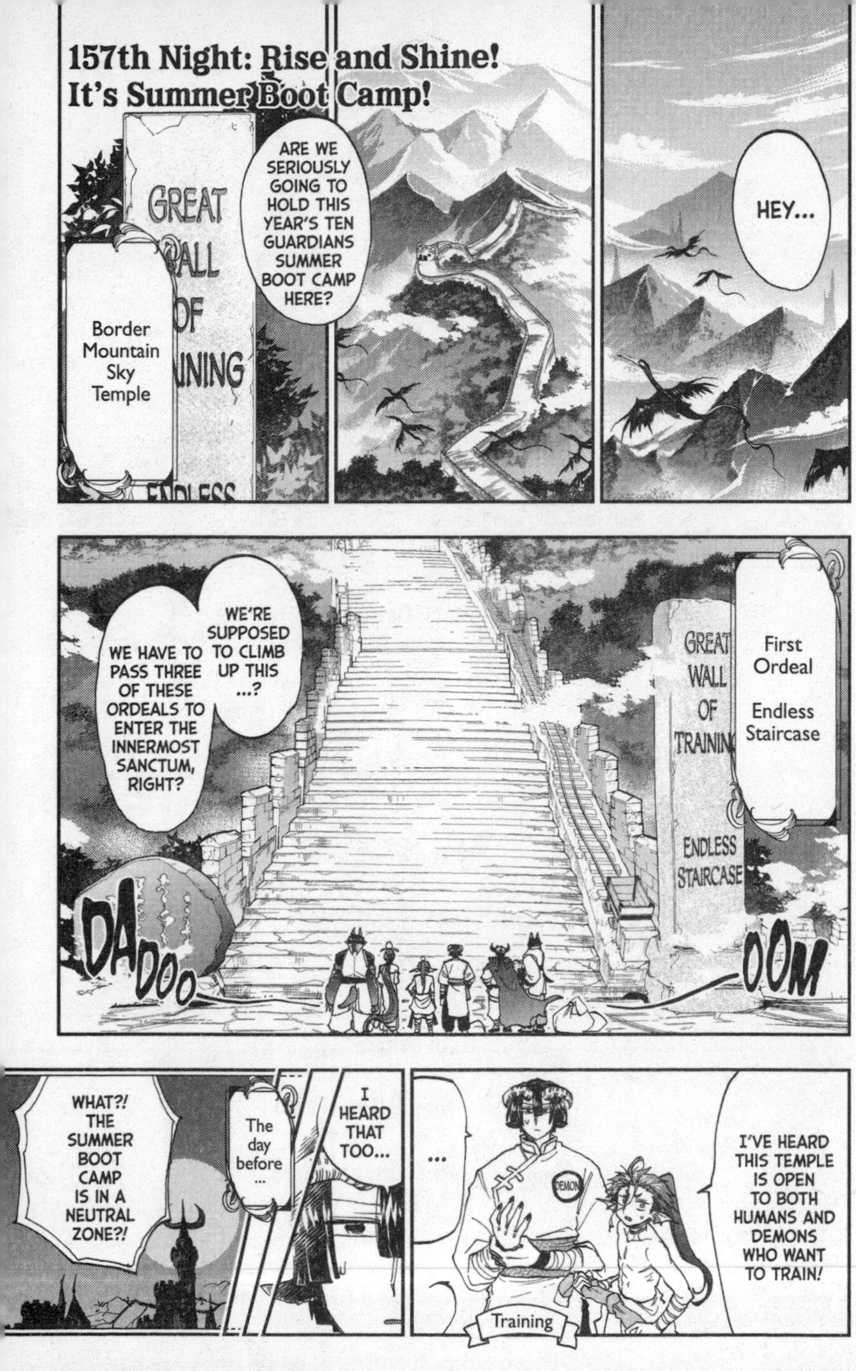
157th Night: Rise and Shine! It's Summer Boot Camp!
HEY...
ARE WE SERIOUSLY GOING TO HOLD THIS YEAR'S TEN GUARDIANS SUMMER BOOT CAMP HERE?
GREAT WALL OF TRAINING ENDLESS
Border Mountain Sky Temple
First Ordeal
Endless Staircase
GREAT WALL OF TRAINING
ENDLESS STAIRCASE
WE'RE SUPPOSED TO CLIMB UP THIS ...?
WE HAVE TO PASS THREE OF THESE ORDEALS TO ENTER THE INNERMOST SANCTUM, RIGHT?
DADOO
OOM
I'VE HEARD THIS TEMPLE IS OPEN TO BOTH HUMANS AND DEMONS WHO WANT TO TRAIN!
...
DEMON
Training
I HEARD THAT TOO...
The day before ...
WHAT?! THE SUMMER BOOT CAMP IS IN A NEUTRAL ZONE?!

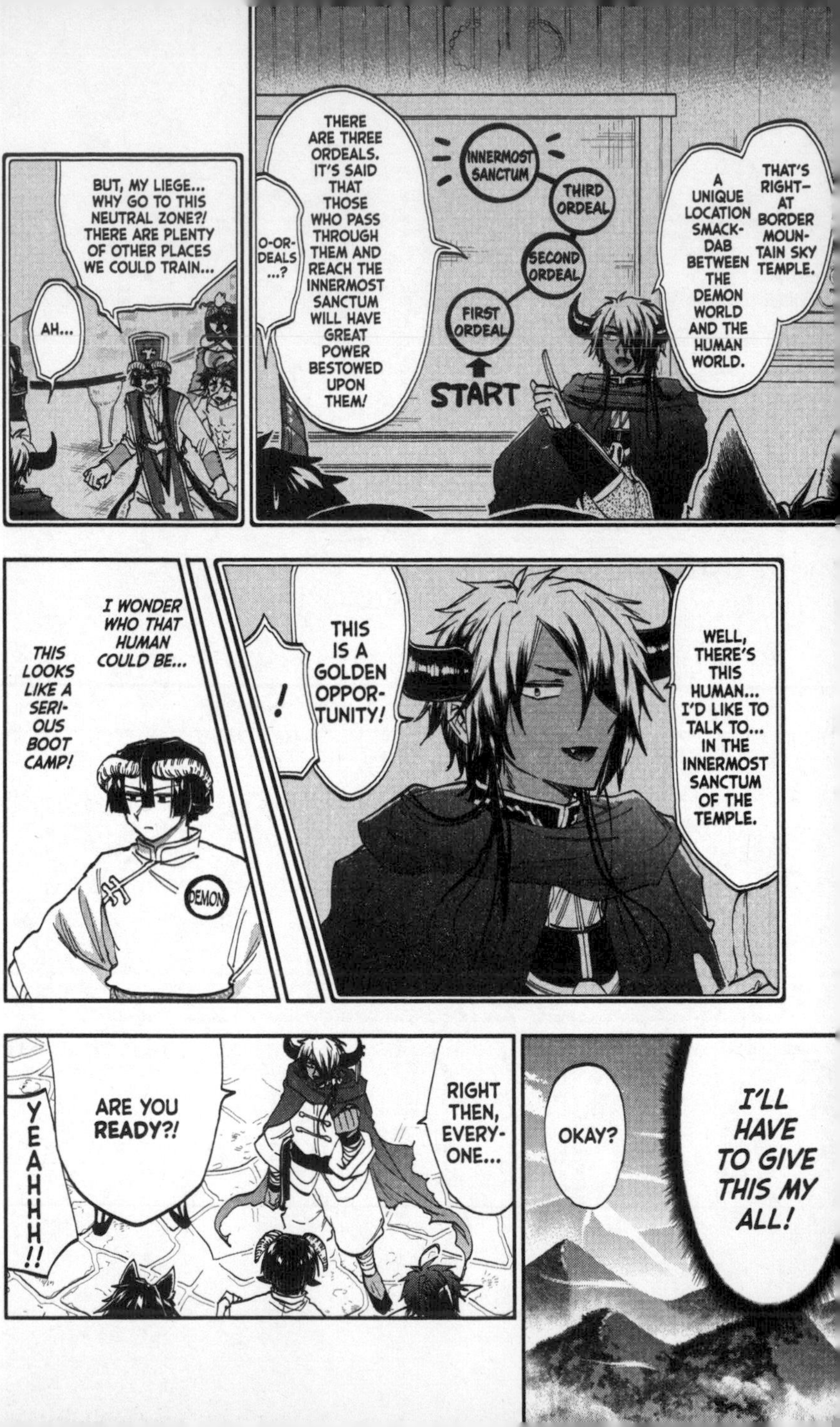
THAT'S RIGHT—AT BORDER MOUNTAIN SKY TEMPLE.
A UNIQUE LOCATION SMACK-DAB BETWEEN THE DEMON WORLD AND THE HUMAN WORLD.
INNERMOST SANCTUM
THIRD ORDEAL
SECOND ORDEAL
FIRST ORDEAL
START
THERE ARE THREE ORDEALS. IT'S SAID THAT THOSE WHO PASS THROUGH THEM AND REACH THE INNERMOST SANCTUM WILL HAVE GREAT POWER BESTOWED UPON THEM!
O-ORDEALS...?
BUT, MY LIEGE... WHY GO TO THIS NEUTRAL ZONE?! THERE ARE PLENTY OF OTHER PLACES WE COULD TRAIN...
AH...
WELL, THERE'S THIS HUMAN... I'D LIKE TO TALK TO... IN THE INNERMOST SANCTUM OF THE TEMPLE.
THIS IS A GOLDEN OPPORTUNITY!
!
I WONDER WHO THAT HUMAN COULD BE...
THIS LOOKS LIKE A SERIOUS BOOT CAMP!
DEMON
I'LL HAVE TO GIVE THIS MY ALL!
OKAY?
RIGHT THEN, EVERYONE...
ARE YOU READY?!
YEAHHHH!!

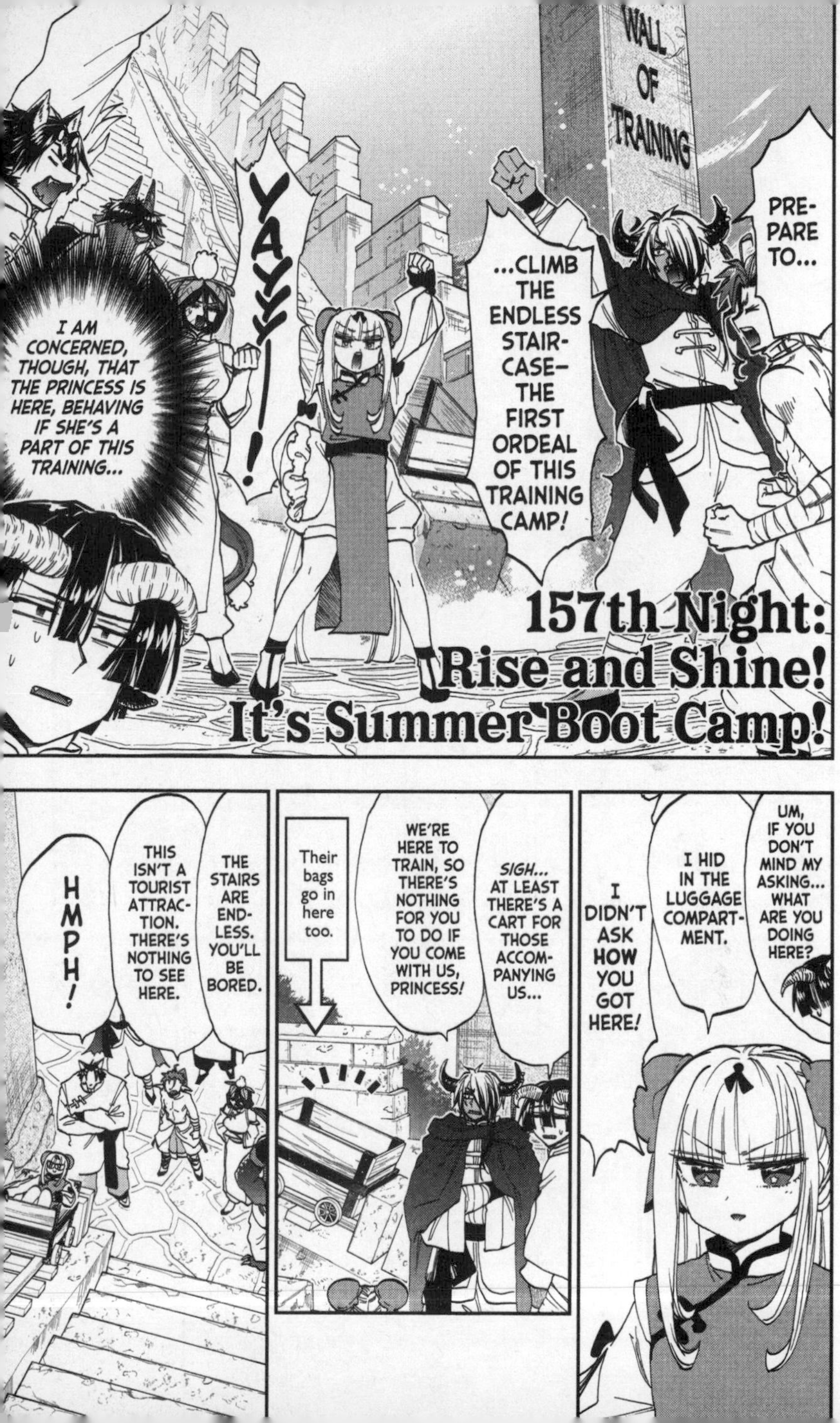
WALL OF TRAINING
PRE-PARE TO...
...CLIMB THE ENDLESS STAIR-CASE— THE FIRST ORDEAL OF THIS TRAINING CAMP!
YAYYY—!
I AM CONCERNED, THOUGH, THAT THE PRINCESS IS HERE, BEHAVING IF SHE'S A PART OF THIS TRAINING...
157th Night: Rise and Shine! It's Summer Boot Camp!
UM, IF YOU DON'T MIND MY ASKING... WHAT ARE YOU DOING HERE?
I HID IN THE LUGGAGE COMPART-MENT.
I DIDN'T ASK HOW YOU GOT HERE!
SIGH... AT LEAST THERE'S A CART FOR THOSE ACCOM-PANYING US...
WE'RE HERE TO TRAIN, SO THERE'S NOTHING FOR YOU TO DO IF YOU COME WITH US, PRINCESS!
Their bags go in here too.
THE STAIRS ARE END-LESS. YOU'LL BE BORED.
THIS ISN'T A TOURIST ATTRAC-TION. THERE'S NOTHING TO SEE HERE.
HMPH!

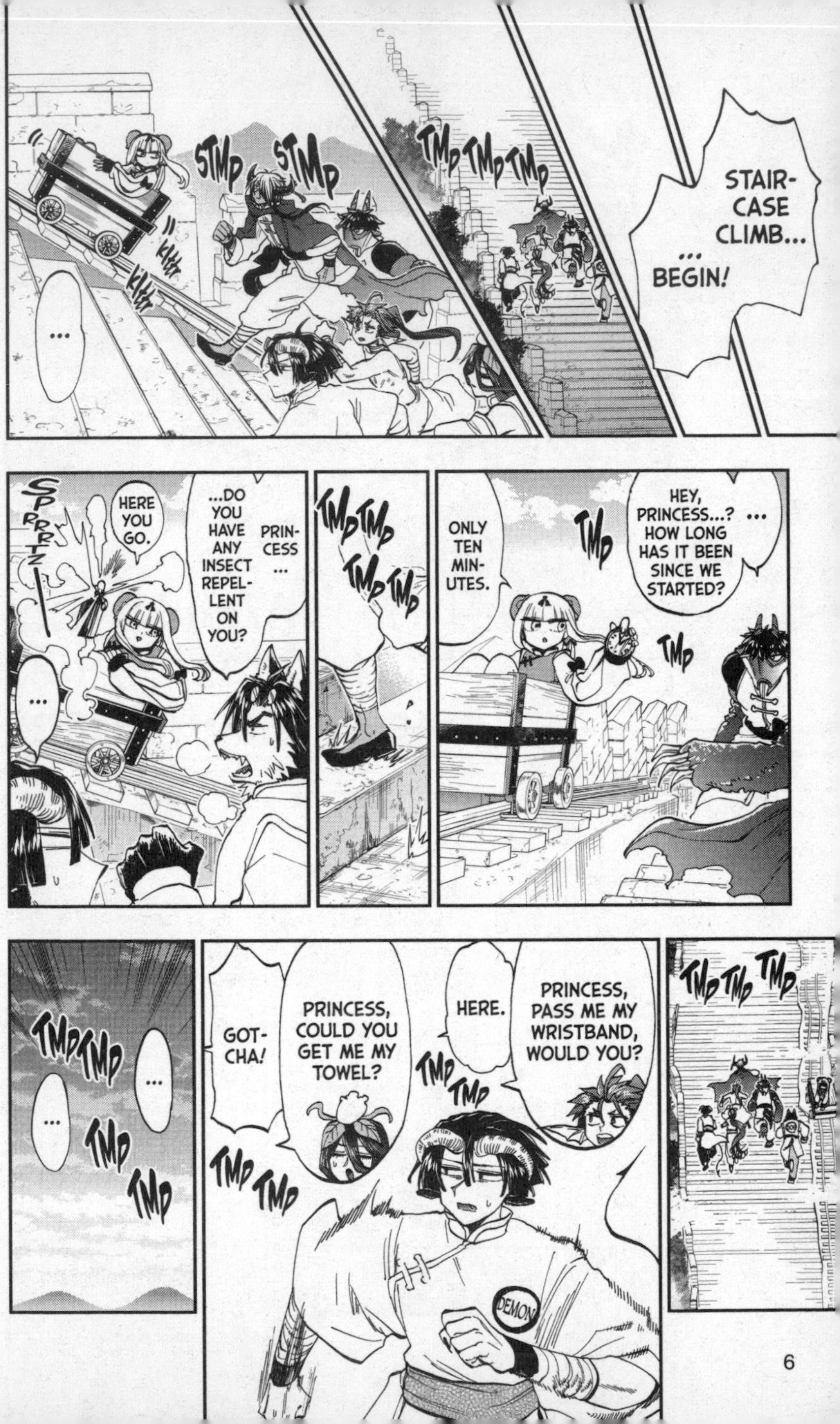
STAIR-CASE CLIMB...
... BEGIN!
TMP TMP TMP
STIMP STIMP
KLITTER KLITTER
...
HEY, PRINCESS...? HOW LONG HAS IT BEEN SINCE WE STARTED?
...
TMP
TMP
ONLY TEN MIN-UTES.
TMP TMP TMP TMP
PRIN-CESS ...
...DO YOU HAVE ANY INSECT REPEL-LENT ON YOU?
HERE YOU GO.
SPRRRTZ
...
TMP TMP TMP
PRINCESS, PASS ME MY WRISTBAND, WOULD YOU?
HERE.
TMP TMP
PRINCESS, COULD YOU GET ME MY TOWEL?
GOT-CHA!
TMP TMP
DEMON
TMP TMP
...
...
TMP
TMP

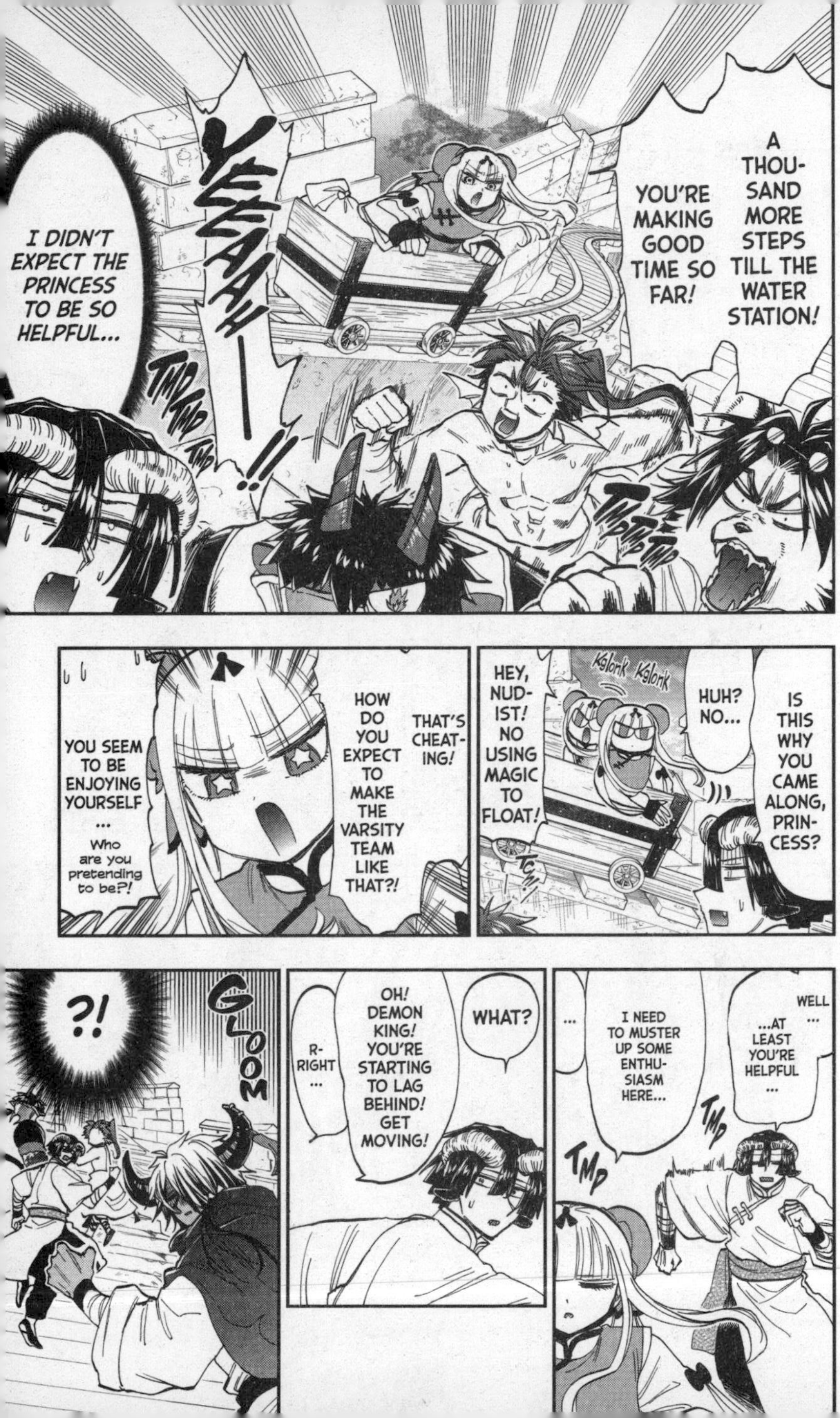
A THOUSAND MORE STEPS TILL THE WATER STATION!
YOU'RE MAKING GOOD TIME SO FAR!
YEEAAAH—!!
TMP TMP TMP
TMPTMPTMP
I DIDN'T EXPECT THE PRINCESS TO BE SO HELPFUL...
IS THIS WHY YOU CAME ALONG, PRINCESS?
HUH? NO...
Kglonk Kglonk
HEY, NUDIST! NO USING MAGIC TO FLOAT!
THAT'S CHEATING!
HOW DO YOU EXPECT TO MAKE THE VARSITY TEAM LIKE THAT?!
YOU SEEM TO BE ENJOYING YOURSELF ... Who are you pretending to be?!
WELL ...
...AT LEAST YOU'RE HELPFUL ...
TMP
I NEED TO MUSTER UP SOME ENTHUSIASM HERE...
...
TMP
WHAT?
OH! DEMON KING! YOU'RE STARTING TO LAG BEHIND! GET MOVING!
R-RIGHT ...
GLOOM
?!

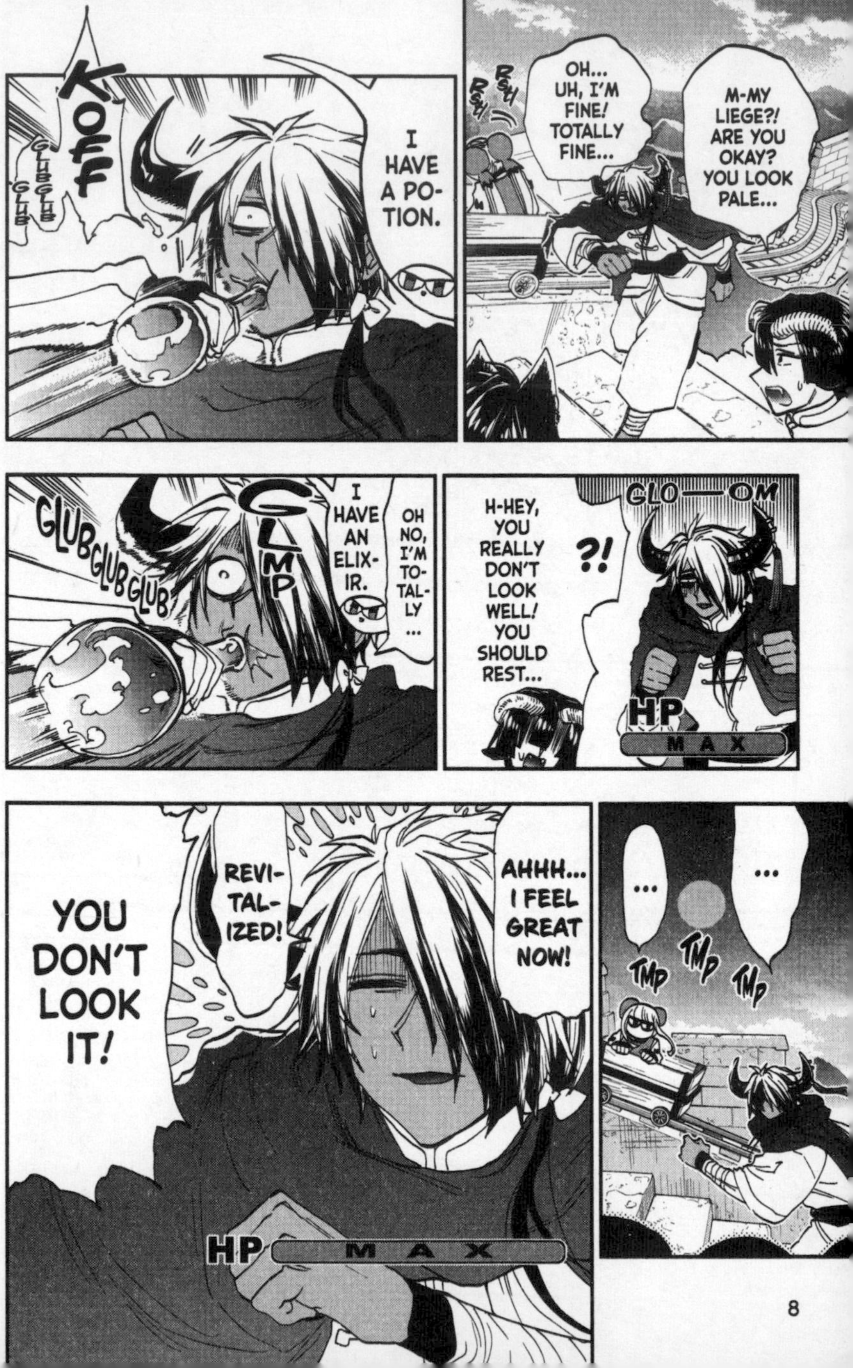
M-MY LIEGE?! ARE YOU OKAY? YOU LOOK PALE...
OH... UH, I'M FINE! TOTALLY FINE...
RSH RSH
I HAVE A PO-TION.
KOFF
GLUB GLUB GLUB
GLO—OM
H-HEY, YOU REALLY DON'T LOOK WELL! YOU SHOULD REST...
?!
HP MAX
OH NO, I'M TO-TAL-LY ...
I HAVE AN ELIX-IR.
GLMP
GLUBGLUBGLUB
...
...
TMP TMP TMP
AHHH... I FEEL GREAT NOW!
REVI-TAL-IZED!
YOU DON'T LOOK IT!
HP MAX

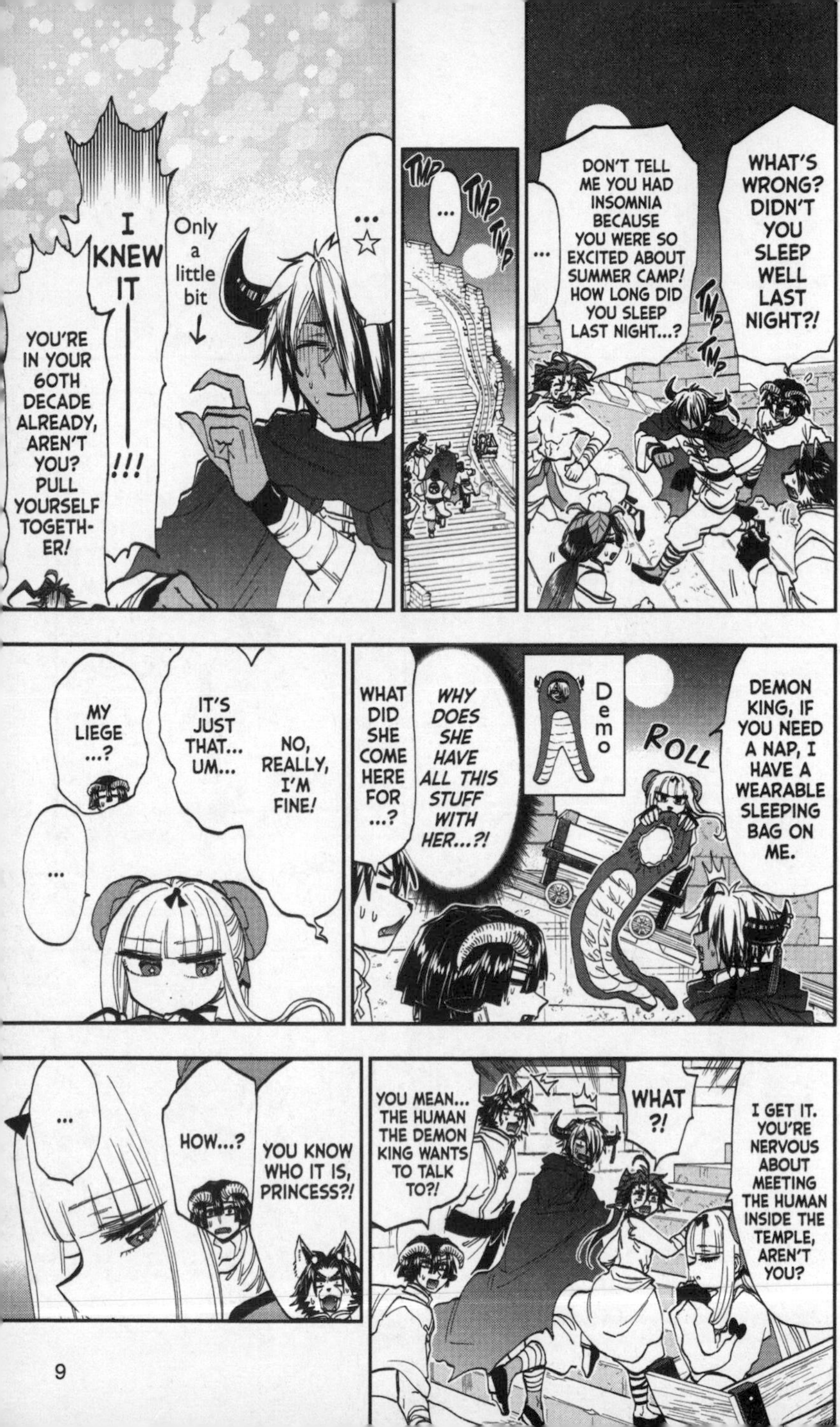
WHAT'S WRONG? DIDN'T YOU SLEEP WELL LAST NIGHT?!
TMP TMP
DON'T TELL ME YOU HAD INSOMNIA BECAUSE YOU WERE SO EXCITED ABOUT SUMMER CAMP! HOW LONG DID YOU SLEEP LAST NIGHT...?
...
TMP TMP TMP
...
...☆
Only a little bit ↓
I KNEW IT—!!!
YOU'RE IN YOUR 60TH DECADE ALREADY, AREN'T YOU? PULL YOURSELF TOGETHER!
DEMON KING, IF YOU NEED A NAP, I HAVE A WEARABLE SLEEPING BAG ON ME.
ROLL
Demo
WHY DOES SHE HAVE ALL THIS STUFF WITH HER...?!
WHAT DID SHE COME HERE FOR ...?
NO, REALLY, I'M FINE!
IT'S JUST THAT... UM...
MY LIEGE ...?
...
I GET IT. YOU'RE NERVOUS ABOUT MEETING THE HUMAN INSIDE THE TEMPLE, AREN'T YOU?
WHAT ?!
YOU MEAN... THE HUMAN THE DEMON KING WANTS TO TALK TO?!
YOU KNOW WHO IT IS, PRINCESS?!
HOW...?
...

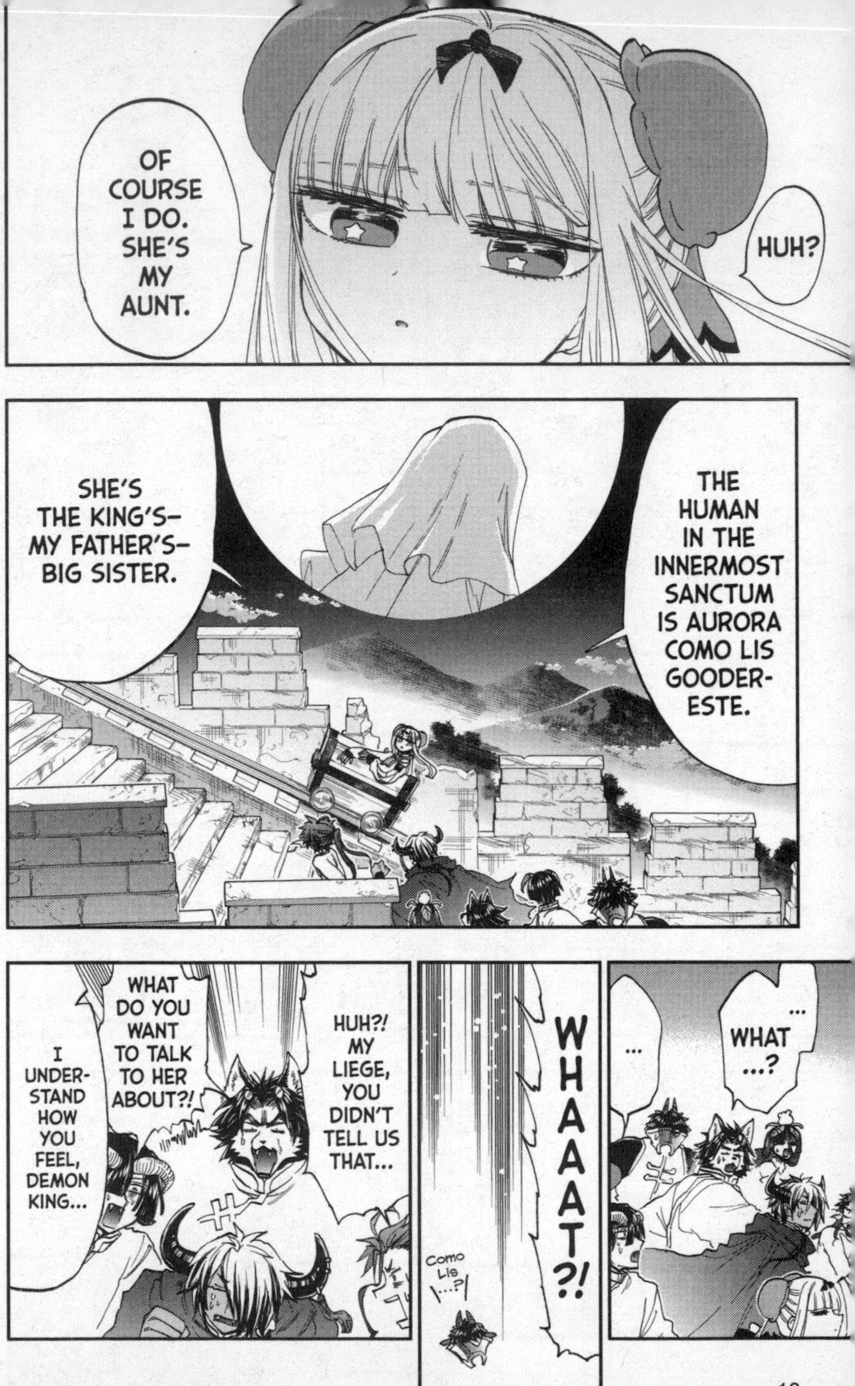
HUH?
OF COURSE I DO. SHE'S MY AUNT.
THE HUMAN IN THE INNERMOST SANCTUM IS AURORA COMO LIS GOODER-ESTE.
SHE'S THE KING'S—MY FATHER'S—BIG SISTER.
... WHAT ...?
...
WHAAAAT?!
Como Lis \...?/
HUH?! MY LIEGE, YOU DIDN'T TELL US THAT...
WHAT DO YOU WANT TO TALK TO HER ABOUT?!
I UNDER-STAND HOW YOU FEEL, DEMON KING...

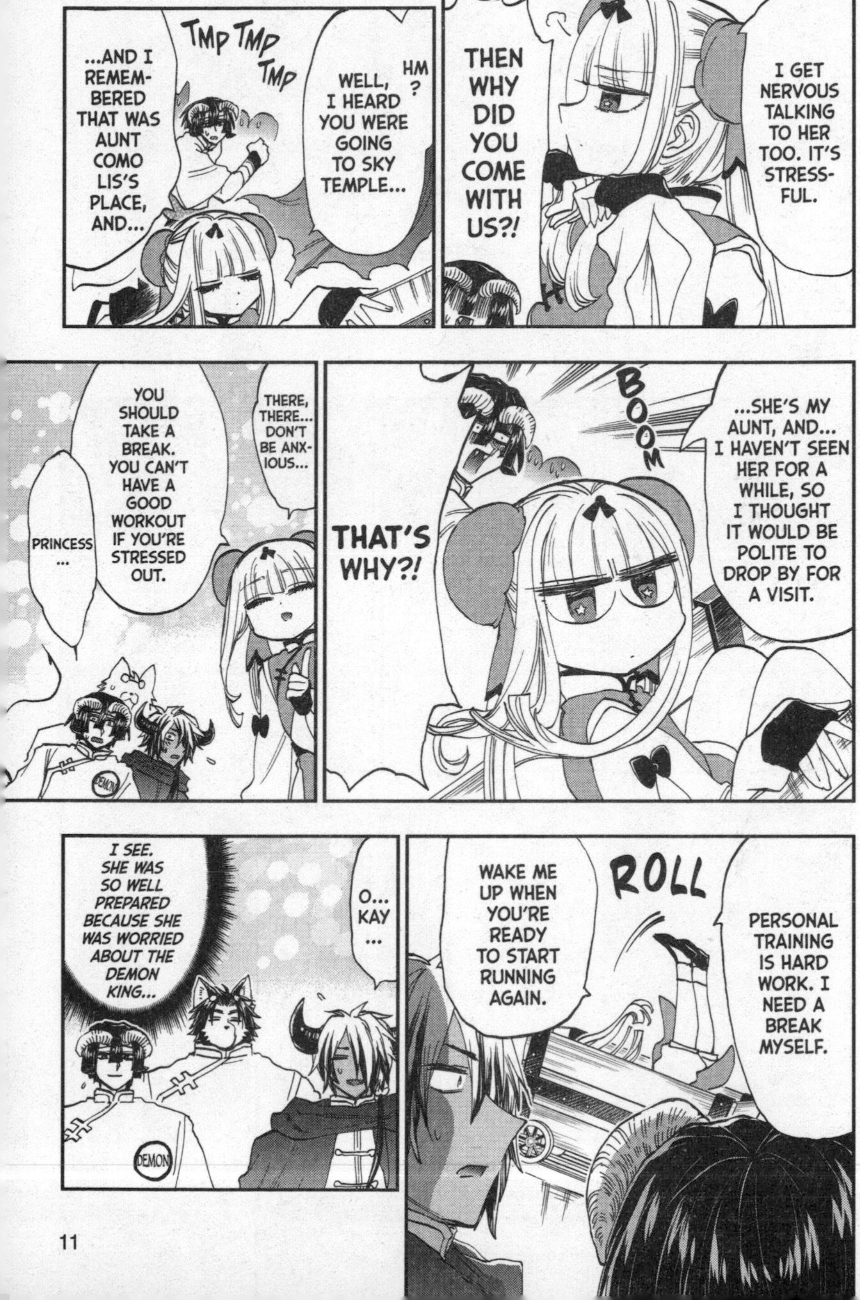
I GET NERVOUS TALKING TO HER TOO. IT'S STRESSFUL.
THEN WHY DID YOU COME WITH US?!
HM?
WELL, I HEARD YOU WERE GOING TO SKY TEMPLE...
TMP TMP TMP
...AND I REMEMBERED THAT WAS AUNT COMO LIS'S PLACE, AND...
...SHE'S MY AUNT, AND... I HAVEN'T SEEN HER FOR A WHILE, SO I THOUGHT IT WOULD BE POLITE TO DROP BY FOR A VISIT.
BOOM
THAT'S WHY?!
THERE, THERE... DON'T BE ANXIOUS...
YOU SHOULD TAKE A BREAK. YOU CAN'T HAVE A GOOD WORKOUT IF YOU'RE STRESSED OUT.
PRINCESS...
DEMON
PERSONAL TRAINING IS HARD WORK. I NEED A BREAK MYSELF.
ROLL
WAKE ME UP WHEN YOU'RE READY TO START RUNNING AGAIN.
O... KAY...
I SEE. SHE WAS SO WELL PREPARED BECAUSE SHE WAS WORRIED ABOUT THE DEMON KING...
DEMON

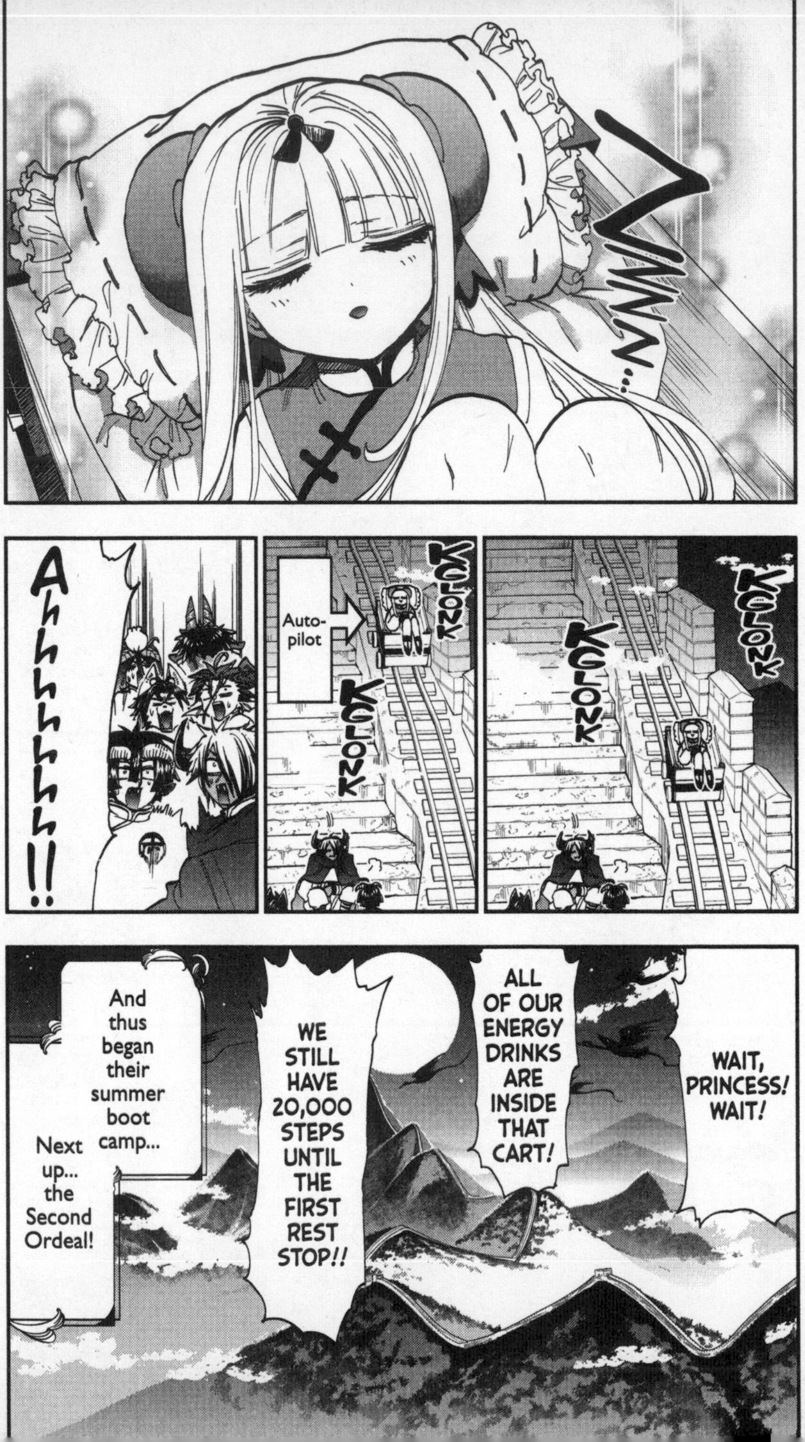
ZZZZ...
KGLONK
KGLONK
KGLONK
Auto-pilot
KGLONK
Ahhhhhhhh!!
WAIT, PRINCESS! WAIT!
ALL OF OUR ENERGY DRINKS ARE INSIDE THAT CART!
WE STILL HAVE 20,000 STEPS UNTIL THE FIRST REST STOP!!
And thus began their summer boot camp...
Next up... the Second Ordeal!

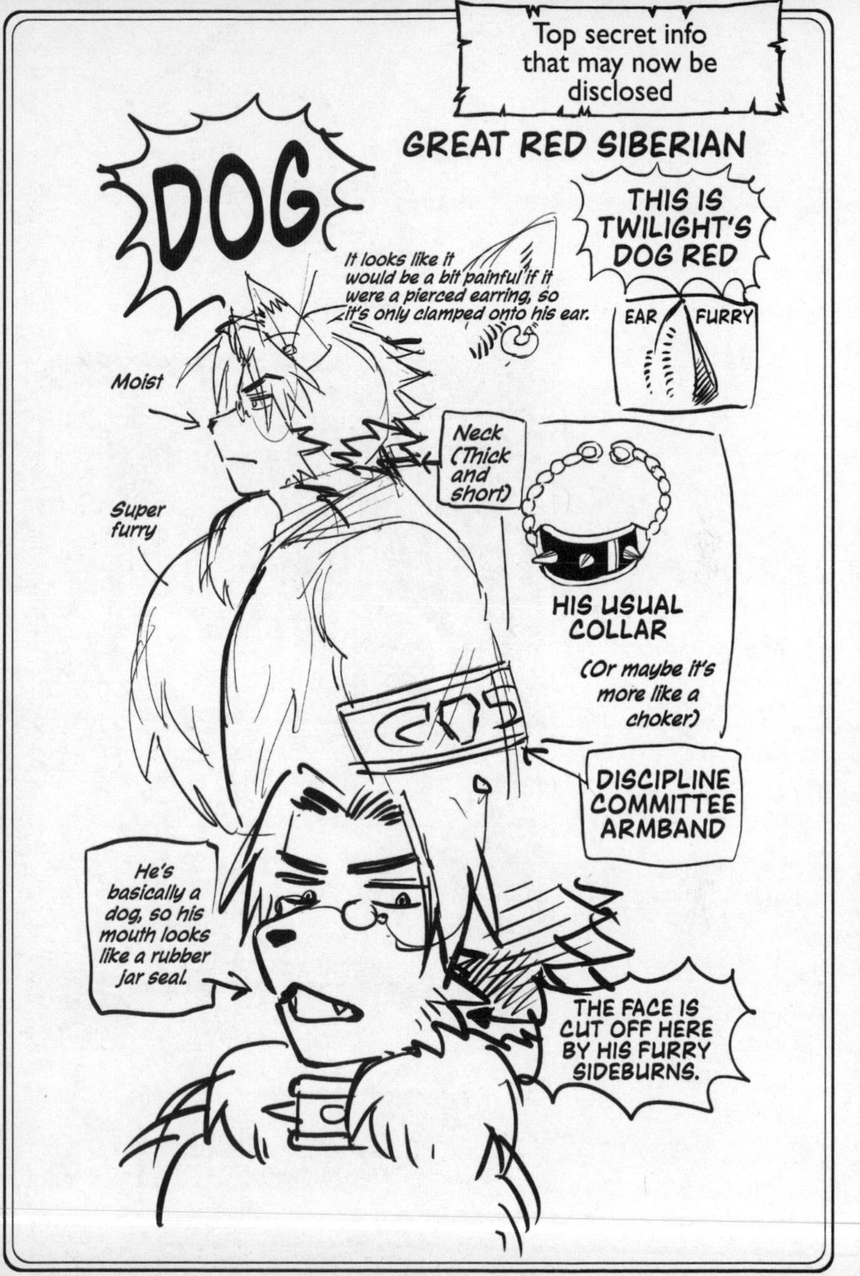
Top secret info that may now be disclosed
GREAT RED SIBERIAN
DOG
THIS IS TWILIGHT'S DOG RED
It looks like it would be a bit painful if it were a pierced earring, so it's only clamped onto his ear.
EAR
FURRY
Moist
Neck (Thick and short)
Super furry
HIS USUAL COLLAR
(Or maybe it's more like a choker)
DISCIPLINE COMMITTEE ARMBAND
THE FACE IS CUT OFF HERE BY HIS FURRY SIDEBURNS.
He's basically a dog, so his mouth looks like a rubber jar seal.

Would you like to change your class?

11 changes remaining

▶Yes

No ▼

Weaver

"This textile isn't made of Ghost Shroud. ♡"

▼

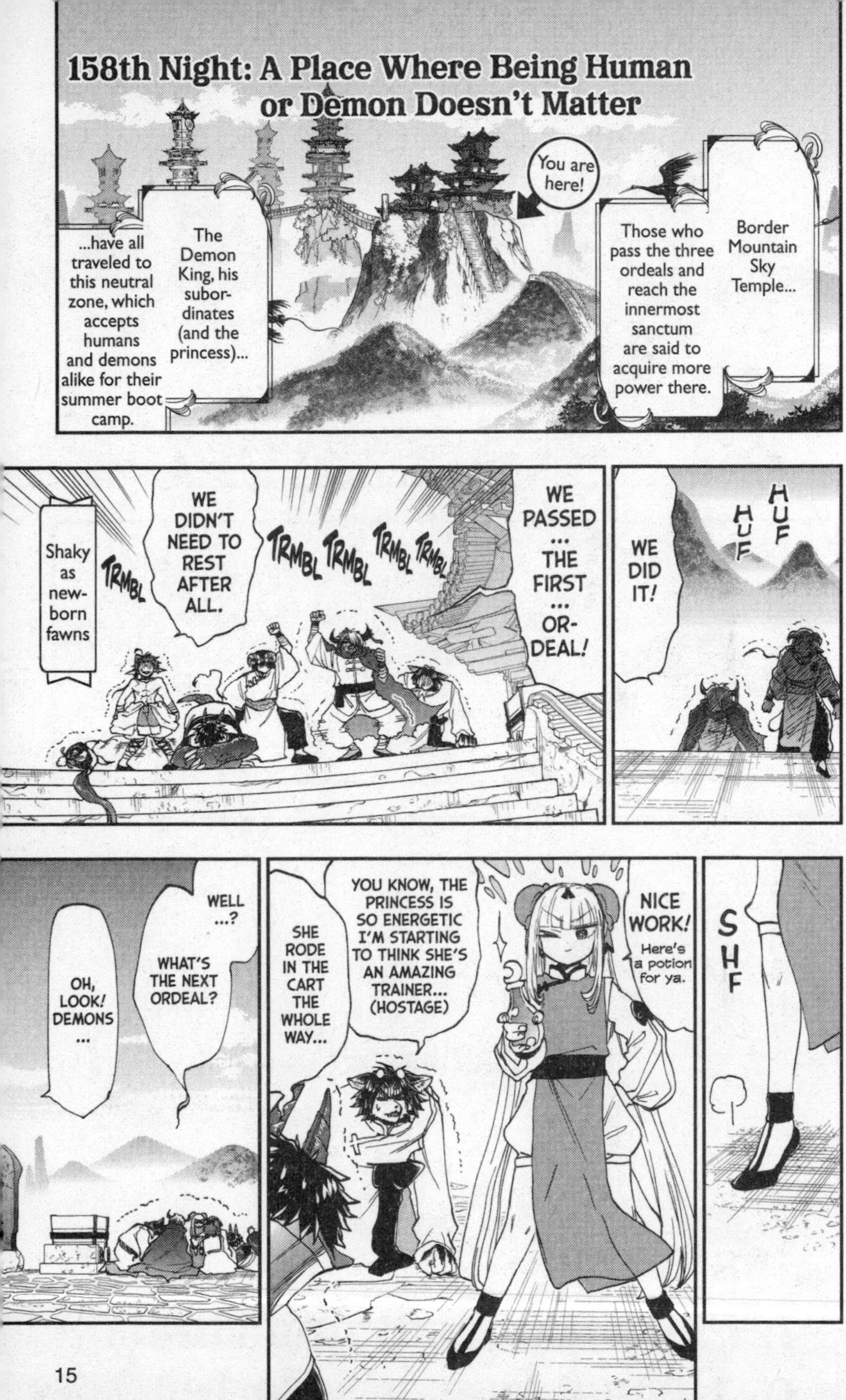
158th Night: A Place Where Being Human or Demon Doesn't Matter
Border Mountain Sky Temple...
Those who pass the three ordeals and reach the innermost sanctum are said to acquire more power there.
You are here!
The Demon King, his subor-dinates (and the princess)...
...have all traveled to this neutral zone, which accepts humans and demons alike for their summer boot camp.
HUF HUF
HUF
WE DID IT!
WE PASSED... THE FIRST... OR-DEAL!
TRMBL TRMBL TRMBL TRMBL
WE DIDN'T NEED TO REST AFTER ALL.
TRMBL
Shaky as new-born fawns
SHF
NICE WORK!
Here's a potion for ya.
YOU KNOW, THE PRINCESS IS SO ENERGETIC I'M STARTING TO THINK SHE'S AN AMAZING TRAINER... (HOSTAGE)
SHE RODE IN THE CART THE WHOLE WAY...
WELL...?
WHAT'S THE NEXT ORDEAL?
OH, LOOK! DEMONS...

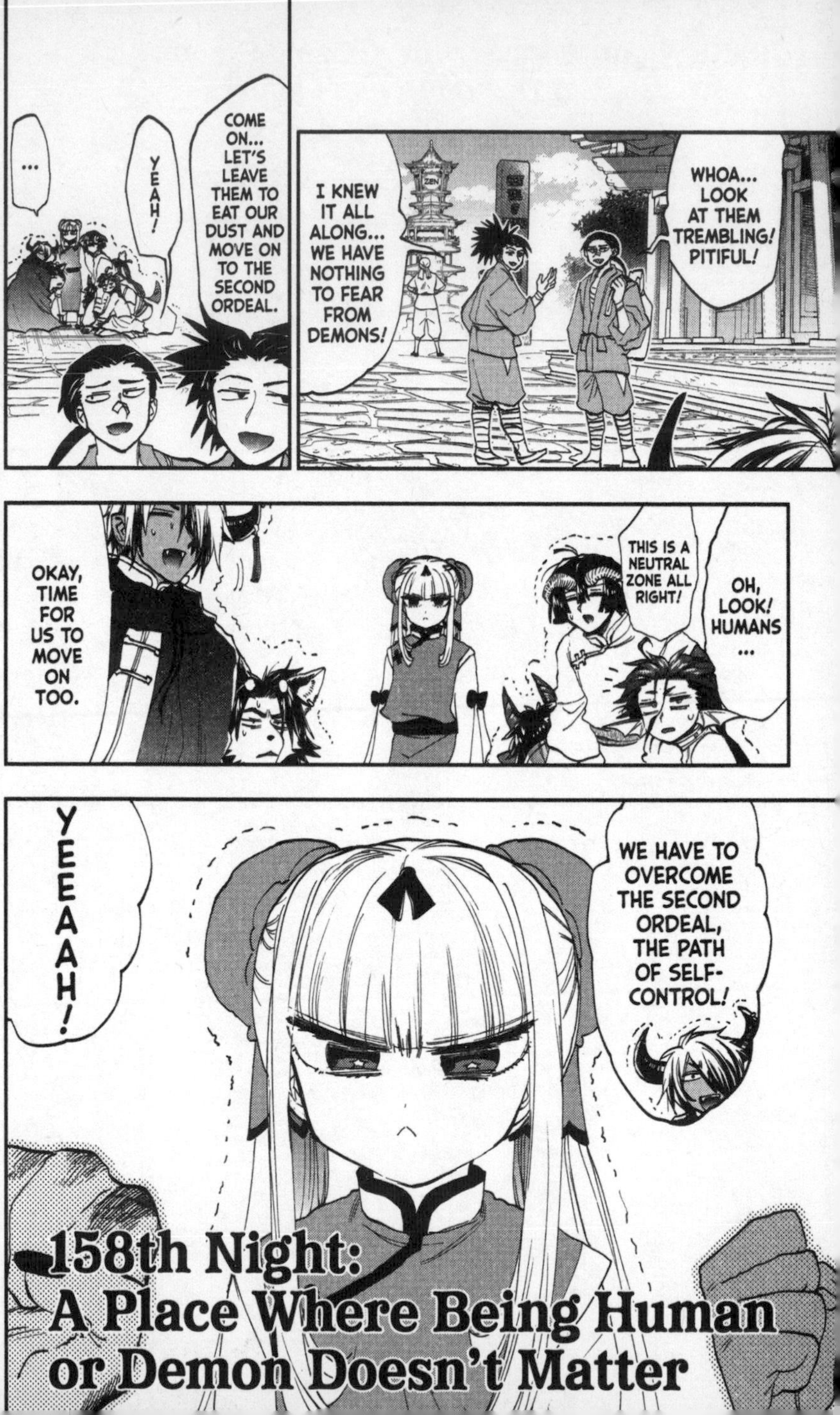
WHOA... LOOK AT THEM TREMBLING! PITIFUL!
ZEN
I KNEW IT ALL ALONG... WE HAVE NOTHING TO FEAR FROM DEMONS!
COME ON... LET'S LEAVE THEM TO EAT OUR DUST AND MOVE ON TO THE SECOND ORDEAL.
YEAH!
...
OH, LOOK! HUMANS...
THIS IS A NEUTRAL ZONE ALL RIGHT!
OKAY, TIME FOR US TO MOVE ON TOO.
WE HAVE TO OVERCOME THE SECOND ORDEAL, THE PATH OF SELF-CONTROL!
YEEAAAH!
158th Night:
A Place Where Being Human or Demon Doesn't Matter

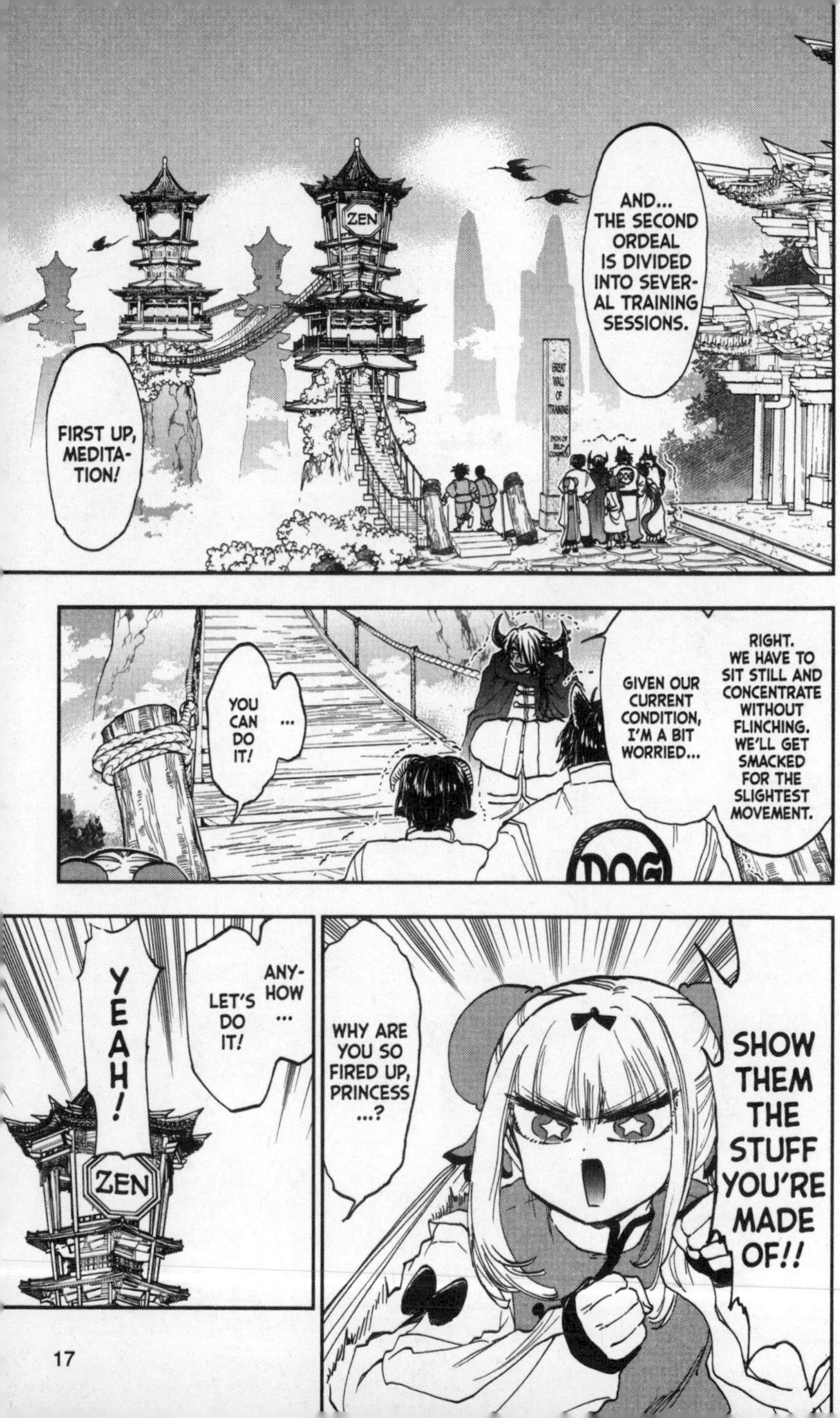
AND... THE SECOND ORDEAL IS DIVIDED INTO SEVER-AL TRAINING SESSIONS.
ZEN
GREAT WALL OF TRAINING
FIRST UP, MEDITA-TION!
RIGHT. WE HAVE TO SIT STILL AND CONCENTRATE WITHOUT FLINCHING. WE'LL GET SMACKED FOR THE SLIGHTEST MOVEMENT.
GIVEN OUR CURRENT CONDITION, I'M A BIT WORRIED...
...
YOU CAN DO IT!
DOG
SHOW THEM THE STUFF YOU'RE MADE OF!!
WHY ARE YOU SO FIRED UP, PRINCESS ...?
ANY-HOW ...
LET'S DO IT!
YEAH!
ZEN

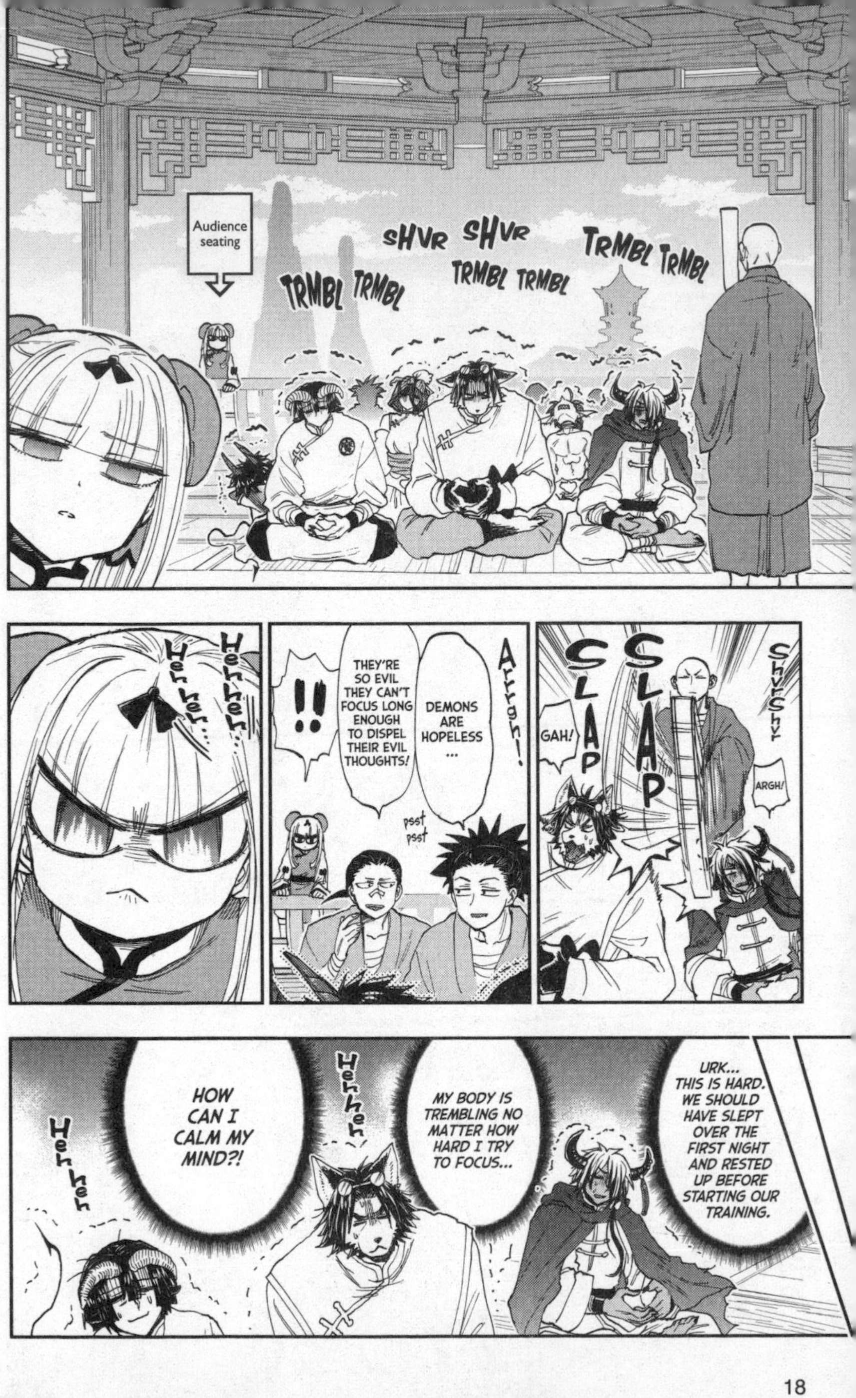
TRMBL TRMBL
SHVR SHVR
TRMBL TRMBL
TRMBL TRMBL
Audience seating
Shvr Shvr
SLAP
SLAP
GAH!
ARGH!
Arrgh!
DEMONS ARE HOPELESS...
THEY'RE SO EVIL THEY CAN'T FOCUS LONG ENOUGH TO DISPEL THEIR EVIL THOUGHTS!
!!
psst psst
Heh heh heh...
Heh heh...
URK... THIS IS HARD. WE SHOULD HAVE SLEPT OVER THE FIRST NIGHT AND RESTED UP BEFORE STARTING OUR TRAINING.
MY BODY IS TREMBLING NO MATTER HOW HARD I TRY TO FOCUS...
Heh heh
HOW CAN I CALM MY MIND?!
Heh heh

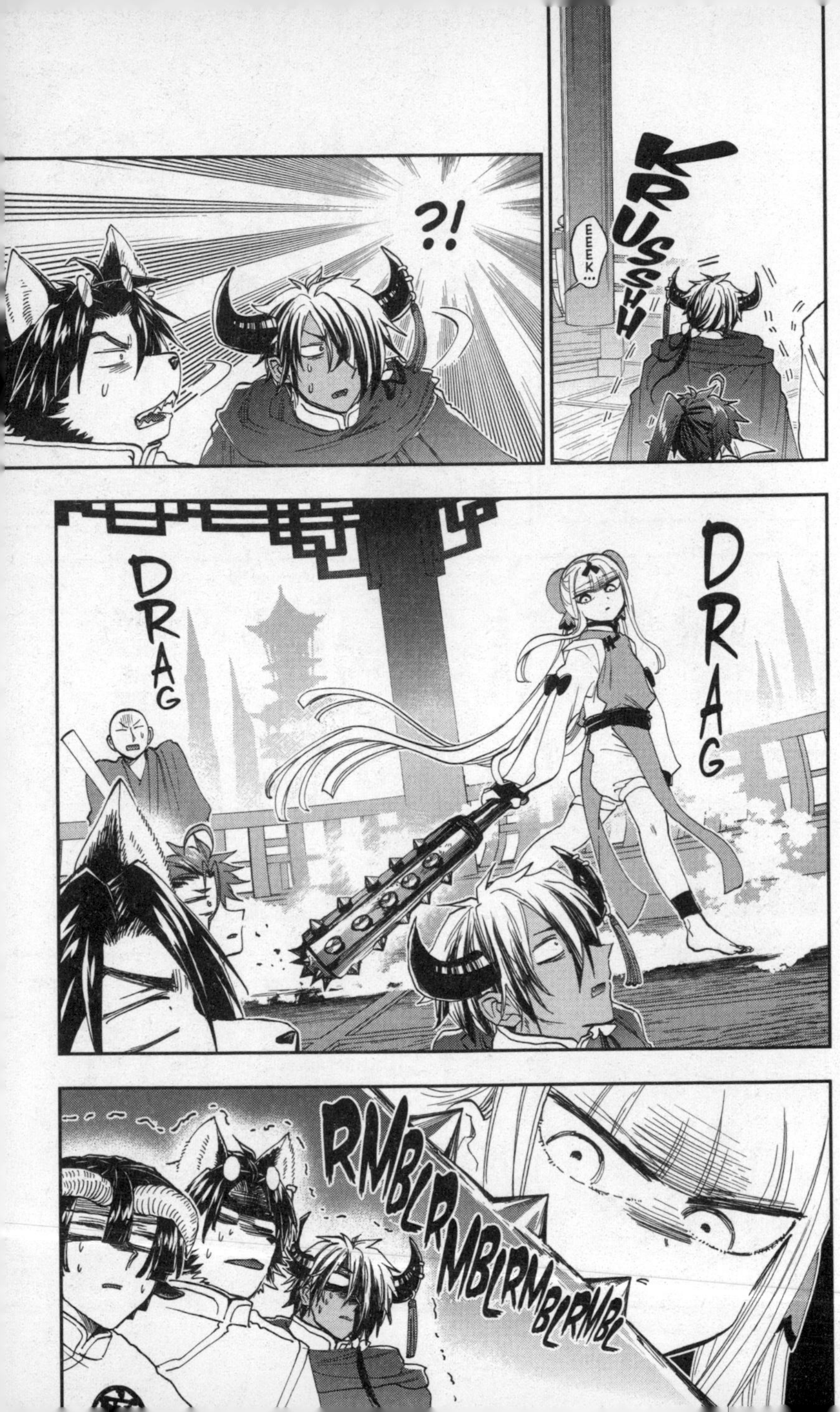
KRUSSHH
EEEK...
?!
DRAG
DRAG
RMBLRMBLRMBLRMBLRMBL

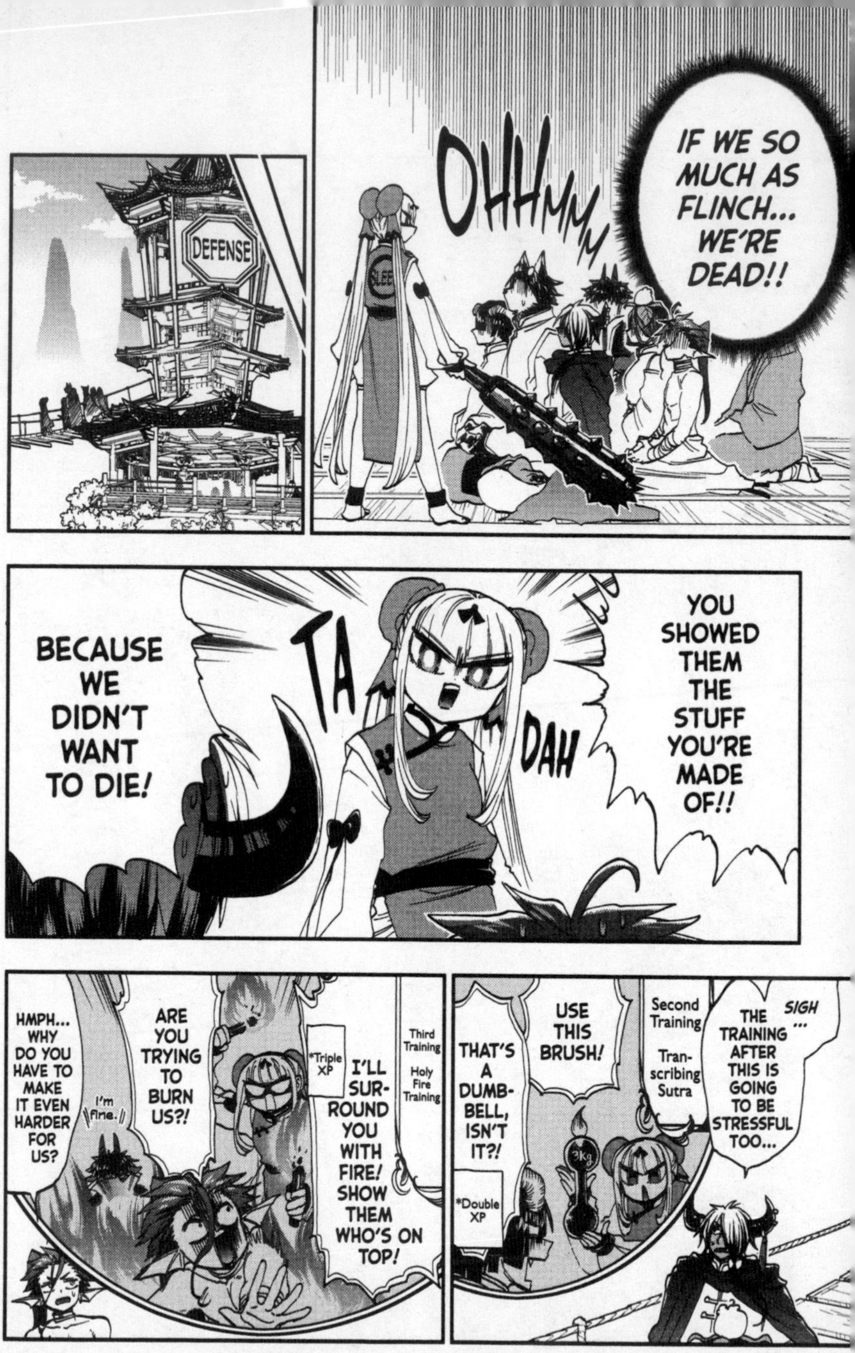
IF WE SO MUCH AS FLINCH... WE'RE DEAD!!
OHHMMMM
DEFENSE
YOU SHOWED THEM THE STUFF YOU'RE MADE OF!!
TA
DAH
BECAUSE WE DIDN'T WANT TO DIE!
SIGH...
THE TRAINING AFTER THIS IS GOING TO BE STRESSFUL TOO...
Second Training
Tran-scribing Sutra
USE THIS BRUSH!
THAT'S A DUMB-BELL, ISN'T IT?!
3kg
*Double XP
Third Training
Holy Fire Training
I'LL SUR-ROUND YOU WITH FIRE! SHOW THEM WHO'S ON TOP!
*Triple XP
ARE YOU TRYING TO BURN US?!
I'm fine.
HMPH... WHY DO YOU HAVE TO MAKE IT EVEN HARDER FOR US?

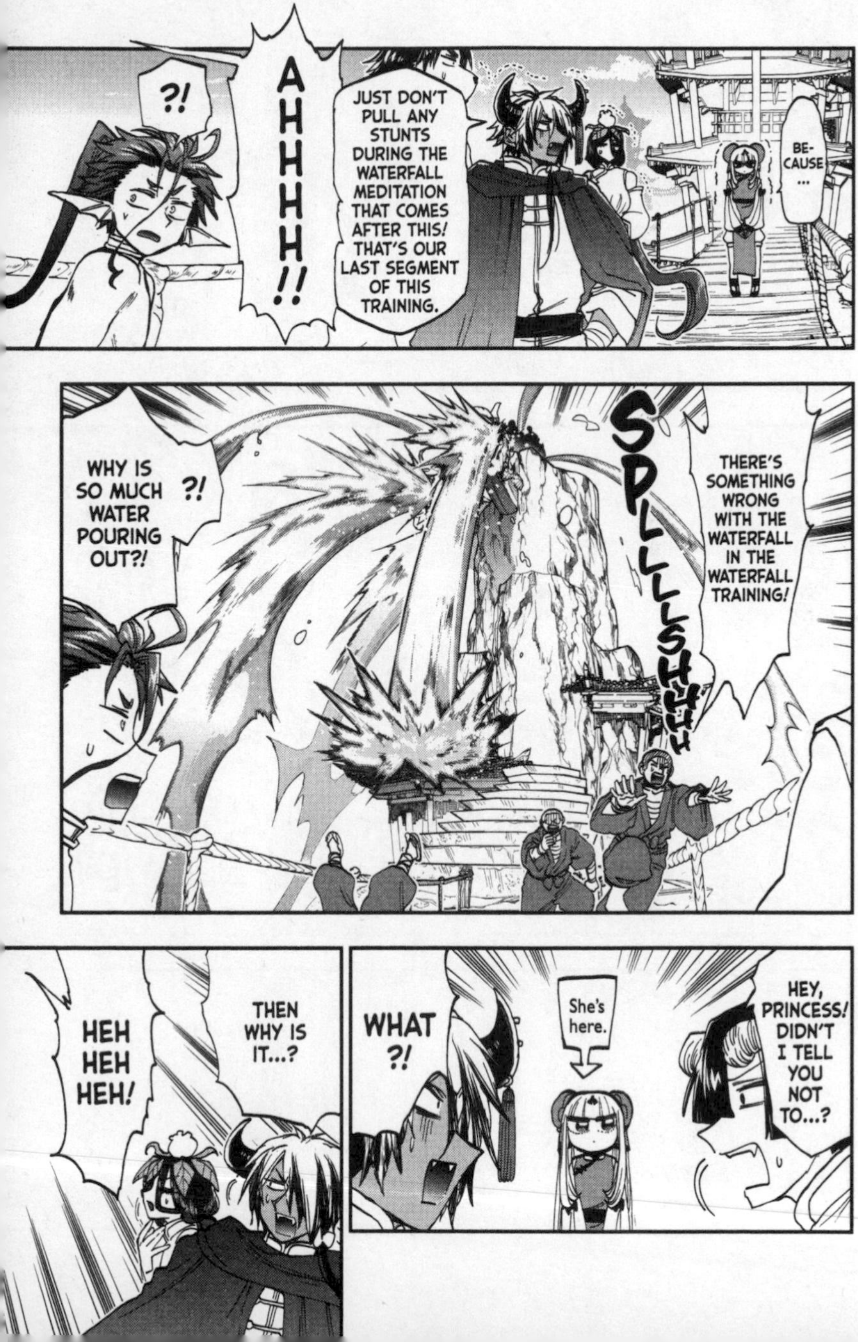
BE-CAUSE ...
JUST DON'T PULL ANY STUNTS DURING THE WATERFALL MEDITATION THAT COMES AFTER THIS! THAT'S OUR LAST SEGMENT OF THIS TRAINING.
AHHHH!!
?!
THERE'S SOMETHING WRONG WITH THE WATERFALL IN THE WATERFALL TRAINING!
SPLLLLSHHHH
WHY IS SO MUCH WATER POURING OUT?!
?!
HEY, PRINCESS! DIDN'T I TELL YOU NOT TO...?
She's here.
WHAT ?!
THEN WHY IS IT...?
HEH HEH HEH!

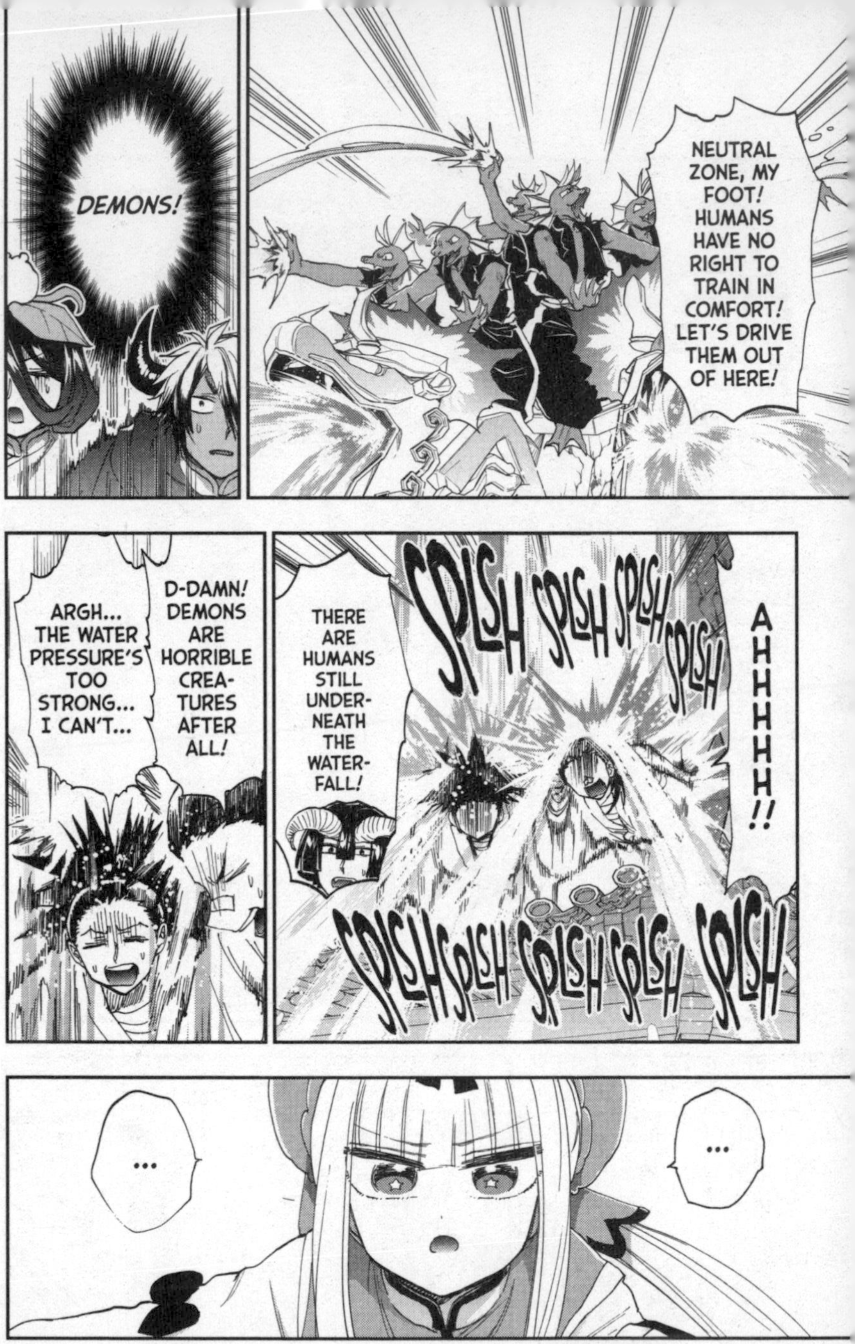
NEUTRAL ZONE, MY FOOT! HUMANS HAVE NO RIGHT TO TRAIN IN COMFORT! LET'S DRIVE THEM OUT OF HERE!
DEMONS!
SPLSH SPLSH SPLSH SPLSH
AHHHHH!!
SPLSH SPLSH SPLSH SPLSH SPLSH
THERE ARE HUMANS STILL UNDERNEATH THE WATERFALL!
D-DAMN! DEMONS ARE HORRIBLE CREATURES AFTER ALL!
ARGH... THE WATER PRESSURE'S TOO STRONG... I CAN'T...
...
...

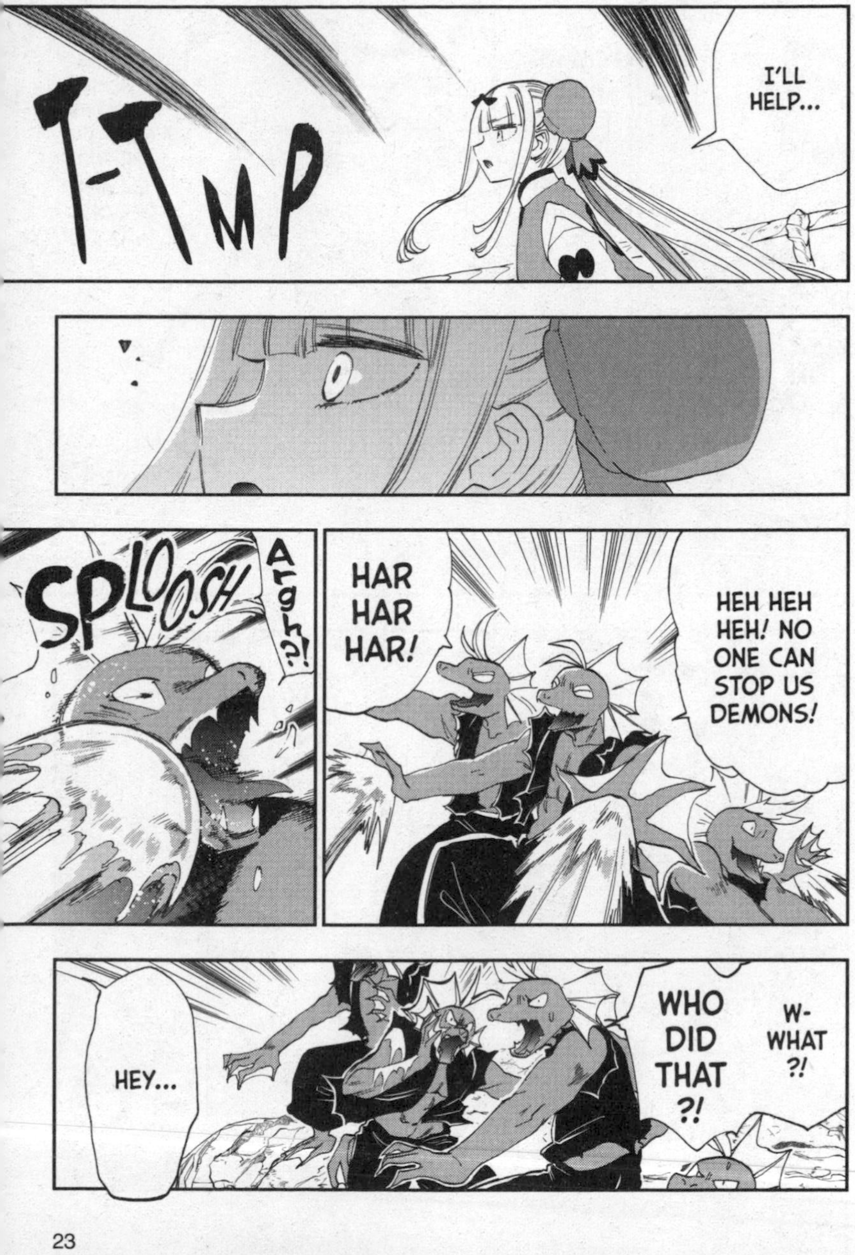
I'LL HELP...
T-TMP
HEH HEH HEH! NO ONE CAN STOP US DEMONS!
HAR HAR HAR!
Argh?!
SPLOOSH
W-WHAT?!
WHO DID THAT?!
HEY...

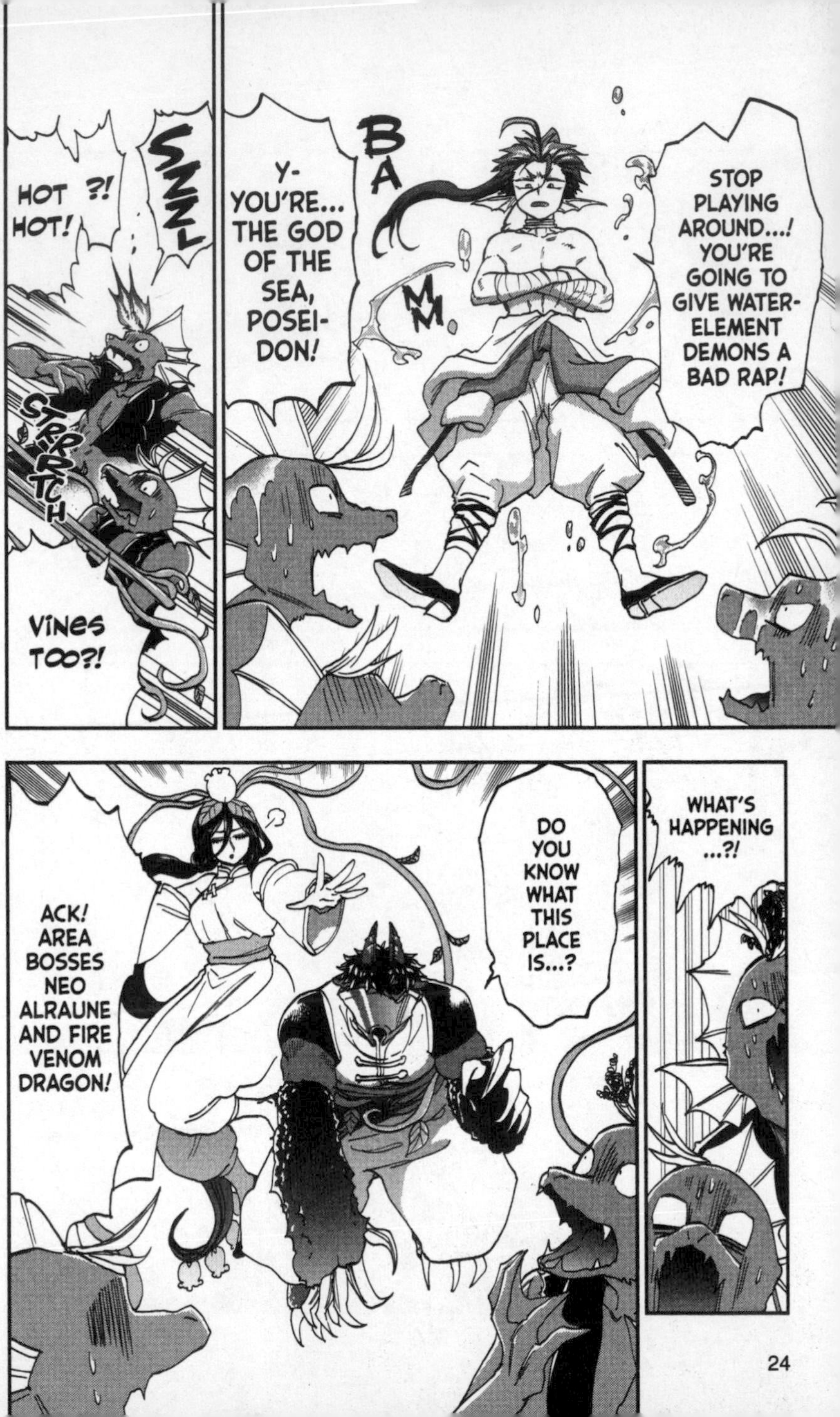
STOP PLAYING AROUND...! YOU'RE GOING TO GIVE WATER-ELEMENT DEMONS A BAD RAP!
BAMM
Y-YOU'RE... THE GOD OF THE SEA, POSEIDON!
SZZZL
HOT ?! HOT!
STRRRTCH
VINES TOO?!
WHAT'S HAPPENING ...?!
DO YOU KNOW WHAT THIS PLACE IS...?
ACK! AREA BOSSES NEO ALRAUNE AND FIRE VENOM DRAGON!

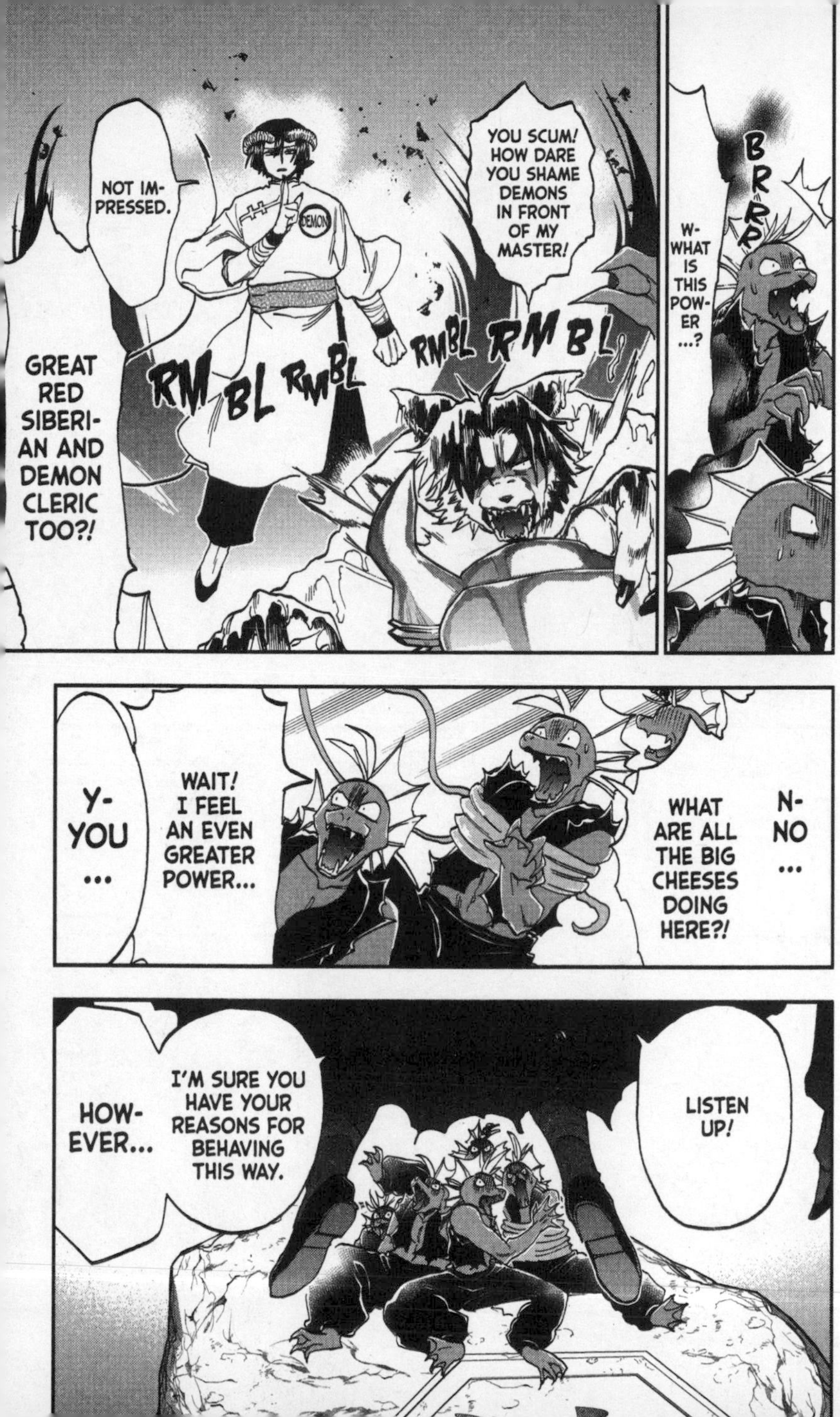
BRRR
W-WHAT IS THIS POWER ...?
YOU SCUM! HOW DARE YOU SHAME DEMONS IN FRONT OF MY MASTER!
RMBL RMBL
RMBL RMBL
NOT IMPRESSED.
DEMON
GREAT RED SIBERIAN AND DEMON CLERIC TOO?!
N-NO ...
WHAT ARE ALL THE BIG CHEESES DOING HERE?!
WAIT! I FEEL AN EVEN GREATER POWER...
Y-YOU ...
LISTEN UP!
I'M SURE YOU HAVE YOUR REASONS FOR BEHAVING THIS WAY.
HOWEVER...

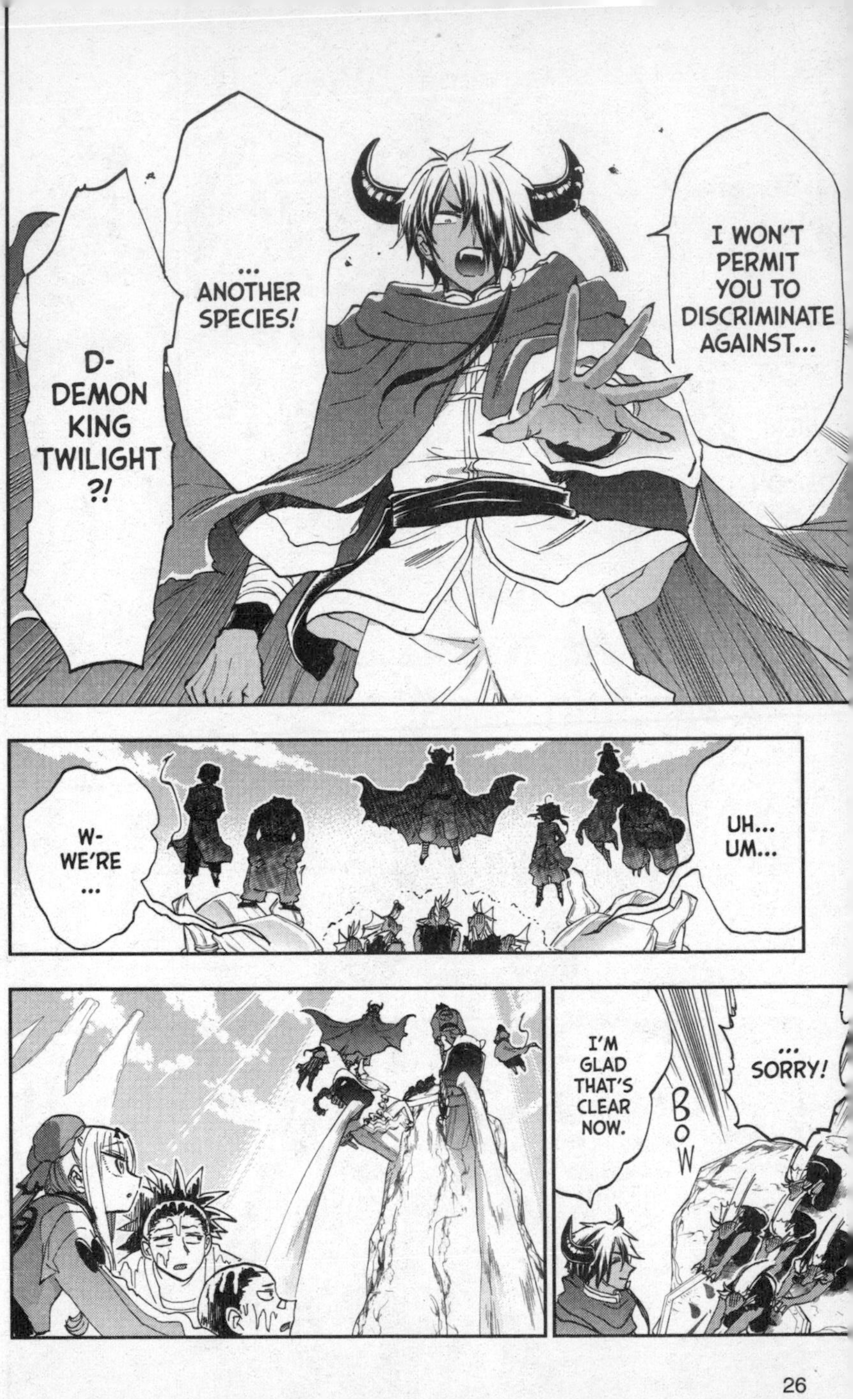
I WON'T PERMIT YOU TO DISCRIMINATE AGAINST...
... ANOTHER SPECIES!
D-DEMON KING TWILIGHT ?!
UH... UM...
W-WE'RE ...
... SORRY!
BOW
I'M GLAD THAT'S CLEAR NOW.

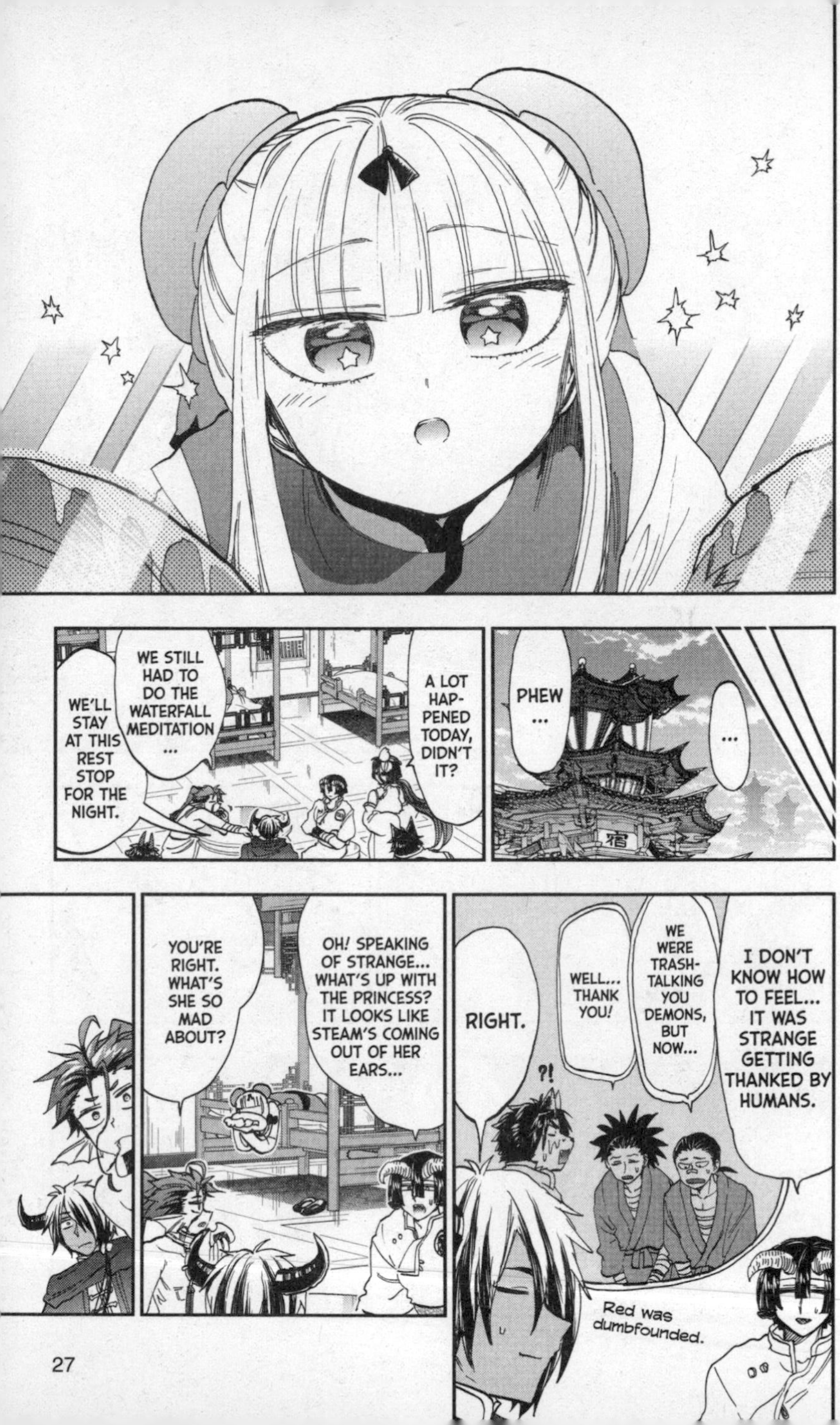
...
PHEW ...
A LOT HAPPENED TODAY, DIDN'T IT?
WE STILL HAD TO DO THE WATERFALL MEDITATION ...
WE'LL STAY AT THIS REST STOP FOR THE NIGHT.
I DON'T KNOW HOW TO FEEL... IT WAS STRANGE GETTING THANKED BY HUMANS.
WE WERE TRASH-TALKING YOU DEMONS, BUT NOW...
WELL... THANK YOU!
RIGHT.
?!
Red was dumbfounded.
OH! SPEAKING OF STRANGE... WHAT'S UP WITH THE PRINCESS? IT LOOKS LIKE STEAM'S COMING OUT OF HER EARS...
YOU'RE RIGHT. WHAT'S SHE SO MAD ABOUT?

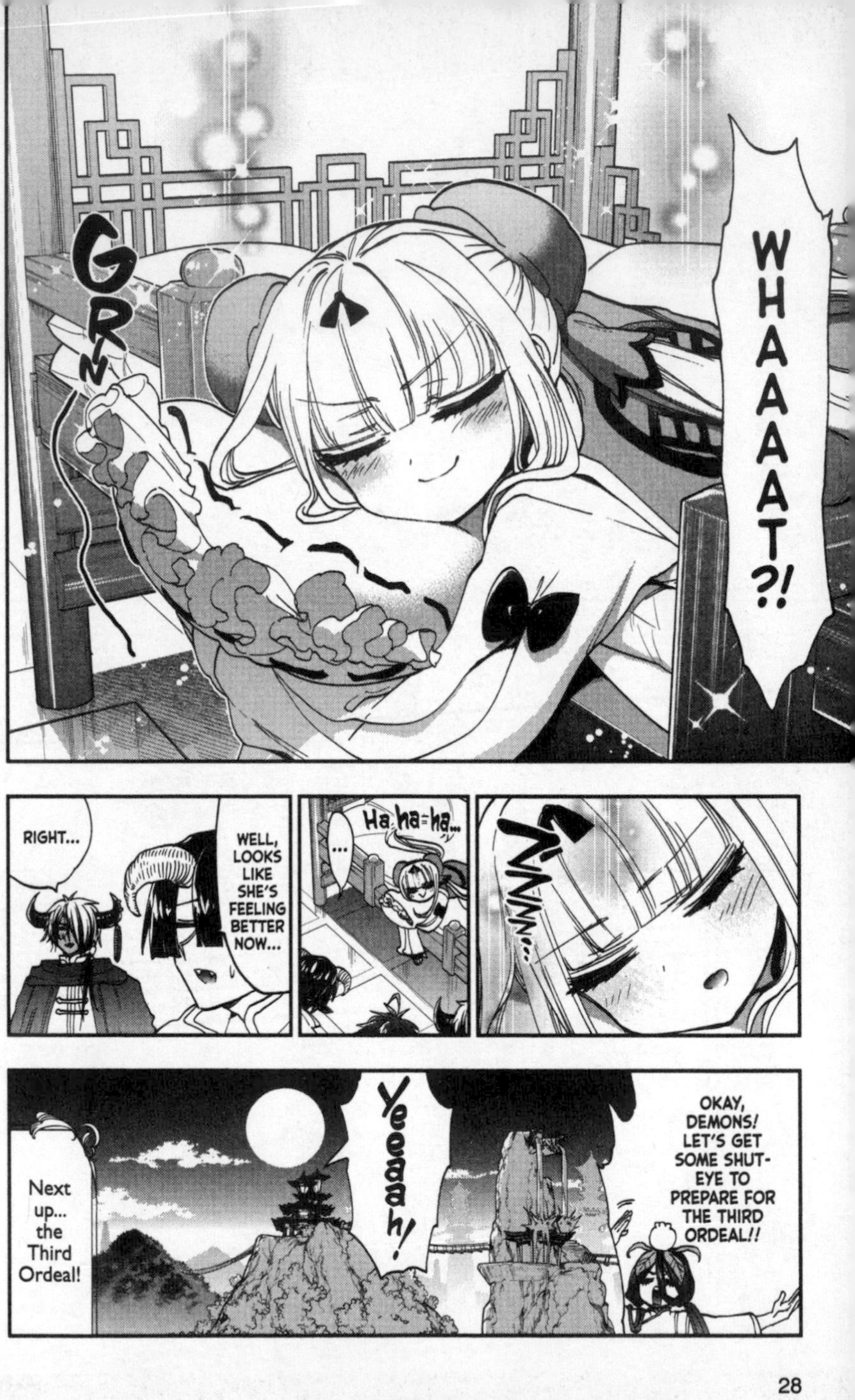
WHAAAAAAT?!
GRIN
Ha ha ha...
...
WELL, LOOKS LIKE SHE'S FEELING BETTER NOW...
RIGHT...
OKAY, DEMONS! LET'S GET SOME SHUT-EYE TO PREPARE FOR THE THIRD ORDEAL!!
Yeeaaah!
Next up... the Third Ordeal!

Border Mountain Sky Temple

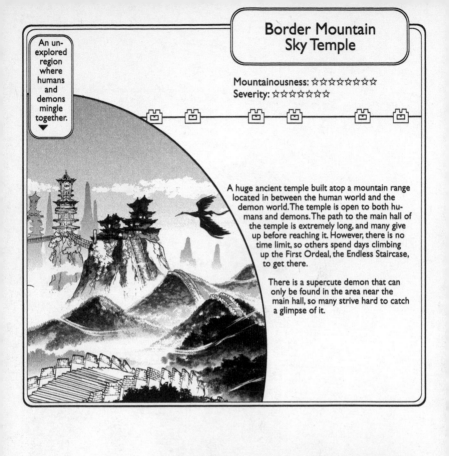

An unexplored region where humans and demons mingle together.

Mountainousness: ☆☆☆☆☆☆☆☆☆
Severity: ☆☆☆☆☆☆☆

A huge ancient temple built atop a mountain range located in between the human world and the demon world. The temple is open to both humans and demons. The path to the main hall of the temple is extremely long, and many give up before reaching it. However, there is no time limit, so others spend days climbing up the First Ordeal, the Endless Staircase, to get there.

There is a supercute demon that can only be found in the area near the main hall, so many strive hard to catch a glimpse of it.

SHAKKASHAKKA
The dog turns into a sprinkler after jumping into the waterfall!
SPLASHHH
The Demon King is completely used to it.
Meh... Just keep your distance.

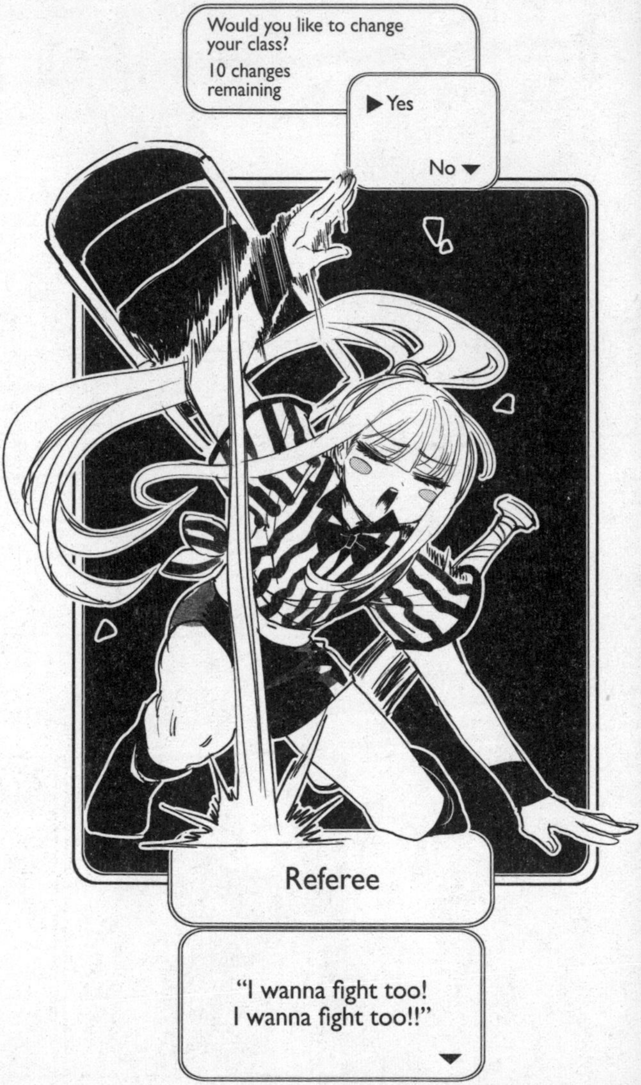
Would you like to change your class?
10 changes remaining
▶Yes
No
Referee
"I wanna fight too! I wanna fight too!!"

159th Night: Falling for My Fallen Panda Angel

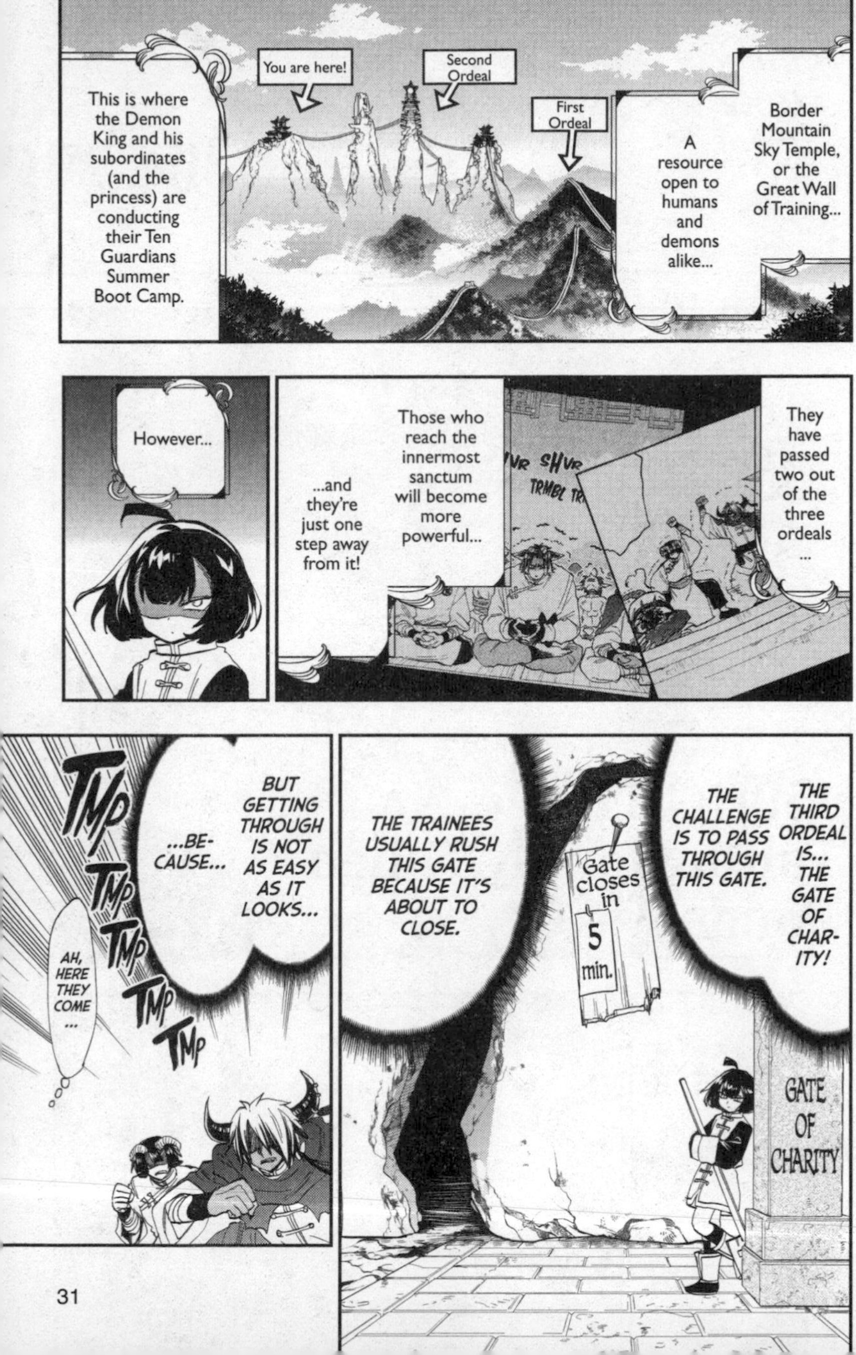
Border Mountain Sky Temple, or the Great Wall of Training...
A resource open to humans and demons alike...
First Ordeal
Second Ordeal
You are here!
This is where the Demon King and his subordinates (and the princess) are conducting their Ten Guardians Summer Boot Camp.
They have passed two out of the three ordeals ...
SHVR
TRMBL
Those who reach the innermost sanctum will become more powerful...
...and they're just one step away from it!
However...
THE THIRD ORDEAL IS... THE GATE OF CHARITY!
THE CHALLENGE IS TO PASS THROUGH THIS GATE.
Gate closes in 5 min.
THE TRAINEES USUALLY RUSH THIS GATE BECAUSE IT'S ABOUT TO CLOSE.
GATE OF CHARITY
BUT GETTING THROUGH IS NOT AS EASY AS IT LOOKS...
...BE-CAUSE...
TMP TMP TMP TMP TMP
AH, HERE THEY COME ...

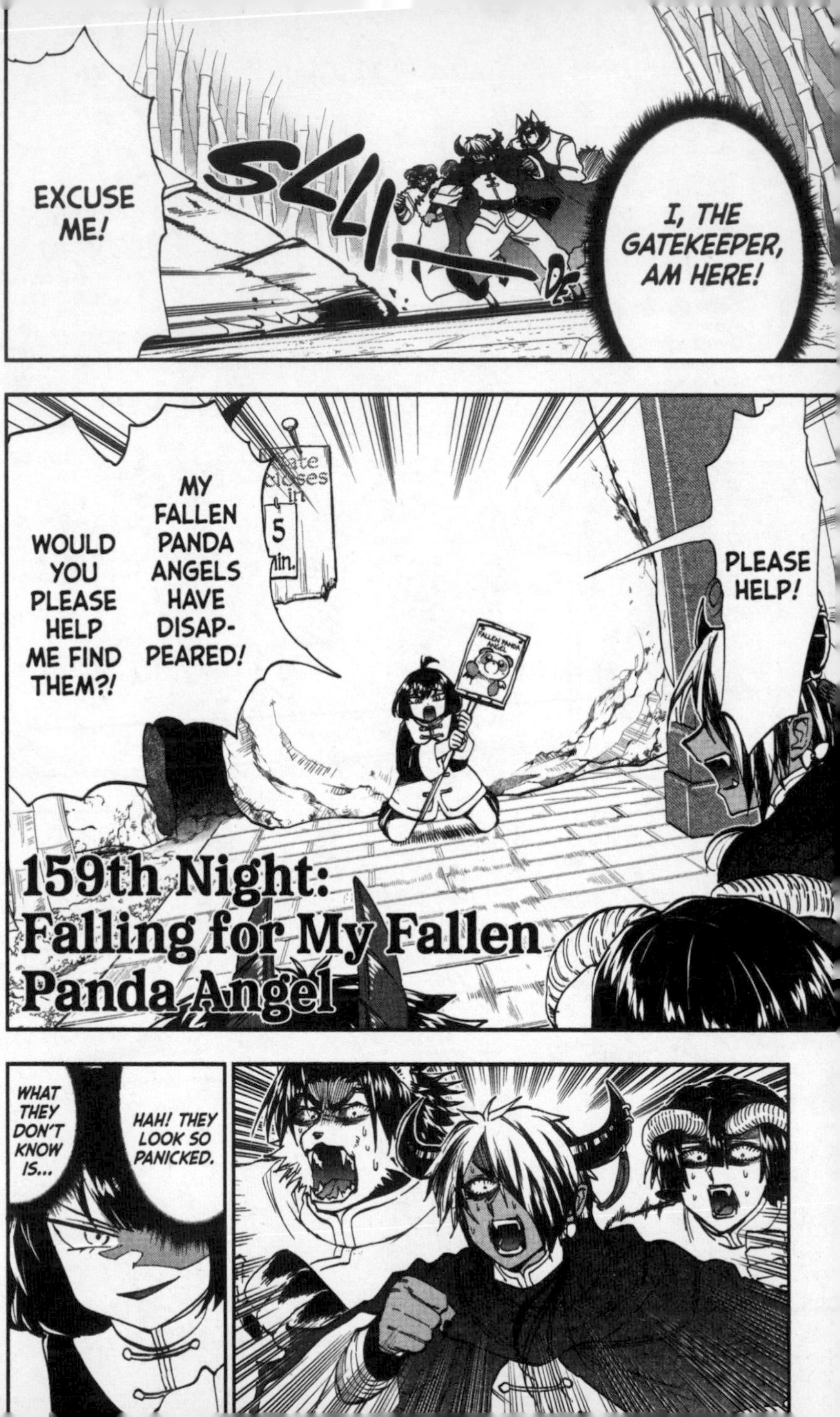
I, THE GATEKEEPER, AM HERE!
EXCUSE ME!
PLEASE HELP!
MY FALLEN PANDA ANGELS HAVE DISAPPEARED!
WOULD YOU PLEASE HELP ME FIND THEM?!
closes in 5
FALLEN PANDA ANGEL
159th Night: Falling for My Fallen Panda Angel
HAH! THEY LOOK SO PANICKED.
WHAT THEY DON'T KNOW IS...

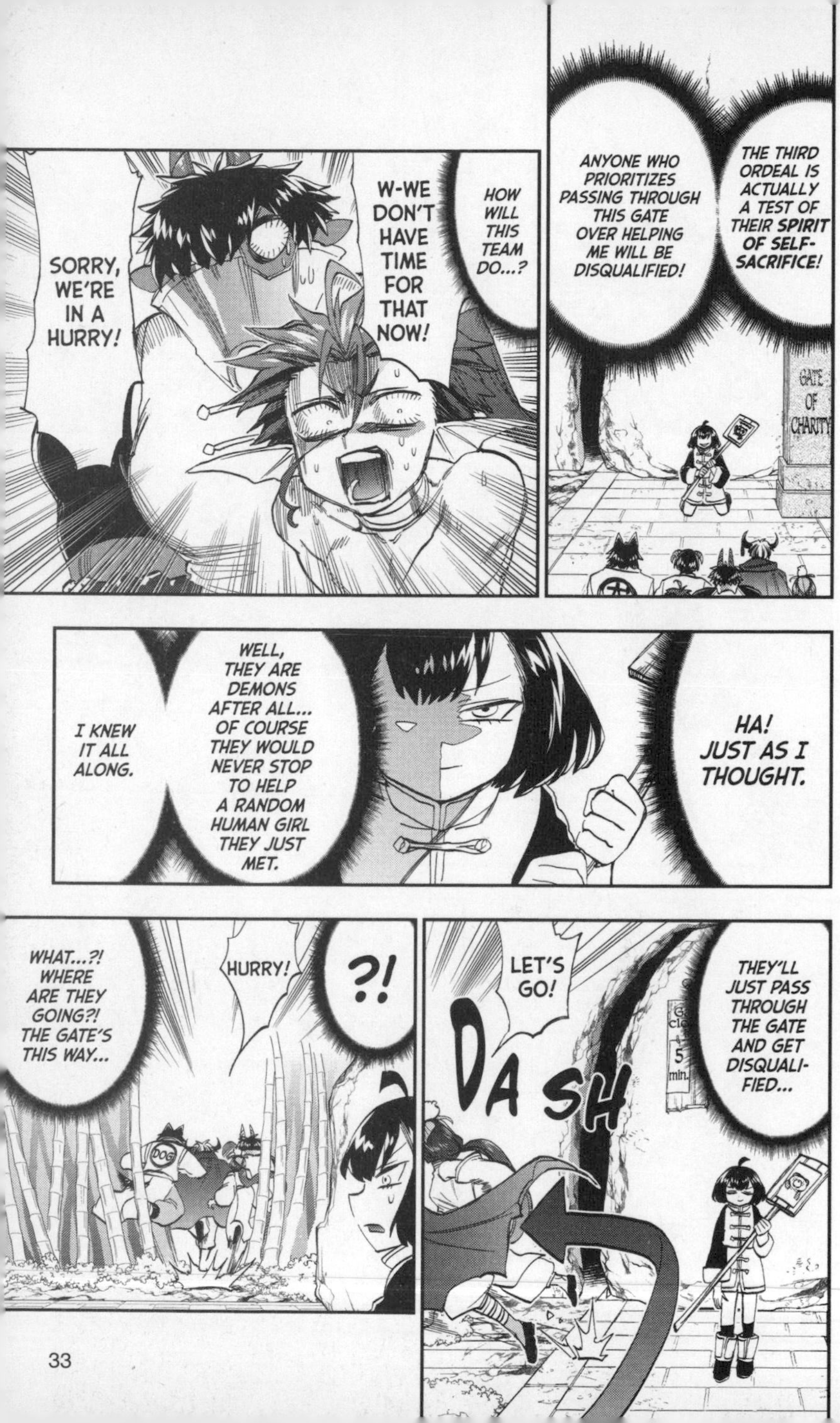
THE THIRD ORDEAL IS ACTUALLY A TEST OF THEIR SPIRIT OF SELF-SACRIFICE!
ANYONE WHO PRIORITIZES PASSING THROUGH THIS GATE OVER HELPING ME WILL BE DISQUALIFIED!
GATE OF CHARITY
HOW WILL THIS TEAM DO...?
W-WE DON'T HAVE TIME FOR THAT NOW!
SORRY, WE'RE IN A HURRY!
HA! JUST AS I THOUGHT.
WELL, THEY ARE DEMONS AFTER ALL... OF COURSE THEY WOULD NEVER STOP TO HELP A RANDOM HUMAN GIRL THEY JUST MET.
I KNEW IT ALL ALONG.
THEY'LL JUST PASS THROUGH THE GATE AND GET DISQUALIFIED...
LET'S GO!
DASH
?!
HURRY!
WHAT...?! WHERE ARE THEY GOING?! THE GATE'S THIS WAY...
DOG

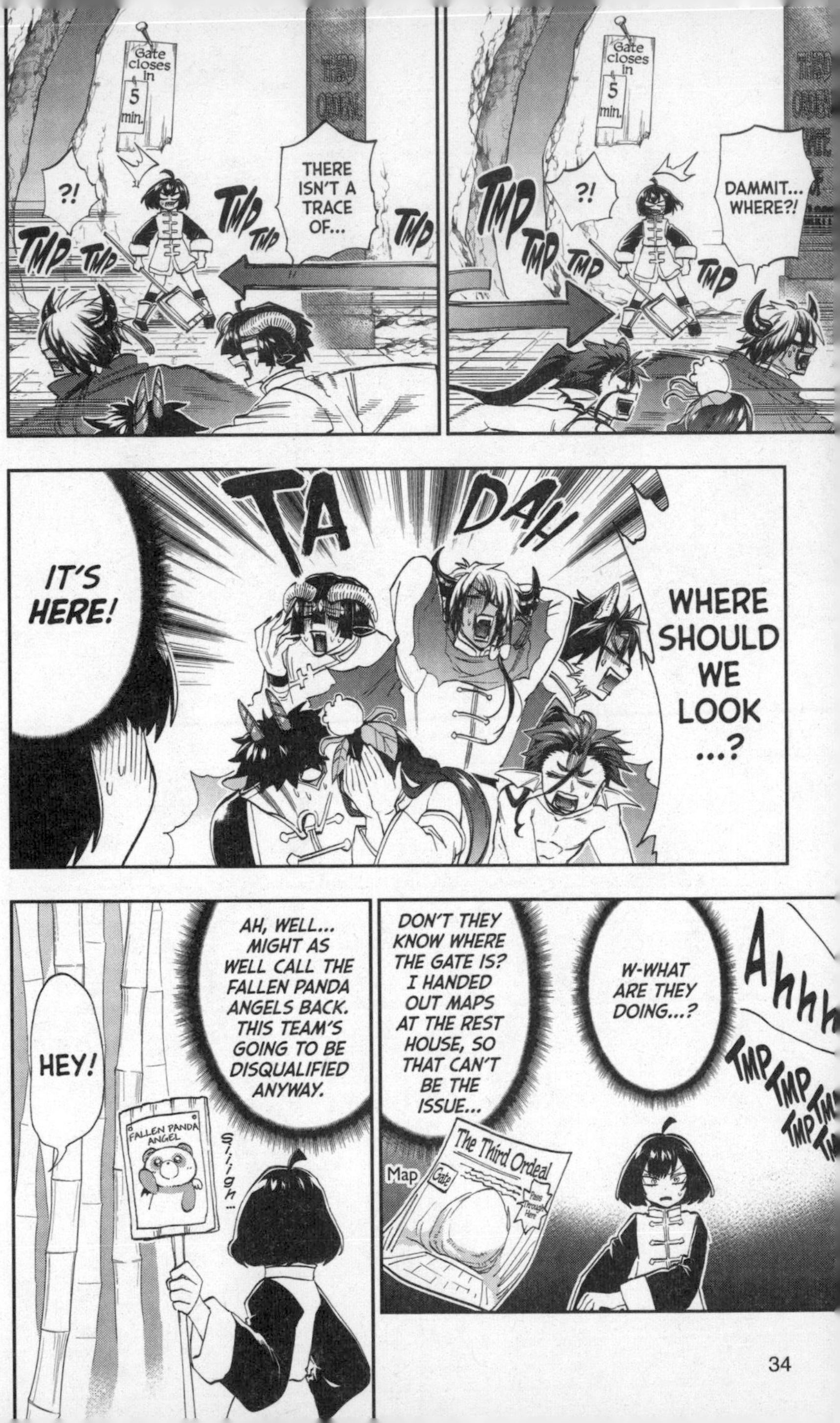
Gate closes in 5 min.
DAMMIT... WHERE?!
?!
TMP TMP TMP TMP
Gate closes in 5 min.
THERE ISN'T A TRACE OF...
?!
TMP TMP TMP TMP TMP
WHERE SHOULD WE LOOK ...?
TA DAH
IT'S HERE!
Ahhh
TMP TMP TMP TMP
W-WHAT ARE THEY DOING...?
DON'T THEY KNOW WHERE THE GATE IS? I HANDED OUT MAPS AT THE REST HOUSE, SO THAT CAN'T BE THE ISSUE...
The Third Ordeal
Map
Gate
Pass Through Here
AH, WELL... MIGHT AS WELL CALL THE FALLEN PANDA ANGELS BACK. THIS TEAM'S GOING TO BE DISQUALIFIED ANYWAY.
Siiigh...
HEY!
FALLEN PANDA ANGEL

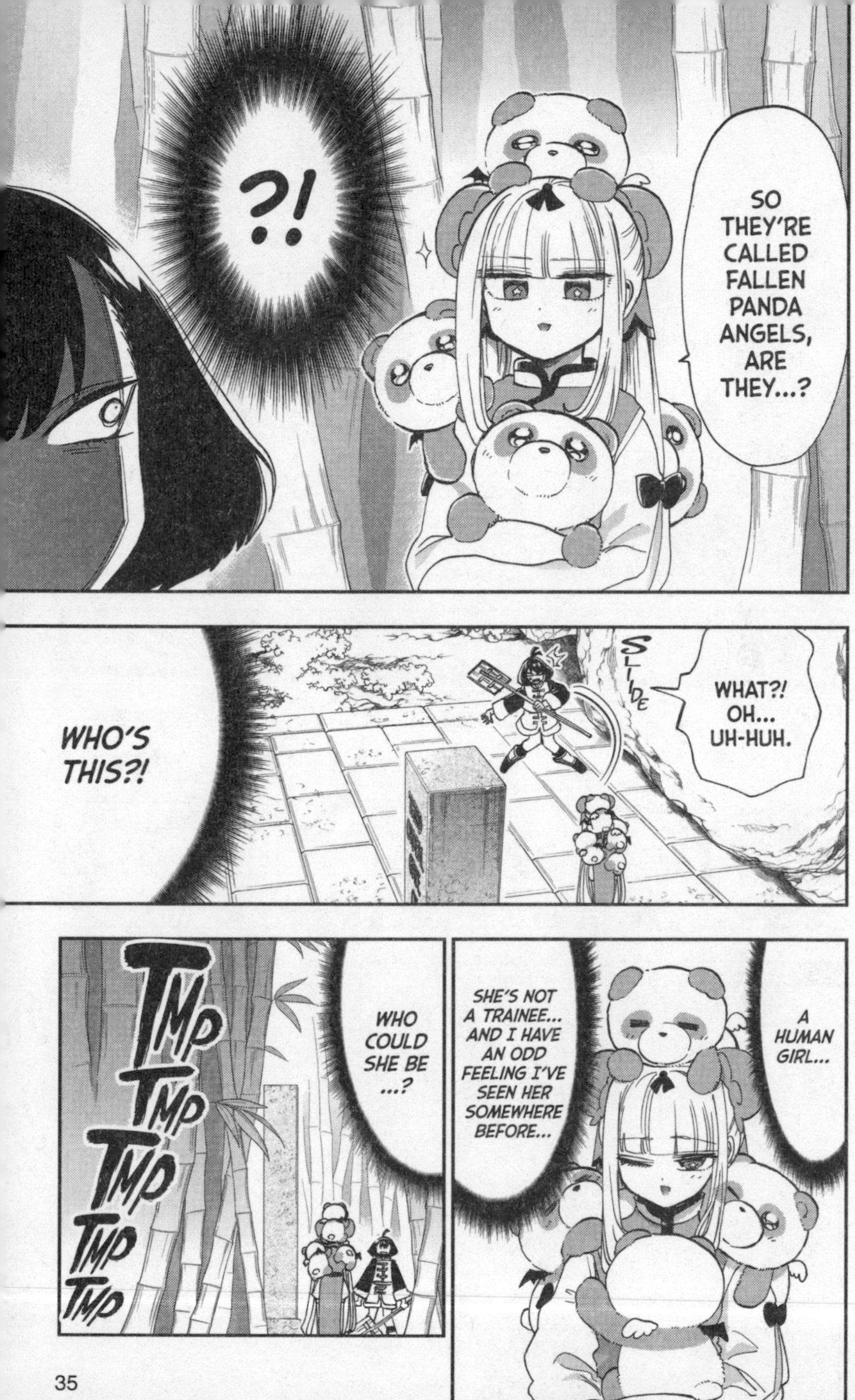
SO THEY'RE CALLED FALLEN PANDA ANGELS, ARE THEY...?
?!
WHAT?! OH... UH-HUH.
SLIIDE
WHO'S THIS?!
A HUMAN GIRL...
SHE'S NOT A TRAINEE... AND I HAVE AN ODD FEELING I'VE SEEN HER SOMEWHERE BEFORE...
WHO COULD SHE BE ...?
TMP TMP TMP TMP TMP

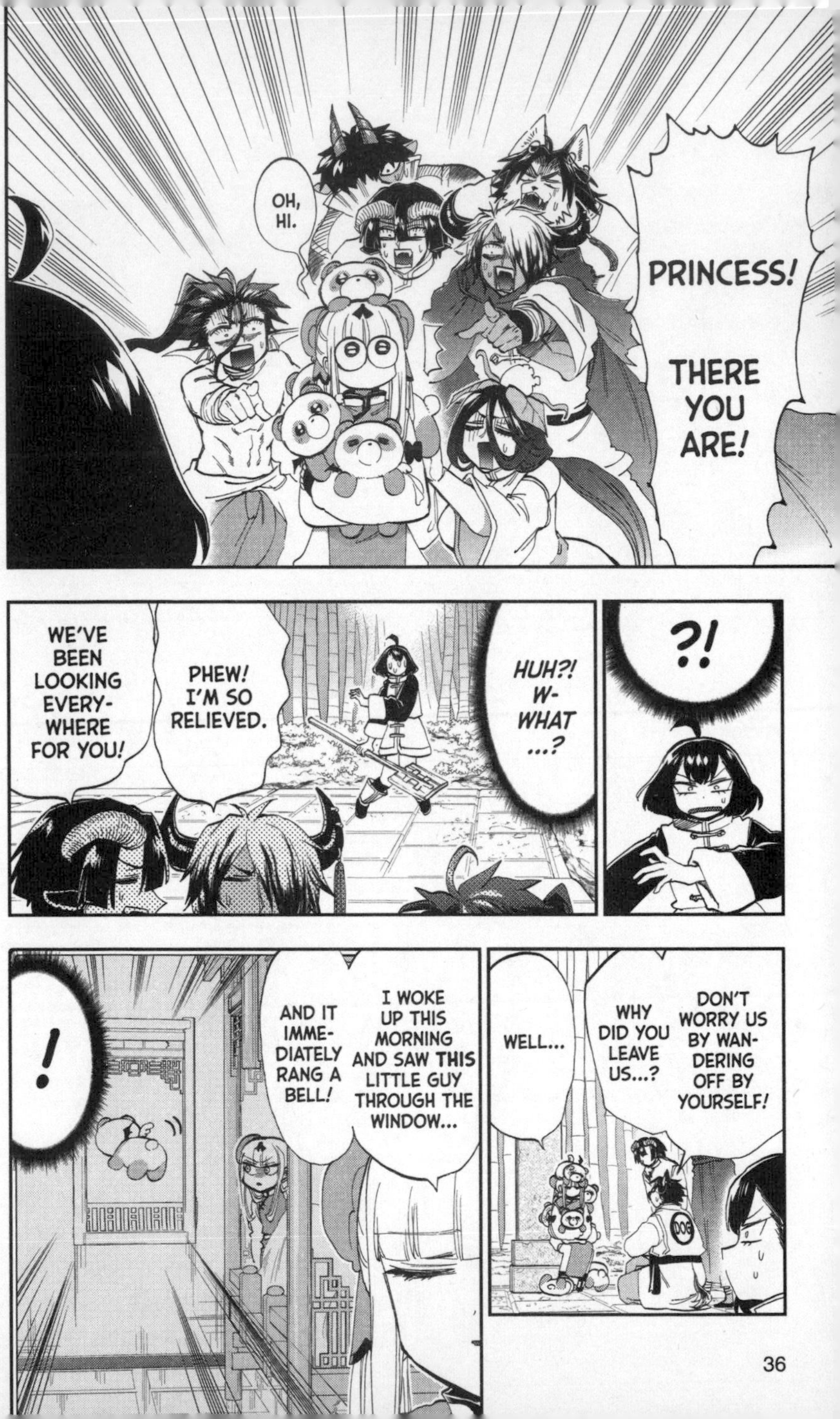
PRINCESS!
THERE YOU ARE!
OH, HI.
?!
HUH?! W-WHAT...?
PHEW! I'M SO RELIEVED.
WE'VE BEEN LOOKING EVERY-WHERE FOR YOU!
DON'T WORRY US BY WAN-DERING OFF BY YOURSELF!
WHY DID YOU LEAVE US...?
WELL...
I WOKE UP THIS MORNING AND SAW THIS LITTLE GUY THROUGH THE WINDOW...
AND IT IMME-DIATELY RANG A BELL!
!

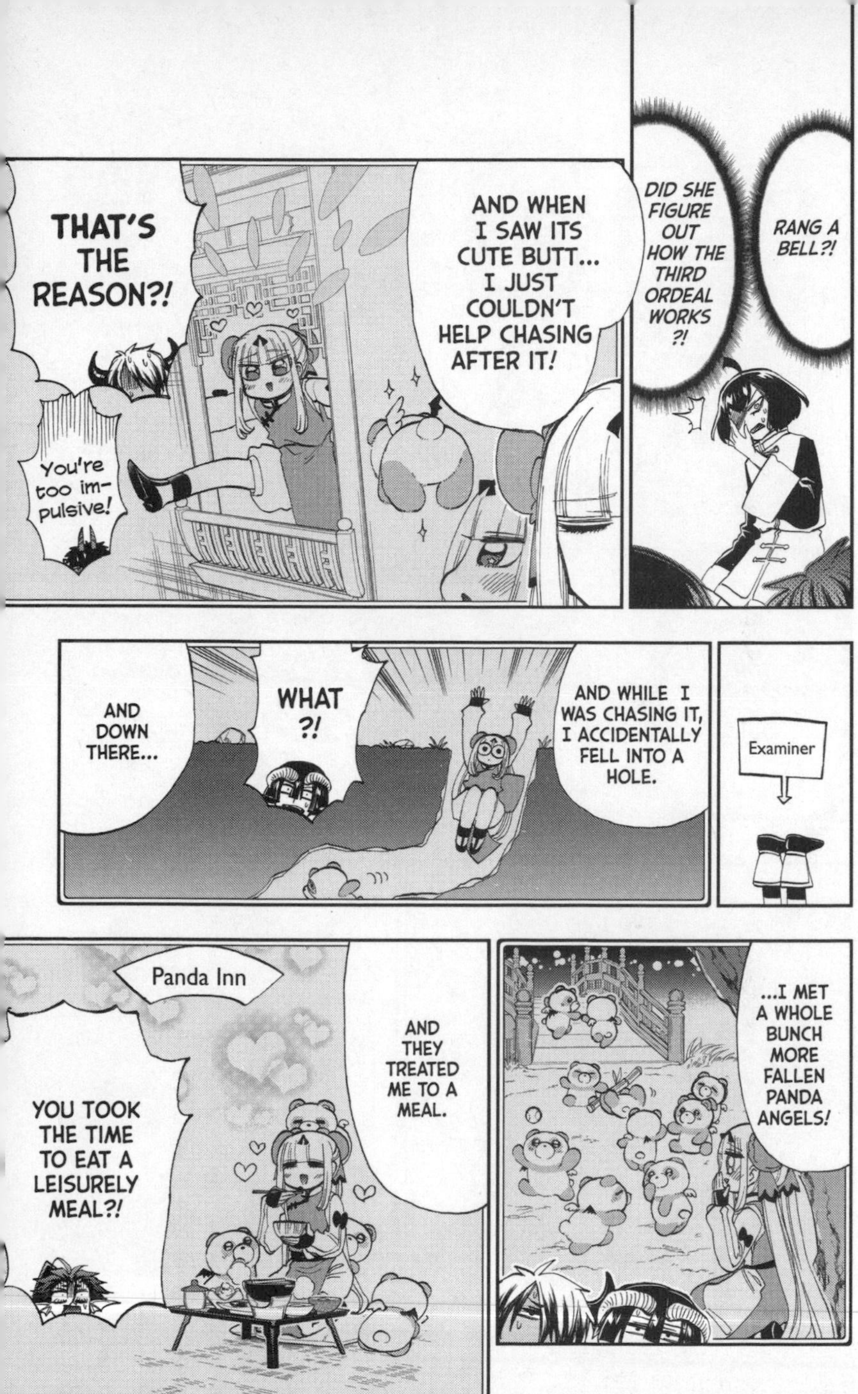
RANG A BELL?!
DID SHE FIGURE OUT HOW THE THIRD ORDEAL WORKS ?!
AND WHEN I SAW ITS CUTE BUTT... I JUST COULDN'T HELP CHASING AFTER IT!
THAT'S THE REASON?!
You're too impulsive!
Examiner
AND WHILE I WAS CHASING IT, I ACCIDENTALLY FELL INTO A HOLE.
WHAT ?!
AND DOWN THERE...
...I MET A WHOLE BUNCH MORE FALLEN PANDA ANGELS!
Panda Inn
AND THEY TREATED ME TO A MEAL.
YOU TOOK THE TIME TO EAT A LEISURELY MEAL?!

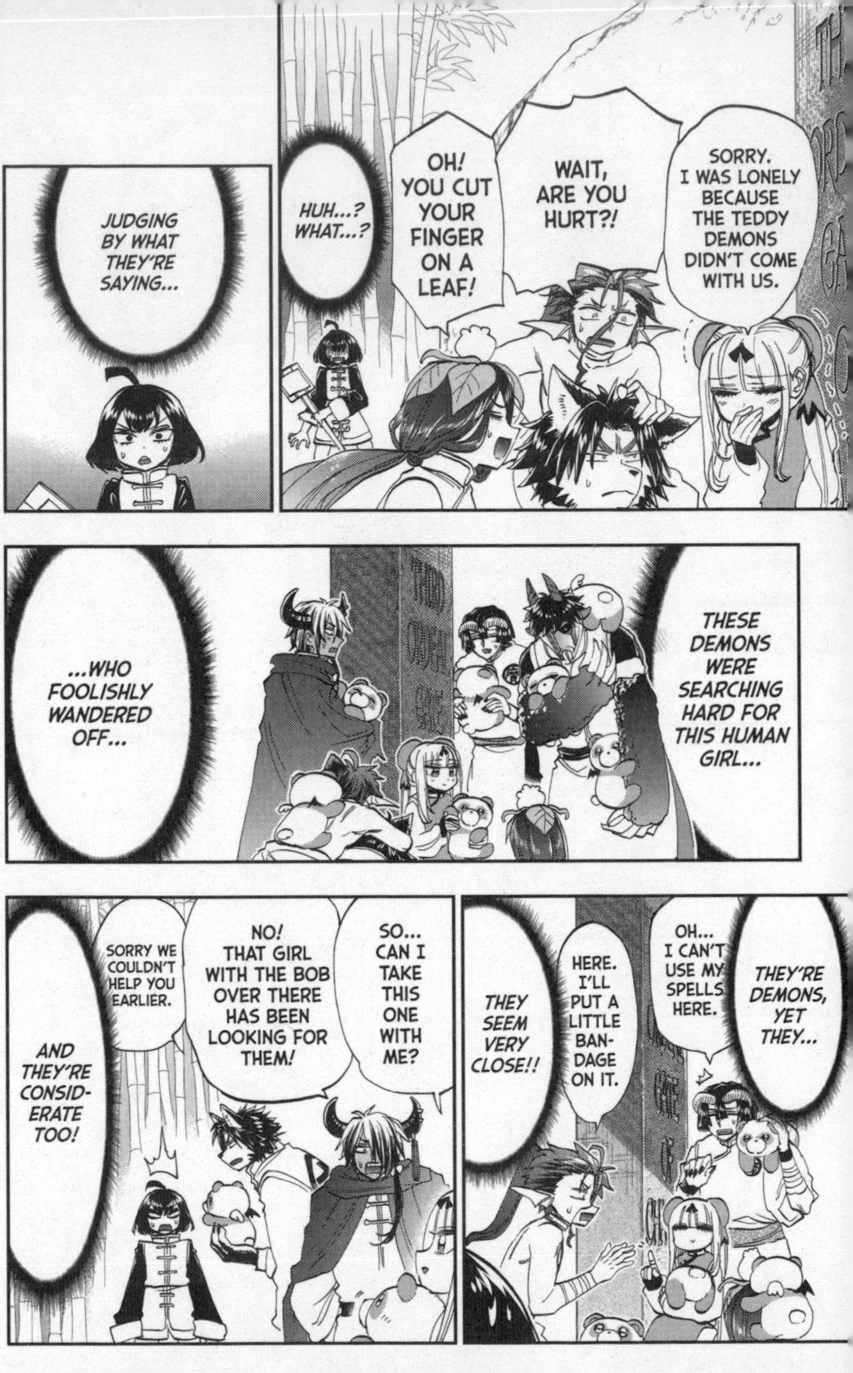
SORRY. I WAS LONELY BECAUSE THE TEDDY DEMONS DIDN'T COME WITH US.
WAIT, ARE YOU HURT?!
OH! YOU CUT YOUR FINGER ON A LEAF!
HUH...? WHAT...?
JUDGING BY WHAT THEY'RE SAYING...
THESE DEMONS WERE SEARCHING HARD FOR THIS HUMAN GIRL...
...WHO FOOLISHLY WANDERED OFF...
THEY'RE DEMONS, YET THEY...
OH... I CAN'T USE MY SPELLS HERE.
HERE. I'LL PUT A LITTLE BAN-DAGE ON IT.
THEY SEEM VERY CLOSE!!
SO... CAN I TAKE THIS ONE WITH ME?
NO! THAT GIRL WITH THE BOB OVER THERE HAS BEEN LOOKING FOR THEM!
SORRY WE COULDN'T HELP YOU EARLIER.
AND THEY'RE CONSID-ERATE TOO!

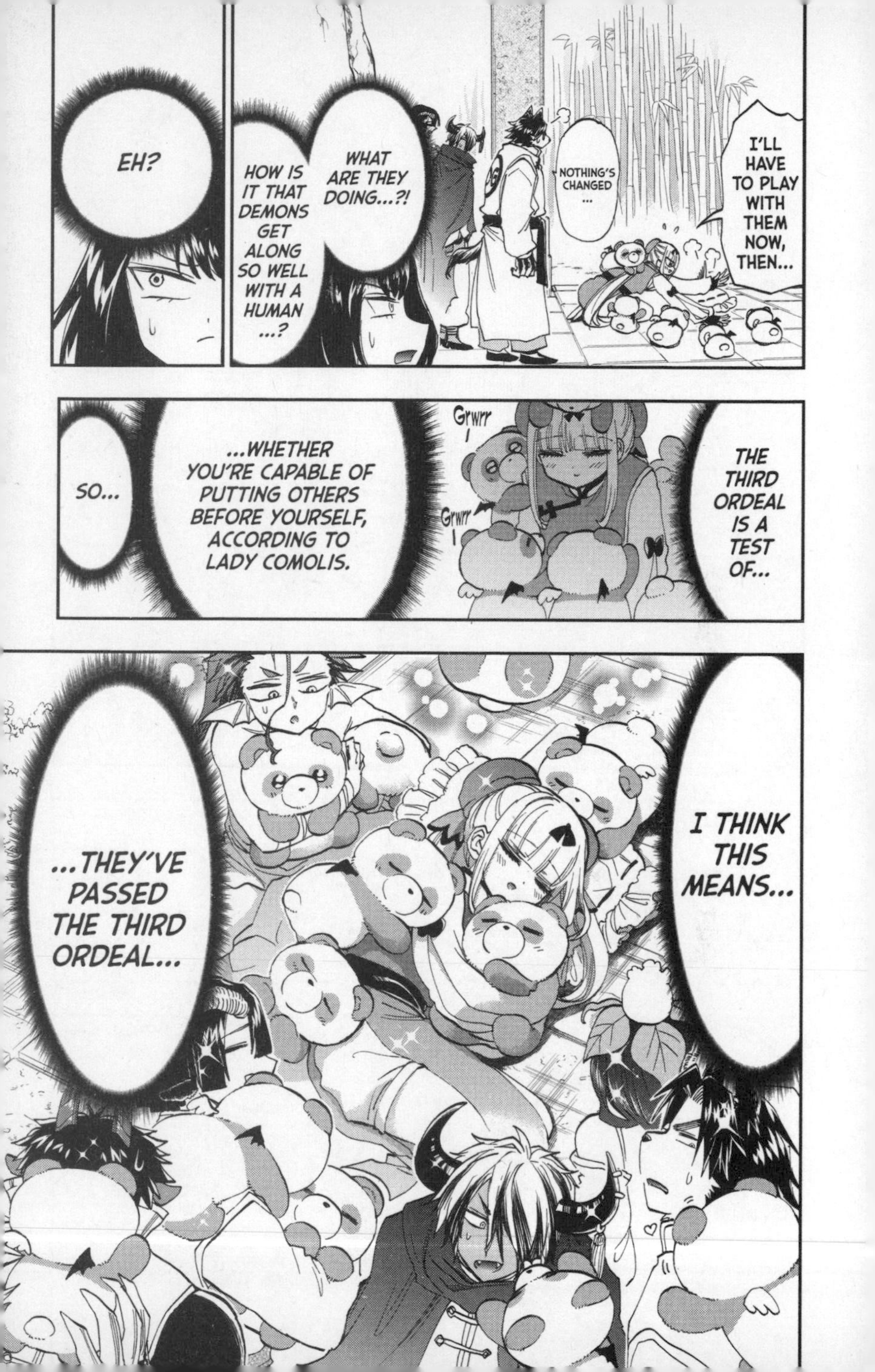
I'LL HAVE TO PLAY WITH THEM NOW, THEN...
NOTHING'S CHANGED ...
WHAT ARE THEY DOING...?!
HOW IS IT THAT DEMONS GET ALONG SO WELL WITH A HUMAN ...?
EH?
THE THIRD ORDEAL IS A TEST OF...
Grwrr
Grwrr
...WHETHER YOU'RE CAPABLE OF PUTTING OTHERS BEFORE YOURSELF, ACCORDING TO LADY COMOLIS.
SO...
I THINK THIS MEANS...
...THEY'VE PASSED THE THIRD ORDEAL...

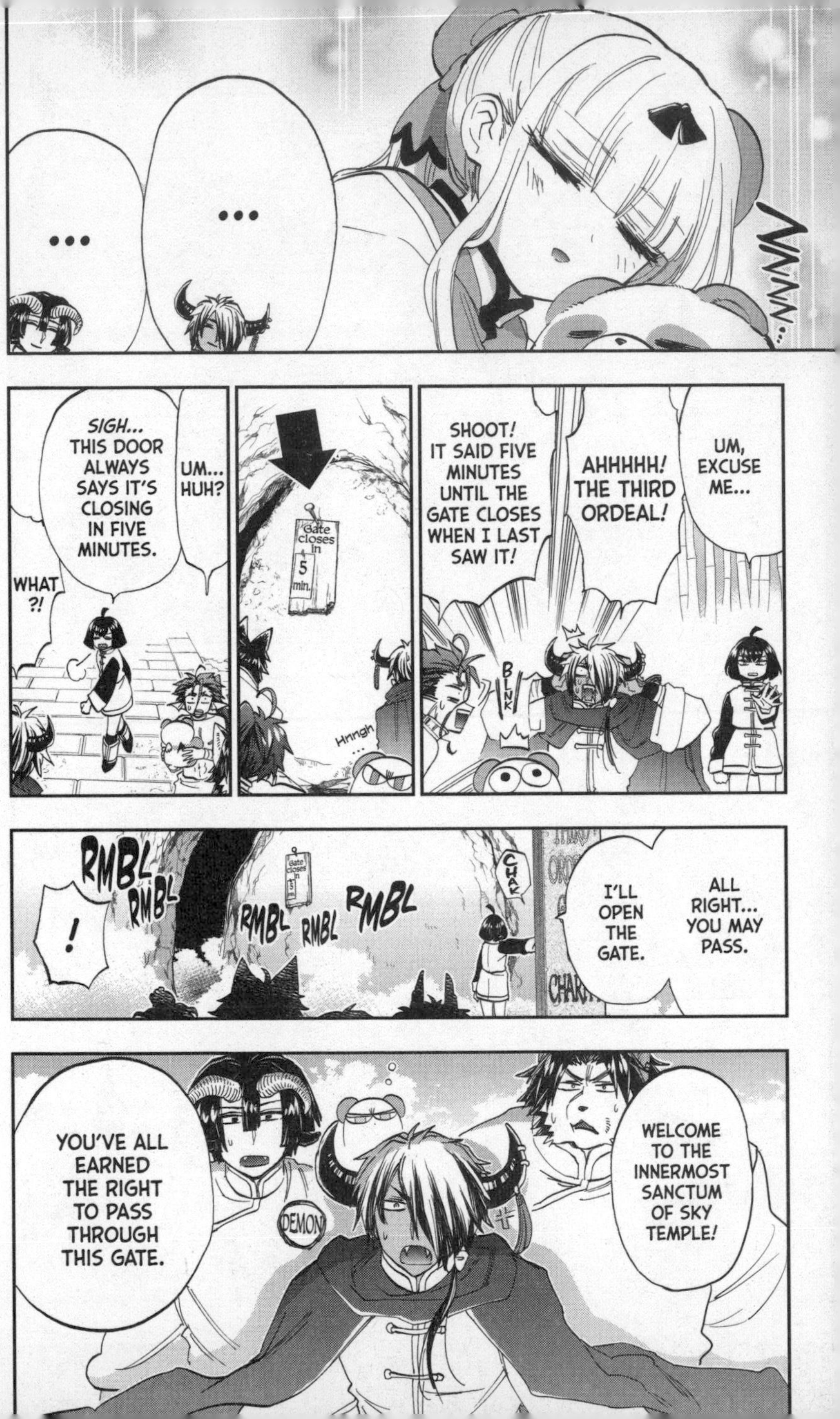
NNNN...
...
...
UM, EXCUSE ME...
AHHHHH! THE THIRD ORDEAL!
SHOOT! IT SAID FIVE MINUTES UNTIL THE GATE CLOSES WHEN I LAST SAW IT!
BLNK
Gate closes in 5 min.
Hrnngh...
UM... HUH?
SIGH... THIS DOOR ALWAYS SAYS IT'S CLOSING IN FIVE MINUTES.
WHAT?!
ALL RIGHT... YOU MAY PASS.
I'LL OPEN THE GATE.
CHAK
RMBL RMBL RMBL
RMBL RMBL RMBL
!
WELCOME TO THE INNERMOST SANCTUM OF SKY TEMPLE!
DEMON
YOU'VE ALL EARNED THE RIGHT TO PASS THROUGH THIS GATE.

Fallen Panda Angel

Furry and cuddly.

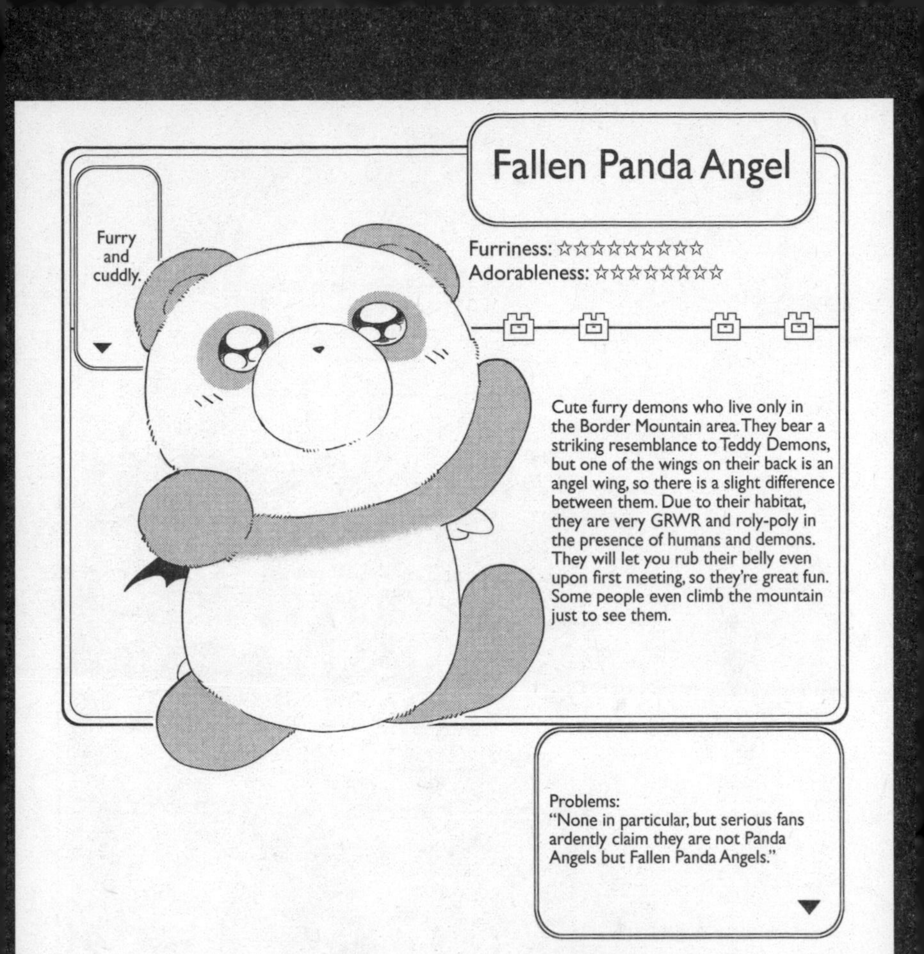

Furriness: ☆☆☆☆☆☆☆☆☆
Adorableness: ☆☆☆☆☆☆☆☆

Cute furry demons who live only in the Border Mountain area. They bear a striking resemblance to Teddy Demons, but one of the wings on their back is an angel wing, so there is a slight difference between them. Due to their habitat, they are very GRWR and roly-poly in the presence of humans and demons. They will let you rub their belly even upon first meeting, so they're great fun. Some people even climb the mountain just to see them.

Problems:
"None in particular, but serious fans ardently claim they are not Panda Angels but Fallen Panda Angels."

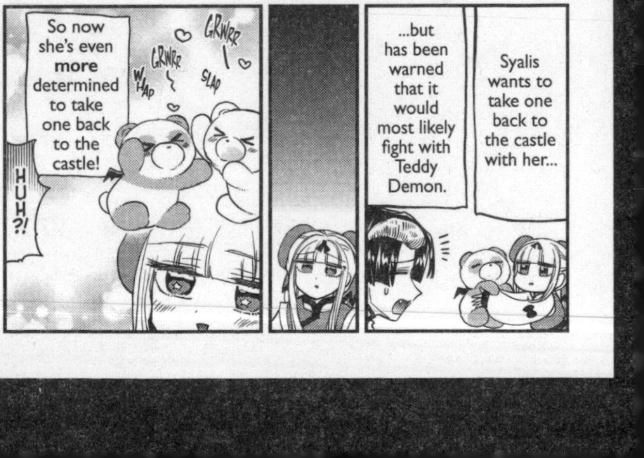
Syalis wants to take one back to the castle with her...
...but has been warned that it would most likely fight with Teddy Demon.
So now she's even **more** determined to take one back to the castle!
GRWRR
WHAP
GRWRR
SLAP
HUH?!

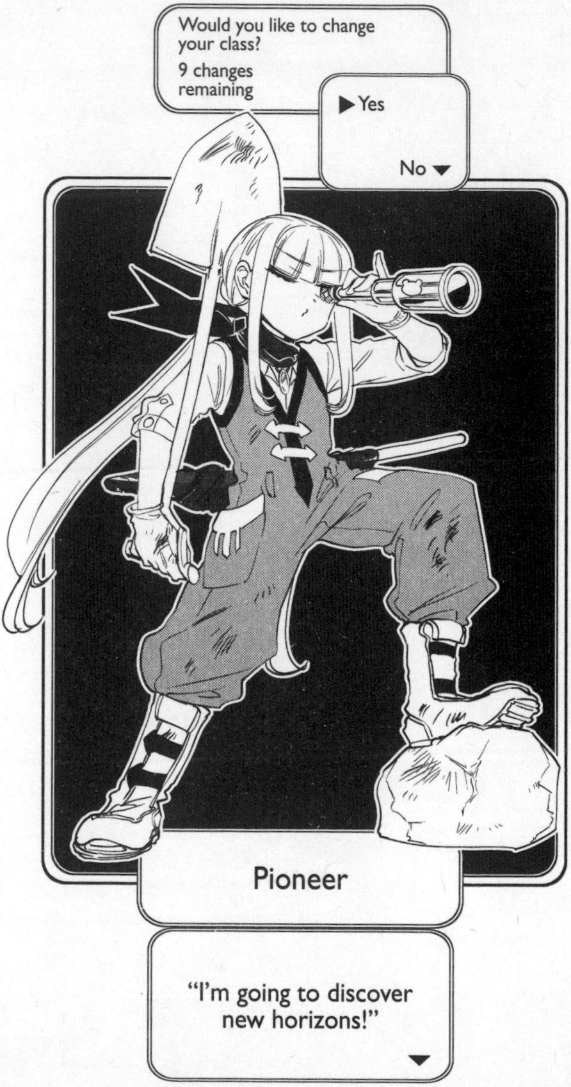
Would you like to change your class?
9 changes remaining
▶Yes
No
Pioneer
"I'm going to discover new horizons!"

160th Night: I Want Her to Wake Up, and Then Again I Don't

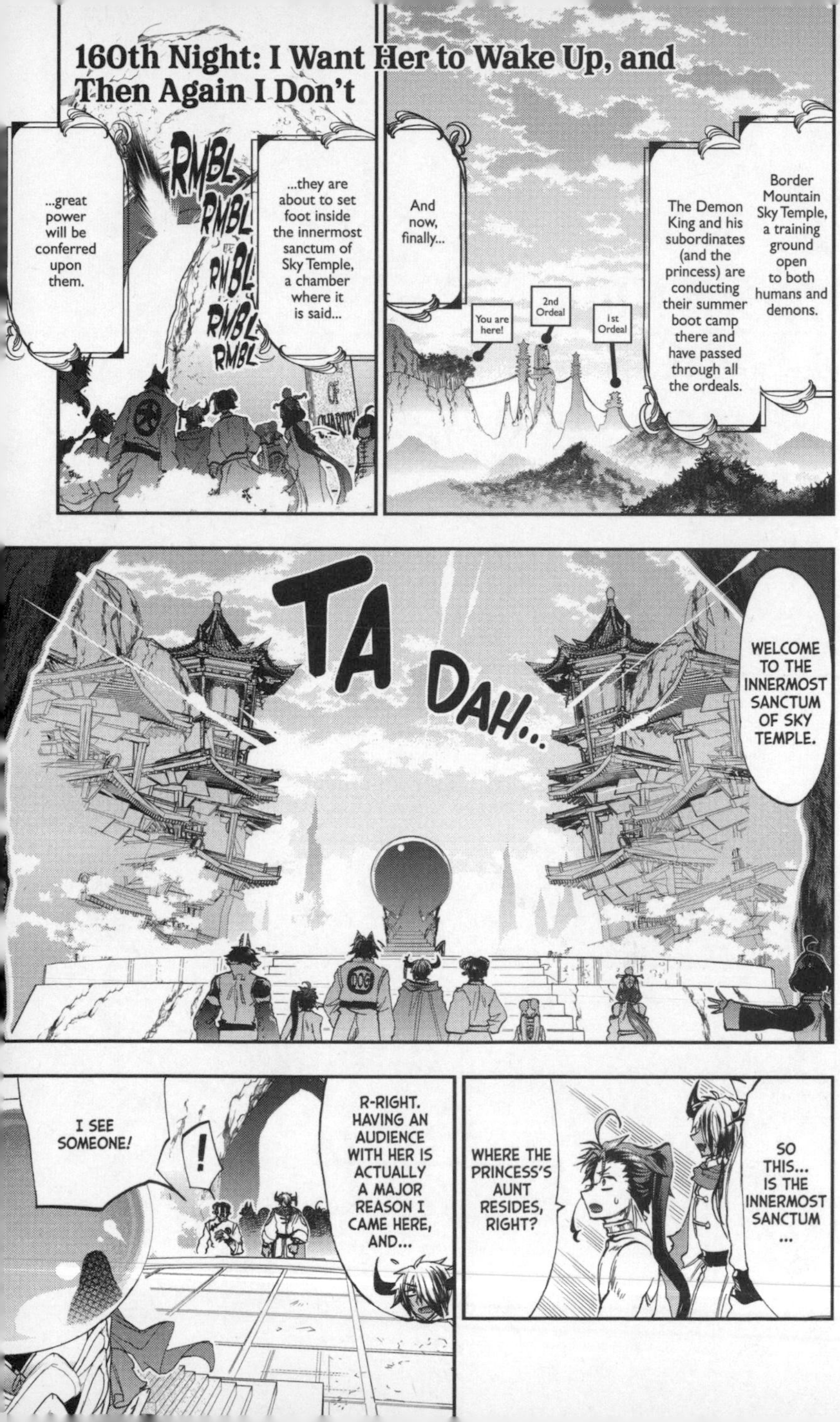
Border Mountain Sky Temple, a training ground open to both humans and demons.
The Demon King and his subordinates (and the princess) are conducting their summer boot camp there and have passed through all the ordeals.
1st Ordeal
2nd Ordeal
You are here!
And now, finally...
...they are about to set foot inside the innermost sanctum of Sky Temple, a chamber where it is said...
...great power will be conferred upon them.
RMBL RMBL RMBL RMBL RMBL
TA DAH...
WELCOME TO THE INNERMOST SANCTUM OF SKY TEMPLE.
SO THIS... IS THE INNERMOST SANCTUM...
WHERE THE PRINCESS'S AUNT RESIDES, RIGHT?
R-RIGHT. HAVING AN AUDIENCE WITH HER IS ACTUALLY A MAJOR REASON I CAME HERE, AND...
!
I SEE SOMEONE!

160th Night: I Want Her to Wake Up, and Then Again I Don't

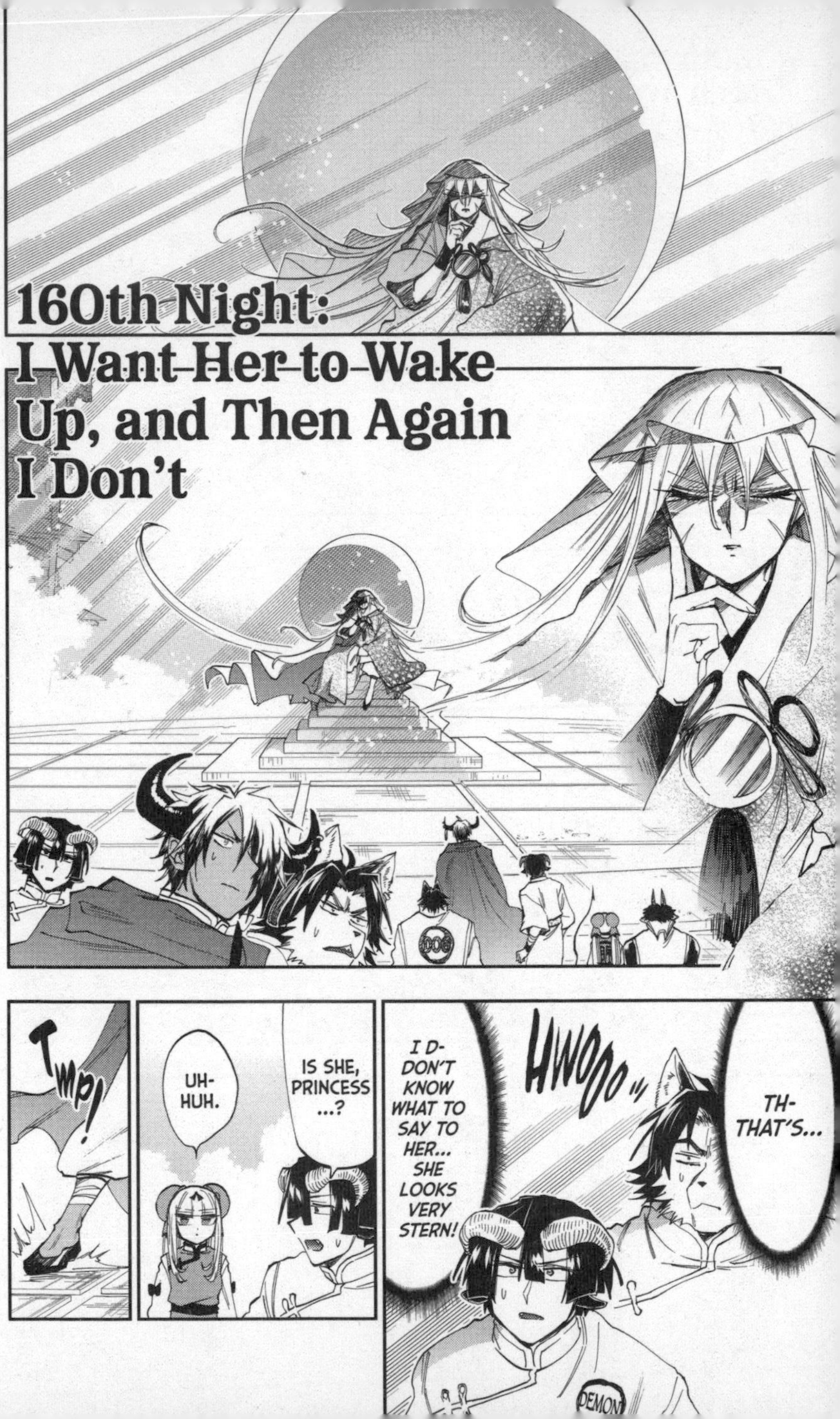

TH-THAT'S...
UHWOOO
I D-DON'T KNOW WHAT TO SAY TO HER... SHE LOOKS VERY STERN!
DEMON
IS SHE, PRINCESS ...?
UH-HUH.
TMP!

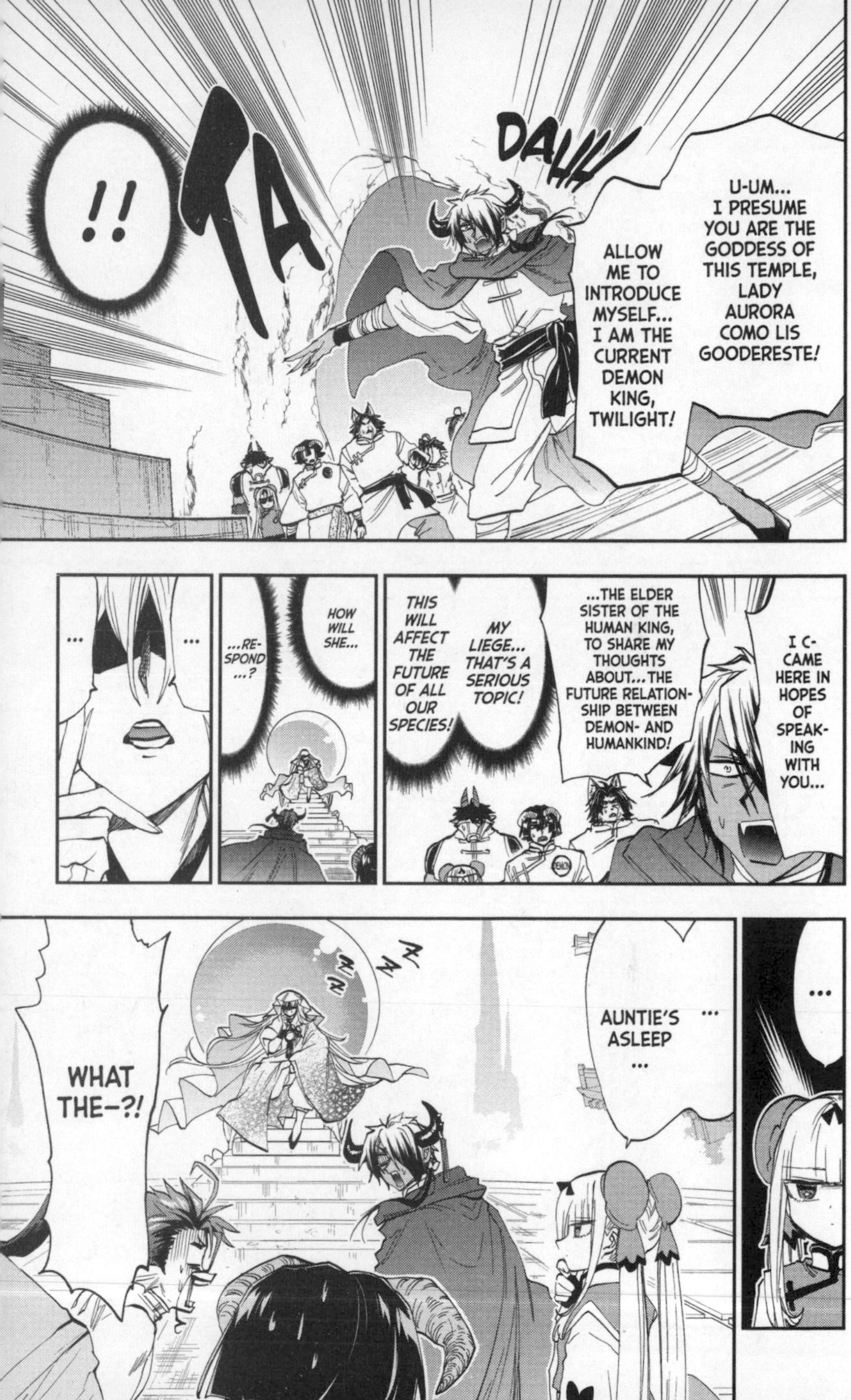
U-UM... I PRESUME YOU ARE THE GODDESS OF THIS TEMPLE, LADY AURORA COMO LIS GOODERESTE!
ALLOW ME TO INTRODUCE MYSELF... I AM THE CURRENT DEMON KING, TWILIGHT!
DAHH
TA
!!
I C-CAME HERE IN HOPES OF SPEAK-ING WITH YOU...
...THE ELDER SISTER OF THE HUMAN KING, TO SHARE MY THOUGHTS ABOUT...THE FUTURE RELATION-SHIP BETWEEN DEMON- AND HUMANKIND!
MY LIEGE... THAT'S A SERIOUS TOPIC!
THIS WILL AFFECT THE FUTURE OF ALL OUR SPECIES!
HOW WILL SHE...
...RE-SPOND ...?
... ...
...
...
AUNTIE'S ASLEEP ...
Z Z Z
WHAT THE–?!

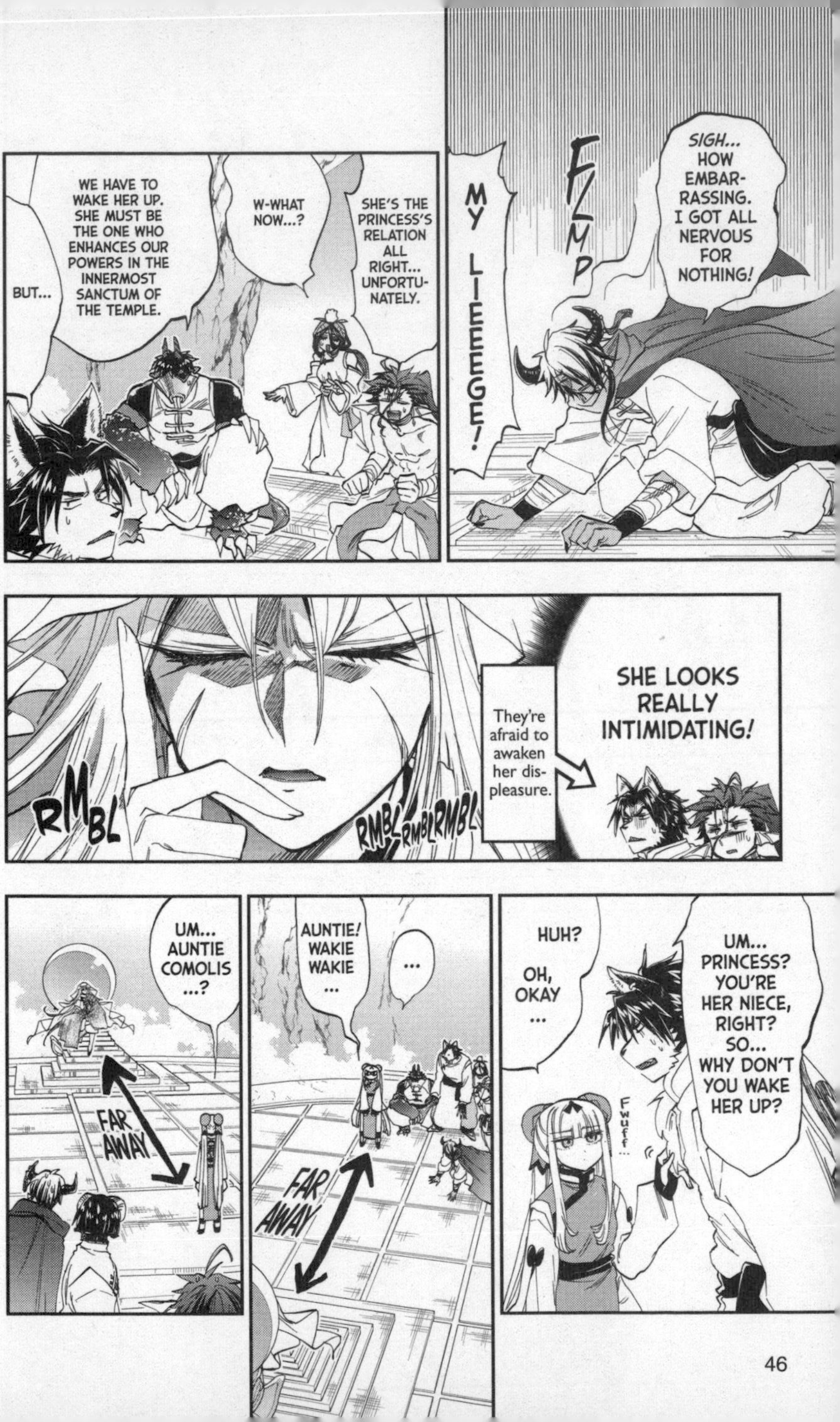
SIGH... HOW EMBAR-RASSING. I GOT ALL NERVOUS FOR NOTHING!
FLMP
MY LIEEEGE!
SHE'S THE PRINCESS'S RELATION ALL RIGHT... UNFORTU-NATELY.
W-WHAT NOW...?
WE HAVE TO WAKE HER UP. SHE MUST BE THE ONE WHO ENHANCES OUR POWERS IN THE INNERMOST SANCTUM OF THE TEMPLE.
BUT...
SHE LOOKS REALLY INTIMIDATING!
They're afraid to awaken her dis-pleasure.
RMBL RMBL RMBL
RMBL
UM... PRINCESS? YOU'RE HER NIECE, RIGHT? SO... WHY DON'T YOU WAKE HER UP?
HUH?
OH, OKAY ...
Fwuff...
...
AUNTIE! WAKIE WAKIE ...
FAR AWAY
UM... AUNTIE COMOLIS ...?
FAR AWAY

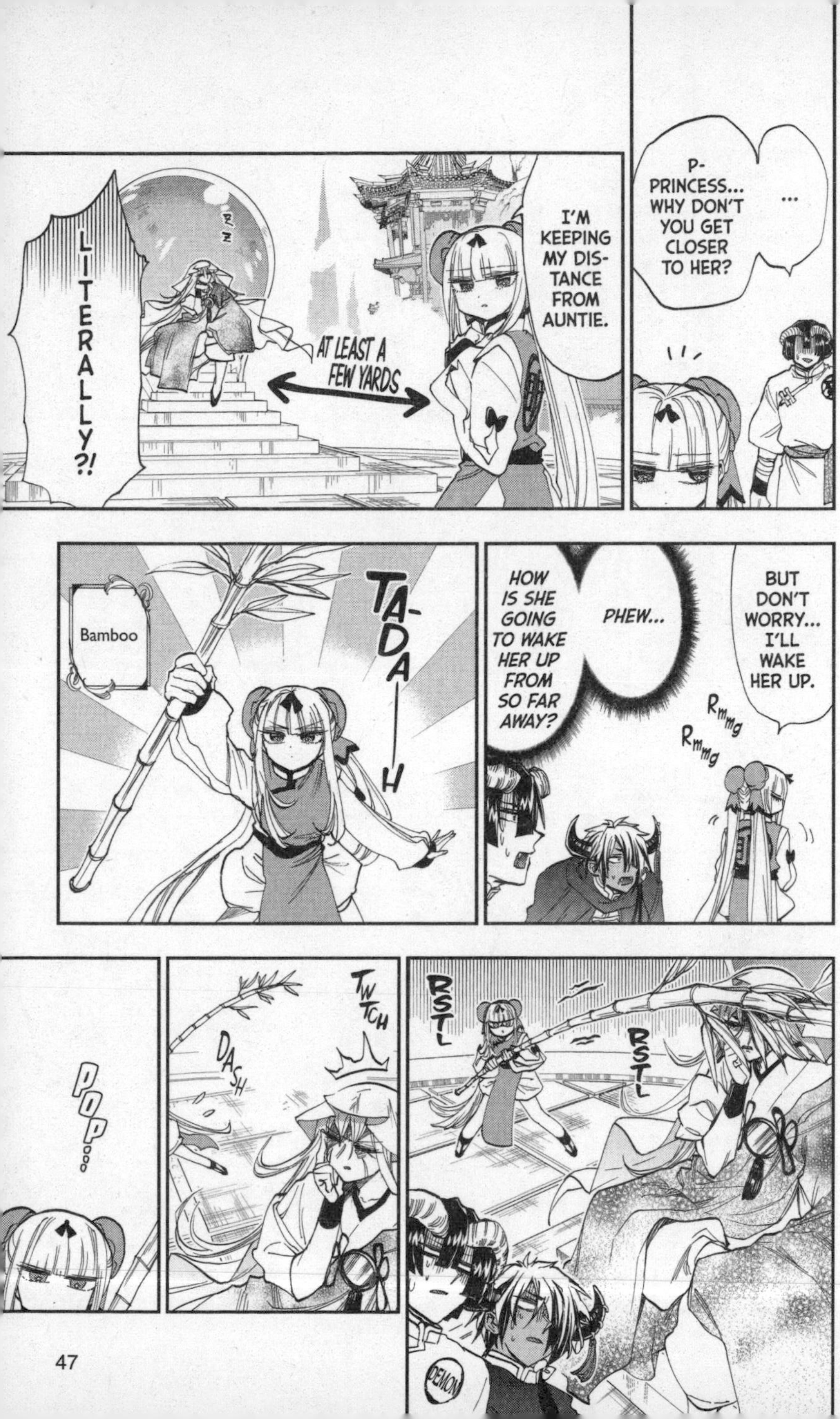
P-PRINCESS... WHY DON'T YOU GET CLOSER TO HER?
...
I'M KEEPING MY DIS-TANCE FROM AUNTIE.
AT LEAST A FEW YARDS
LITERALLY?!
BUT DON'T WORRY... I'LL WAKE HER UP.
Rmmg
Rmmg
PHEW...
HOW IS SHE GOING TO WAKE HER UP FROM SO FAR AWAY?
TA-DA-H
Bamboo
RSTL
RSTL
DEMON
TWTCH
DASH
POPooo

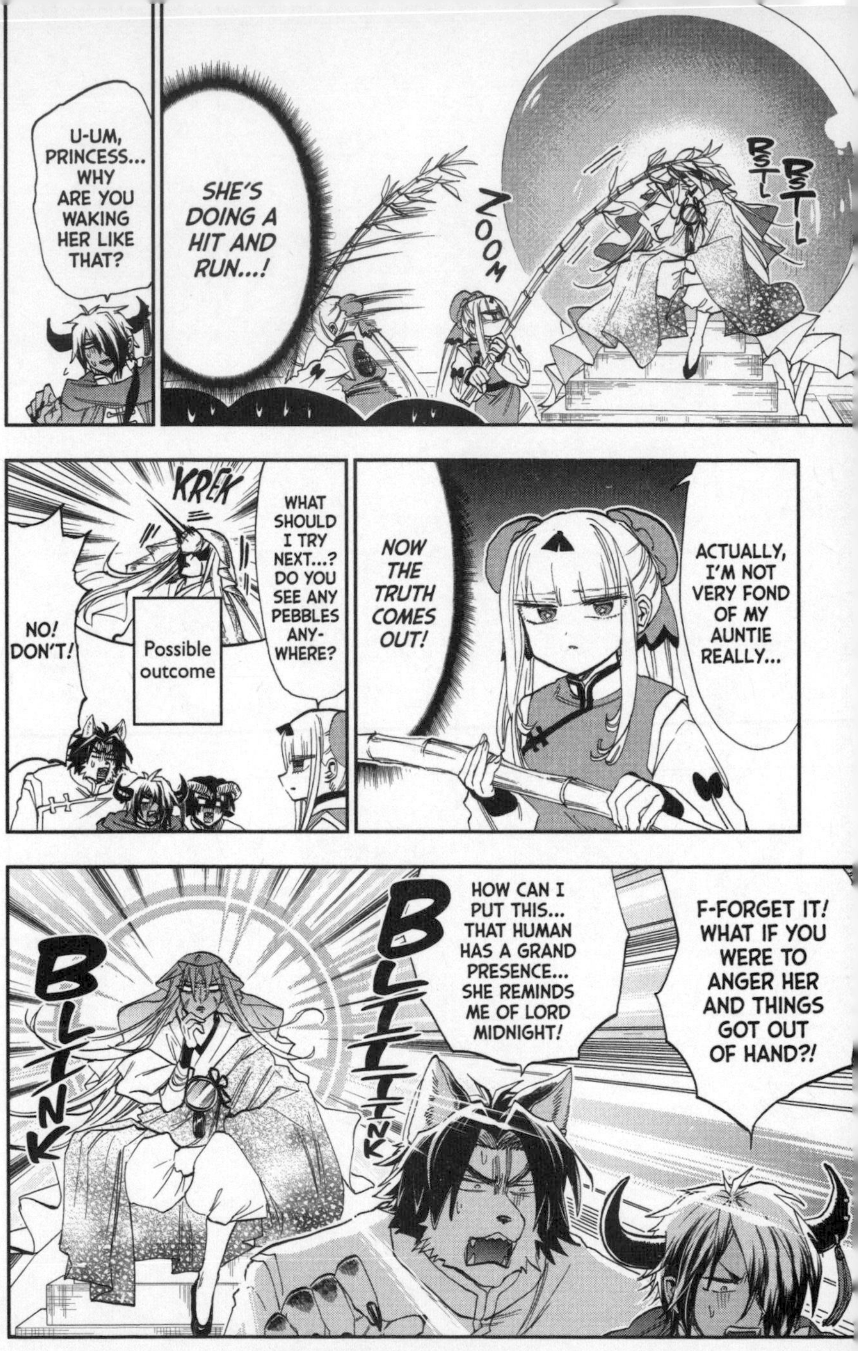
RSTL RSTL
ZOOM
SHE'S DOING A HIT AND RUN...!
U-UM, PRINCESS... WHY ARE YOU WAKING HER LIKE THAT?
ACTUALLY, I'M NOT VERY FOND OF MY AUNTIE REALLY...
NOW THE TRUTH COMES OUT!
WHAT SHOULD I TRY NEXT...? DO YOU SEE ANY PEBBLES ANY-WHERE?
KREK
Possible outcome
NO! DON'T!
F-FORGET IT! WHAT IF YOU WERE TO ANGER HER AND THINGS GOT OUT OF HAND?!
HOW CAN I PUT THIS... THAT HUMAN HAS A GRAND PRESENCE... SHE REMINDS ME OF LORD MIDNIGHT!
BLIIIINK
BLINK

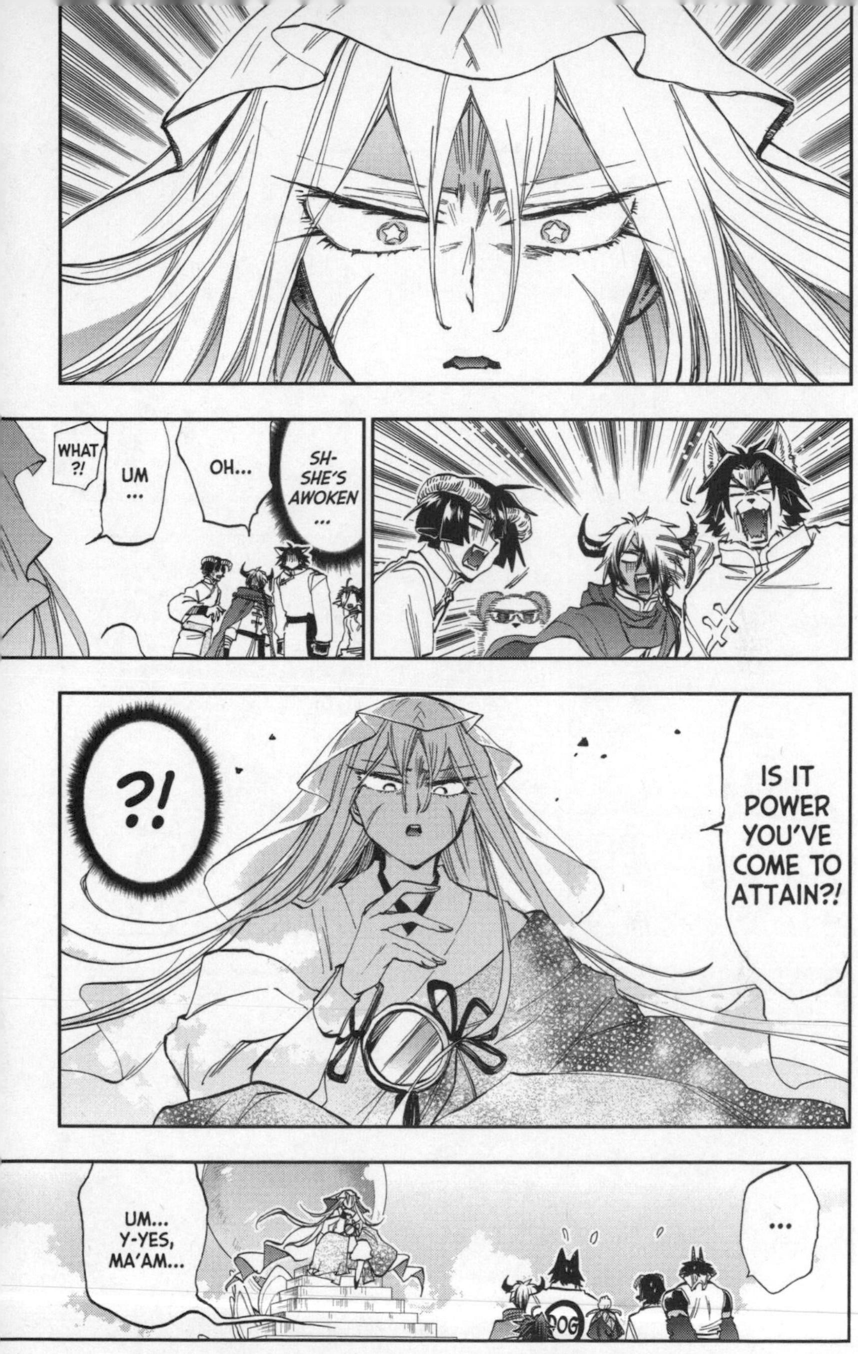
SH-SHE'S AWOKEN...
OH...
UM...
WHAT?!
IS IT POWER YOU'VE COME TO ATTAIN?!
?!
...
DOG
UM... Y-YES, MA'AM...

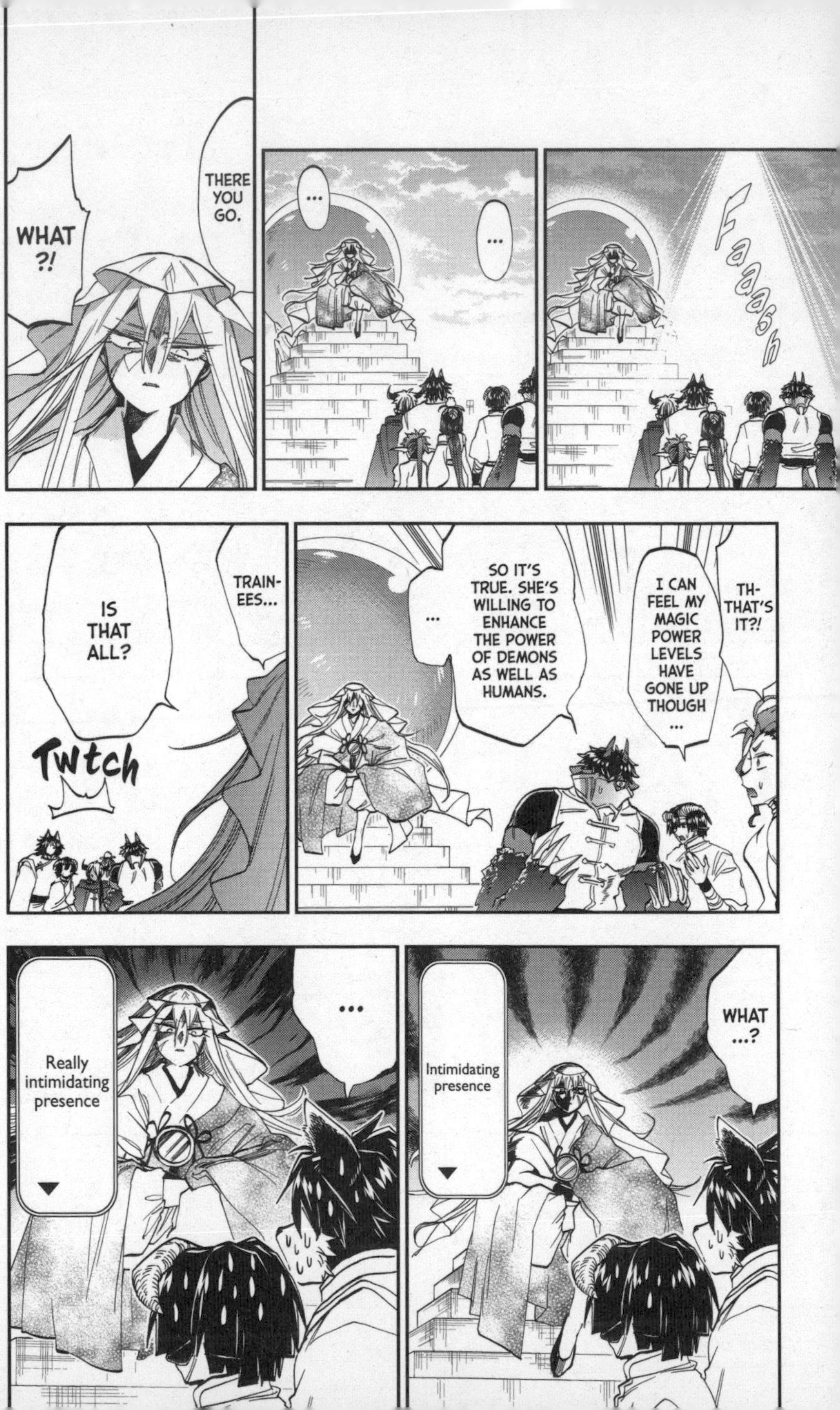

Faaash
...
...
THERE YOU GO.
WHAT ?!
TH-THAT'S IT?!
I CAN FEEL MY MAGIC POWER LEVELS HAVE GONE UP THOUGH ...
SO IT'S TRUE. SHE'S WILLING TO ENHANCE THE POWER OF DEMONS AS WELL AS HUMANS.
...
TRAIN-EES...
IS THAT ALL?
Twtch
WHAT ...?
Intimidating presence
...
Really intimidating presence

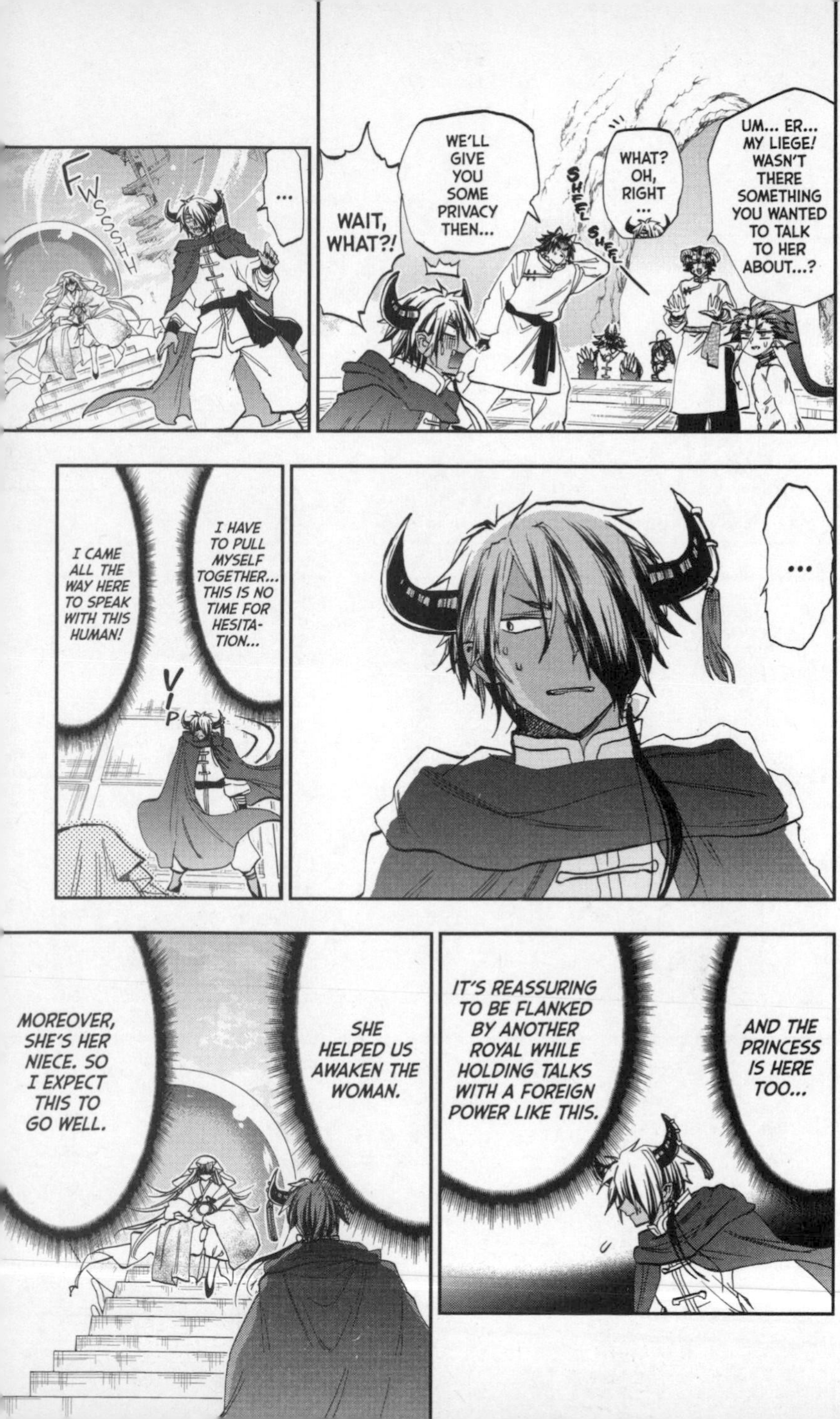
UM... ER... MY LIEGE! WASN'T THERE SOMETHING YOU WANTED TO TALK TO HER ABOUT...?
WHAT? OH, RIGHT ...
SHEF SHEF
WE'LL GIVE YOU SOME PRIVACY THEN...
WAIT, WHAT?!
...
FWSSSHH
...
I HAVE TO PULL MYSELF TOGETHER... THIS IS NO TIME FOR HESITATION...
I CAME ALL THE WAY HERE TO SPEAK WITH THIS HUMAN!
VIP
AND THE PRINCESS IS HERE TOO...
IT'S REASSURING TO BE FLANKED BY ANOTHER ROYAL WHILE HOLDING TALKS WITH A FOREIGN POWER LIKE THIS.
SHE HELPED US AWAKEN THE WOMAN.
MOREOVER, SHE'S HER NIECE. SO I EXPECT THIS TO GO WELL.

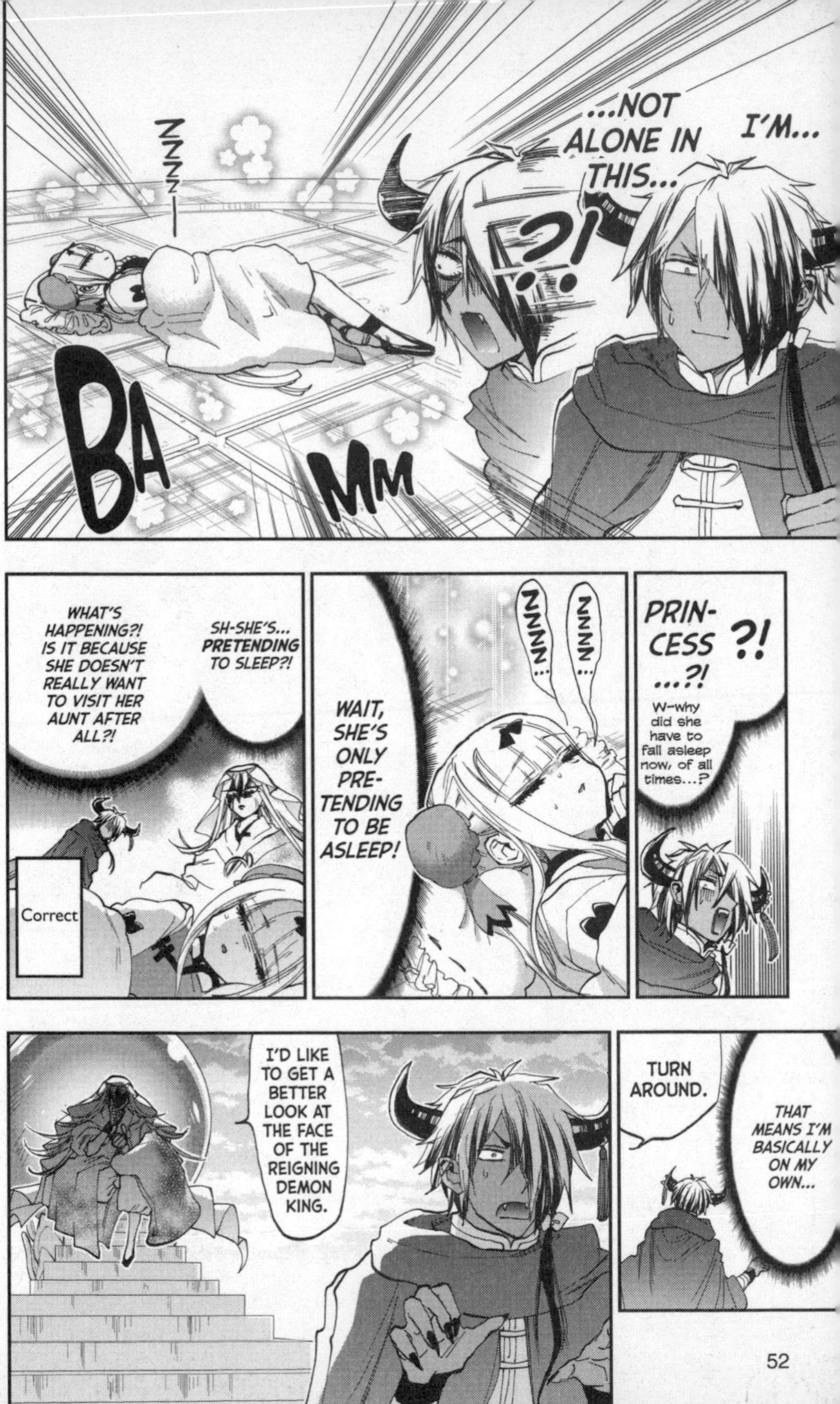
I'M...
...NOT ALONE IN THIS...
?!
ZZZZ—
BAMM
PRINCESS ...?!
?!
W-why did she have to fall asleep now, of all times...?
NNNN...
NNNN...
WAIT, SHE'S ONLY PRETENDING TO BE ASLEEP!
SH-SHE'S... PRETENDING TO SLEEP?!
WHAT'S HAPPENING?! IS IT BECAUSE SHE DOESN'T REALLY WANT TO VISIT HER AUNT AFTER ALL?!
Correct
THAT MEANS I'M BASICALLY ON MY OWN...
TURN AROUND.
I'D LIKE TO GET A BETTER LOOK AT THE FACE OF THE REIGNING DEMON KING.

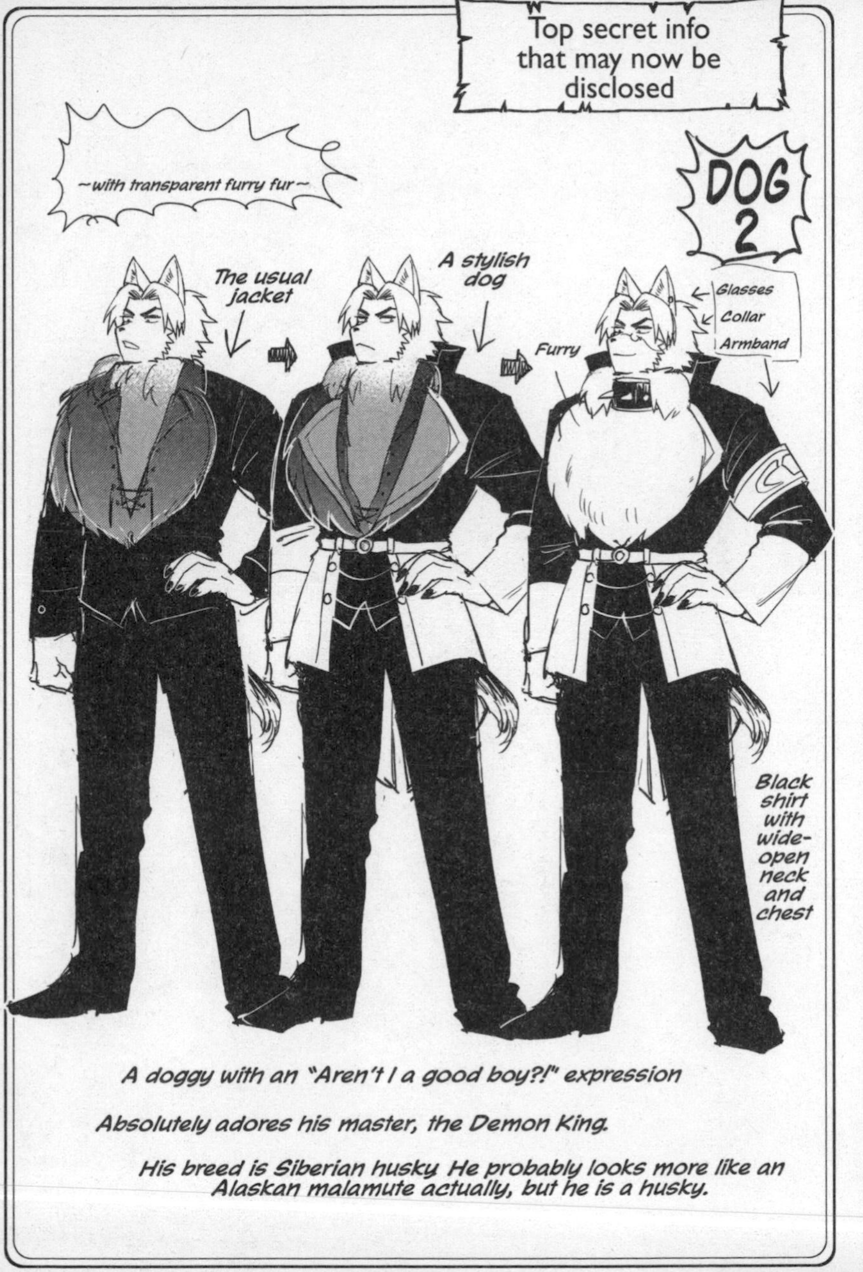
Top secret info that may now be disclosed
DOG 2
~with transparent furry fur~
The usual jacket
A stylish dog
Furry
Glasses
Collar
Armband
Black shirt with wide-open neck and chest
A doggy with an "Aren't I a good boy?!" expression
Absolutely adores his master, the Demon King.
His breed is Siberian husky. He probably looks more like an Alaskan malamute actually, but he is a husky.

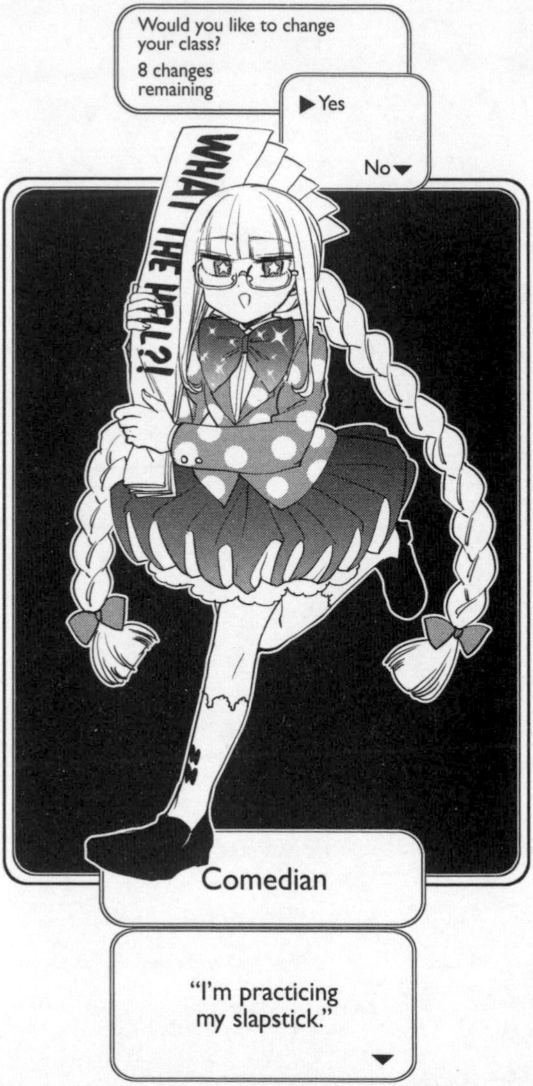
Would you like to change your class?
8 changes remaining
▶Yes
No▼
Comedian
"I'm practicing my slapstick."

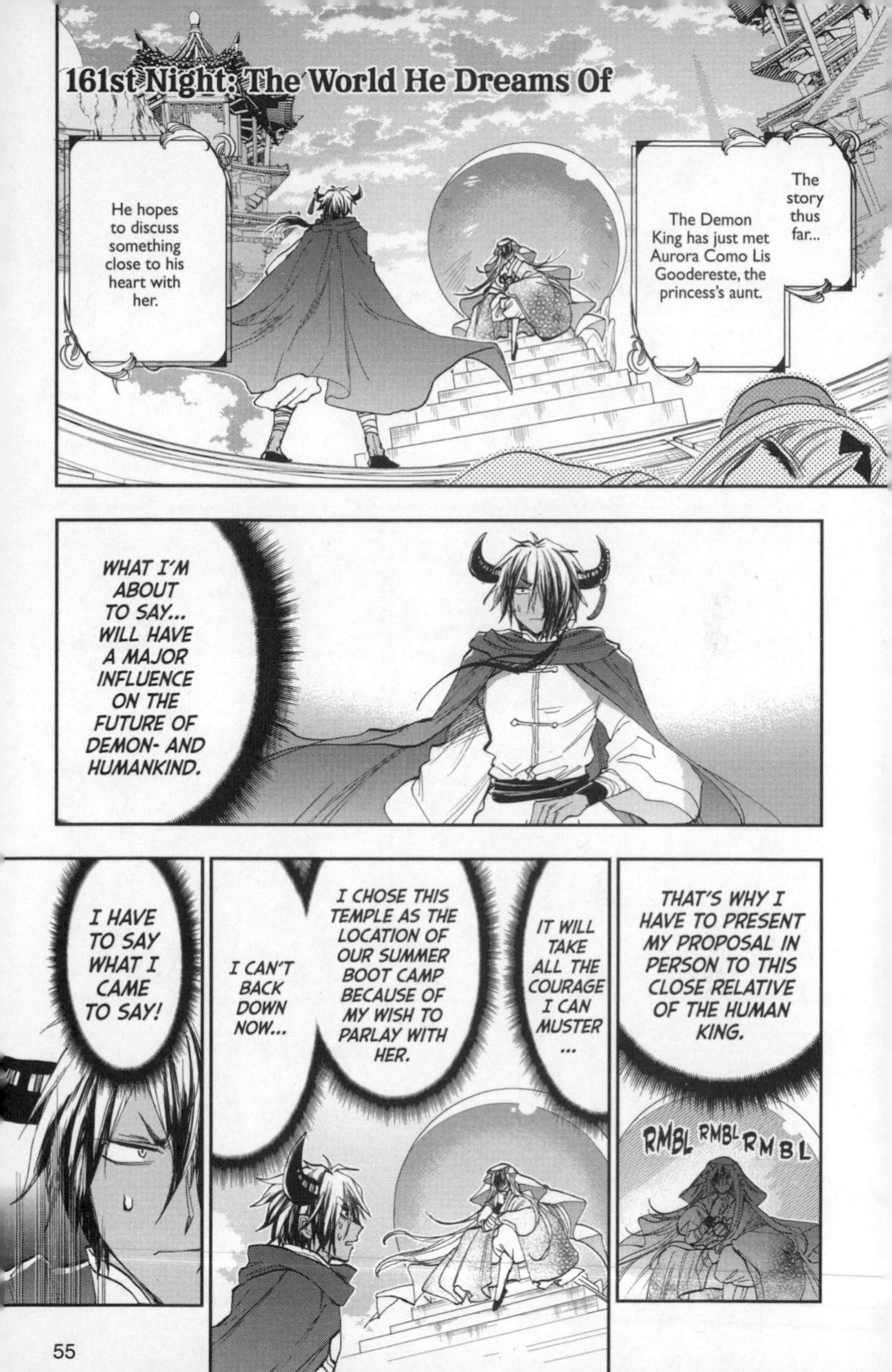
161st Night: The World He Dreams Of
The story thus far...
The Demon King has just met Aurora Como Lis Gooderestе, the princess's aunt.
He hopes to discuss something close to his heart with her.
WHAT I'M ABOUT TO SAY... WILL HAVE A MAJOR INFLUENCE ON THE FUTURE OF DEMON- AND HUMANKIND.
THAT'S WHY I HAVE TO PRESENT MY PROPOSAL IN PERSON TO THIS CLOSE RELATIVE OF THE HUMAN KING.
RMBL RMBL RMBL
IT WILL TAKE ALL THE COURAGE I CAN MUSTER...
I CHOSE THIS TEMPLE AS THE LOCATION OF OUR SUMMER BOOT CAMP BECAUSE OF MY WISH TO PARLAY WITH HER.
I CAN'T BACK DOWN NOW...
I HAVE TO SAY WHAT I CAME TO SAY!

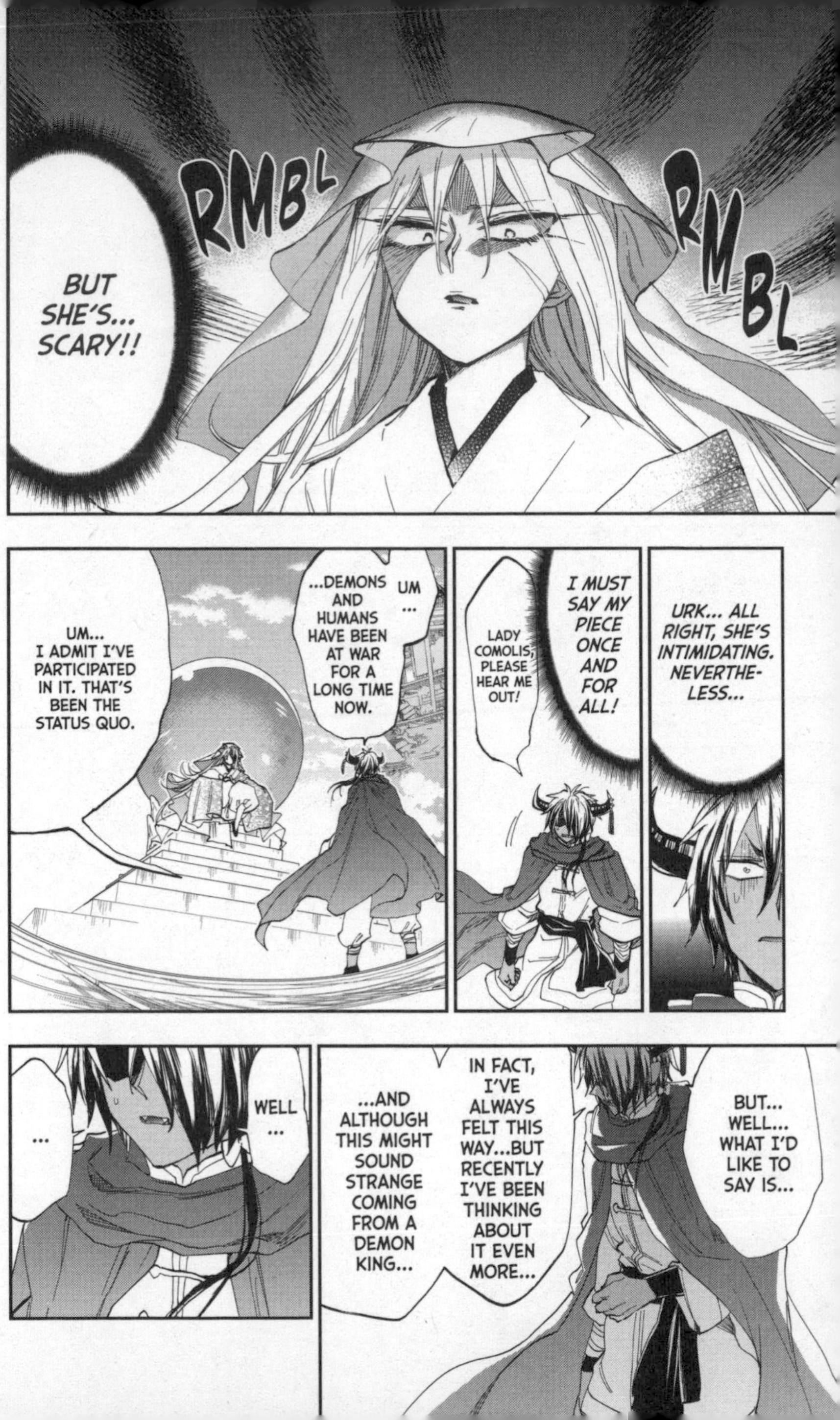
RMBL
RMBL
BUT SHE'S... SCARY!!
URK... ALL RIGHT, SHE'S INTIMIDATING. NEVERTHE-LESS...
I MUST SAY MY PIECE ONCE AND FOR ALL!
LADY COMOLIS, PLEASE HEAR ME OUT!
UM ...
...DEMONS AND HUMANS HAVE BEEN AT WAR FOR A LONG TIME NOW.
UM... I ADMIT I'VE PARTICIPATED IN IT. THAT'S BEEN THE STATUS QUO.
BUT... WELL... WHAT I'D LIKE TO SAY IS...
IN FACT, I'VE ALWAYS FELT THIS WAY...BUT RECENTLY I'VE BEEN THINKING ABOUT IT EVEN MORE...
...AND ALTHOUGH THIS MIGHT SOUND STRANGE COMING FROM A DEMON KING...
WELL ...
...

161st Night: The World He Dreams Of

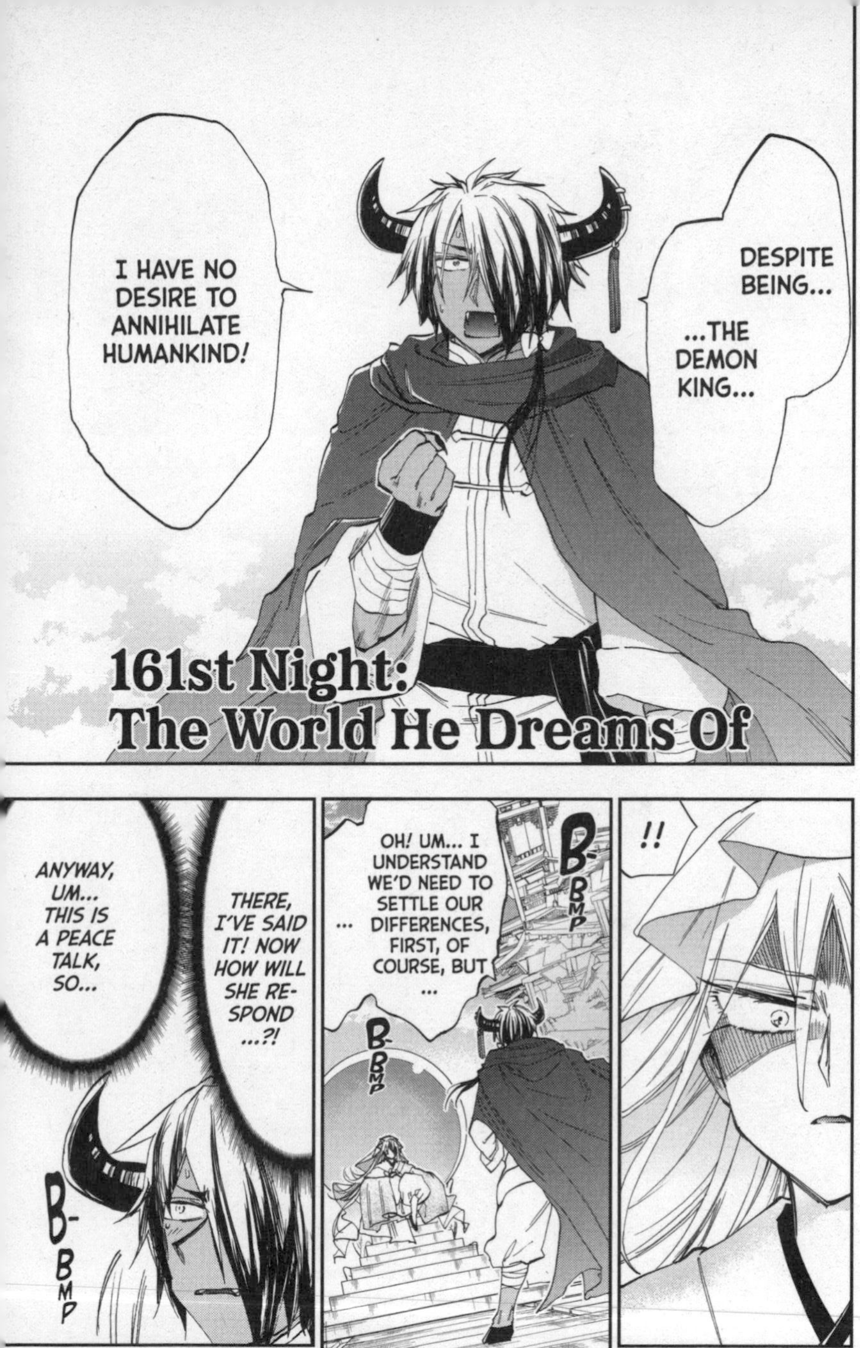
DESPITE BEING...
...THE DEMON KING...
I HAVE NO DESIRE TO ANNIHILATE HUMANKIND!
!!
OH! UM... I UNDERSTAND WE'D NEED TO SETTLE OUR DIFFERENCES, FIRST, OF COURSE, BUT ...
...
B-BMP
B-BMP
THERE, I'VE SAID IT! NOW HOW WILL SHE RE-SPOND ...?!
ANYWAY, UM... THIS IS A PEACE TALK, SO...
B-BMP

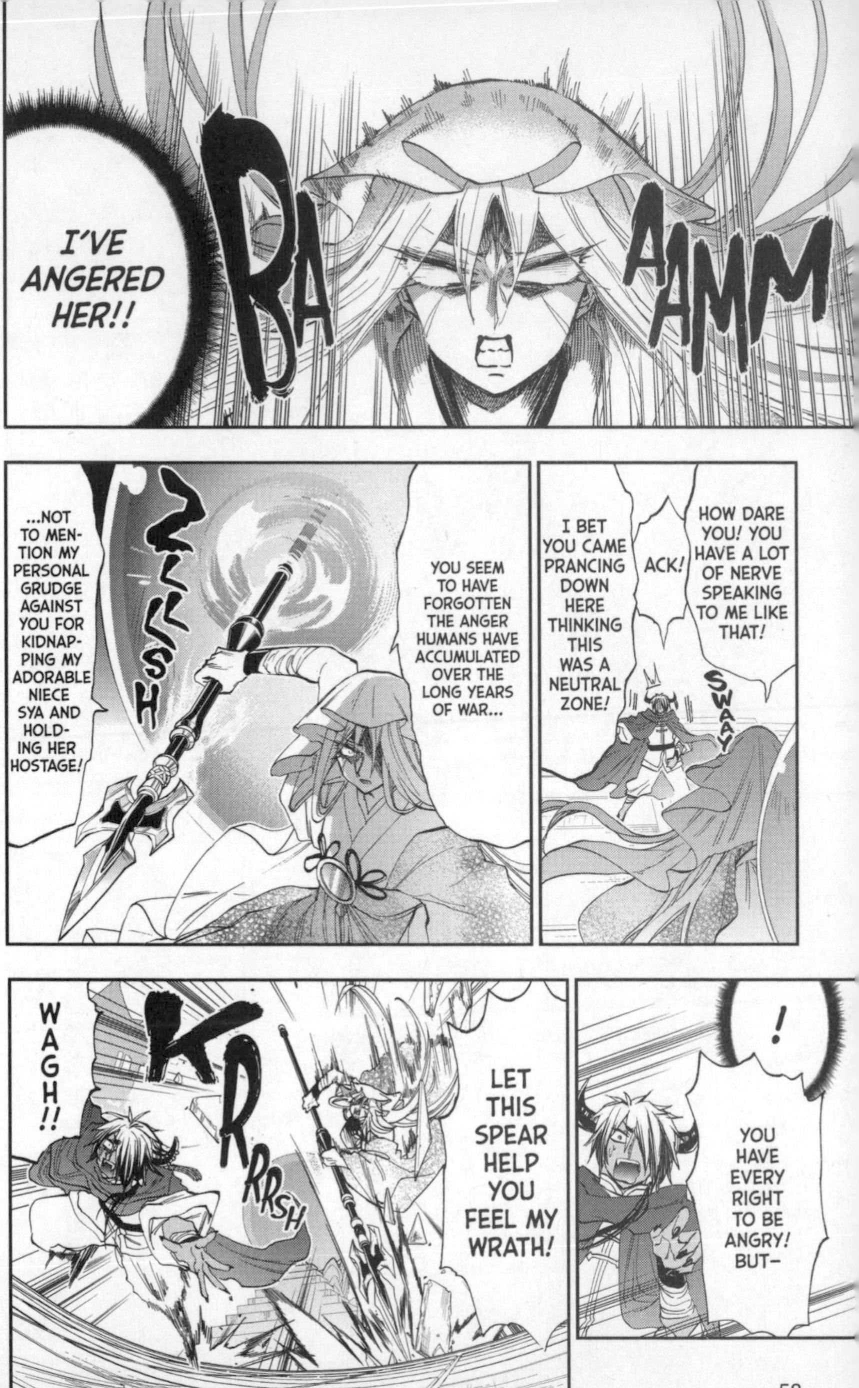
I'VE ANGERED HER!!
BAAAMM
HOW DARE YOU! YOU HAVE A LOT OF NERVE SPEAKING TO ME LIKE THAT!
ACK!
I BET YOU CAME PRANCING DOWN HERE THINKING THIS WAS A NEUTRAL ZONE!
SWAY
YOU SEEM TO HAVE FORGOTTEN THE ANGER HUMANS HAVE ACCUMULATED OVER THE LONG YEARS OF WAR...
...NOT TO MENTION MY PERSONAL GRUDGE AGAINST YOU FOR KIDNAPPING MY ADORABLE NIECE SYA AND HOLDING HER HOSTAGE!
!
YOU HAVE EVERY RIGHT TO BE ANGRY! BUT–
LET THIS SPEAR HELP YOU FEEL MY WRATH!
KRRRSH
WAGH!!

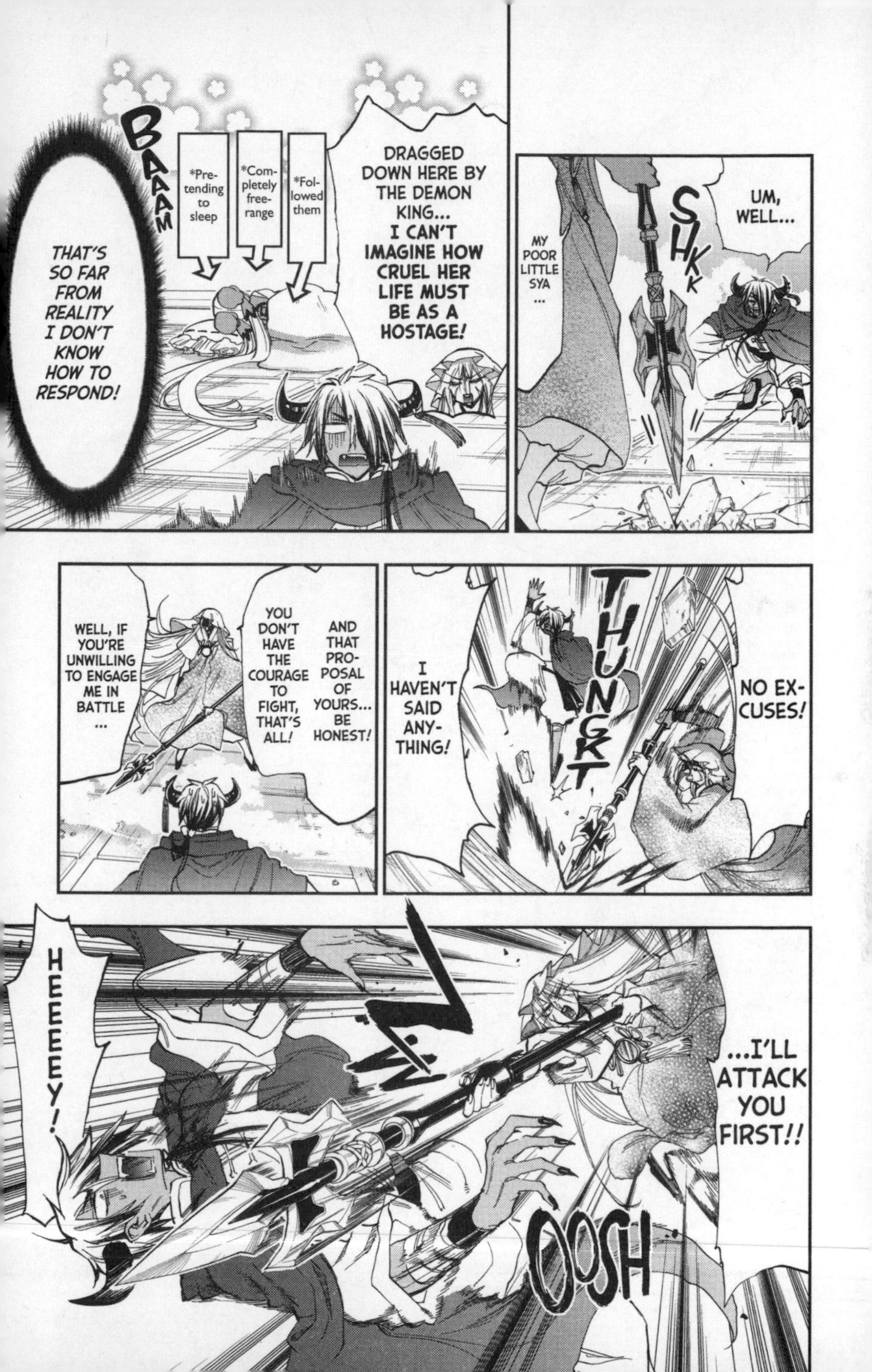
SHKK
UM, WELL...
MY POOR LITTLE SYA...
DRAGGED DOWN HERE BY THE DEMON KING... I CAN'T IMAGINE HOW CRUEL HER LIFE MUST BE AS A HOSTAGE!
*Followed them
*Completely free-range
*Pretending to sleep
BAAAM
THAT'S SO FAR FROM REALITY I DON'T KNOW HOW TO RESPOND!
NO EXCUSES!
THUNGKT
I HAVEN'T SAID ANYTHING!
AND THAT PROPOSAL OF YOURS... BE HONEST!
YOU DON'T HAVE THE COURAGE TO FIGHT, THAT'S ALL!
WELL, IF YOU'RE UNWILLING TO ENGAGE ME IN BATTLE...
...I'LL ATTACK YOU FIRST!!
ZW
OOSH
HEEEEY!

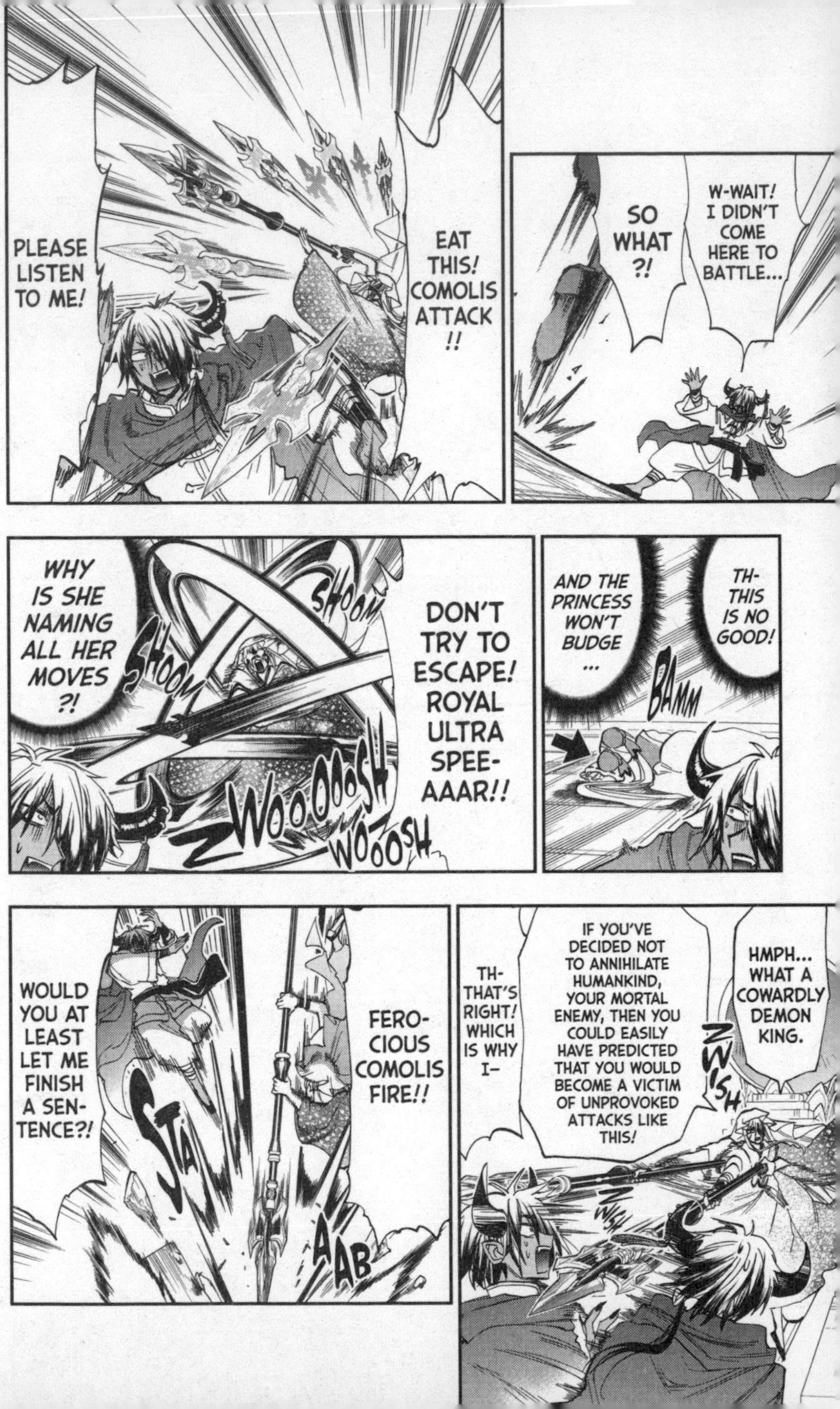
W-WAIT! I DIDN'T COME HERE TO BATTLE...
SO WHAT?!
EAT THIS! COMOLIS ATTACK!!
PLEASE LISTEN TO ME!
TH-THIS IS NO GOOD!
AND THE PRINCESS WON'T BUDGE...
BAMM
DON'T TRY TO ESCAPE! ROYAL ULTRA SPEE-AAAR!!
SHOOM
SHOOM
WHY IS SHE NAMING ALL HER MOVES?!
ZWOOOOOSH
WOOOSH
HMPH... WHAT A COWARDLY DEMON KING.
IF YOU'VE DECIDED NOT TO ANNIHILATE HUMANKIND, YOUR MORTAL ENEMY, THEN YOU COULD EASILY HAVE PREDICTED THAT YOU WOULD BECOME A VICTIM OF UNPROVOKED ATTACKS LIKE THIS!
ZWISH
TH-THAT'S RIGHT! WHICH IS WHY I–
ZWISH
FEROCIOUS COMOLIS FIRE!!
WOULD YOU AT LEAST LET ME FINISH A SENTENCE?!
STA
AAB

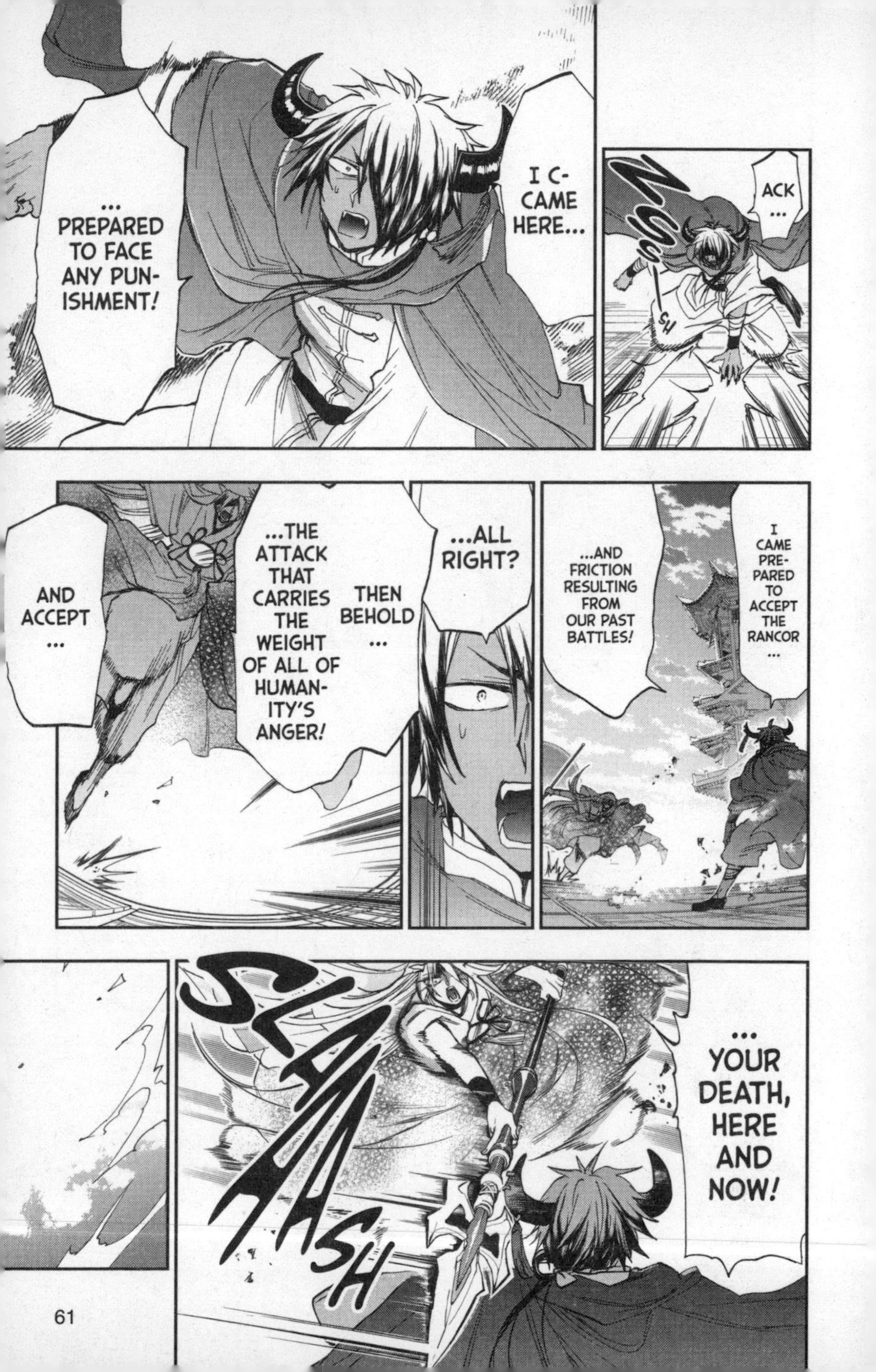
ZSSH
ACK ...
I C- CAME HERE...
... PREPARED TO FACE ANY PUN- ISHMENT!
I CAME PRE- PARED TO ACCEPT THE RANCOR ...
...AND FRICTION RESULTING FROM OUR PAST BATTLES!
...ALL RIGHT?
THEN BEHOLD ...
...THE ATTACK THAT CARRIES THE WEIGHT OF ALL OF HUMAN- ITY'S ANGER!
AND ACCEPT ...
... YOUR DEATH, HERE AND NOW!
SLAAAASH

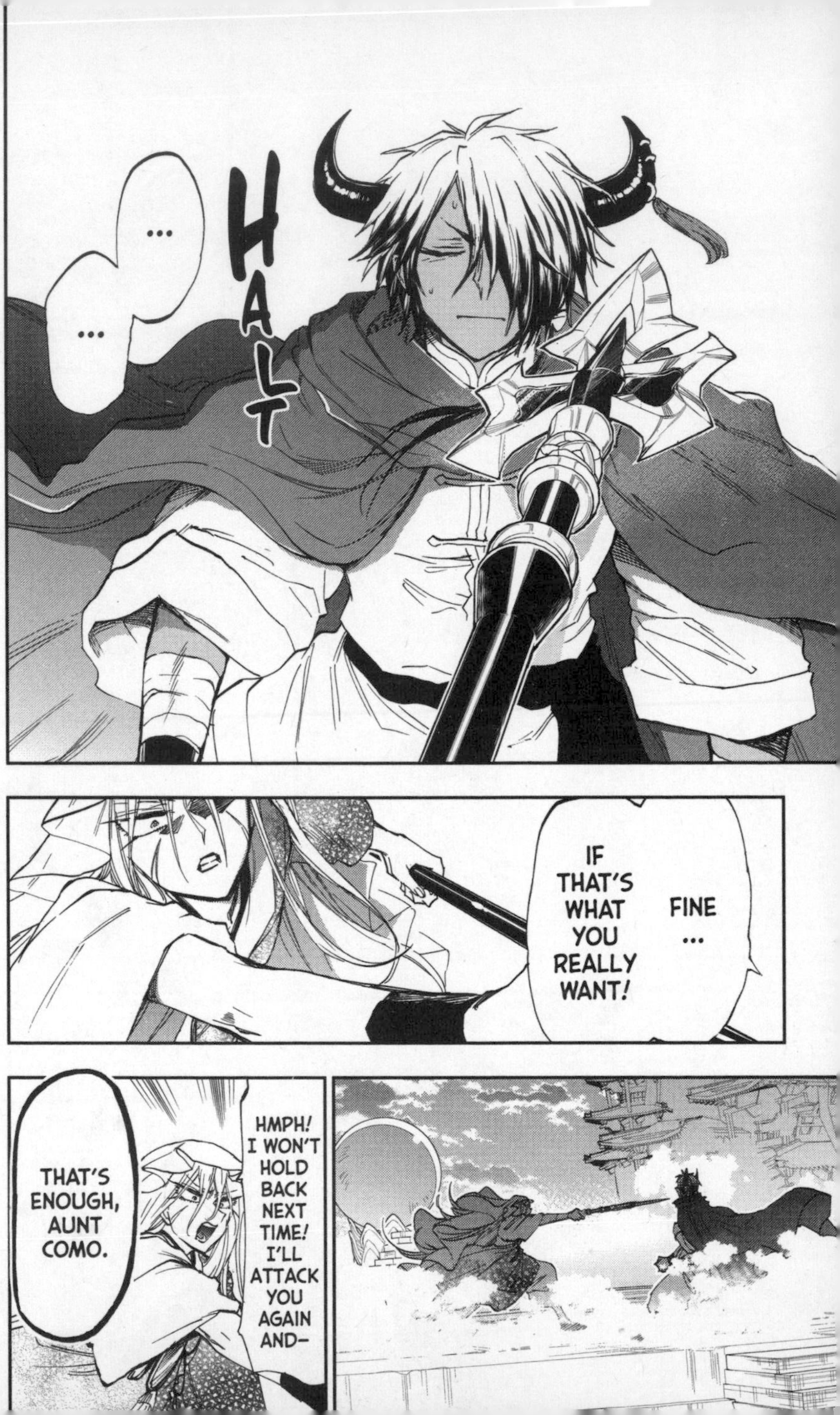

...
HALT
...
FINE...
IF THAT'S WHAT YOU REALLY WANT!
HMPH! I WON'T HOLD BACK NEXT TIME! I'LL ATTACK YOU AGAIN AND—
THAT'S ENOUGH, AUNT COMO.

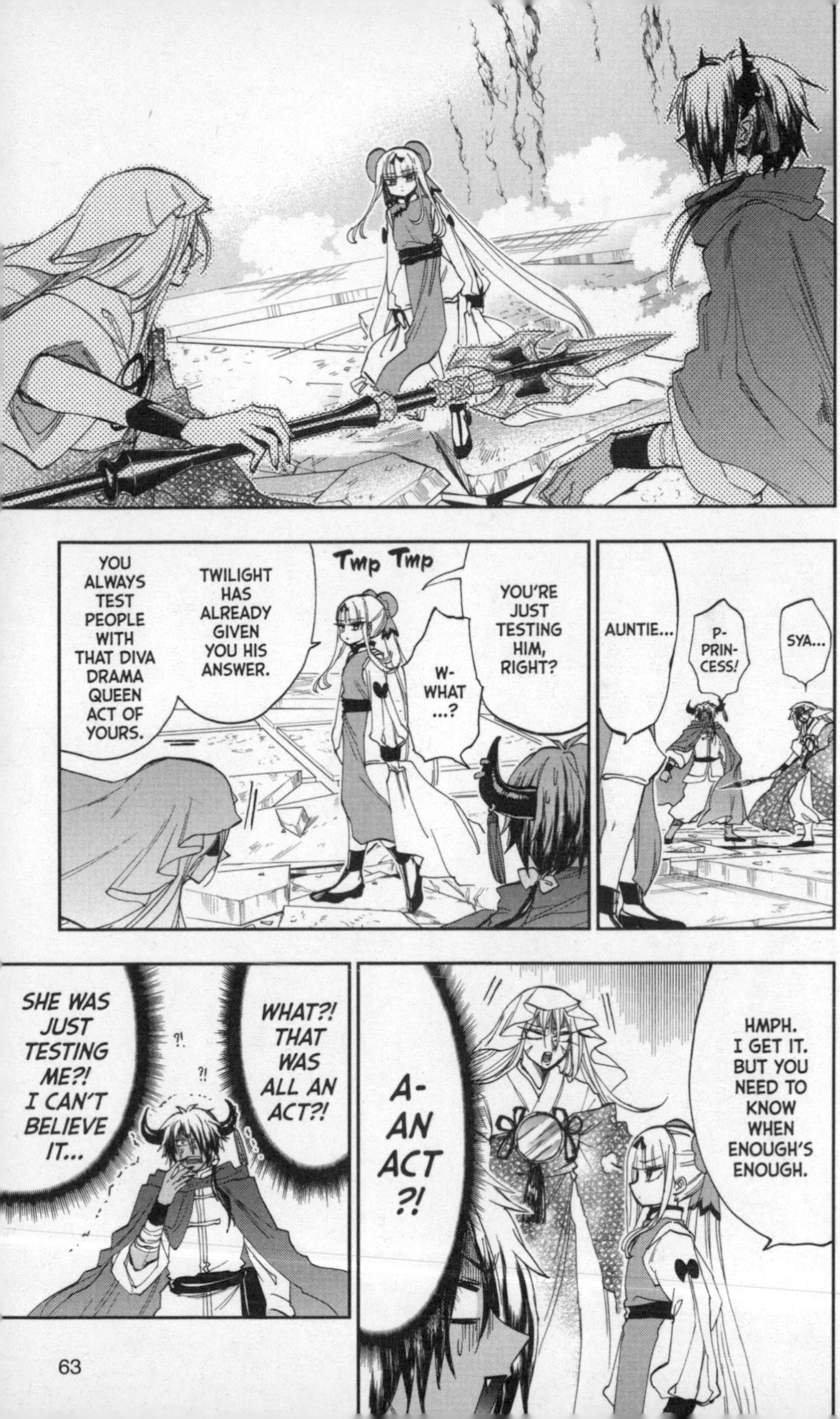
SYA...
P-PRINCESS!
AUNTIE...
Tmp Tmp
YOU'RE JUST TESTING HIM, RIGHT?
W-WHAT ...?
TWILIGHT HAS ALREADY GIVEN YOU HIS ANSWER.
YOU ALWAYS TEST PEOPLE WITH THAT DIVA DRAMA QUEEN ACT OF YOURS.
HMPH. I GET IT. BUT YOU NEED TO KNOW WHEN ENOUGH'S ENOUGH.
A-AN ACT ?!
WHAT?! THAT WAS ALL AN ACT?!
SHE WAS JUST TESTING ME?! I CAN'T BELIEVE IT...
?!
?!

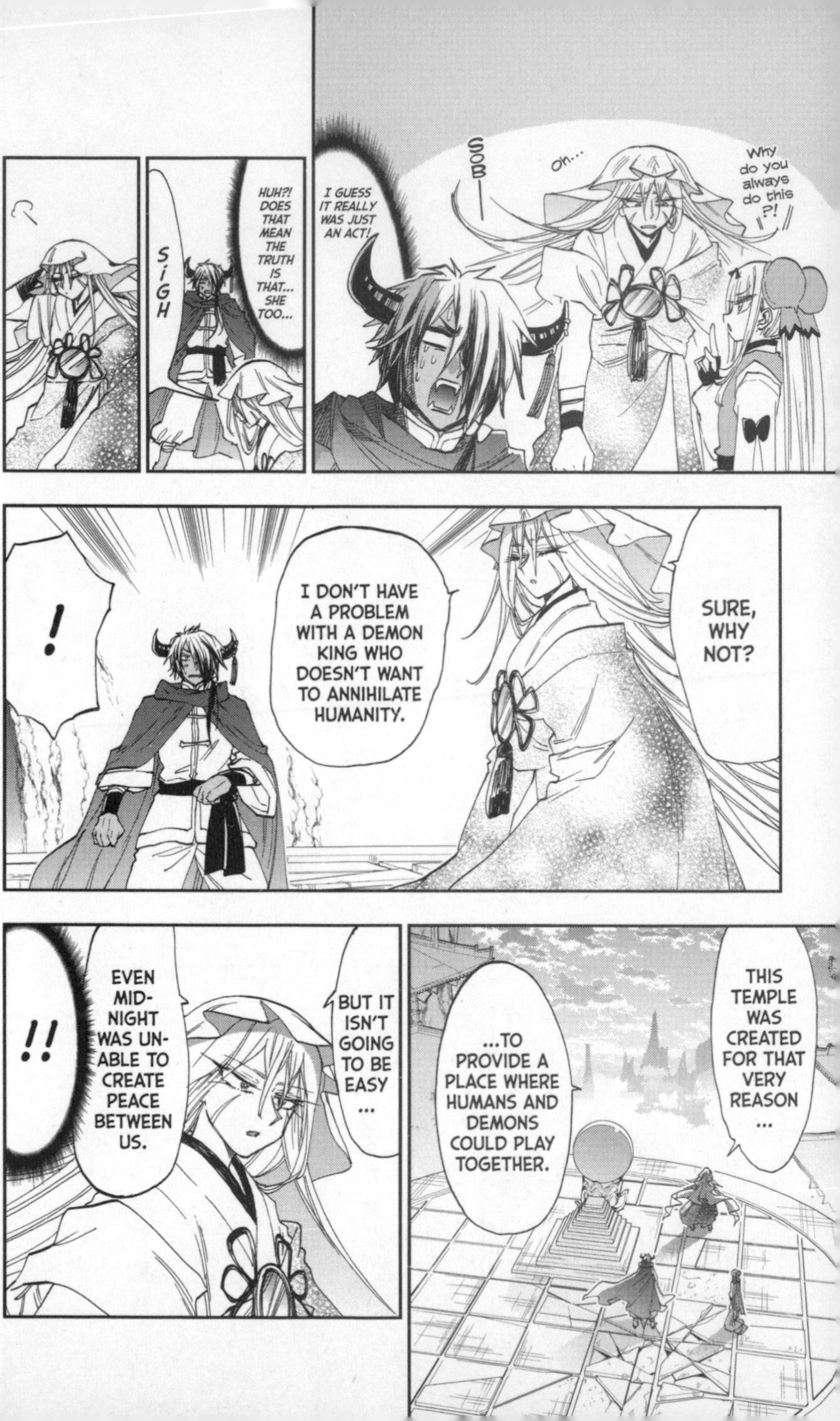
Why do you always do this ?!
Oh...
SOB—
I GUESS IT REALLY WAS JUST AN ACT!
HUH?! DOES THAT MEAN THE TRUTH IS THAT... SHE TOO...
SIGH
SURE, WHY NOT?
I DON'T HAVE A PROBLEM WITH A DEMON KING WHO DOESN'T WANT TO ANNIHILATE HUMANITY.
!
THIS TEMPLE WAS CREATED FOR THAT VERY REASON...
...TO PROVIDE A PLACE WHERE HUMANS AND DEMONS COULD PLAY TOGETHER.
BUT IT ISN'T GOING TO BE EASY...
EVEN MID-NIGHT WAS UN-ABLE TO CREATE PEACE BETWEEN US.
!!

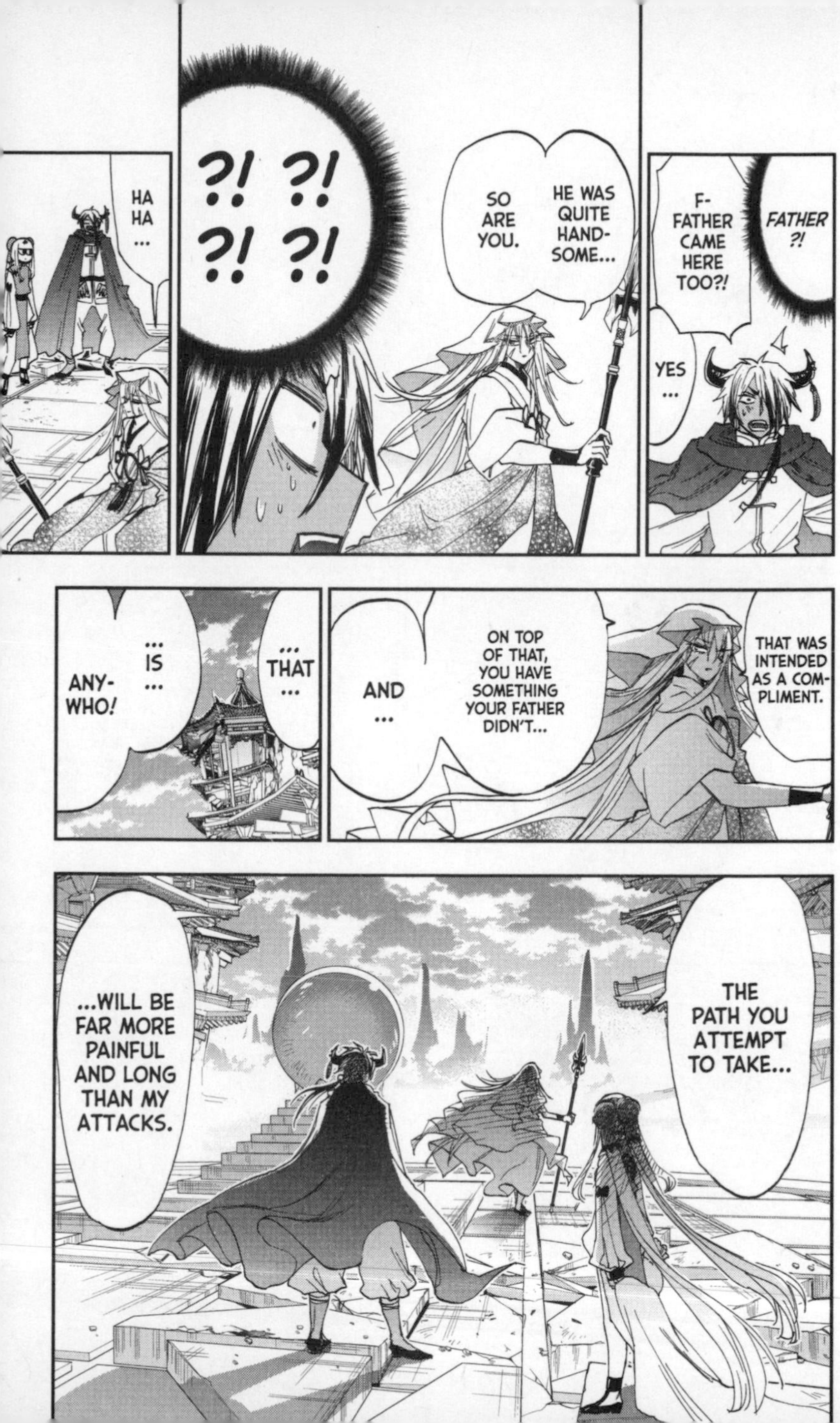
FATHER?!
F-FATHER CAME HERE TOO?!
YES ...
HE WAS QUITE HANDSOME...
SO ARE YOU.
?! ?! ?! ?!
HA HA ...
THAT WAS INTENDED AS A COMPLIMENT.
ON TOP OF THAT, YOU HAVE SOMETHING YOUR FATHER DIDN'T...
AND ...
... THAT ...
... IS ...
ANY-WHO!
THE PATH YOU ATTEMPT TO TAKE...
...WILL BE FAR MORE PAINFUL AND LONG THAN MY ATTACKS.

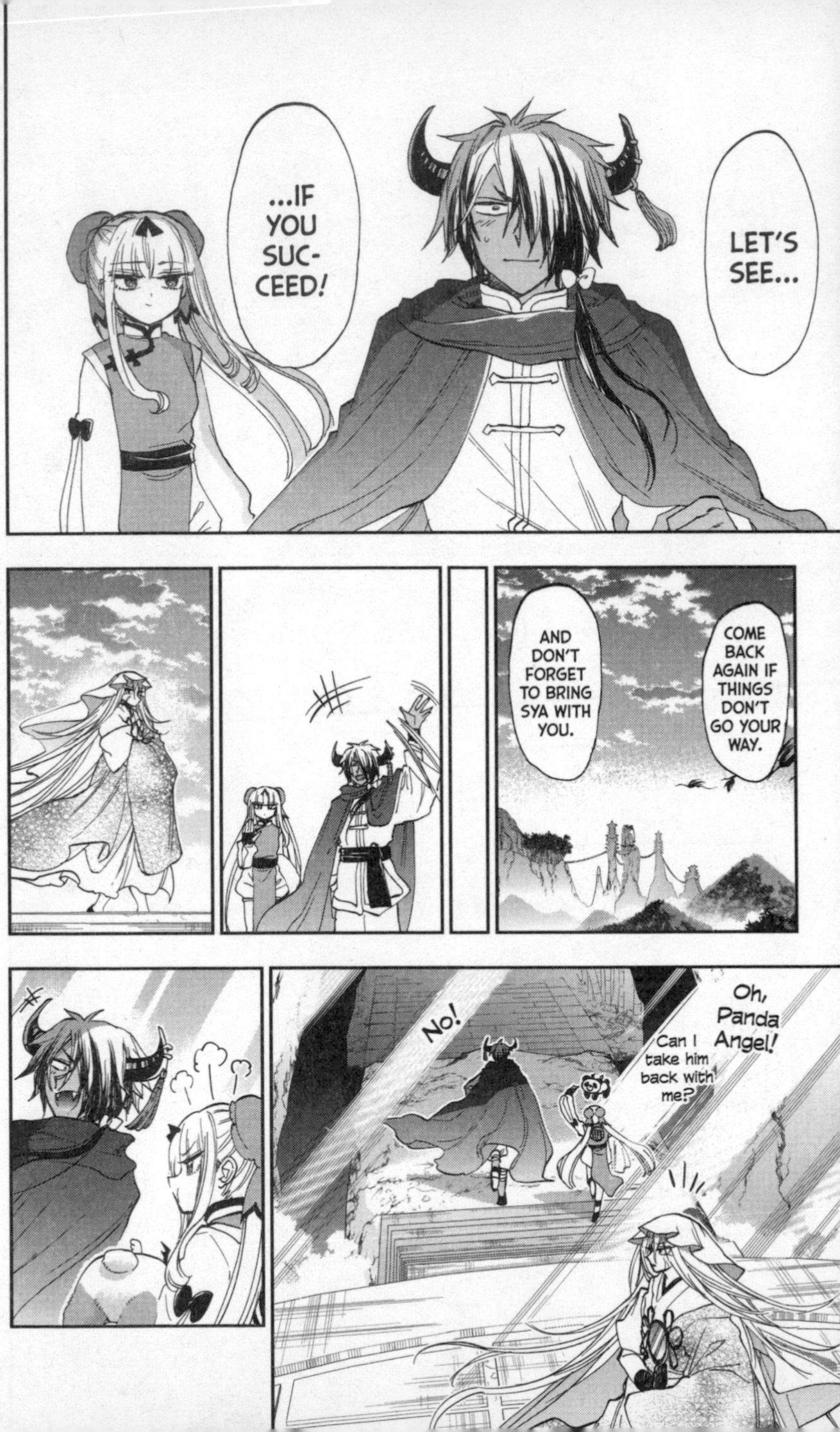
LET'S SEE...
...IF YOU SUC-CEED!
COME BACK AGAIN IF THINGS DON'T GO YOUR WAY.
AND DON'T FORGET TO BRING SYA WITH YOU.
Oh, Panda Angel!
Can I take him back with me?
No!

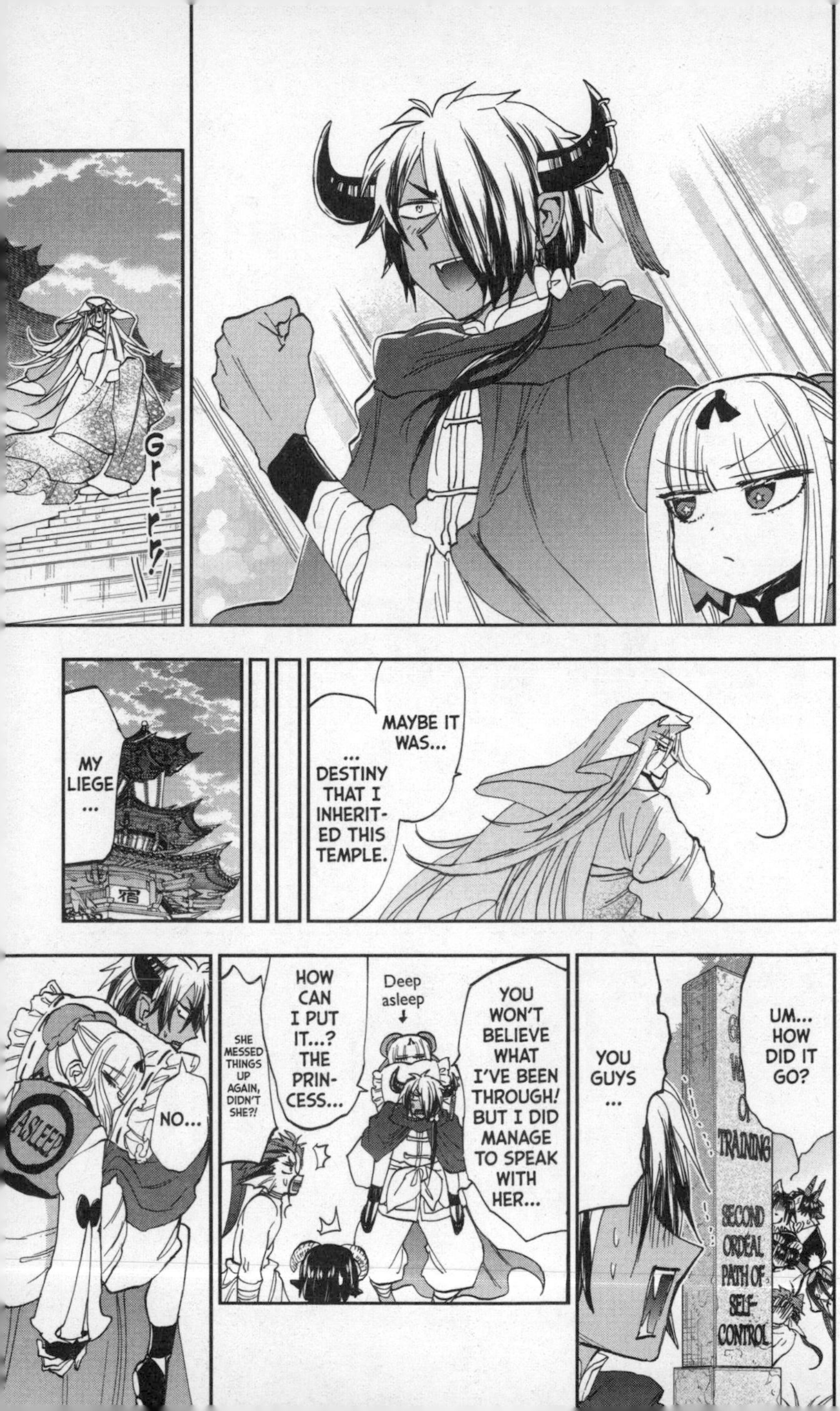
Grrrr!
MAYBE IT WAS...
... DESTINY THAT I INHERITED THIS TEMPLE.
MY LIEGE ...
宿
UM... HOW DID IT GO?
YOU GUYS ...
TRAINING
SECOND ORDEAL PATH OF SELF-CONTROL
YOU WON'T BELIEVE WHAT I'VE BEEN THROUGH! BUT I DID MANAGE TO SPEAK WITH HER...
Deep asleep
HOW CAN I PUT IT...? THE PRINCESS...
SHE MESSED THINGS UP AGAIN, DIDN'T SHE?!
NO...
ASLEEP

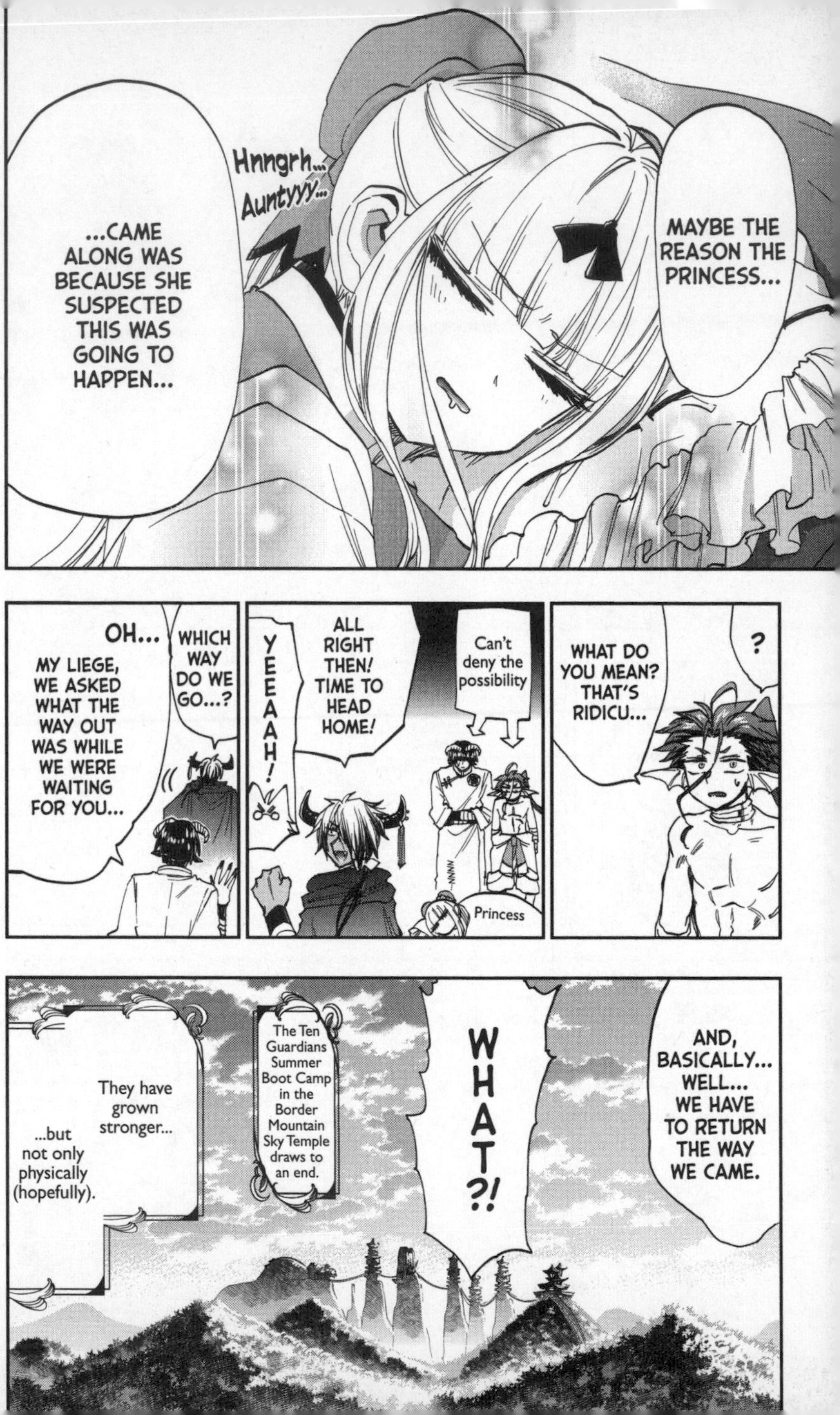
MAYBE THE REASON THE PRINCESS...
Hnngrh... Auntyyy...
...CAME ALONG WAS BECAUSE SHE SUSPECTED THIS WAS GOING TO HAPPEN...
?
WHAT DO YOU MEAN? THAT'S RIDICU...
Can't deny the possibility
Princess
ALL RIGHT THEN! TIME TO HEAD HOME!
YEEAAH!
WHICH WAY DO WE GO...?
OH... MY LIEGE, WE ASKED WHAT THE WAY OUT WAS WHILE WE WERE WAITING FOR YOU...
AND, BASICALLY... WELL... WE HAVE TO RETURN THE WAY WE CAME.
WHAT?!
The Ten Guardians Summer Boot Camp in the Border Mountain Sky Temple draws to an end.
They have grown stronger...
...but not only physically (hopefully).

Aurora Como Lis Goodereste

Sternness: ☆☆☆☆☆☆☆

Grandiosity: ☆☆☆☆☆☆☆☆

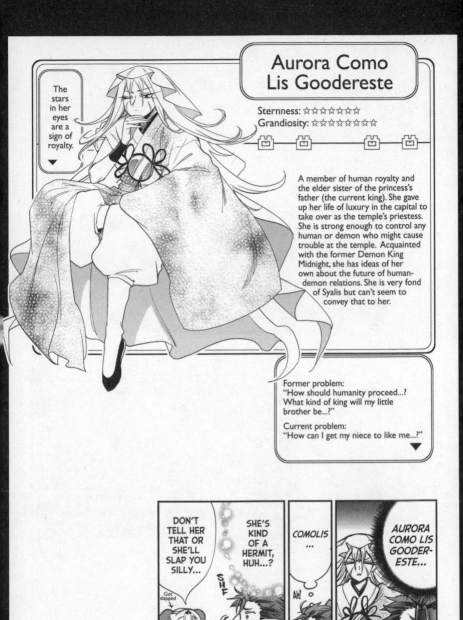

The stars in her eyes are a sign of royalty. ▼

A member of human royalty and the elder sister of the princess's father (the current king). She gave up her life of luxury in the capital to take over as the temple's priestess. She is strong enough to control any human or demon who might cause trouble at the temple. Acquainted with the former Demon King Midnight, she has ideas of her own about the future of human-demon relations. She is very fond of Syalis but can't seem to convey that to her.

Former problem:
"How should humanity proceed...? What kind of king will my little brother be...?"

Current problem:
"How can I get my niece to like me...?" ▼

AURORA COMO LIS GOODER-ESTE...
COMOLIS ...
AH!
SHE'S KIND OF A HERMIT, HUH...?
SHF
DON'T TELL HER THAT OR SHE'LL SLAP YOU SILLY...
Got slapped

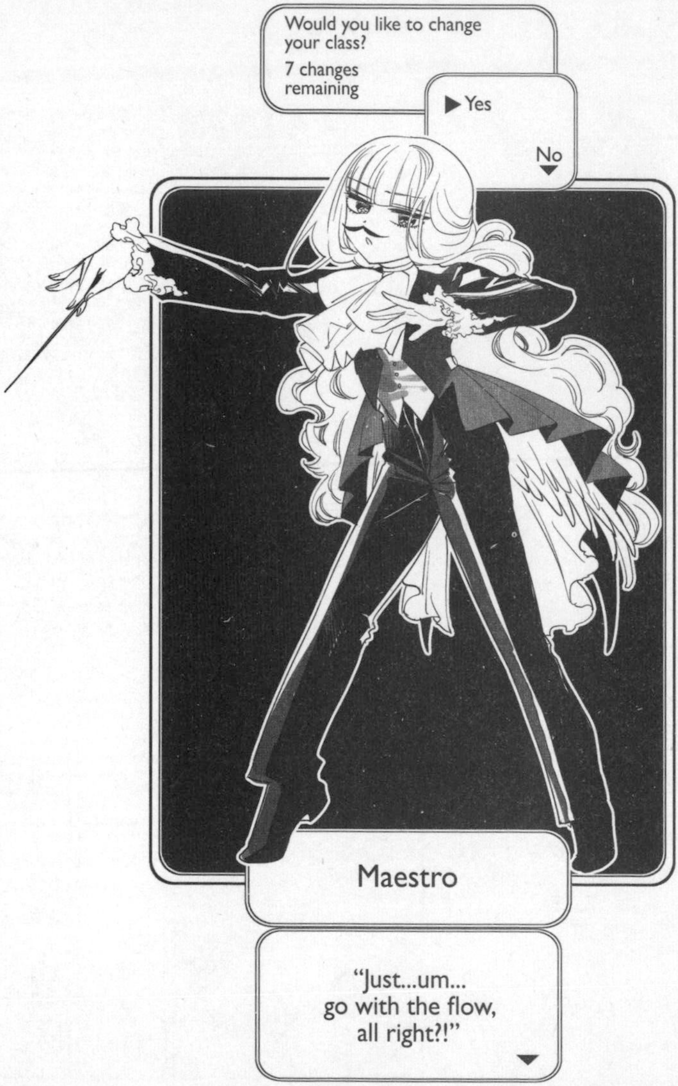
Would you like to change your class?
7 changes remaining
▶Yes
No
Maestro
"Just...um... go with the flow, all right?!"

162nd Night: Please Seal the Deal ASAP

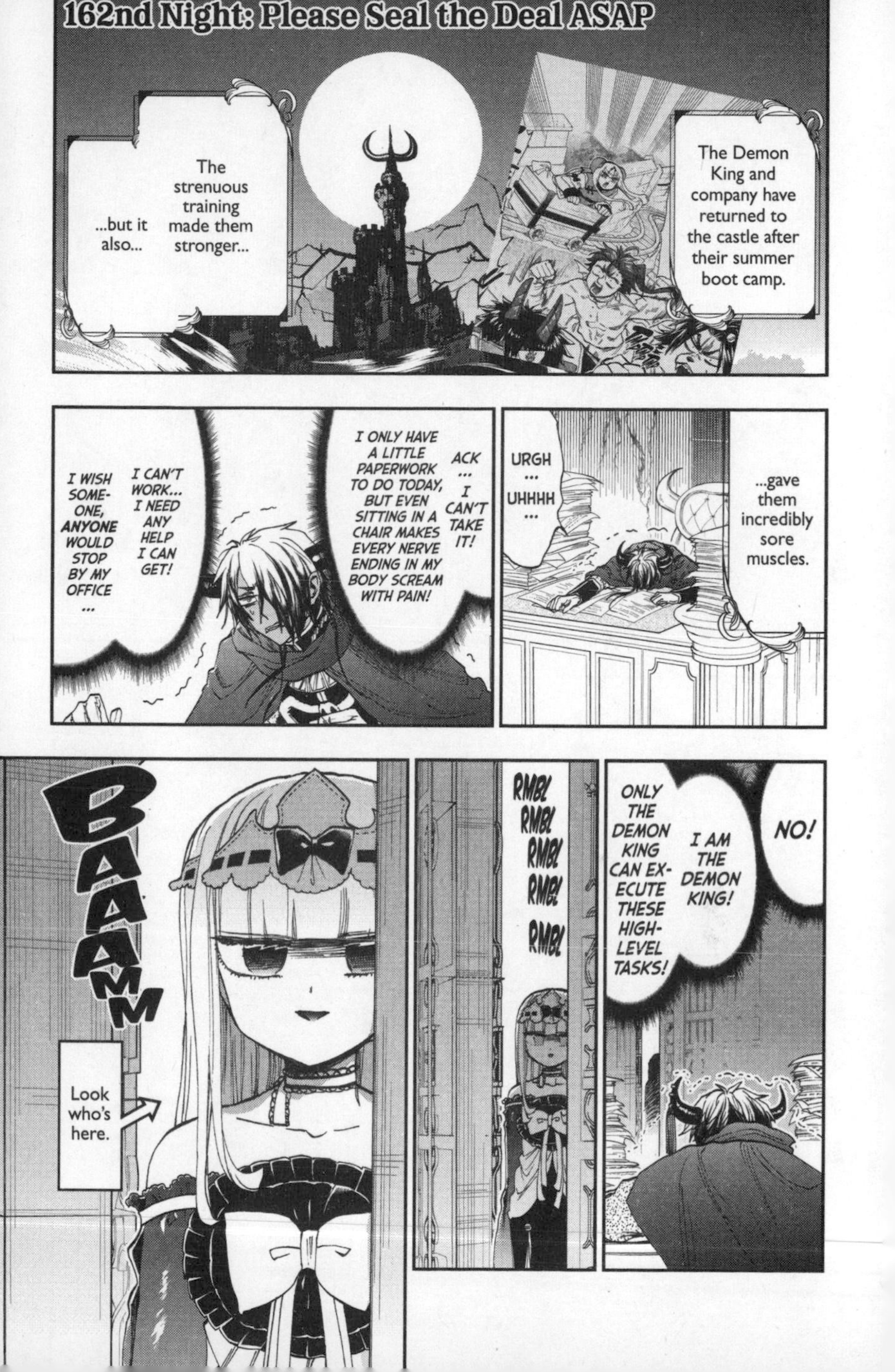
The Demon King and company have returned to the castle after their summer boot camp.
The strenuous training made them stronger...
...but it also...
...gave them incredibly sore muscles.
URGH... UHHHH...
ACK... I CAN'T TAKE IT!
I ONLY HAVE A LITTLE PAPERWORK TO DO TODAY, BUT EVEN SITTING IN A CHAIR MAKES EVERY NERVE ENDING IN MY BODY SCREAM WITH PAIN!
I CAN'T WORK... I NEED ANY HELP I CAN GET!
I WISH SOMEONE, ANYONE WOULD STOP BY MY OFFICE...
NO!
I AM THE DEMON KING!
ONLY THE DEMON KING CAN EXECUTE THESE HIGH-LEVEL TASKS!
RMBL RMBL RMBL RMBL RMBL
BAAAMM
Look who's here.

162nd Night: Please Seal the Deal ASAP

Not an option	Sore muscles	Sore muscles	Sore muscles	Sore muscles

I CAN'T ASK THE HOSTAGE TO FILL IN FOR THE DEMON KING!

RMBL RMBL RMBL RMBL RMBL RMBL

RMBL! RMBL! RMBL! RMBL!

HEY, DO YOU NEED HELP WITH YOUR WORK...?

KLA KK

ACK! WAIT...

!

ARE THESE WORK DOCUMENTS?

B- BUT WHAT COULD THE PRINCESS'S ULTERIOR MOTIVE BE...?!

THUD

*Sore muscles where he didn't even know he had them

ARRRRRGH!

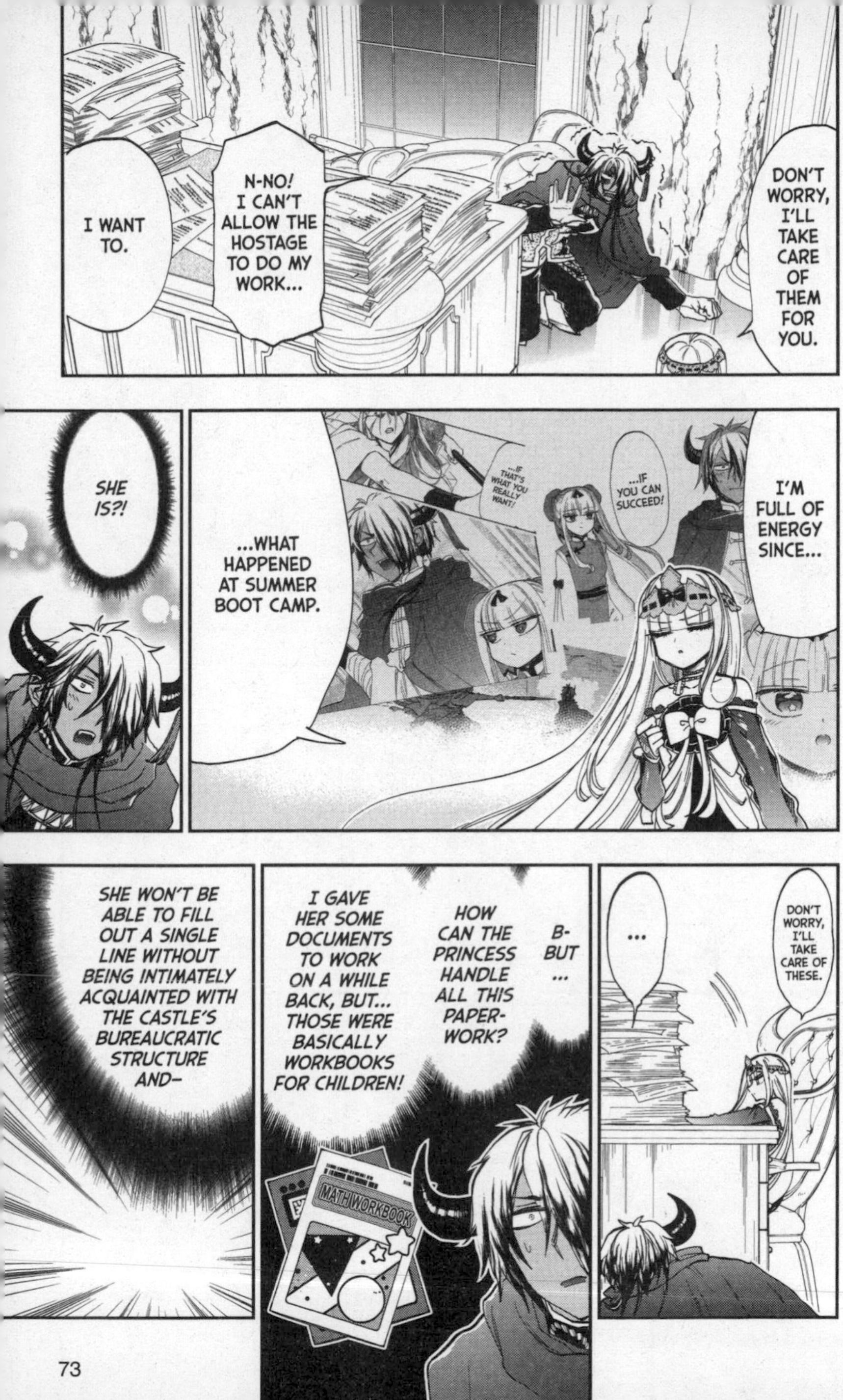
DON'T WORRY, I'LL TAKE CARE OF THEM FOR YOU.
N-NO! I CAN'T ALLOW THE HOSTAGE TO DO MY WORK...
I WANT TO.
I'M FULL OF ENERGY SINCE...
...IF YOU CAN SUCCEED!
...IF THAT'S WHAT YOU REALLY WANT!
...WHAT HAPPENED AT SUMMER BOOT CAMP.
SHE IS?!
DON'T WORRY, I'LL TAKE CARE OF THESE.
...
B-BUT...
HOW CAN THE PRINCESS HANDLE ALL THIS PAPER-WORK?
I GAVE HER SOME DOCUMENTS TO WORK ON A WHILE BACK, BUT... THOSE WERE BASICALLY WORKBOOKS FOR CHILDREN!
MATH WORKBOOK
SHE WON'T BE ABLE TO FILL OUT A SINGLE LINE WITHOUT BEING INTIMATELY ACQUAINTED WITH THE CASTLE'S BUREAUCRATIC STRUCTURE AND–

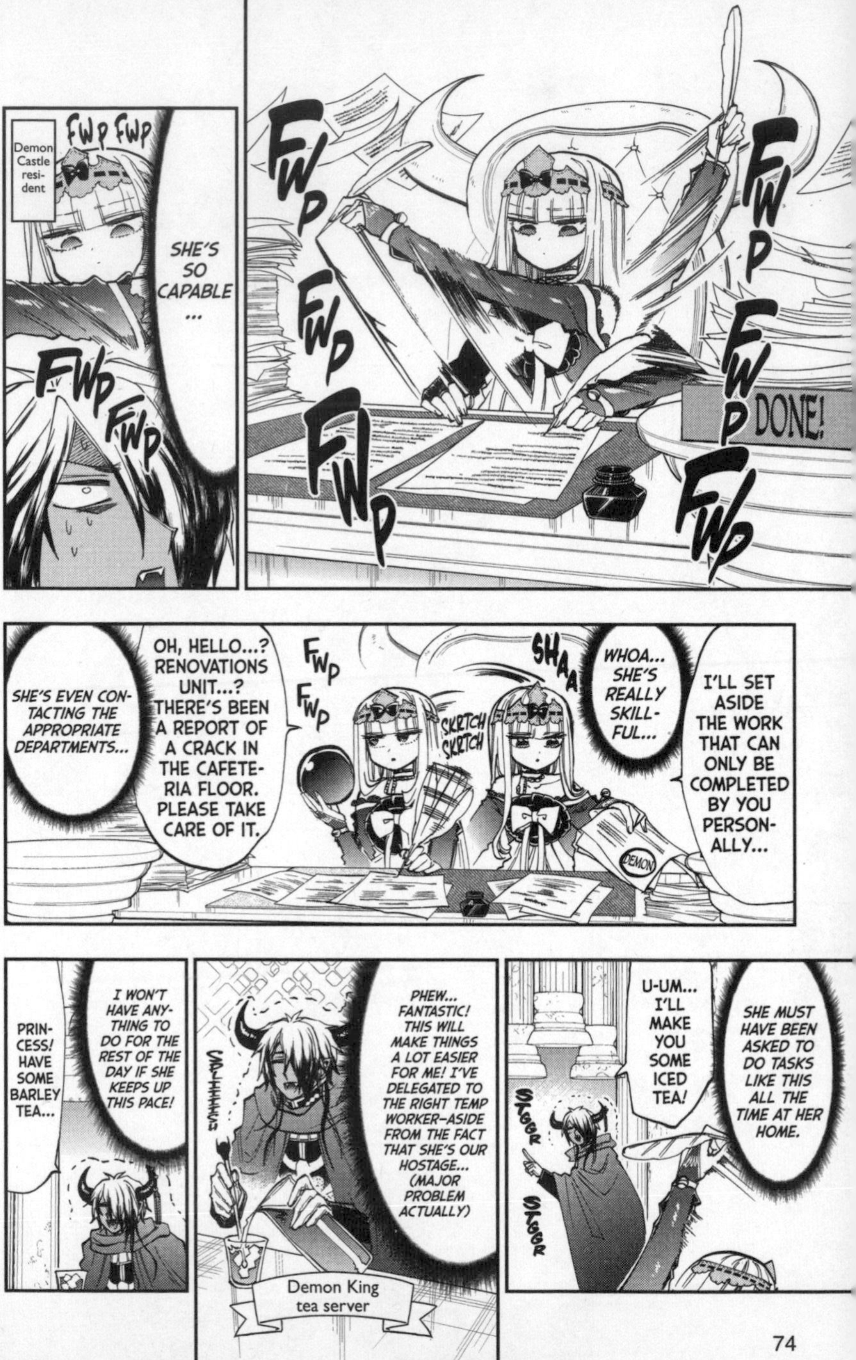
FWP
FWP
FWP
FWP
FWP
FWP
FWP
DONE!
Demon Castle resident
FWP FWP
SHE'S SO CAPABLE...
FWP
FWP
I'LL SET ASIDE THE WORK THAT CAN ONLY BE COMPLETED BY YOU PERSONALLY...
WHOA... SHE'S REALLY SKILLFUL...
SHAA
SKRTCH SKRTCH
DEMON
FWP FWP
OH, HELLO...? RENOVATIONS UNIT...? THERE'S BEEN A REPORT OF A CRACK IN THE CAFETERIA FLOOR. PLEASE TAKE CARE OF IT.
SHE'S EVEN CONTACTING THE APPROPRIATE DEPARTMENTS...
SHE MUST HAVE BEEN ASKED TO DO TASKS LIKE THIS ALL THE TIME AT HER HOME.
U-UM... I'LL MAKE YOU SOME ICED TEA!
STGGR
STGGR
PHEW... FANTASTIC! THIS WILL MAKE THINGS A LOT EASIER FOR ME! I'VE DELEGATED TO THE RIGHT TEMP WORKER—ASIDE FROM THE FACT THAT SHE'S OUR HOSTAGE... (MAJOR PROBLEM ACTUALLY)
Demon King tea server
I WON'T HAVE ANYTHING TO DO FOR THE REST OF THE DAY IF SHE KEEPS UP THIS PACE!
PRINCESS! HAVE SOME BARLEY TEA...

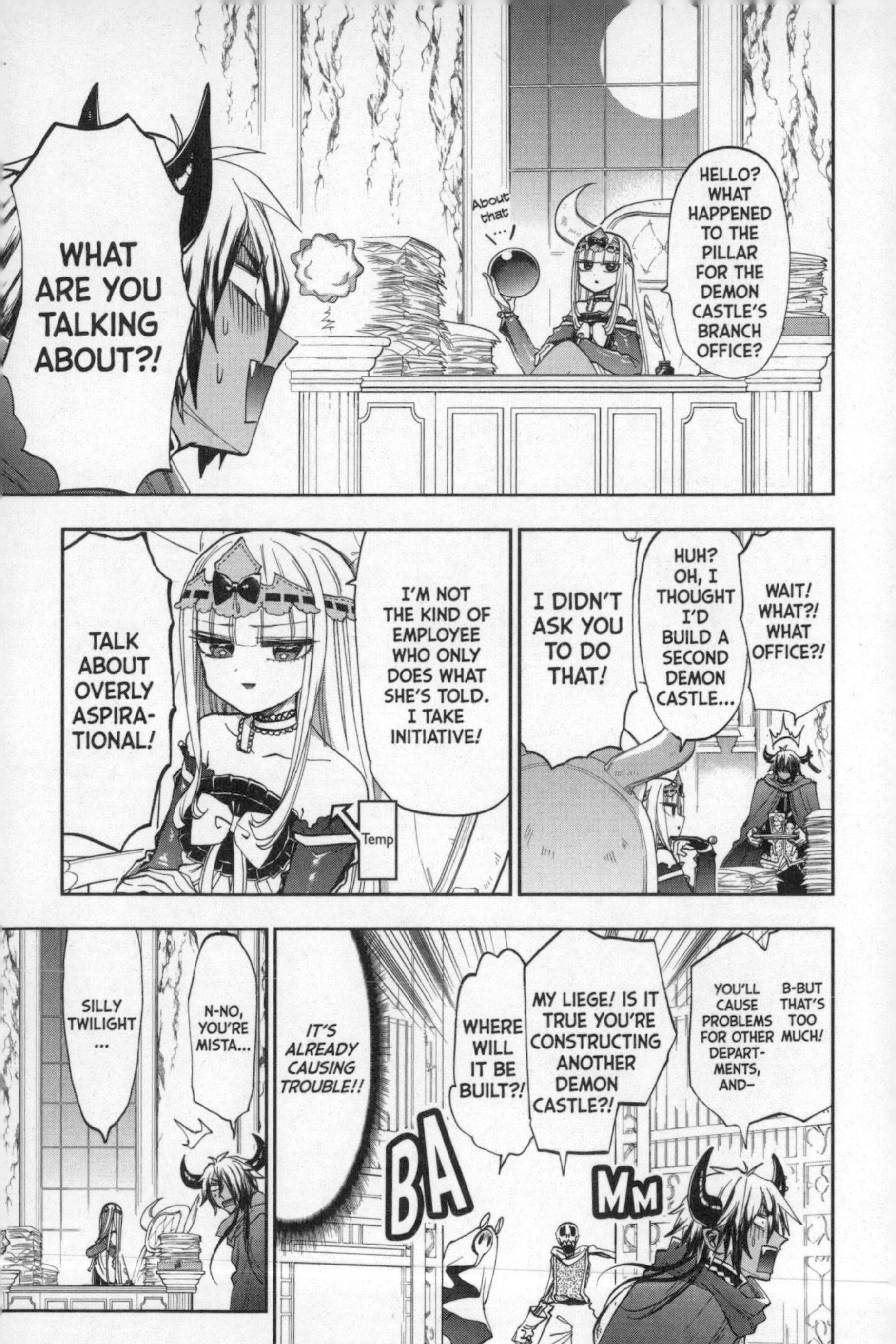
HELLO? WHAT HAPPENED TO THE PILLAR FOR THE DEMON CASTLE'S BRANCH OFFICE?
About that ...
WHAT ARE YOU TALKING ABOUT?!
WAIT! WHAT?! WHAT OFFICE?!
HUH? OH, I THOUGHT I'D BUILD A SECOND DEMON CASTLE...
I DIDN'T ASK YOU TO DO THAT!
I'M NOT THE KIND OF EMPLOYEE WHO ONLY DOES WHAT SHE'S TOLD. I TAKE INITIATIVE!
TALK ABOUT OVERLY ASPIRA-TIONAL!
Temp
B-BUT THAT'S TOO MUCH!
YOU'LL CAUSE PROBLEMS FOR OTHER DEPART-MENTS, AND—
MY LIEGE! IS IT TRUE YOU'RE CONSTRUCTING ANOTHER DEMON CASTLE?!
WHERE WILL IT BE BUILT?!
MM
BA
IT'S ALREADY CAUSING TROUBLE!!
N-NO, YOU'RE MISTA...
SILLY TWILIGHT ...

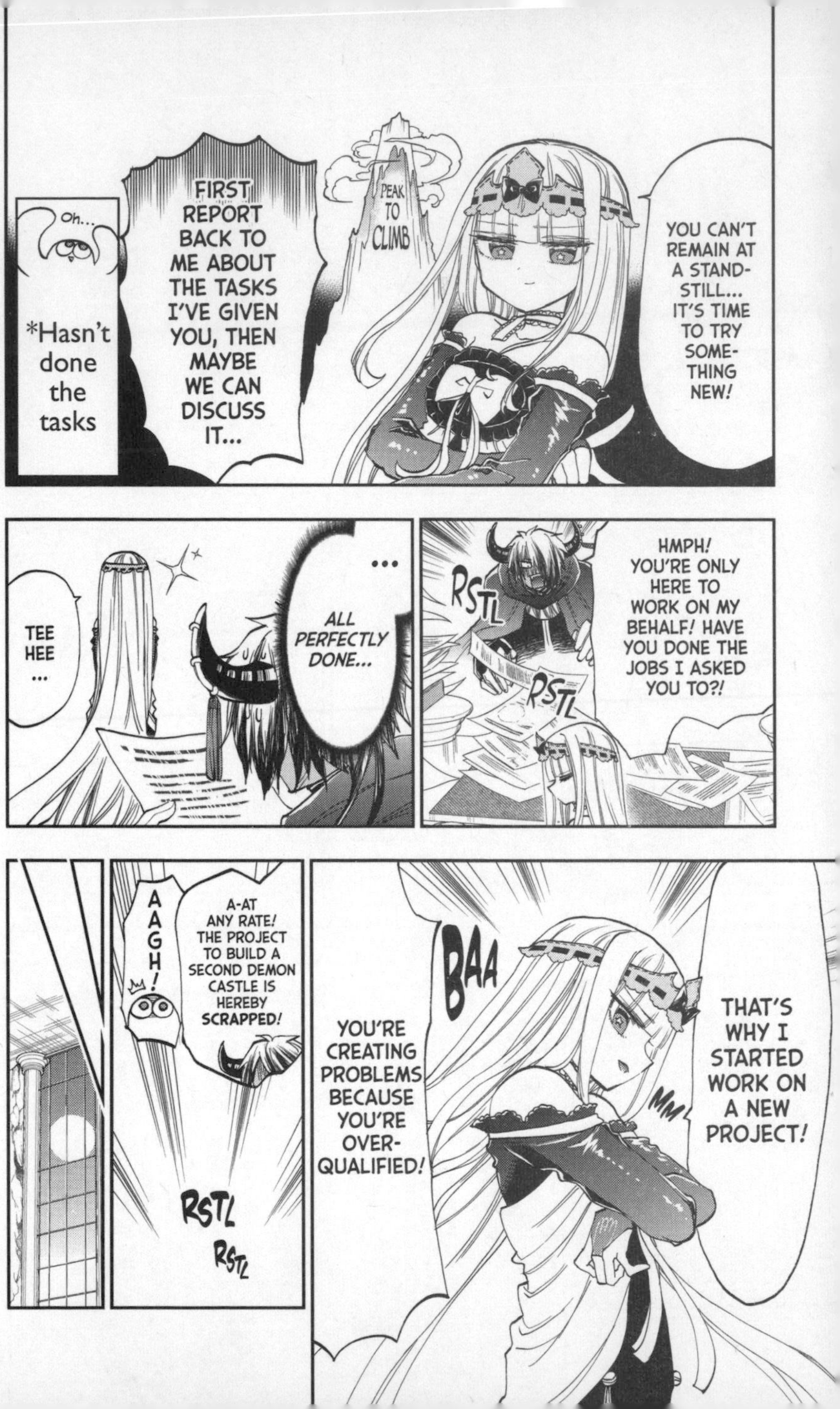
YOU CAN'T REMAIN AT A STAND-STILL... IT'S TIME TO TRY SOME-THING NEW!
PEAK TO CLIMB
FIRST REPORT BACK TO ME ABOUT THE TASKS I'VE GIVEN YOU, THEN MAYBE WE CAN DISCUSS IT...
Oh...
*Hasn't done the tasks
HMPH! YOU'RE ONLY HERE TO WORK ON MY BEHALF! HAVE YOU DONE THE JOBS I ASKED YOU TO?!
RSTL
RSTL
...
ALL PERFECTLY DONE...
TEE HEE ...
THAT'S WHY I STARTED WORK ON A NEW PROJECT!
MM
BAA
YOU'RE CREATING PROBLEMS BECAUSE YOU'RE OVER-QUALIFIED!
A-AT ANY RATE! THE PROJECT TO BUILD A SECOND DEMON CASTLE IS HEREBY SCRAPPED!
AAGH!
RSTL
RSTL

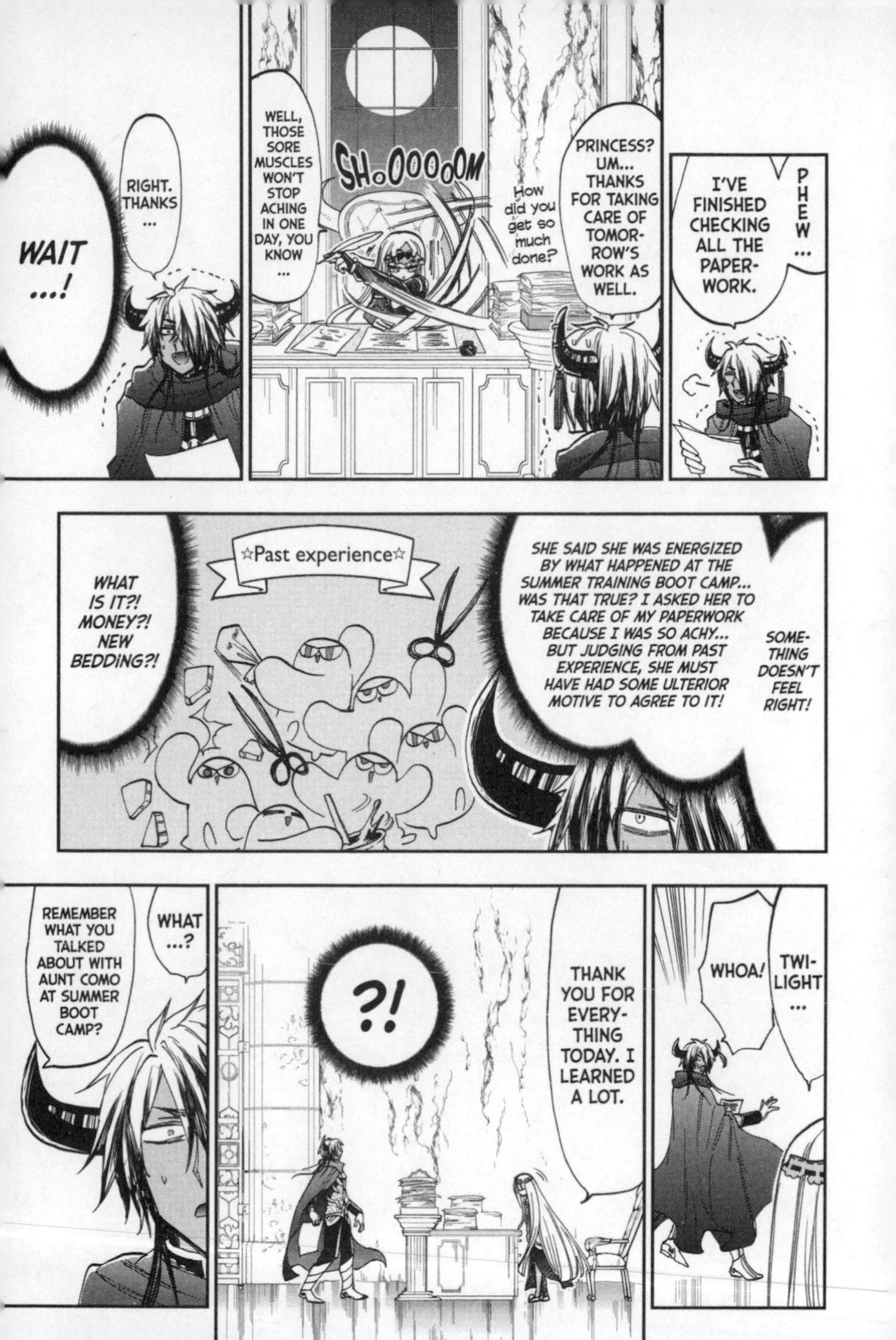
PHEW...
I'VE FINISHED CHECKING ALL THE PAPER-WORK.
PRINCESS? UM... THANKS FOR TAKING CARE OF TOMOR-ROW'S WORK AS WELL.
How did you get so much done?
SHOOOOOOM
WELL, THOSE SORE MUSCLES WON'T STOP ACHING IN ONE DAY, YOU KNOW...
RIGHT. THANKS...
WAIT...!
SOME-THING DOESN'T FEEL RIGHT!
SHE SAID SHE WAS ENERGIZED BY WHAT HAPPENED AT THE SUMMER TRAINING BOOT CAMP... WAS THAT TRUE? I ASKED HER TO TAKE CARE OF MY PAPERWORK BECAUSE I WAS SO ACHY... BUT JUDGING FROM PAST EXPERIENCE, SHE MUST HAVE HAD SOME ULTERIOR MOTIVE TO AGREE TO IT!
WHAT IS IT?! MONEY?! NEW BEDDiNG?!
☆Past experience☆
TWI-LIGHT...
WHOA!
THANK YOU FOR EVERY-THING TODAY. I LEARNED A LOT.
?!
WHAT...?
REMEMBER WHAT YOU TALKED ABOUT WITH AUNT COMO AT SUMMER BOOT CAMP?

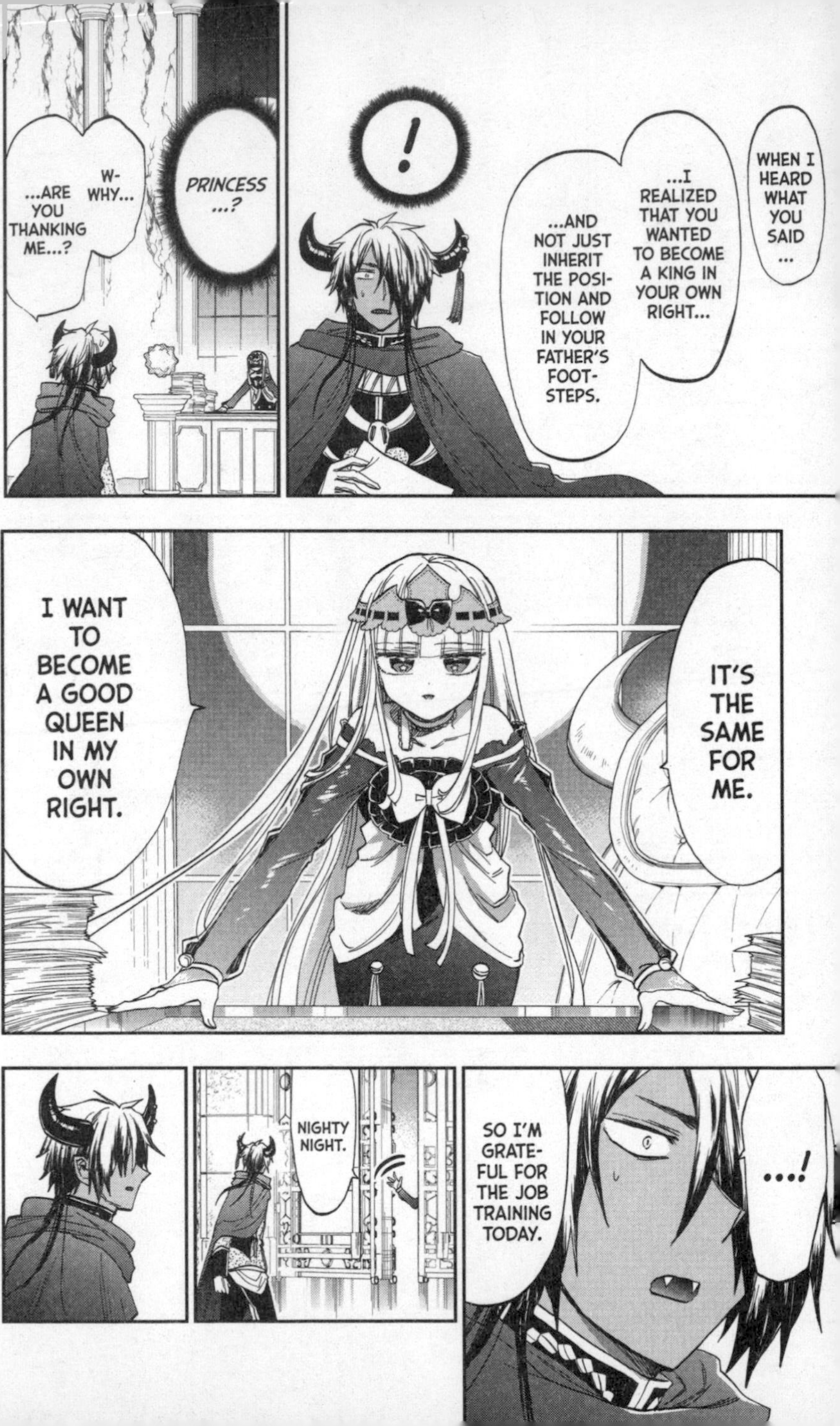
WHEN I HEARD WHAT YOU SAID ...
...I REALIZED THAT YOU WANTED TO BECOME A KING IN YOUR OWN RIGHT...
...AND NOT JUST INHERIT THE POSITION AND FOLLOW IN YOUR FATHER'S FOOTSTEPS.
!
PRINCESS ...?
W- WHY...
...ARE YOU THANKING ME...?
IT'S THE SAME FOR ME.
I WANT TO BECOME A GOOD QUEEN IN MY OWN RIGHT.
...!
SO I'M GRATEFUL FOR THE JOB TRAINING TODAY.
NIGHTY NIGHT.

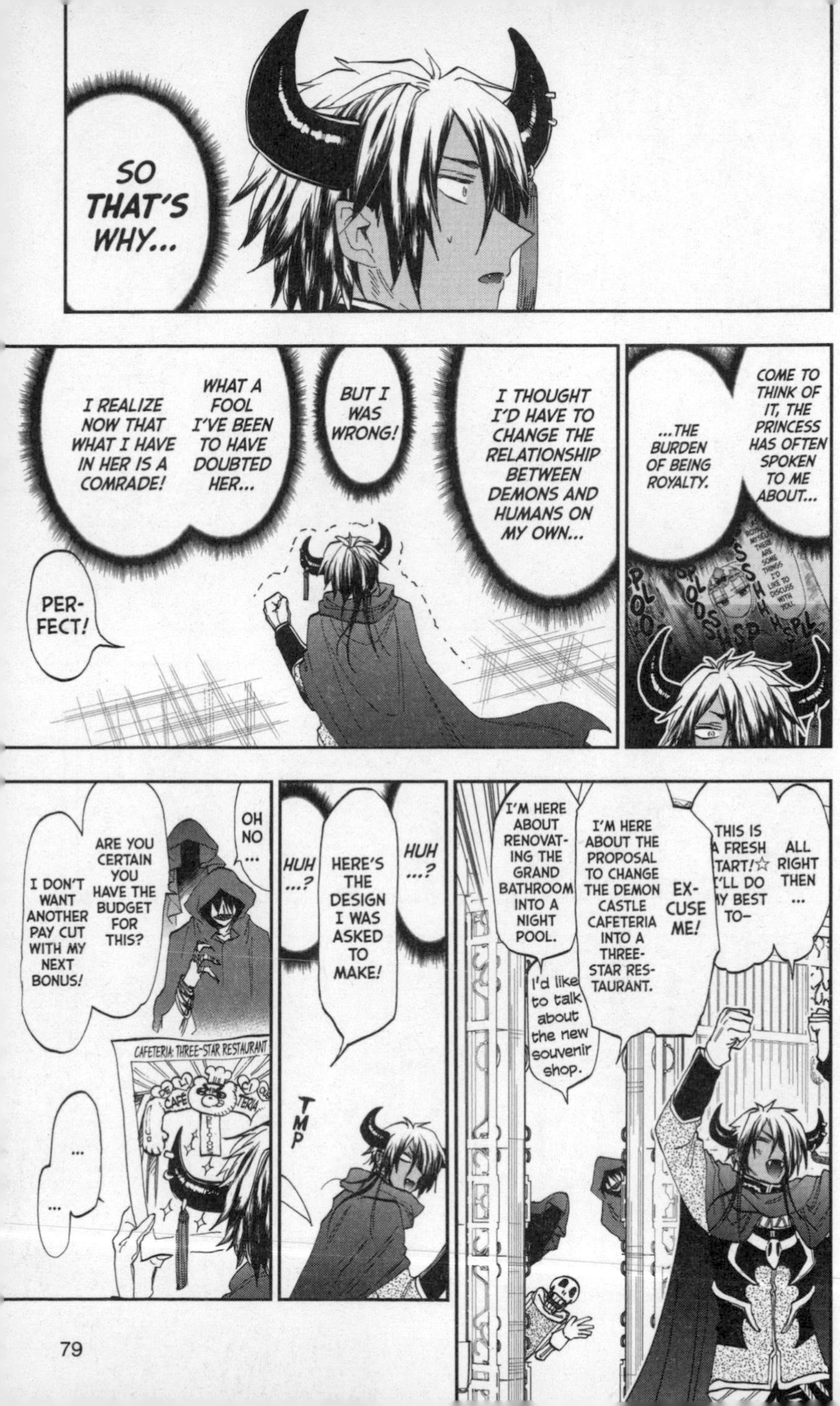
SO THAT'S WHY...
COME TO THINK OF IT, THE PRINCESS HAS OFTEN SPOKEN TO ME ABOUT...
...THE BURDEN OF BEING ROYALTY.
I THOUGHT I'D HAVE TO CHANGE THE RELATIONSHIP BETWEEN DEMONS AND HUMANS ON MY OWN...
BUT I WAS WRONG!
WHAT A FOOL I'VE BEEN TO HAVE DOUBTED HER...
I REALIZE NOW THAT WHAT I HAVE IN HER IS A COMRADE!
PER-FECT!
ALL RIGHT THEN ...
THIS IS A FRESH START!☆ I'LL DO MY BEST TO—
EX-CUSE ME!
I'M HERE ABOUT THE PROPOSAL TO CHANGE THE DEMON CASTLE CAFETERIA INTO A THREE-STAR RESTAURANT.
I'M HERE ABOUT RENOVATING THE GRAND BATHROOM INTO A NIGHT POOL.
I'd like to talk about the new souvenir shop.
HUH ...?
HERE'S THE DESIGN I WAS ASKED TO MAKE!
HUH ...?
TMP
OH NO ...
ARE YOU CERTAIN YOU HAVE THE BUDGET FOR THIS?
I DON'T WANT ANOTHER PAY CUT WITH MY NEXT BONUS!
CAFETERIA: THREE-STAR RESTAURANT
...
...

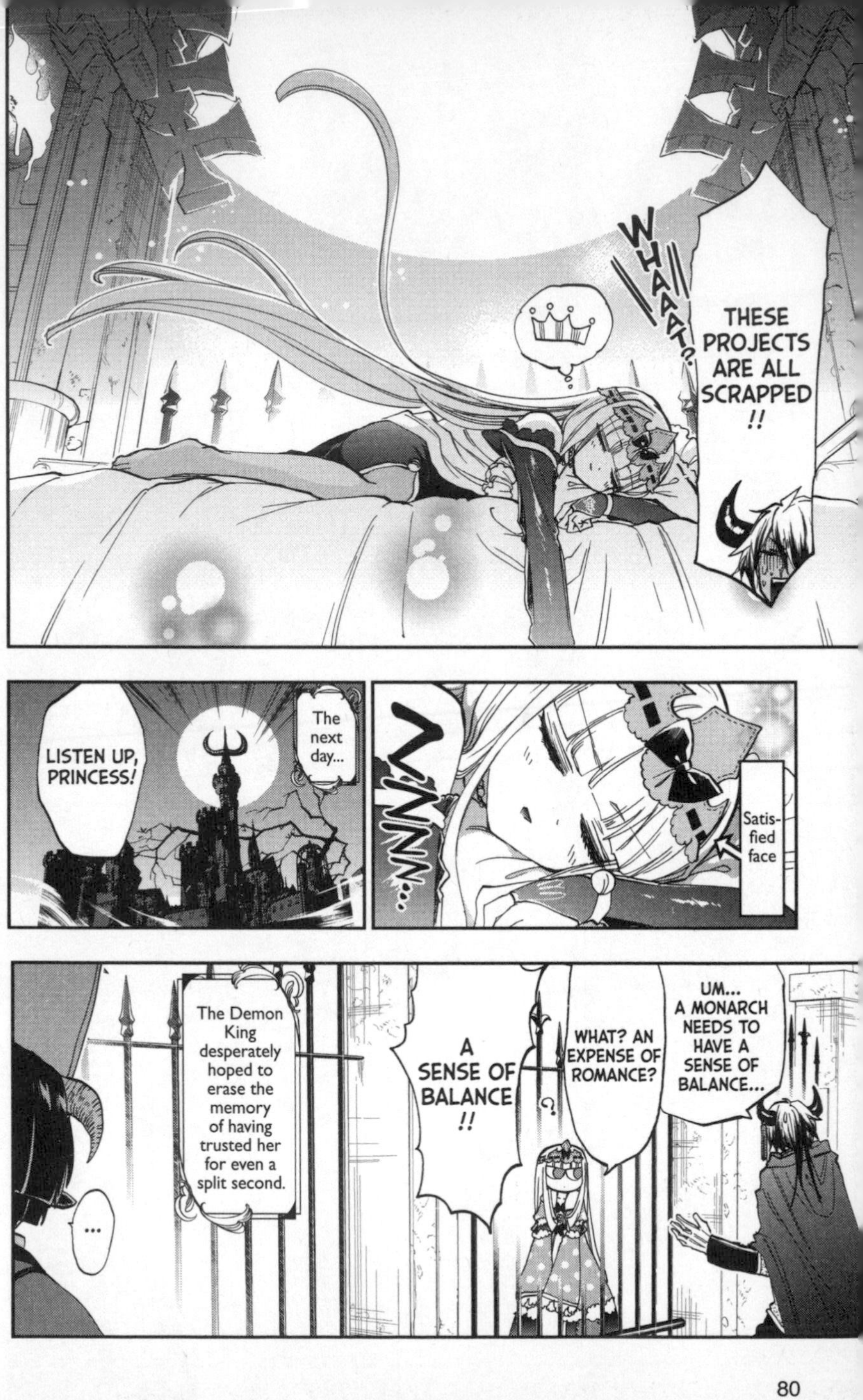
THESE PROJECTS ARE ALL SCRAPPED!!
WHAAAT?
Satis-fied face
NNNN...
The next day...
LISTEN UP, PRINCESS!
UM... A MONARCH NEEDS TO HAVE A SENSE OF BALANCE...
WHAT? AN EXPENSE OF ROMANCE?
A SENSE OF BALANCE!!
The Demon King desperately hoped to erase the memory of having trusted her for even a split second.
...

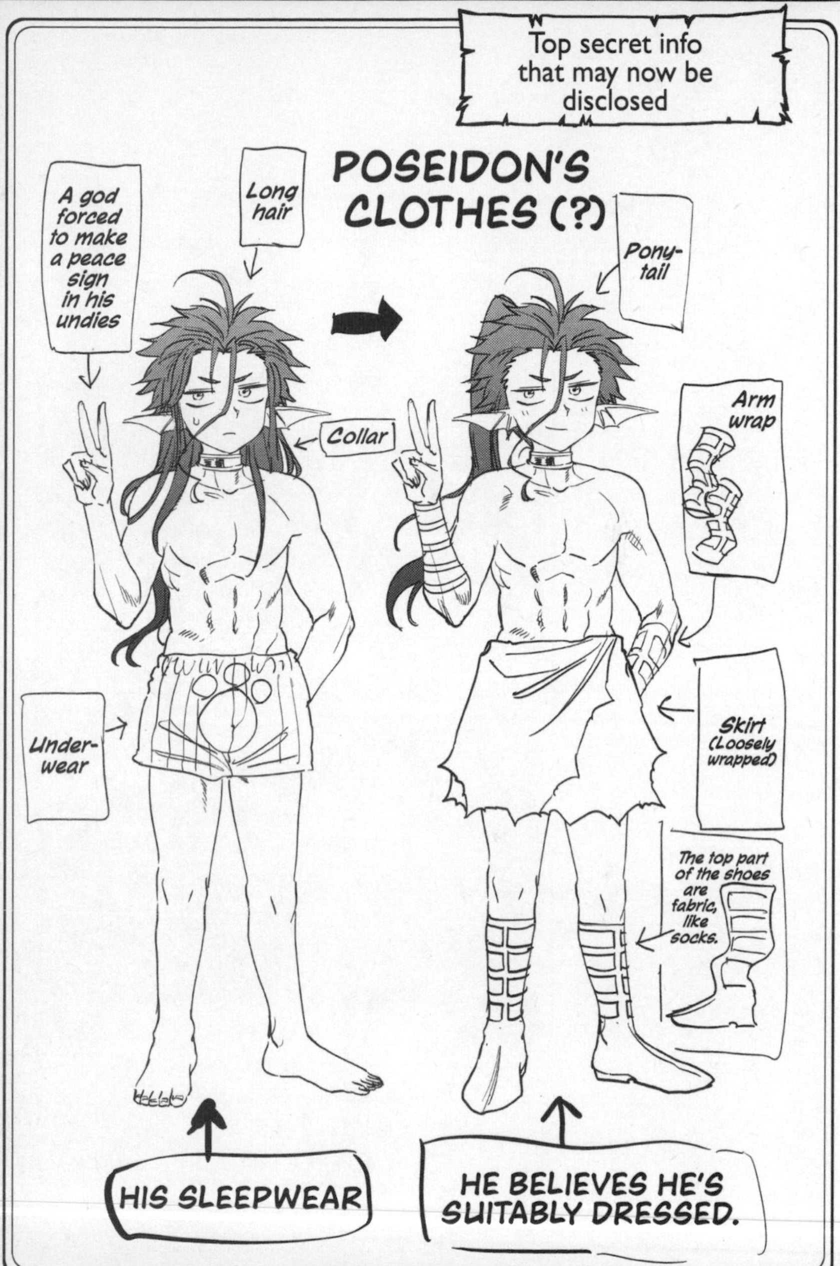
Top secret info that may now be disclosed
POSEIDON'S CLOTHES (?)
Pony-tail
Arm wrap
Skirt (Loosely wrapped)
The top part of the shoes are fabric, like socks.
HE BELIEVES HE'S SUITABLY DRESSED.
Long hair
A god forced to make a peace sign in his undies
Collar
Under-wear
HIS SLEEPWEAR

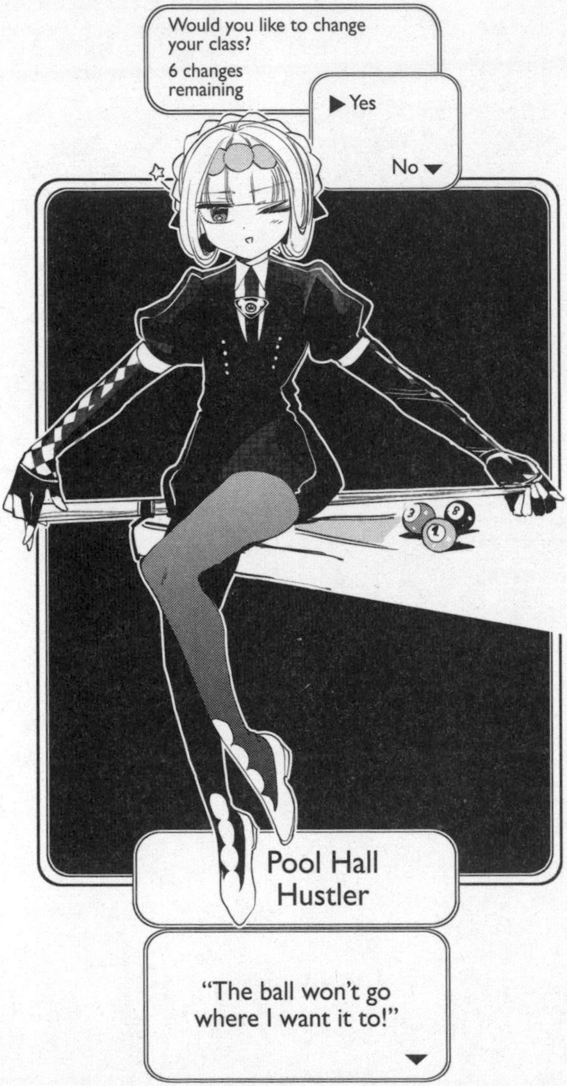
Would you like to change your class?
6 changes remaining
▶ Yes
No
Pool Hall Hustler
"The ball won't go where I want it to!"

163rd Night: Soft and Fluffy Pinballs

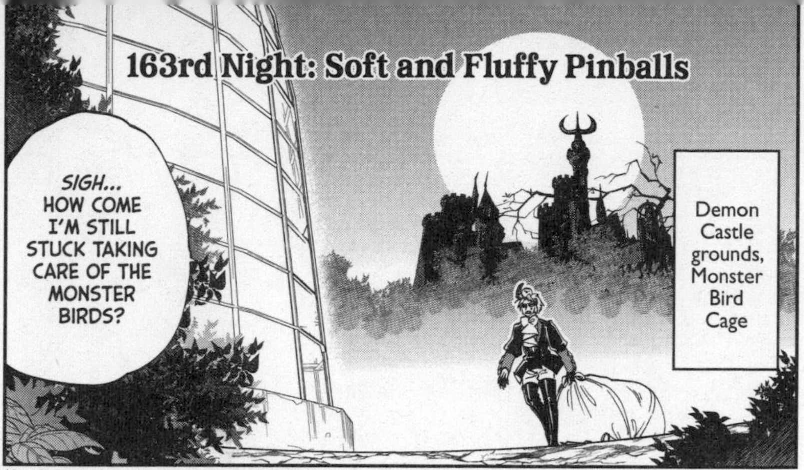
Demon Castle grounds, Monster Bird Cage
SIGH... HOW COME I'M STILL STUCK TAKING CARE OF THE MONSTER BIRDS?

*See *Sleepy Princess in the Demon Castle* Vol.12, 144th Night

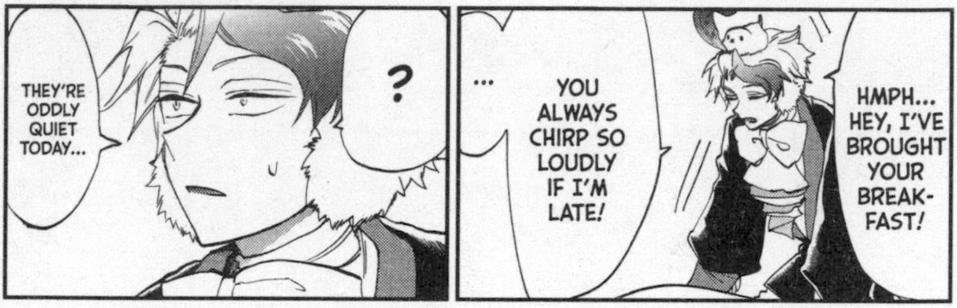
HMPH... HEY, I'VE BROUGHT YOUR BREAK-FAST!
YOU ALWAYS CHIRP SO LOUDLY IF I'M LATE!
...
?
THEY'RE ODDLY QUIET TODAY...

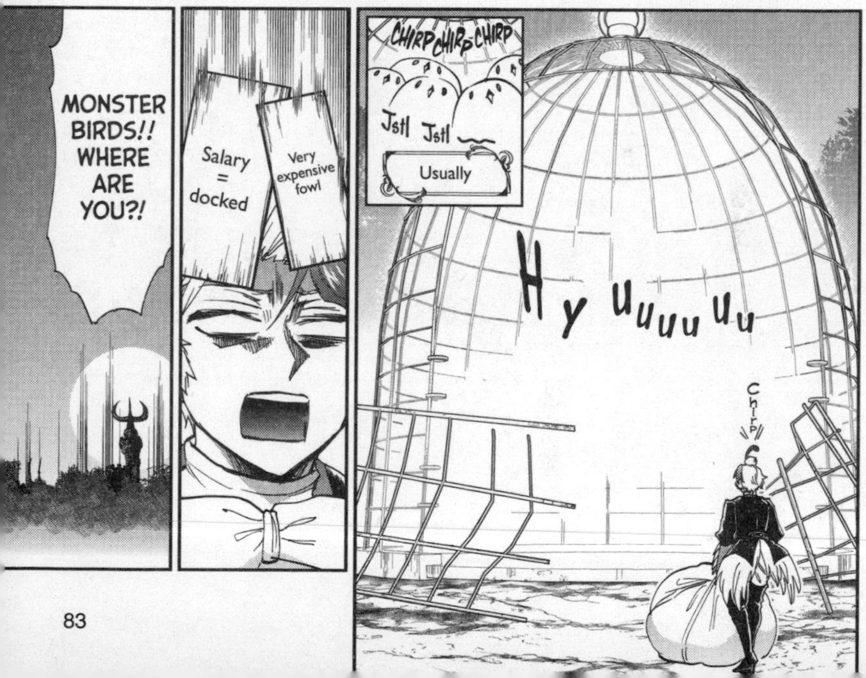
CHIRP CHIRP CHIRP
Jstl Jstl
Usually
Hyuuuuuu
Chirp
Salary = docked
Very expensive fowl
MONSTER BIRDS!! WHERE ARE YOU?!

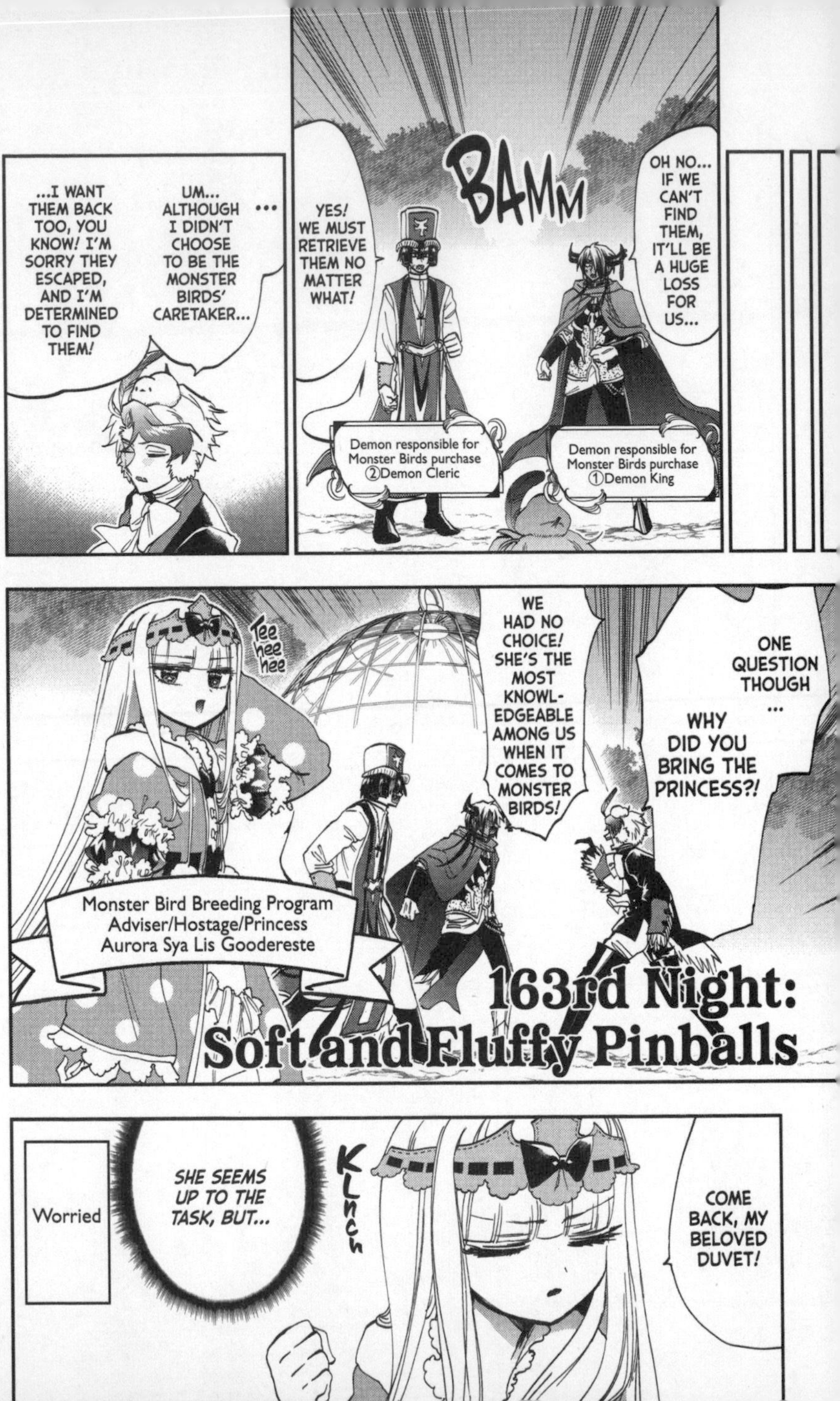
OH NO... IF WE CAN'T FIND THEM, IT'LL BE A HUGE LOSS FOR US...
BAMM
YES! WE MUST RETRIEVE THEM NO MATTER WHAT!
Demon responsible for Monster Birds purchase ①Demon King
Demon responsible for Monster Birds purchase ②Demon Cleric
UM... ALTHOUGH I DIDN'T CHOOSE TO BE THE MONSTER BIRDS' CARETAKER...
...
...I WANT THEM BACK TOO, YOU KNOW! I'M SORRY THEY ESCAPED, AND I'M DETERMINED TO FIND THEM!
ONE QUESTION THOUGH ...
WHY DID YOU BRING THE PRINCESS?!
WE HAD NO CHOICE! SHE'S THE MOST KNOWL-EDGEABLE AMONG US WHEN IT COMES TO MONSTER BIRDS!
Tee hee hee
Monster Bird Breeding Program Adviser/Hostage/Princess Aurora Sya Lis Goodereste
163rd Night: Soft and Fluffy Pinballs
COME BACK, MY BELOVED DUVET!
KLnch
SHE SEEMS UP TO THE TASK, BUT...
Worried

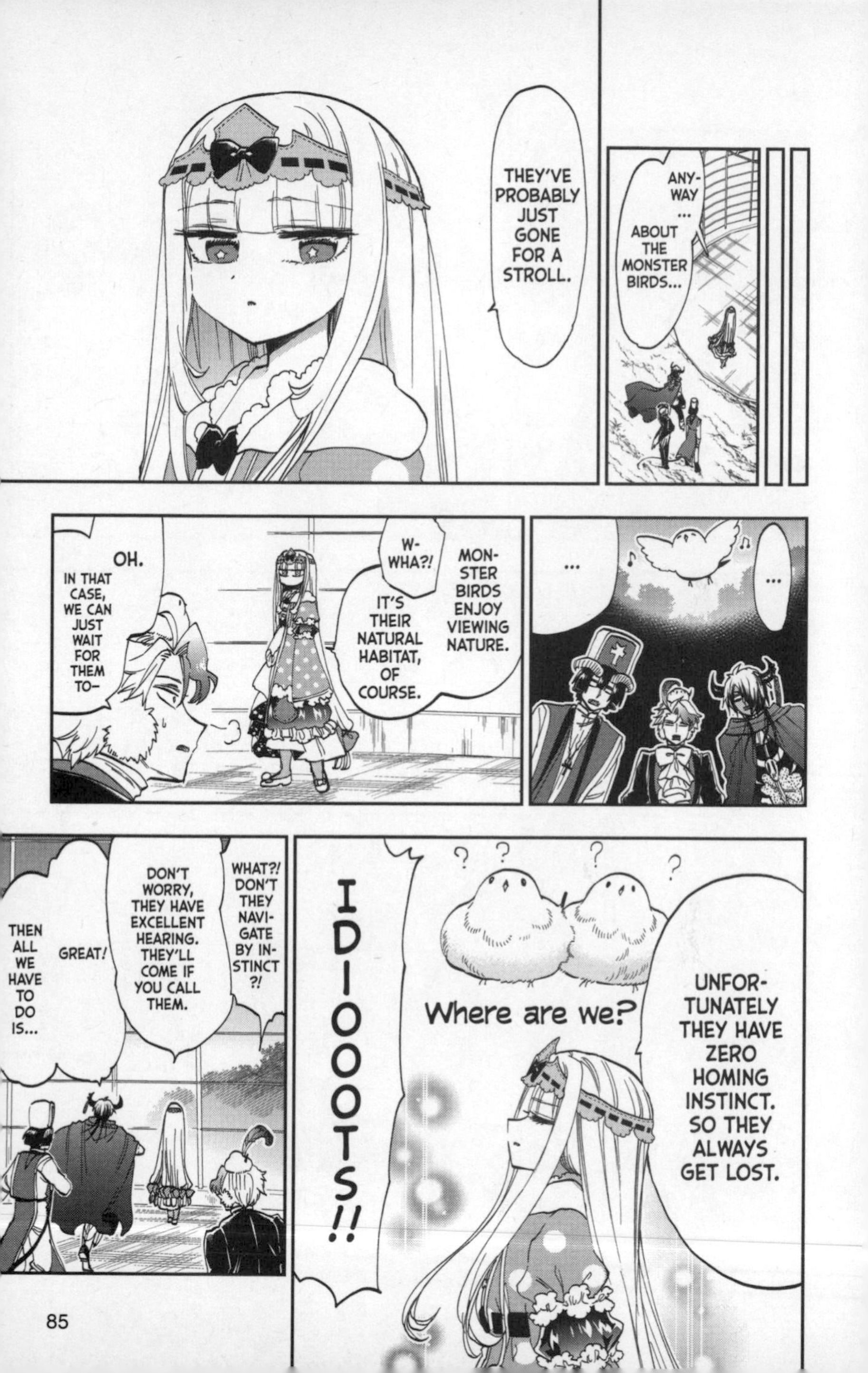
ANYWAY... ABOUT THE MONSTER BIRDS...
THEY'VE PROBABLY JUST GONE FOR A STROLL.
...
...
MONSTER BIRDS ENJOY VIEWING NATURE.
W-WHA?!
IT'S THEIR NATURAL HABITAT, OF COURSE.
OH.
IN THAT CASE, WE CAN JUST WAIT FOR THEM TO–
? ? ? ?
Where are we?
UNFORTUNATELY THEY HAVE ZERO HOMING INSTINCT. SO THEY ALWAYS GET LOST.
IDIOOOTS!!
WHAT?! DON'T THEY NAVIGATE BY INSTINCT?!
DON'T WORRY, THEY HAVE EXCELLENT HEARING. THEY'LL COME IF YOU CALL THEM.
GREAT!
THEN ALL WE HAVE TO DO IS...

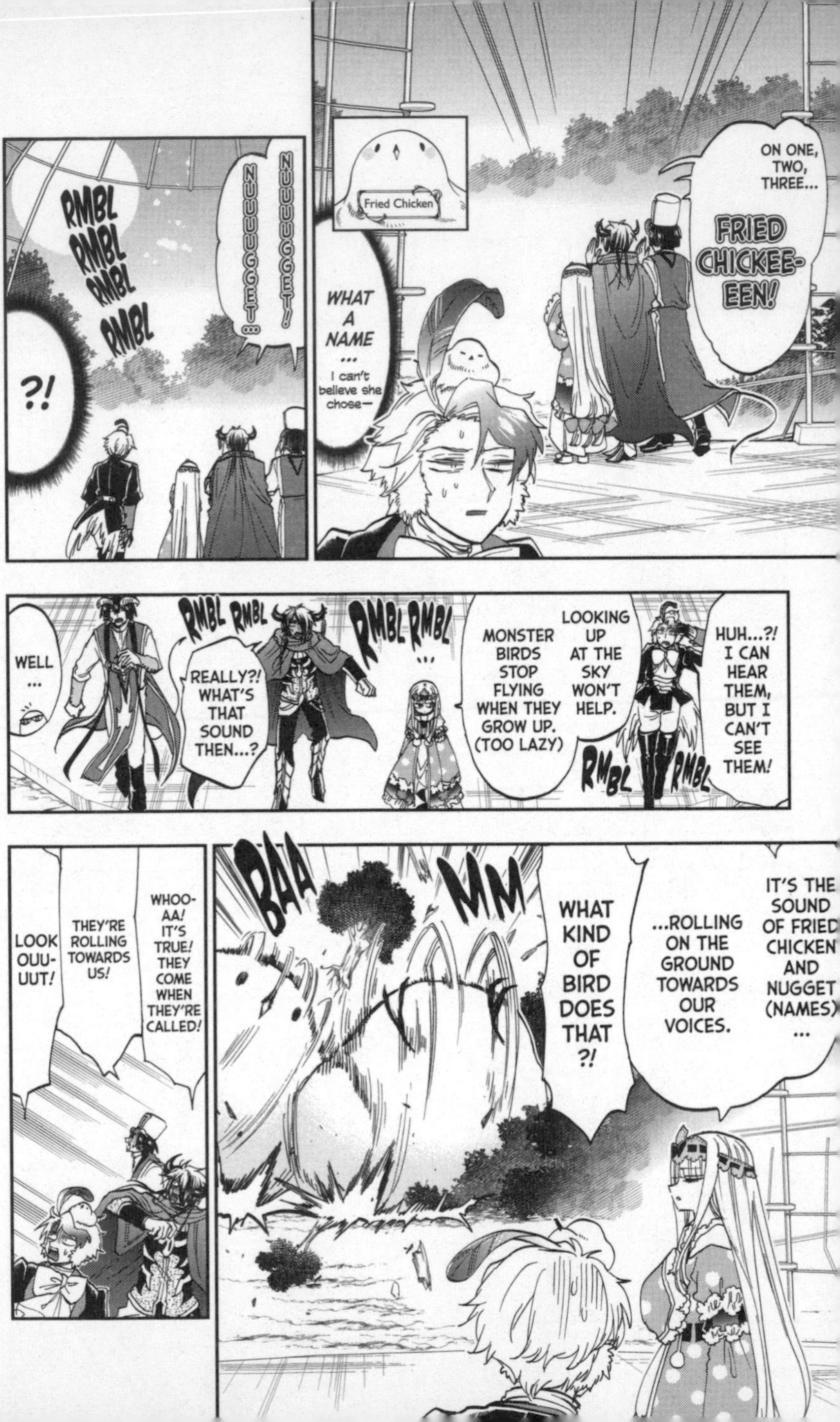
ON ONE, TWO, THREE...
FRIED CHICKEE-EEN!
Fried Chicken
WHAT A NAME... I can't believe she chose—
NUUUUGGET!
NUUUUGGET...
RMBL RMBL RMBL RMBL
?!
HUH...?! I CAN HEAR THEM, BUT I CAN'T SEE THEM!
RMBL
LOOKING UP AT THE SKY WON'T HELP.
MONSTER BIRDS STOP FLYING WHEN THEY GROW UP. (TOO LAZY)
RMBL
RMBL RMBL
...
REALLY?! WHAT'S THAT SOUND THEN...?
RMBL RMBL
WELL...
IT'S THE SOUND OF FRIED CHICKEN AND NUGGET (NAMES)...
...ROLLING ON THE GROUND TOWARDS OUR VOICES.
WHAT KIND OF BIRD DOES THAT?!
BAAMM
WHOO-AA! IT'S TRUE! THEY COME WHEN THEY'RE CALLED!
THEY'RE ROLLING TOWARDS US!
LOOK OUUUUT!

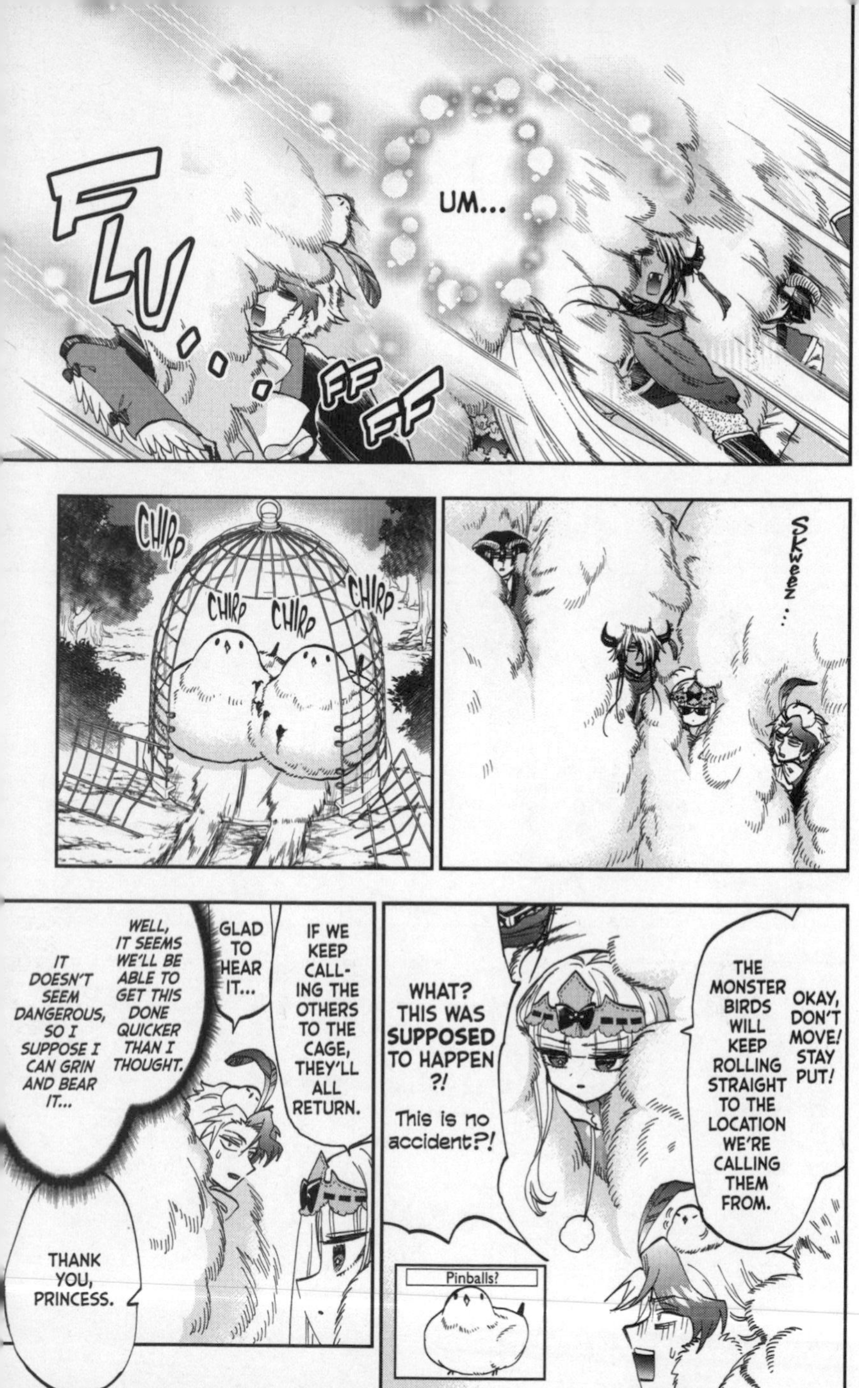
UM...
FLU...
FFFF
SKWEEZ...
CHIRP
CHIRP
CHIRP
CHIRP
OKAY, DON'T MOVE! STAY PUT!
THE MONSTER BIRDS WILL KEEP ROLLING STRAIGHT TO THE LOCATION WE'RE CALLING THEM FROM.
WHAT? THIS WAS **SUPPOSED** TO HAPPEN?!
This is no accident?!
Pinballs?
IF WE KEEP CALL-ING THE OTHERS TO THE CAGE, THEY'LL ALL RETURN.
GLAD TO HEAR IT...
WELL, IT SEEMS WE'LL BE ABLE TO GET THIS DONE QUICKER THAN I THOUGHT.
IT DOESN'T SEEM DANGEROUS, SO I SUPPOSE I CAN GRIN AND BEAR IT...
THANK YOU, PRINCESS.

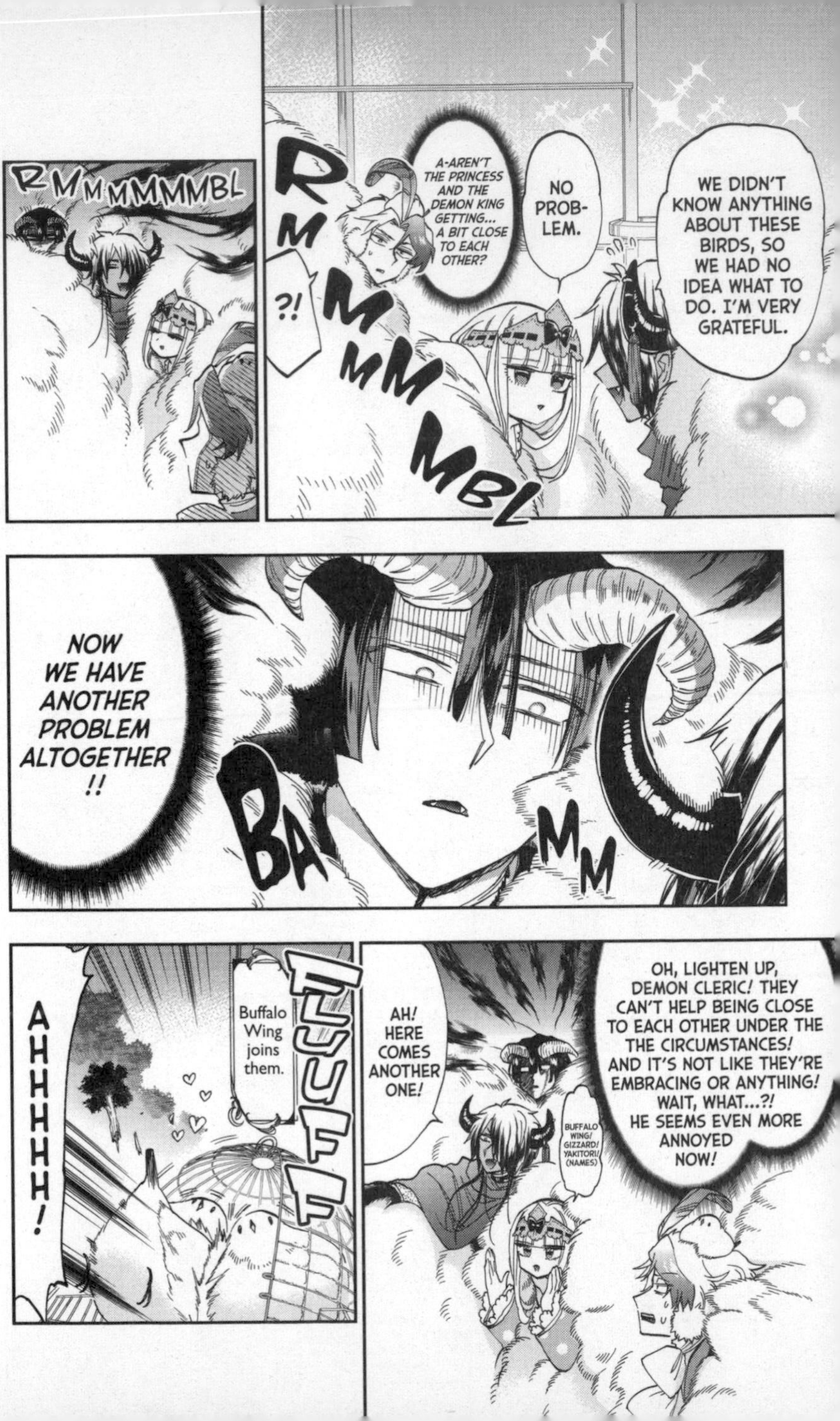
WE DIDN'T KNOW ANYTHING ABOUT THESE BIRDS, SO WE HAD NO IDEA WHAT TO DO. I'M VERY GRATEFUL.
NO PROB-LEM.
A-AREN'T THE PRINCESS AND THE DEMON KING GETTING... A BIT CLOSE TO EACH OTHER?
RMMMMMMBL
?!
RMMMMMMMBL
NOW WE HAVE ANOTHER PROBLEM ALTOGETHER!!
BAMM
OH, LIGHTEN UP, DEMON CLERIC! THEY CAN'T HELP BEING CLOSE TO EACH OTHER UNDER THE THE CIRCUMSTANCES! AND IT'S NOT LIKE THEY'RE EMBRACING OR ANYTHING! WAIT, WHAT...?! HE SEEMS EVEN MORE ANNOYED NOW!
BUFFALO WING/ GIZZARD/ YAKITORI/ (NAMES)
AH! HERE COMES ANOTHER ONE!
FLUUFF
Buffalo Wing joins them.
AHHHHH!

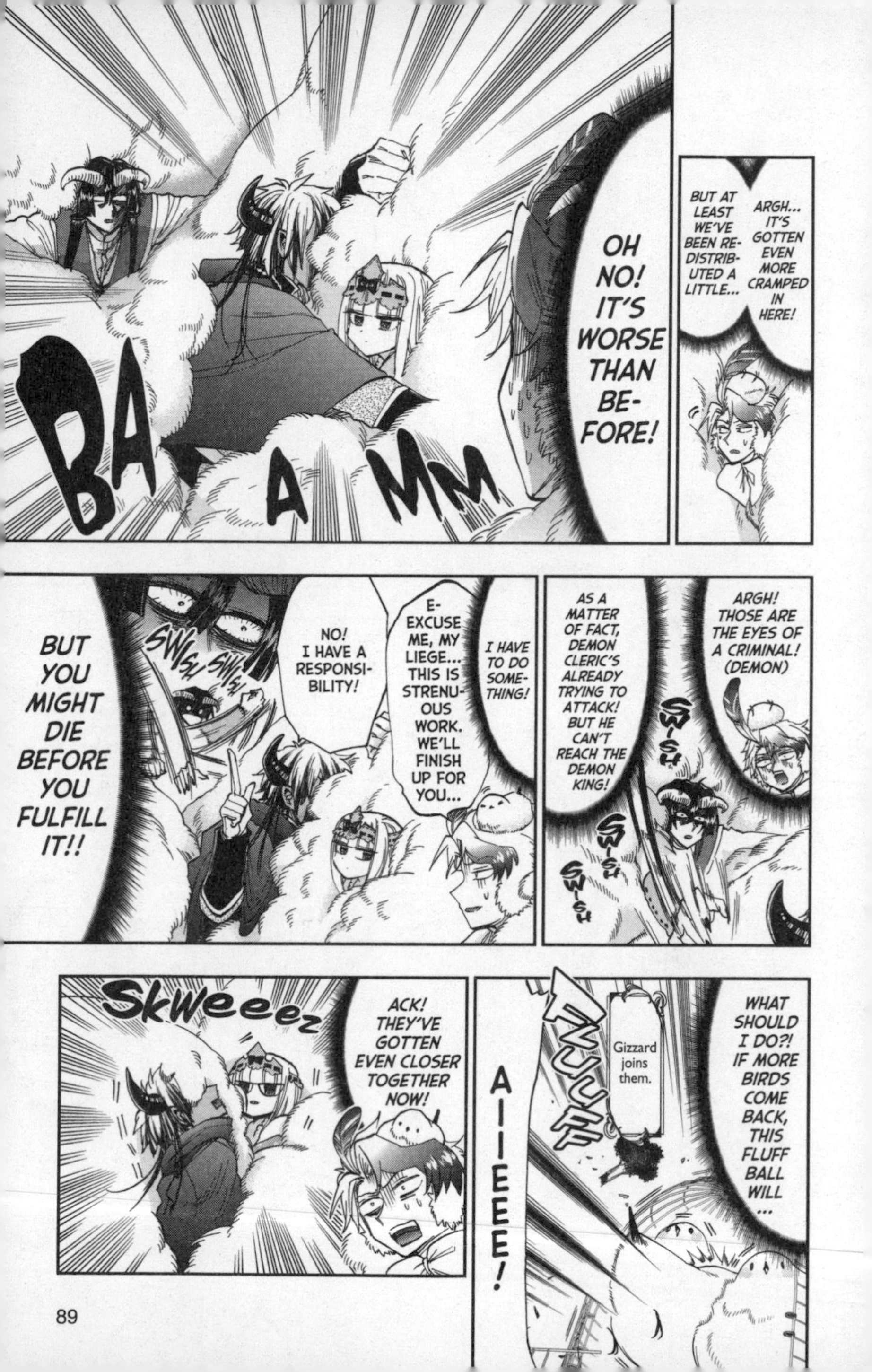
ARGH... IT'S GOTTEN EVEN MORE CRAMPED IN HERE!
BUT AT LEAST WE'VE BEEN RE-DISTRIB-UTED A LITTLE...
OH NO! IT'S WORSE THAN BE-FORE!
BAAMM
ARGH! THOSE ARE THE EYES OF A CRIMINAL! (DEMON)
AS A MATTER OF FACT, DEMON CLERIC'S ALREADY TRYING TO ATTACK! BUT HE CAN'T REACH THE DEMON KING!
SWISH
SWISH
SWISH
I HAVE TO DO SOME-THING!
E-EXCUSE ME, MY LIEGE... THIS IS STRENU-OUS WORK. WE'LL FINISH UP FOR YOU...
NO! I HAVE A RESPONSI-BILITY!
SWISH SWISH
BUT YOU MIGHT DIE BEFORE YOU FULFILL IT!!
WHAT SHOULD I DO?! IF MORE BIRDS COME BACK, THIS FLUFF BALL WILL ...
FZUUFF
Gizzard joins them.
AIIEEE!
ACK! THEY'VE GOTTEN EVEN CLOSER TOGETHER NOW!
Skweeez

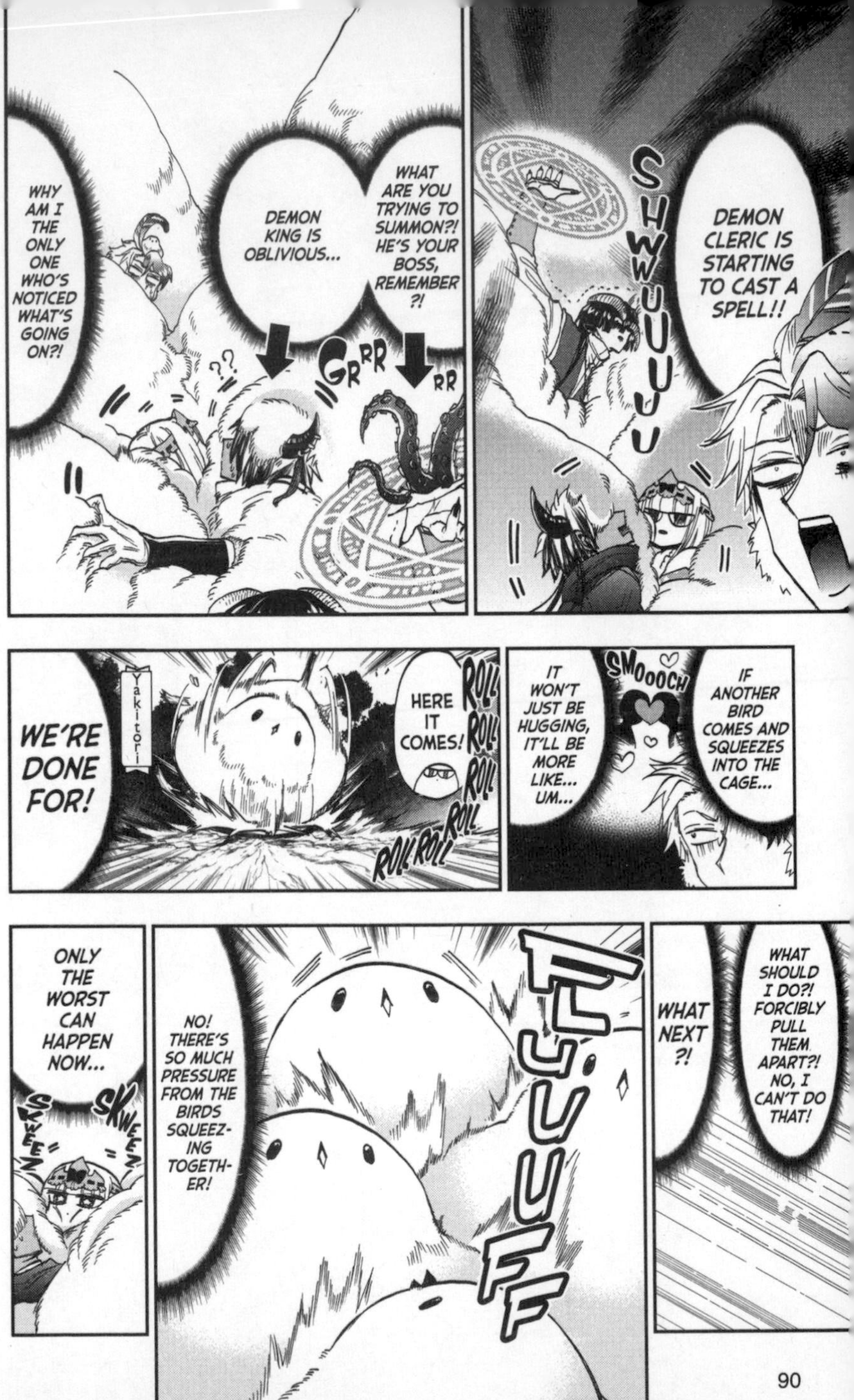
DEMON CLERIC IS STARTING TO CAST A SPELL!!
SHWWUUUUUU
WHAT ARE YOU TRYING TO SUMMON?! HE'S YOUR BOSS, REMEMBER?!
DEMON KING IS OBLIVIOUS...
WHY AM I THE ONLY ONE WHO'S NOTICED WHAT'S GOING ON?!
GRRRRR
IF ANOTHER BIRD COMES AND SQUEEZES INTO THE CAGE...
SMOOOCH
IT WON'T JUST BE HUGGING, IT'LL BE MORE LIKE... UM...
HERE IT COMES!
ROLL ROLL ROLL ROLL ROLL ROLL
Yakitori
WE'RE DONE FOR!
WHAT SHOULD I DO?! FORCIBLY PULL THEM APART?! NO, I CAN'T DO THAT!
WHAT NEXT?!
FLUUUFF
NO! THERE'S SO MUCH PRESSURE FROM THE BIRDS SQUEEZING TOGETHER!
ONLY THE WORST CAN HAPPEN NOW...
SKWEEZ
SKWEEZ

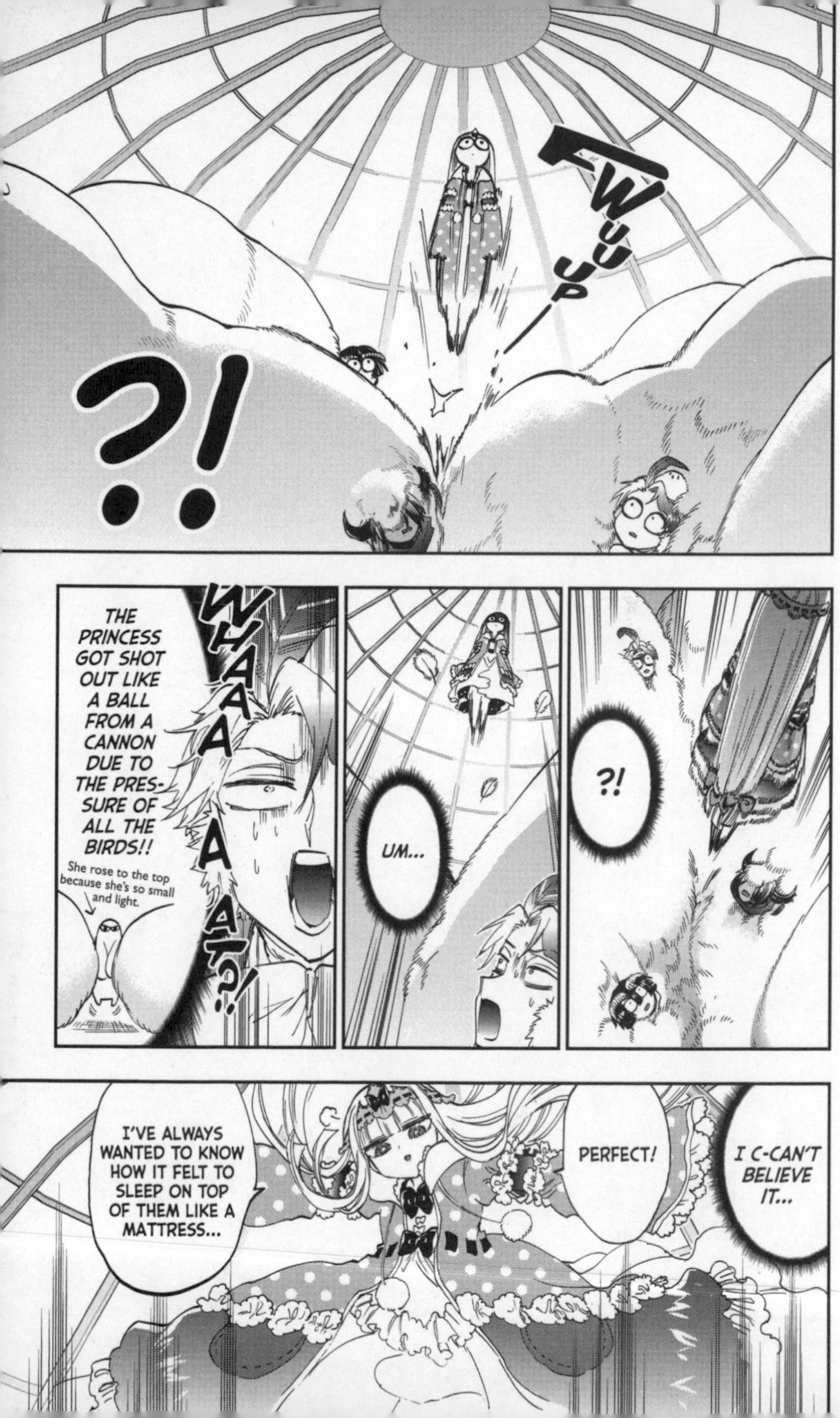
TWUUUP
?!
?!
UM...
WHAAAAAT?!
THE PRINCESS GOT SHOT OUT LIKE A BALL FROM A CANNON DUE TO THE PRES-SURE OF ALL THE BIRDS!!
She rose to the top because she's so small and light.
I C-CAN'T BELIEVE IT...
PERFECT!
I'VE ALWAYS WANTED TO KNOW HOW IT FELT TO SLEEP ON TOP OF THEM LIKE A MATTRESS...

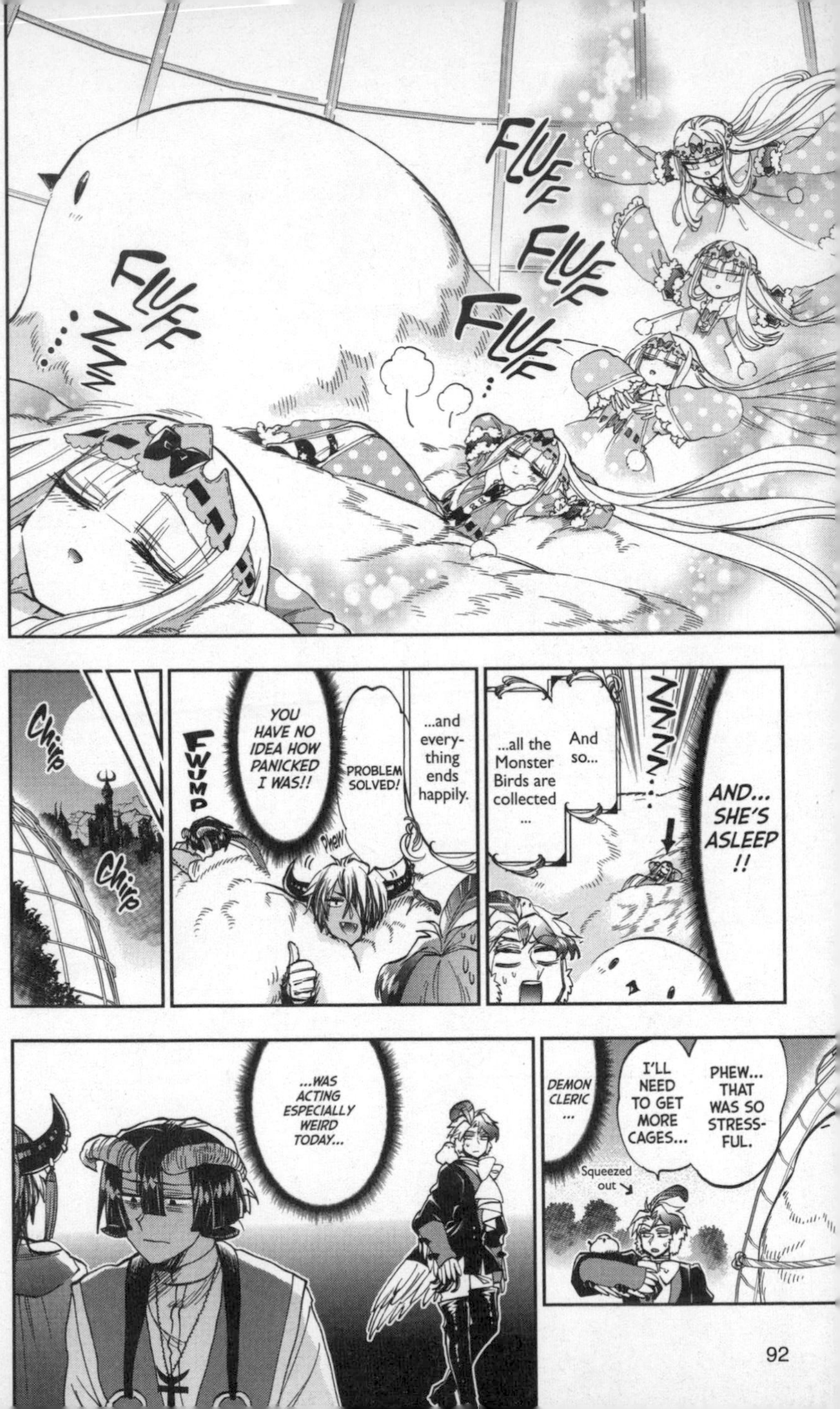
FLUFF
FLUFF
FLUFF
FLUFF
ZZZ...
ZZZZ...
AND... SHE'S ASLEEP !!
And so...
...all the Monster Birds are collected ...
...and every-thing ends happily.
PROBLEM SOLVED!
YOU HAVE NO IDEA HOW PANICKED I WAS!!
Phew
FWUMP
Chirp
Chirp
PHEW... THAT WAS SO STRESS-FUL.
I'LL NEED TO GET MORE CAGES...
Squeezed out
DEMON CLERIC ...
...WAS ACTING ESPECIALLY WEIRD TODAY...

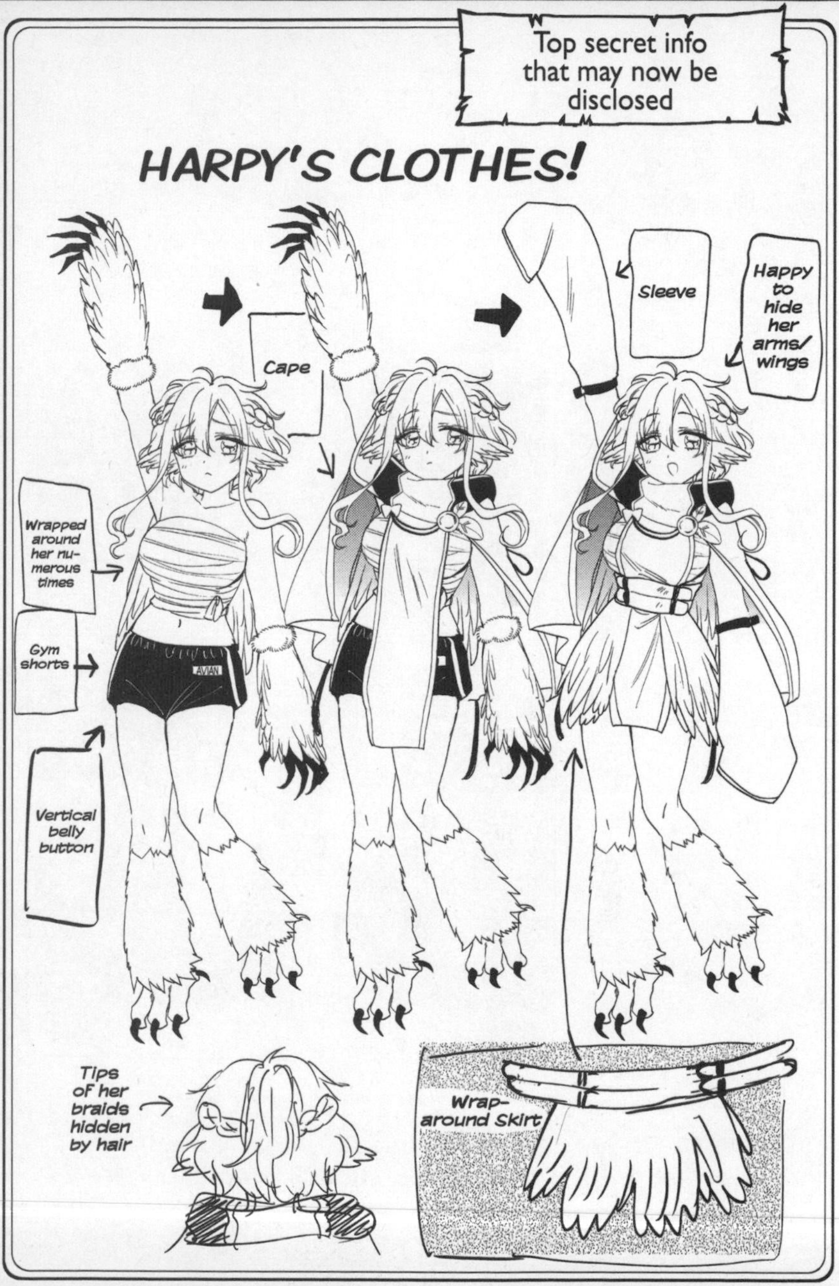
Top secret info that may now be disclosed
HARPY'S CLOTHES!
Cape
Sleeve
Happy to hide her arms/wings
Wrapped around her numerous times
Gym shorts
AVIAN
Vertical belly button
Tips of her braids hidden by hair
Wrap-around Skirt

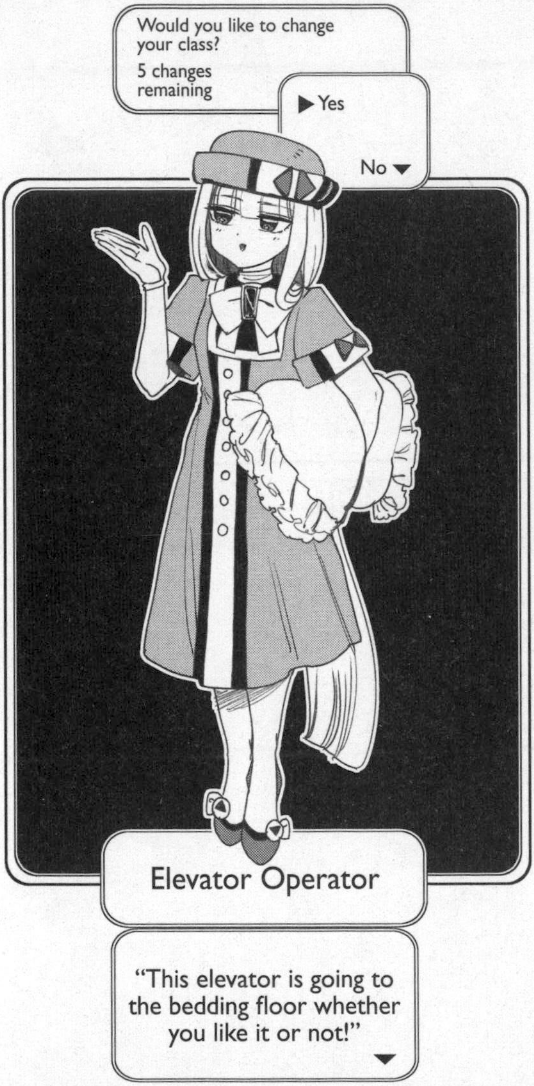

Would you like to change your class?
5 changes remaining
▶ Yes
No
Elevator Operator
"This elevator is going to the bedding floor whether you like it or not!"

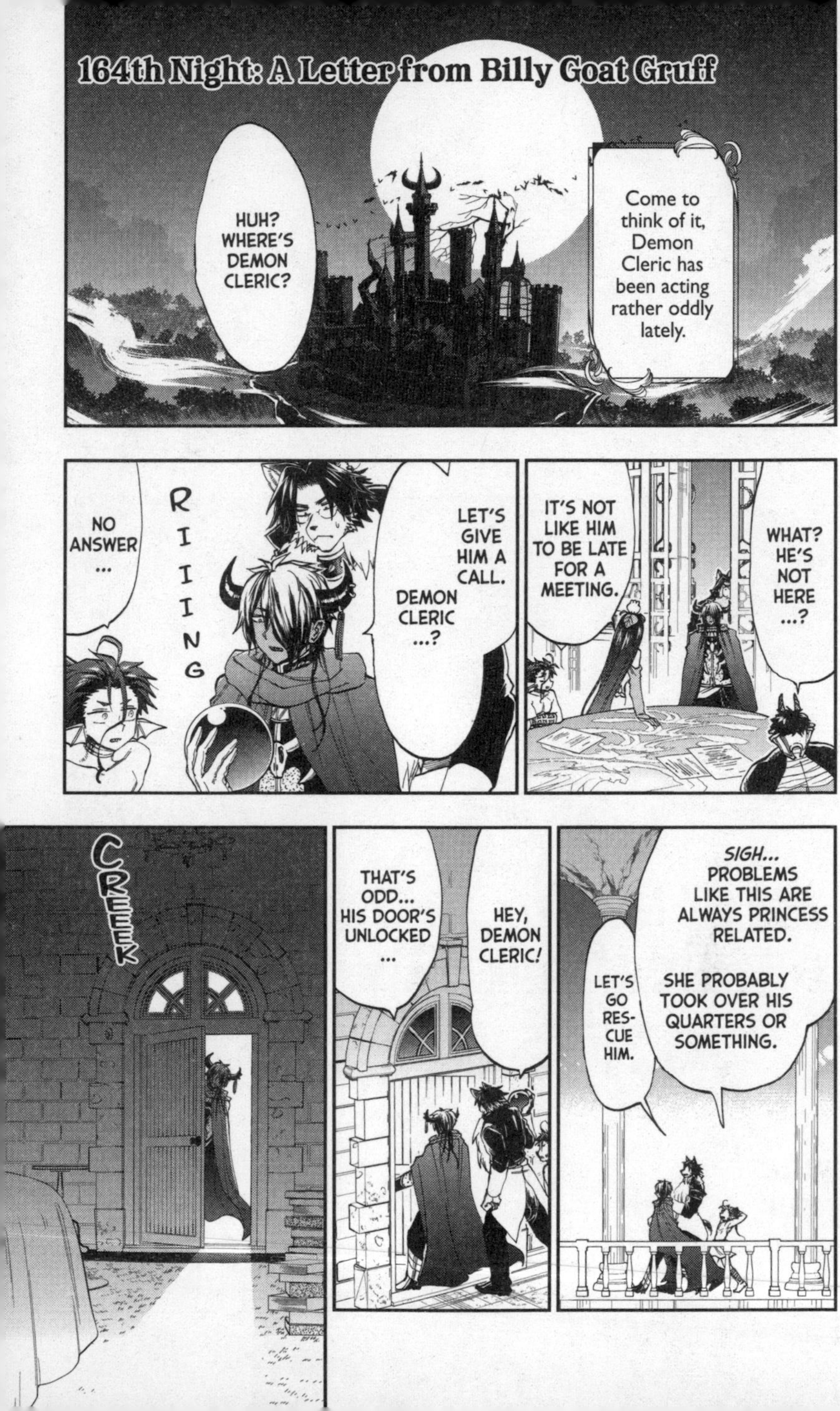
164th Night: A Letter from Billy Goat Gruff
Come to think of it, Demon Cleric has been acting rather oddly lately.
HUH? WHERE'S DEMON CLERIC?
WHAT? HE'S NOT HERE...?
IT'S NOT LIKE HIM TO BE LATE FOR A MEETING.
LET'S GIVE HIM A CALL.
DEMON CLERIC...?
RIIING
NO ANSWER...
SIGH... PROBLEMS LIKE THIS ARE ALWAYS PRINCESS RELATED.
SHE PROBABLY TOOK OVER HIS QUARTERS OR SOMETHING.
LET'S GO RES-CUE HIM.
HEY, DEMON CLERIC!
THAT'S ODD... HIS DOOR'S UNLOCKED...
CREEEK

164th Night: A Letter from Billy Goat Gruff

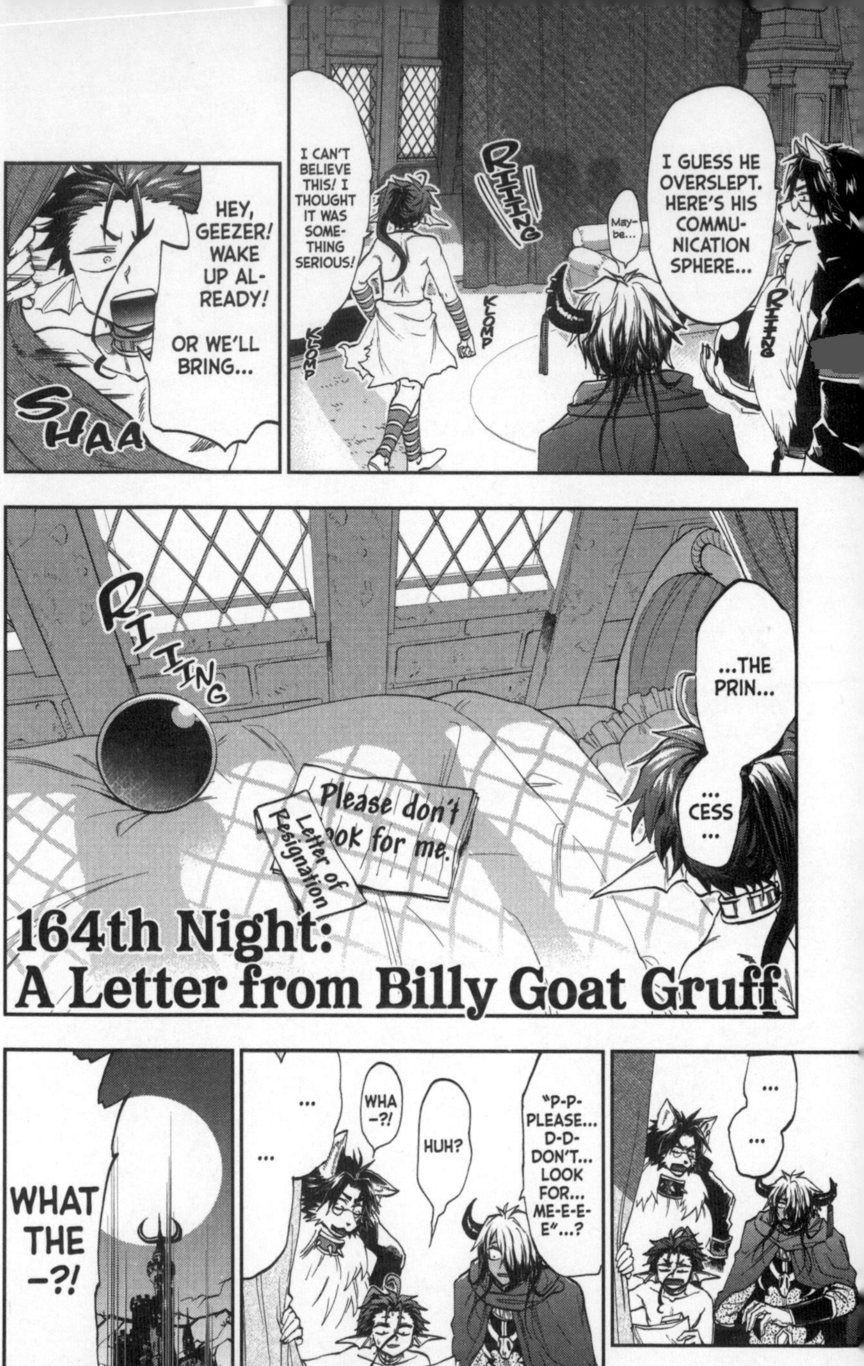
I GUESS HE OVERSLEPT. HERE'S HIS COMMUNICATION SPHERE...
RIIING
May-be...
RIIING
I CAN'T BELIEVE THIS! I THOUGHT IT WAS SOMETHING SERIOUS!
KLOMP
KLOMP
HEY, GEEZER! WAKE UP ALREADY!
OR WE'LL BRING...
SHAA
...THE PRIN...
...CESS...
RIIING
Please don't look for me.
Letter of Resignation
164th Night: A Letter from Billy Goat Gruff
...
...
"P-P-PLEASE... D-D-DON'T... LOOK FOR... ME-E-E-E"...?
HUH?
WHA-?!
...
...
WHAT THE-?!

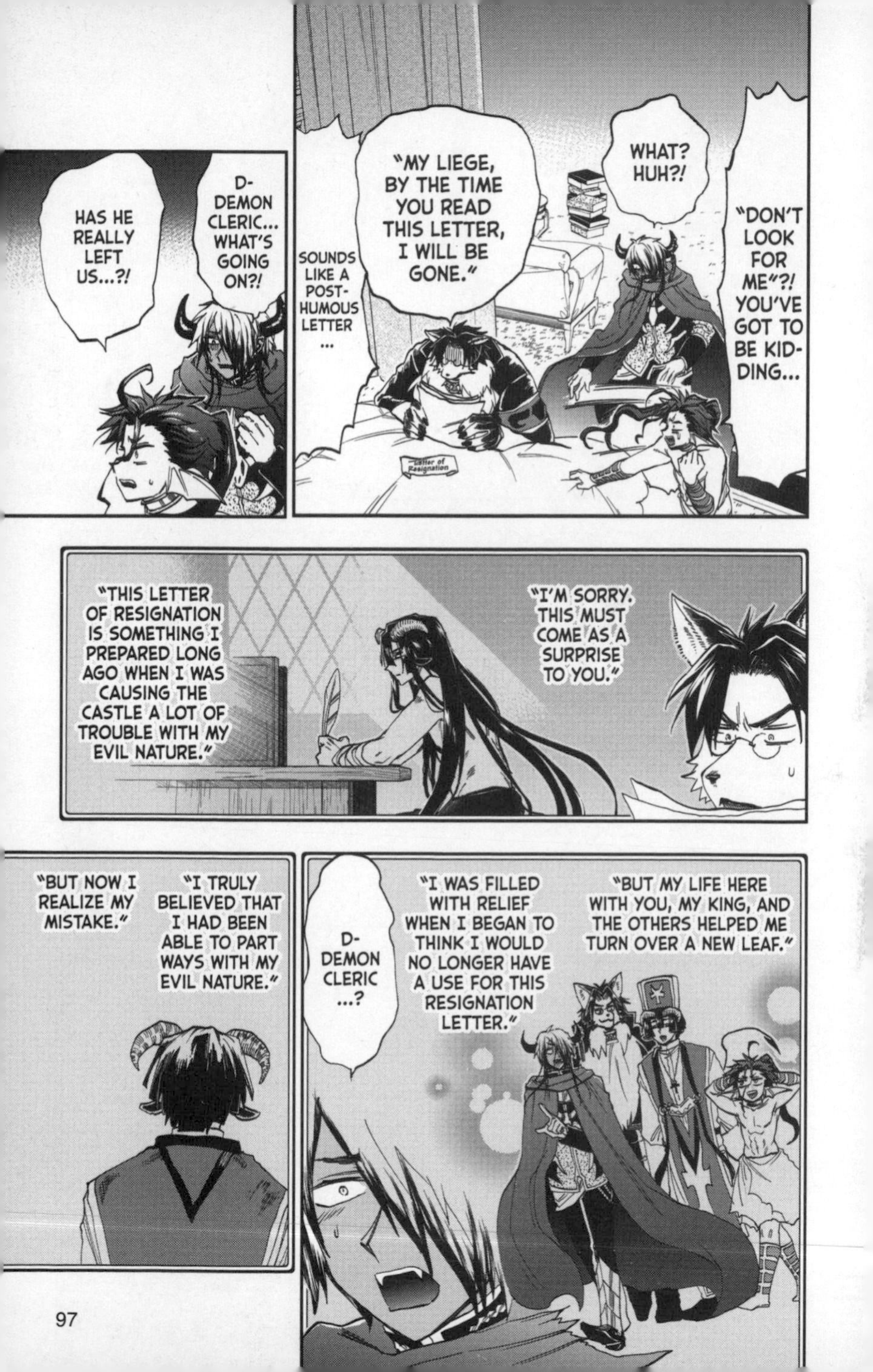
WHAT? HUH?!
"DON'T LOOK FOR ME"?! YOU'VE GOT TO BE KID-DING...
"MY LIEGE, BY THE TIME YOU READ THIS LETTER, I WILL BE GONE."
SOUNDS LIKE A POST-HUMOUS LETTER...
Letter of Resignation
D-DEMON CLERIC... WHAT'S GOING ON?!
HAS HE REALLY LEFT US...?!
"I'M SORRY. THIS MUST COME AS A SURPRISE TO YOU."
"THIS LETTER OF RESIGNATION IS SOMETHING I PREPARED LONG AGO WHEN I WAS CAUSING THE CASTLE A LOT OF TROUBLE WITH MY EVIL NATURE."
"BUT MY LIFE HERE WITH YOU, MY KING, AND THE OTHERS HELPED ME TURN OVER A NEW LEAF."
"I WAS FILLED WITH RELIEF WHEN I BEGAN TO THINK I WOULD NO LONGER HAVE A USE FOR THIS RESIGNATION LETTER."
D-DEMON CLERIC...?
"I TRULY BELIEVED THAT I HAD BEEN ABLE TO PART WAYS WITH MY EVIL NATURE."
"BUT NOW I REALIZE MY MISTAKE."

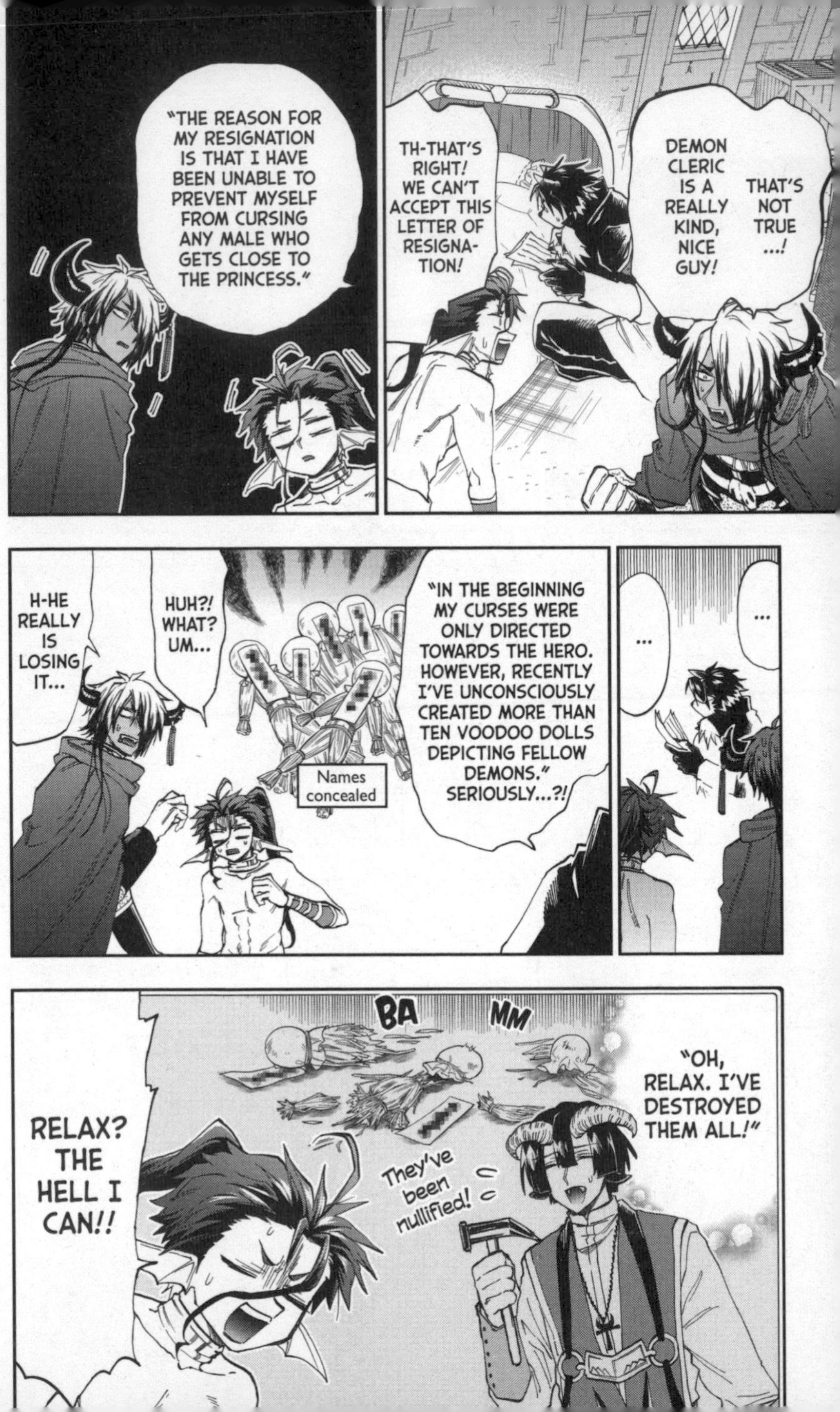
THAT'S NOT TRUE ...!
DEMON CLERIC IS A REALLY KIND, NICE GUY!
TH-THAT'S RIGHT! WE CAN'T ACCEPT THIS LETTER OF RESIGNATION!
"THE REASON FOR MY RESIGNATION IS THAT I HAVE BEEN UNABLE TO PREVENT MYSELF FROM CURSING ANY MALE WHO GETS CLOSE TO THE PRINCESS."
...
...
"IN THE BEGINNING MY CURSES WERE ONLY DIRECTED TOWARDS THE HERO. HOWEVER, RECENTLY I'VE UNCONSCIOUSLY CREATED MORE THAN TEN VOODOO DOLLS DEPICTING FELLOW DEMONS."
SERIOUSLY...?!
HUH?! WHAT? UM...
H-HE REALLY IS LOSING IT...
Names concealed
BAMM
"OH, RELAX. I'VE DESTROYED THEM ALL!"
They've been nullified!
RELAX? THE HELL I CAN!!

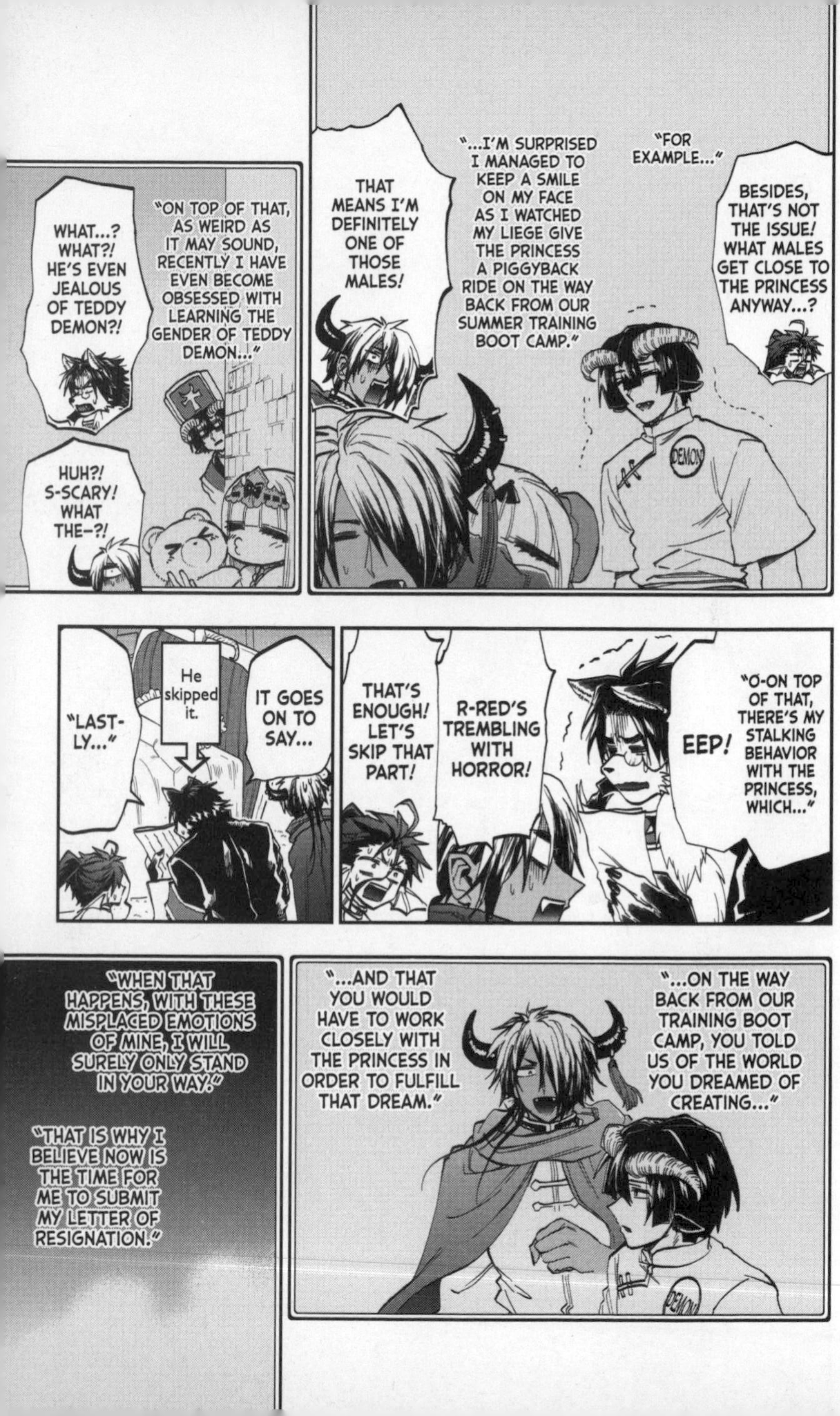
BESIDES, THAT'S NOT THE ISSUE! WHAT MALES GET CLOSE TO THE PRINCESS ANYWAY...?
"FOR EXAMPLE..."
"...I'M SURPRISED I MANAGED TO KEEP A SMILE ON MY FACE AS I WATCHED MY LIEGE GIVE THE PRINCESS A PIGGYBACK RIDE ON THE WAY BACK FROM OUR SUMMER TRAINING BOOT CAMP."
THAT MEANS I'M DEFINITELY ONE OF THOSE MALES!
"ON TOP OF THAT, AS WEIRD AS IT MAY SOUND, RECENTLY I HAVE EVEN BECOME OBSESSED WITH LEARNING THE GENDER OF TEDDY DEMON..."
WHAT...? WHAT?! HE'S EVEN JEALOUS OF TEDDY DEMON?!
HUH?! S-SCARY! WHAT THE-?!
DEMON
"O-ON TOP OF THAT, THERE'S MY STALKING BEHAVIOR WITH THE PRINCESS, WHICH..."
EEP!
R-RED'S TREMBLING WITH HORROR!
THAT'S ENOUGH! LET'S SKIP THAT PART!
IT GOES ON TO SAY...
He skipped it.
"LAST-LY..."
"...ON THE WAY BACK FROM OUR TRAINING BOOT CAMP, YOU TOLD US OF THE WORLD YOU DREAMED OF CREATING..."
"...AND THAT YOU WOULD HAVE TO WORK CLOSELY WITH THE PRINCESS IN ORDER TO FULFILL THAT DREAM."
"WHEN THAT HAPPENS, WITH THESE MISPLACED EMOTIONS OF MINE, I WILL SURELY ONLY STAND IN YOUR WAY."
"THAT IS WHY I BELIEVE NOW IS THE TIME FOR ME TO SUBMIT MY LETTER OF RESIGNATION."
DEMON

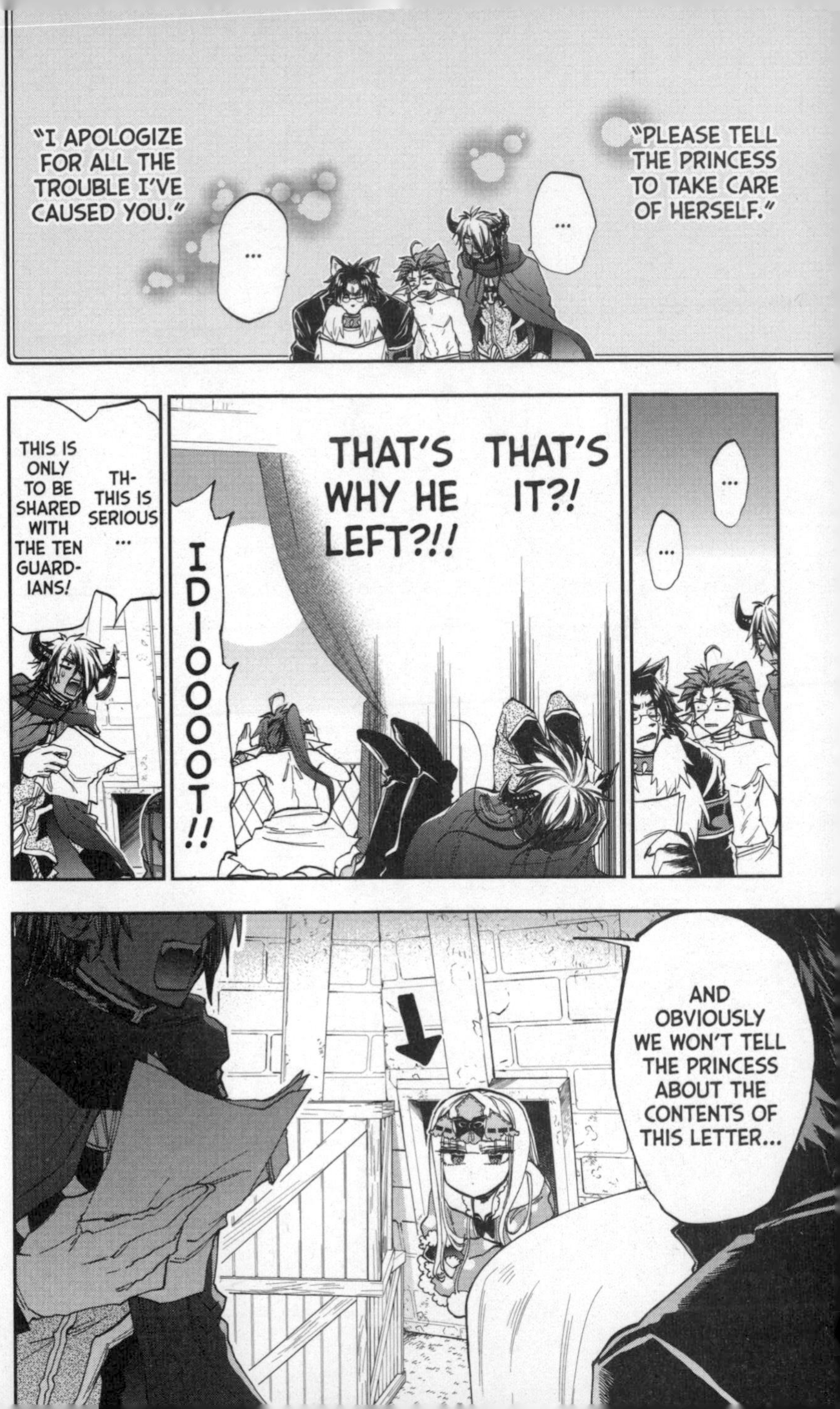
"PLEASE TELL THE PRINCESS TO TAKE CARE OF HERSELF."
...
"I APOLOGIZE FOR ALL THE TROUBLE I'VE CAUSED YOU."
...
...
...
THAT'S IT?!
THAT'S WHY HE LEFT?!!
IDIOOOOOT!!
TH- THIS IS SERIOUS...
THIS IS ONLY TO BE SHARED WITH THE TEN GUARD-IANS!
AND OBVIOUSLY WE WON'T TELL THE PRINCESS ABOUT THE CONTENTS OF THIS LETTER...

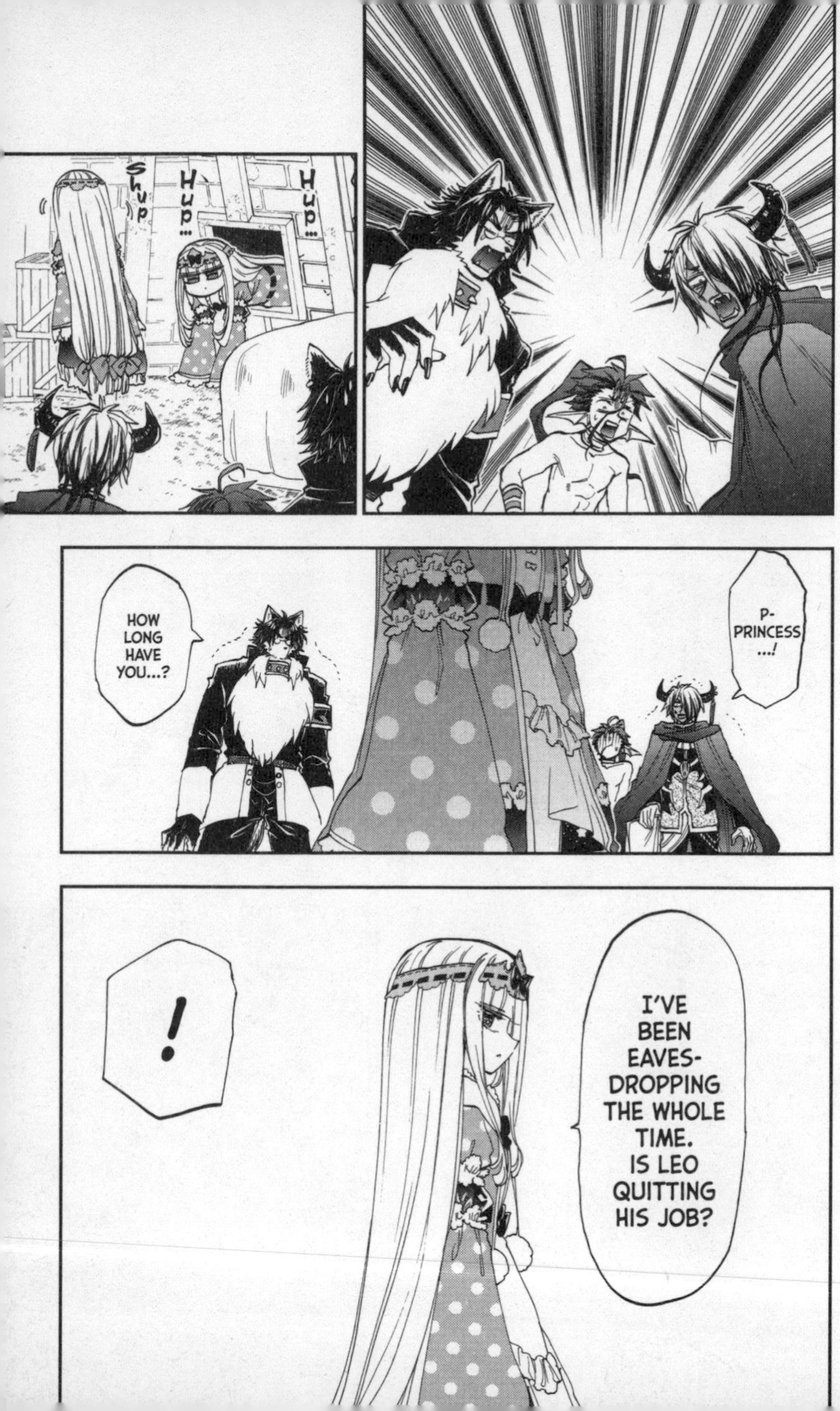
Hup...
Hup...
Shup
P-PRINCESS...!
HOW LONG HAVE YOU...?
I'VE BEEN EAVES-DROPPING THE WHOLE TIME. IS LEO QUITTING HIS JOB?
!

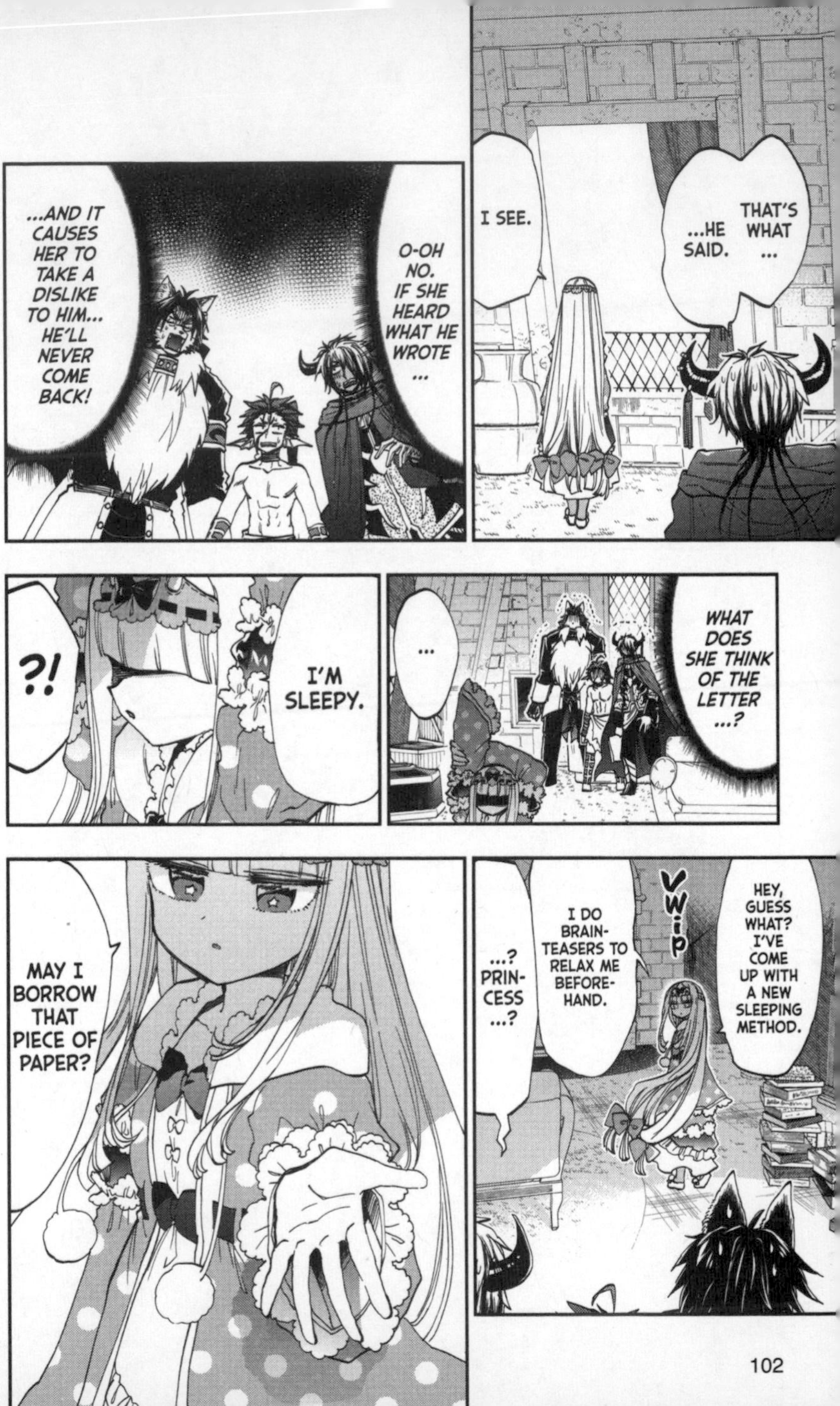
THAT'S WHAT ...
...HE SAID.
I SEE.
O-OH NO. IF SHE HEARD WHAT HE WROTE ...
...AND IT CAUSES HER TO TAKE A DISLIKE TO HIM... HE'LL NEVER COME BACK!
WHAT DOES SHE THINK OF THE LETTER ...?
...
I'M SLEEPY.
?!
HEY, GUESS WHAT? I'VE COME UP WITH A NEW SLEEPING METHOD.
VWIP
I DO BRAIN-TEASERS TO RELAX ME BEFORE-HAND.
...? PRIN-CESS ...?
MAY I BORROW THAT PIECE OF PAPER?

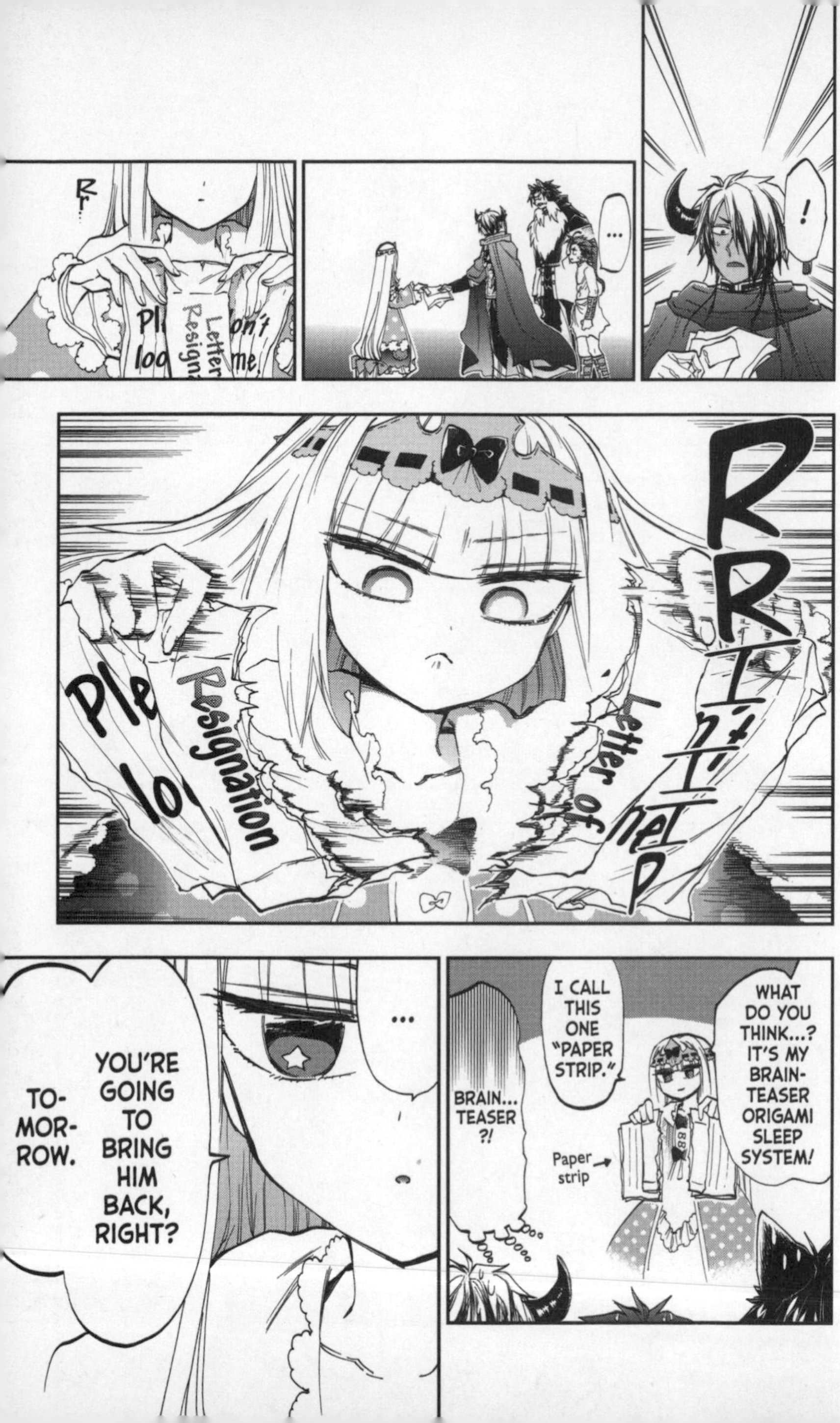

!
...
Rr...
Pl on't
loo me.
Letter
Resigna
RRIIIIP
Letter of
Resignation
Ple
loo
WHAT DO YOU THINK...? IT'S MY BRAIN-TEASER ORIGAMI SLEEP SYSTEM!
I CALL THIS ONE "PAPER STRIP."
BRAIN... TEASER?!
Paper strip
...
YOU'RE GOING TO BRING HIM BACK, RIGHT?
TO-MOR-ROW.

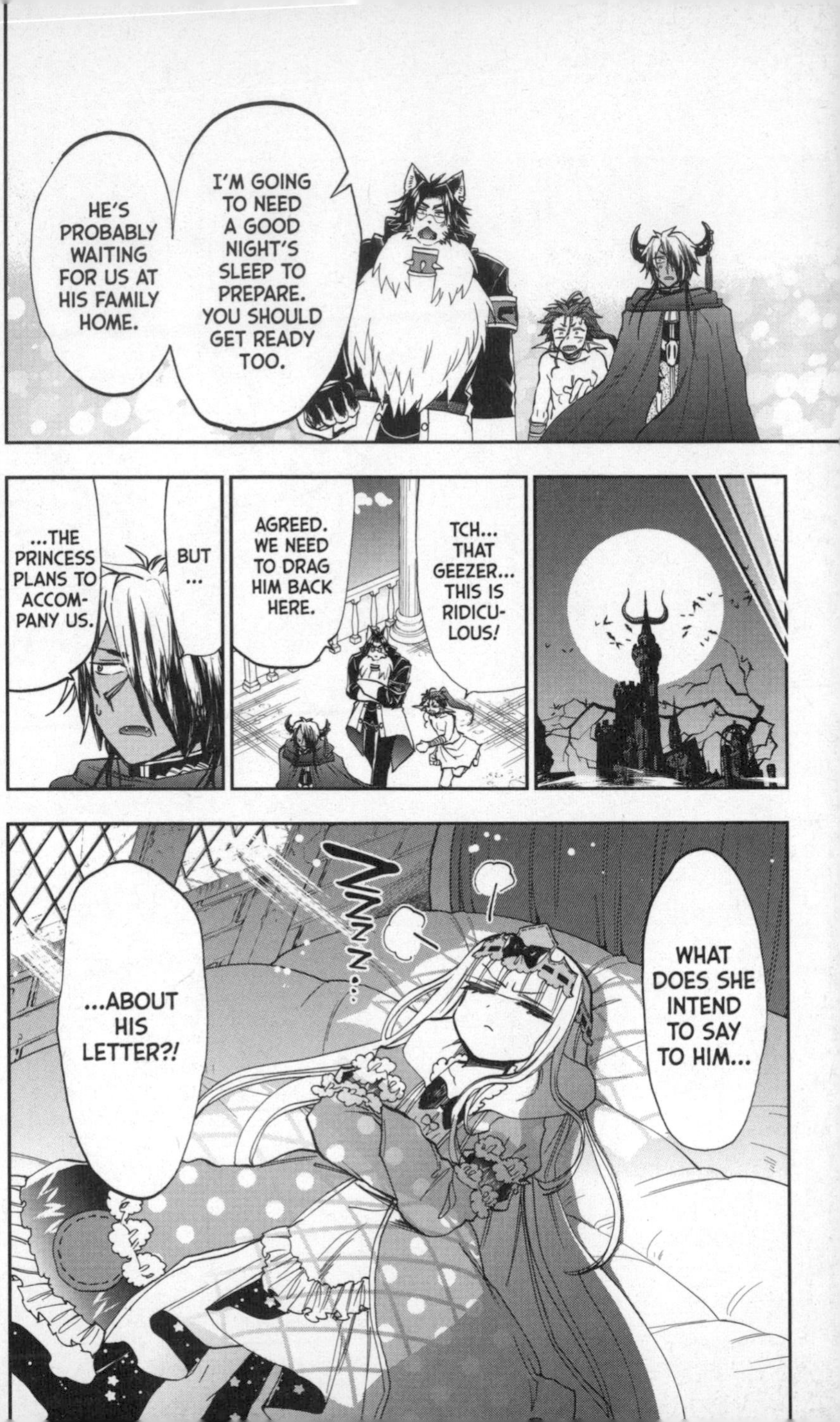
I'M GOING TO NEED A GOOD NIGHT'S SLEEP TO PREPARE. YOU SHOULD GET READY TOO.
HE'S PROBABLY WAITING FOR US AT HIS FAMILY HOME.
TCH... THAT GEEZER... THIS IS RIDICULOUS!
AGREED. WE NEED TO DRAG HIM BACK HERE.
BUT...
...THE PRINCESS PLANS TO ACCOMPANY US.
WHAT DOES SHE INTEND TO SAY TO HIM...
NNNZZZ...
...ABOUT HIS LETTER?!

DEMON CASTLE QUESTION CORNER

1

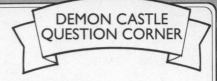

I asked for questions on Twitter and received tons of them, so there are four pages of answers in this volume. That's a lot! But I'll ask for questions again someday.

I've abbreviated the questions, so they're not exactly the same as your originals. Please forgive me.

- Is Demon Cleric's favorite pain reliever patch Fe*tas or Sal*npas?

A It's Vo*taren.

- What is Leonard's favorite and least favorite food?

A He likes seasoned rice and seasoned sticky rice. I'm not sure there's any food he dislikes.

- There are so many questions about Demon Cleric, aren't there? (From Kumanomata)

A *I know!*

- The princess's star-shaped pupil is so cute! I'd love to learn about the eye designs of the other characters!

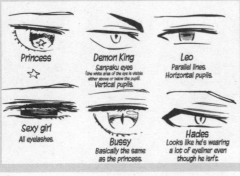

Princess
Demon King
Sanpaku eyes
(the white area of the eye is visible either above or below the pupil).
Vertical pupils.
Leo
Parallel lines.
Horizontal pupils.
Sexy girl
All eyelashes.
Bussy
Basically the same as the princess.
Hades
Looks like he's wearing a lot of eyeliner even though he isn't.

A Most of them have pretty ordinary eyes, but some have pupils that are vertical or horizontal.

- What are the princess's three favorite outfits?!

A Probably her Teddy Demon pajamas, the white dress from back home (cover of vol. 7), and the camper outfit (vol. 11, "Would you like to change your class?" page).

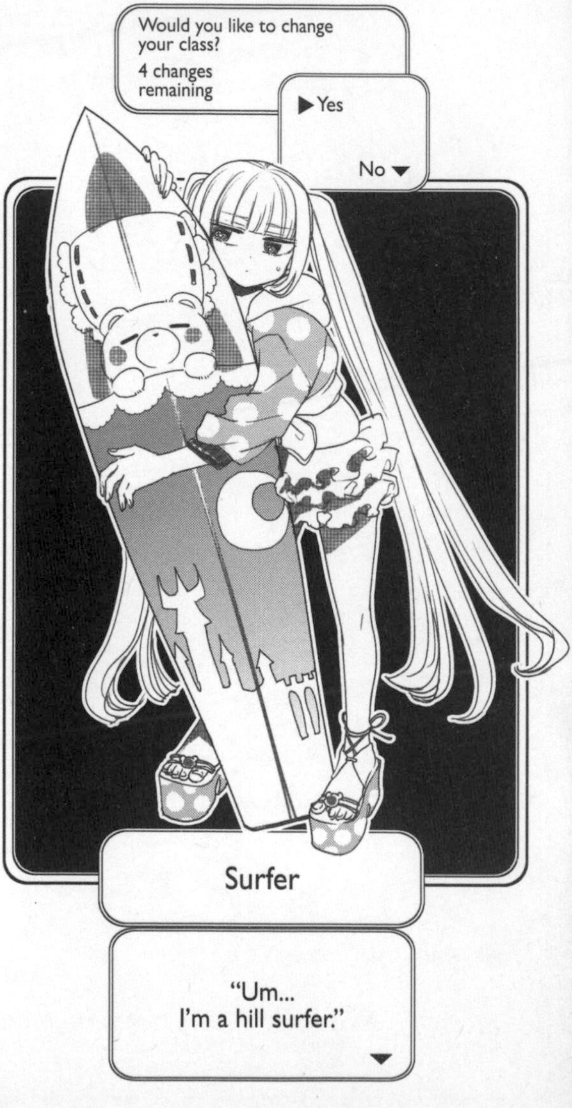
Would you like to change your class?
4 changes remaining
▶Yes
No
Surfer
"Um...
I'm a hill surfer."

165th Night: Travel by Sleeper Choo Choo

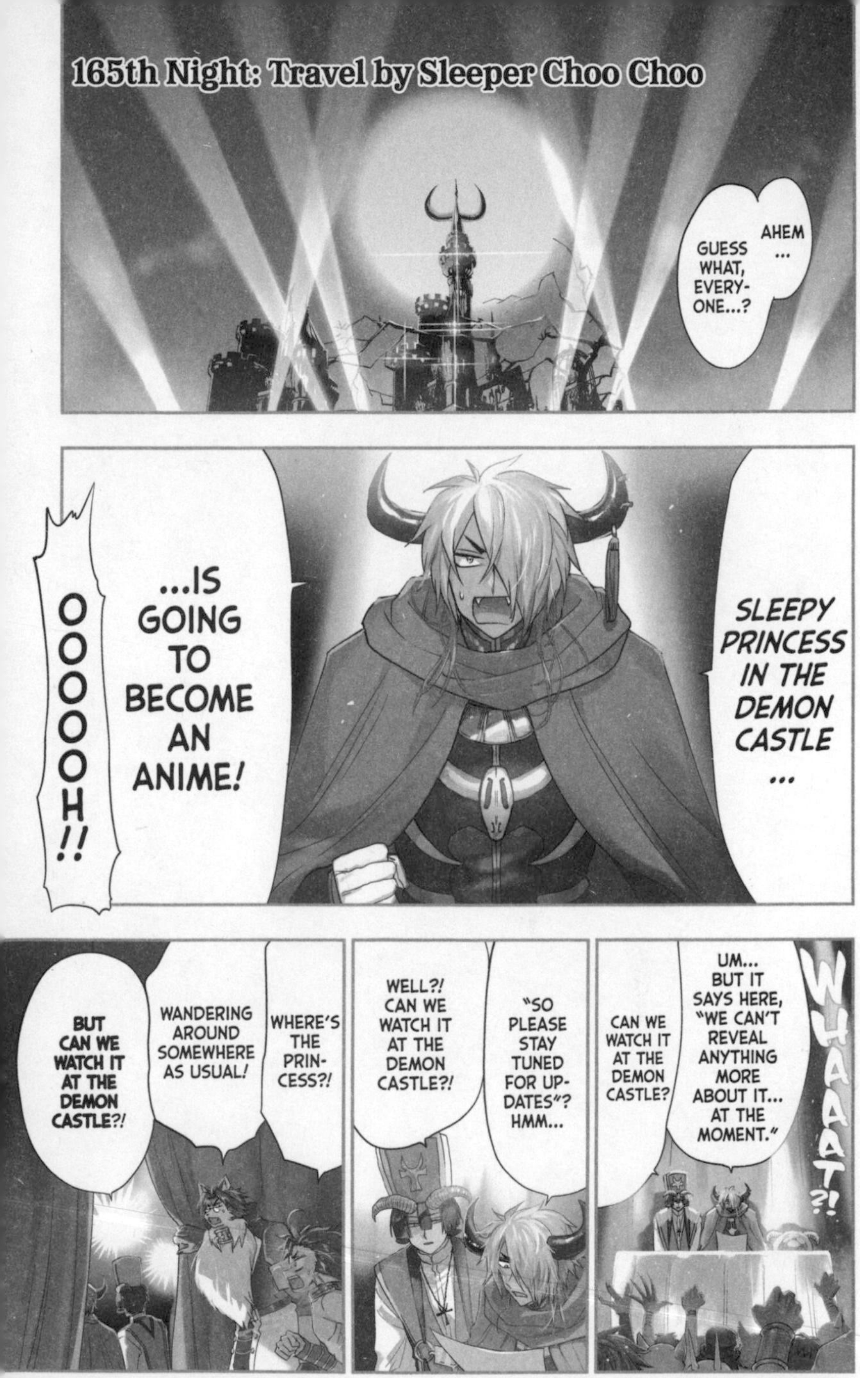
AHEM...
GUESS WHAT, EVERYONE...?
SLEEPY PRINCESS IN THE DEMON CASTLE...
...IS GOING TO BECOME AN ANIME!
OOOOOOH!!
WHAAAT?!
UM... BUT IT SAYS HERE, "WE CAN'T REVEAL ANYTHING MORE ABOUT IT... AT THE MOMENT."
CAN WE WATCH IT AT THE DEMON CASTLE?
"SO PLEASE STAY TUNED FOR UPDATES"? HMM...
WELL?! CAN WE WATCH IT AT THE DEMON CASTLE?!
WHERE'S THE PRINCESS?!
WANDERING AROUND SOMEWHERE AS USUAL!
BUT CAN WE WATCH IT AT THE DEMON CASTLE?!

*From Issue 42 of *Shonen Sunday*, published September 18, 2019

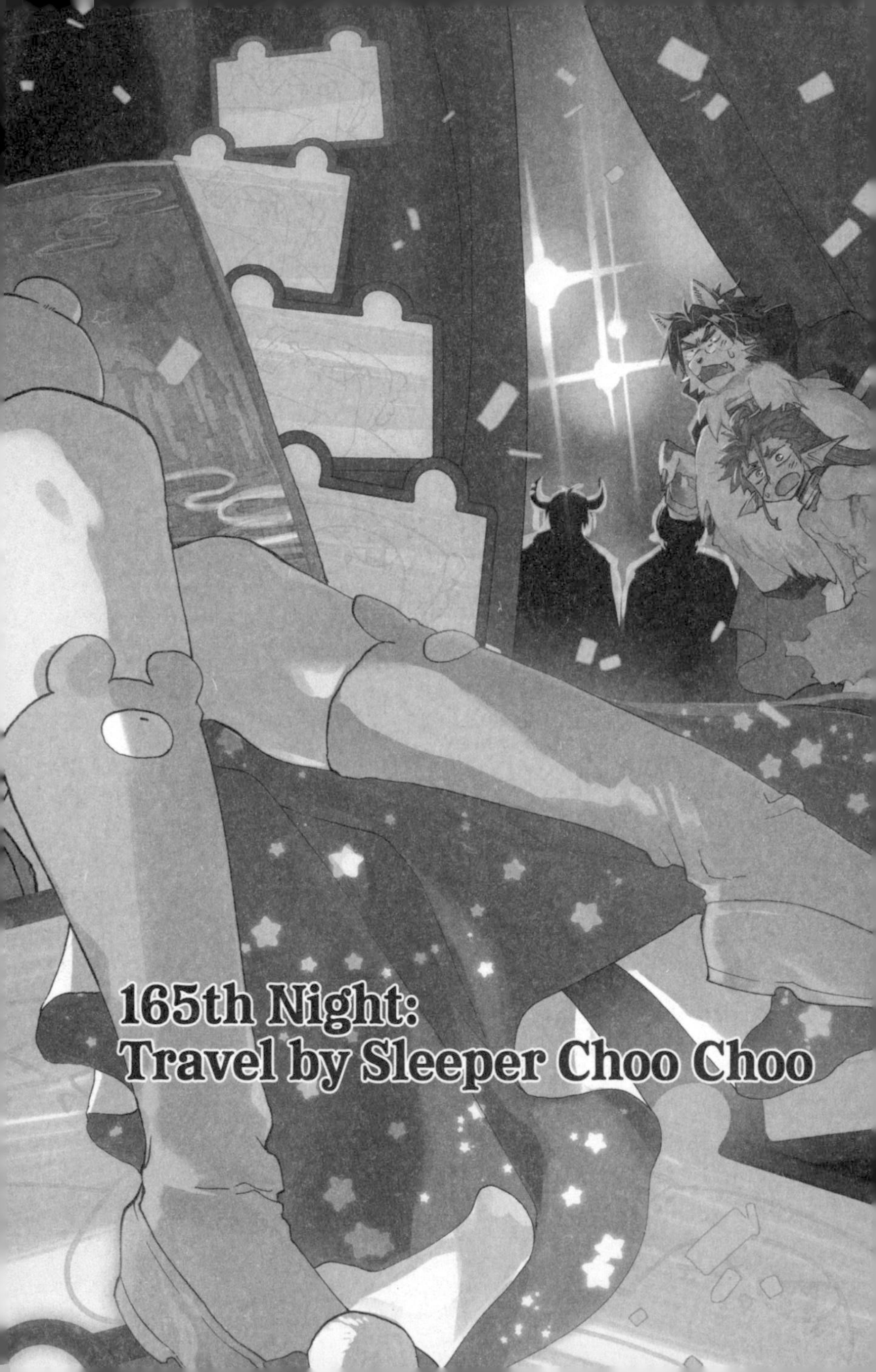
165th Night:
Travel by Sleeper Choo Choo

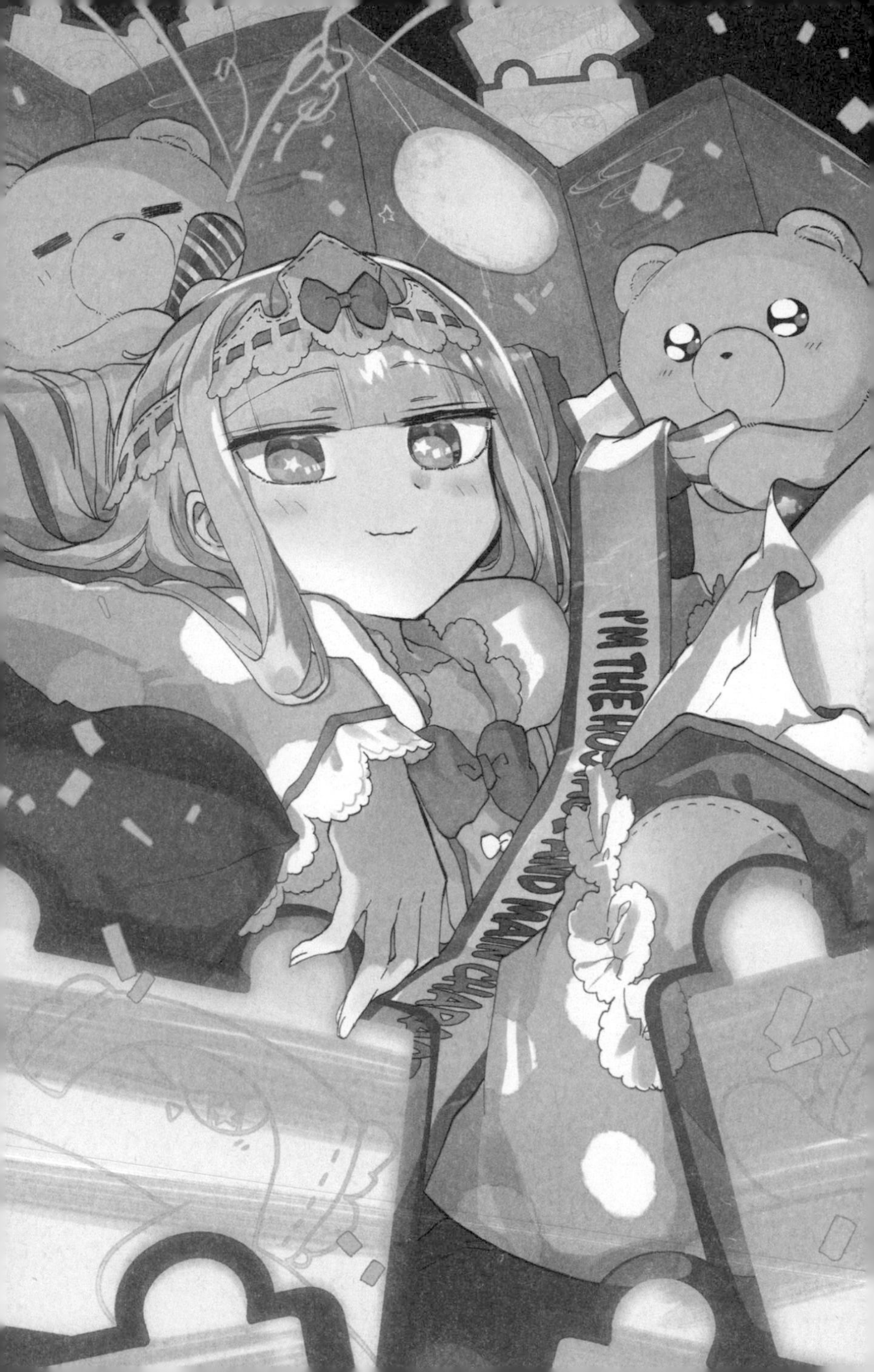
I'M THE HO
AND MAIN CHA

SLEEPY PRINCESS IN THE DEMON CASTLE

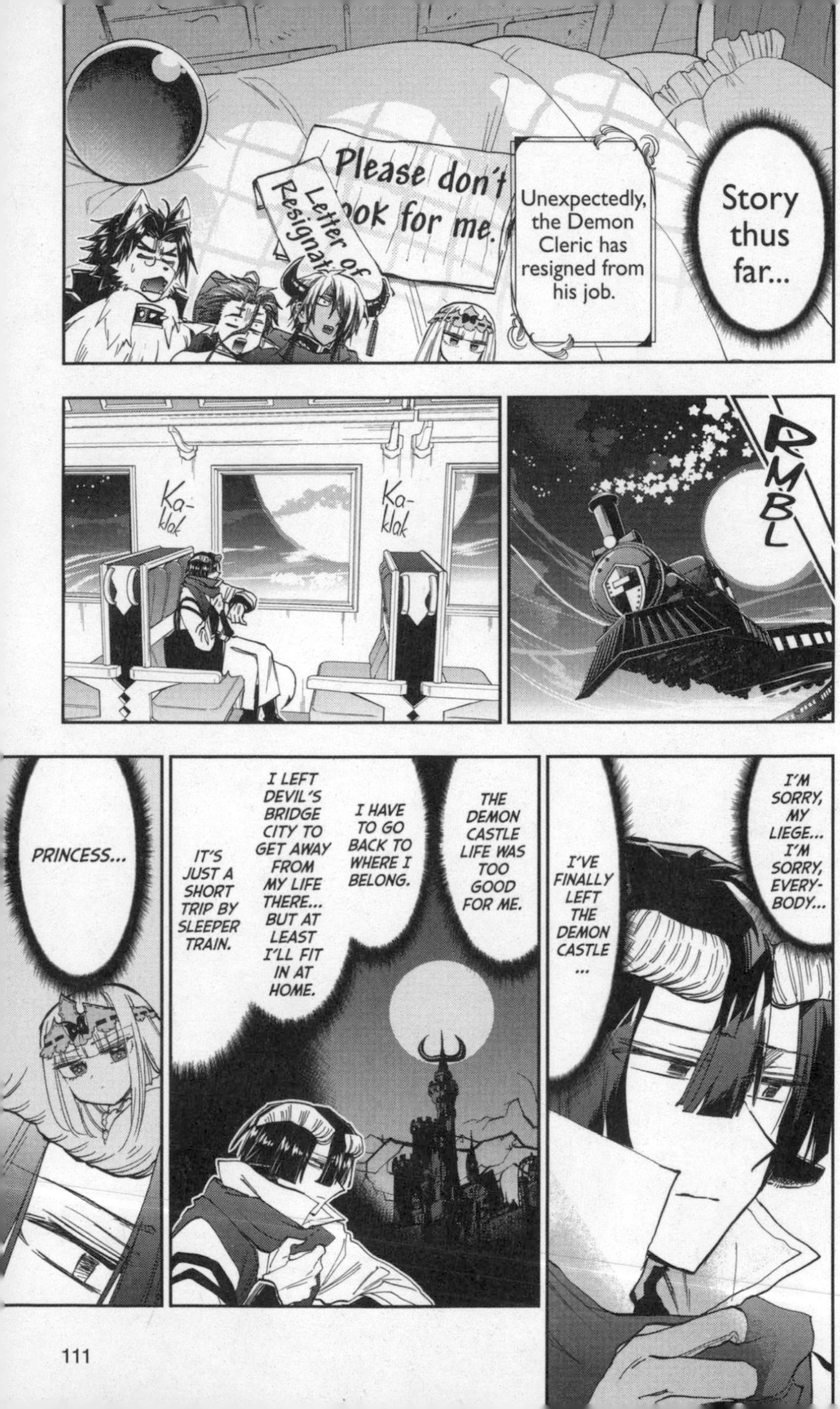
Story thus far...
Unexpectedly, the Demon Cleric has resigned from his job.
Please don't
ook for me.
Letter of Resignat
RMBL
Ka-klak
Ka-klak
I'M SORRY, MY LIEGE... I'M SORRY, EVERYBODY...
I'VE FINALLY LEFT THE DEMON CASTLE...
THE DEMON CASTLE LIFE WAS TOO GOOD FOR ME.
I HAVE TO GO BACK TO WHERE I BELONG.
I LEFT DEVIL'S BRIDGE CITY TO GET AWAY FROM MY LIFE THERE... BUT AT LEAST I'LL FIT IN AT HOME.
IT'S JUST A SHORT TRIP BY SLEEPER TRAIN.
PRINCESS...

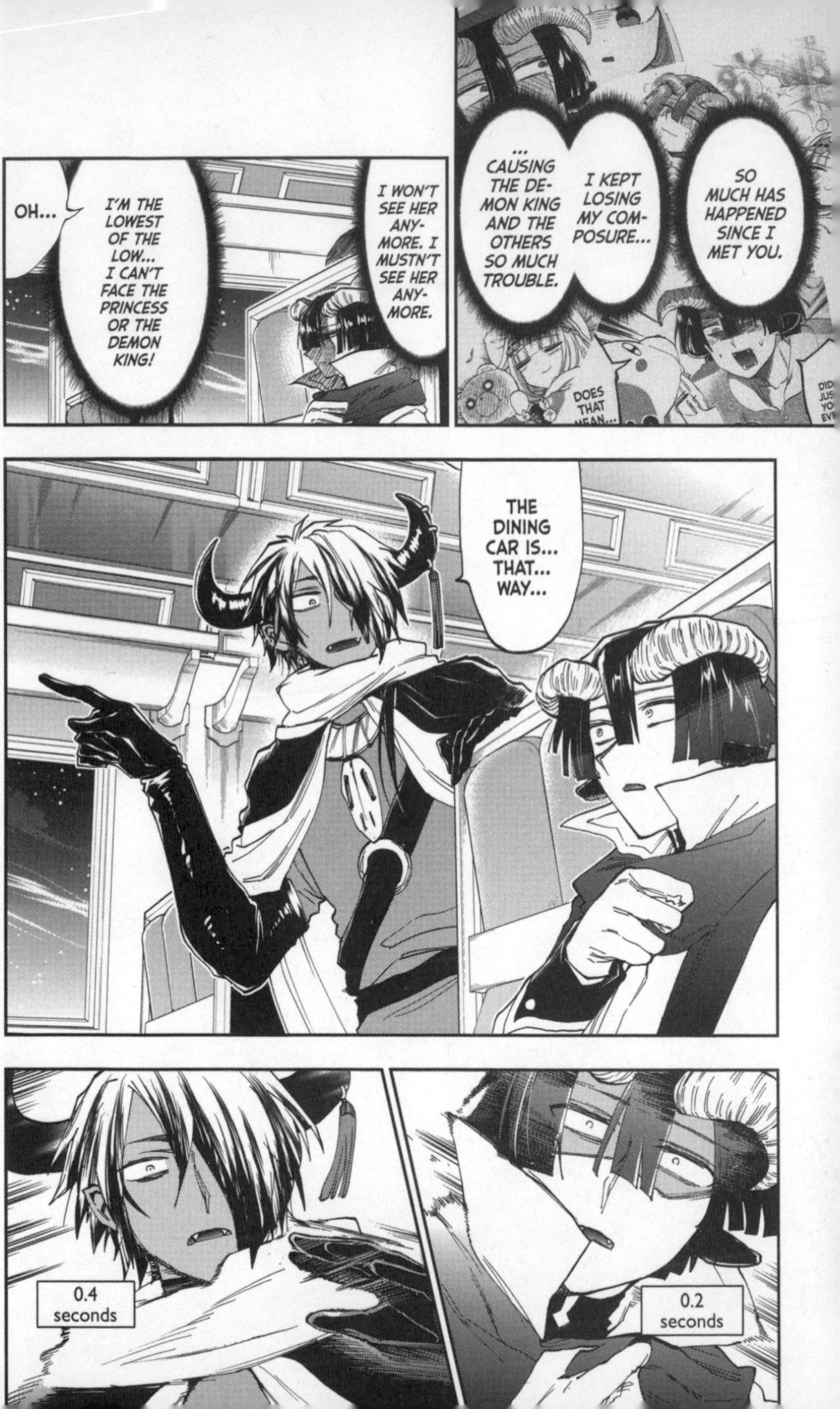
SO MUCH HAS HAPPENED SINCE I MET YOU.
I KEPT LOSING MY COMPOSURE...
... CAUSING THE DEMON KING AND THE OTHERS SO MUCH TROUBLE.
DOES THAT
I WON'T SEE HER ANYMORE. I MUSTN'T SEE HER ANYMORE.
I'M THE LOWEST OF THE LOW... I CAN'T FACE THE PRINCESS OR THE DEMON KING!
OH...
THE DINING CAR IS... THAT... WAY...
0.2 seconds
0.4 seconds

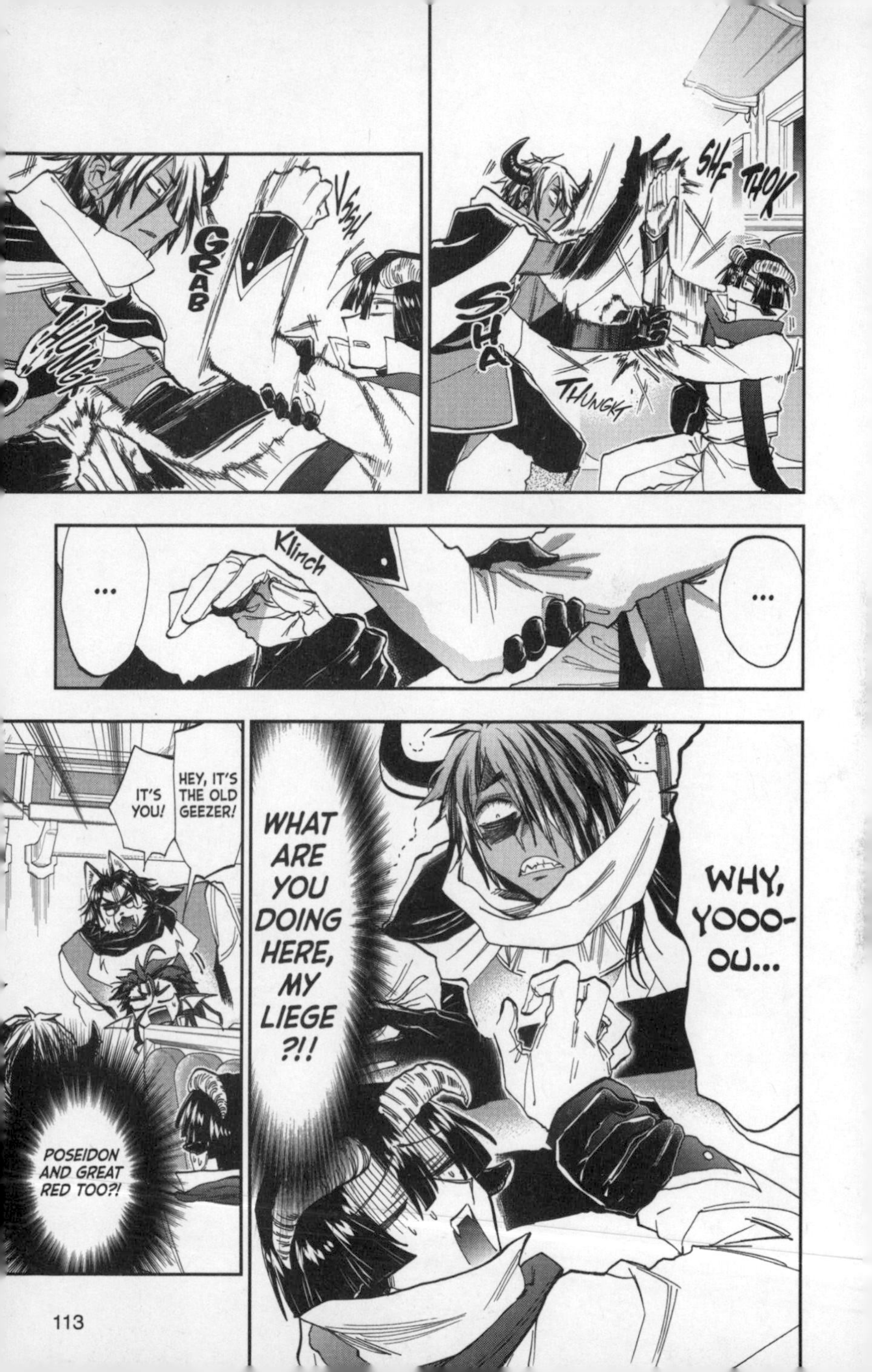
SHF THOK
SHA
THUNGK!
VSSH
GRAB
THUNGK!
...
Klinch
...
WHY, YOOO-OU...
WHAT ARE YOU DOING HERE, MY LIEGE?!!
HEY, IT'S THE OLD GEEZER!
IT'S YOU!
POSEIDON AND GREAT RED TOO?!

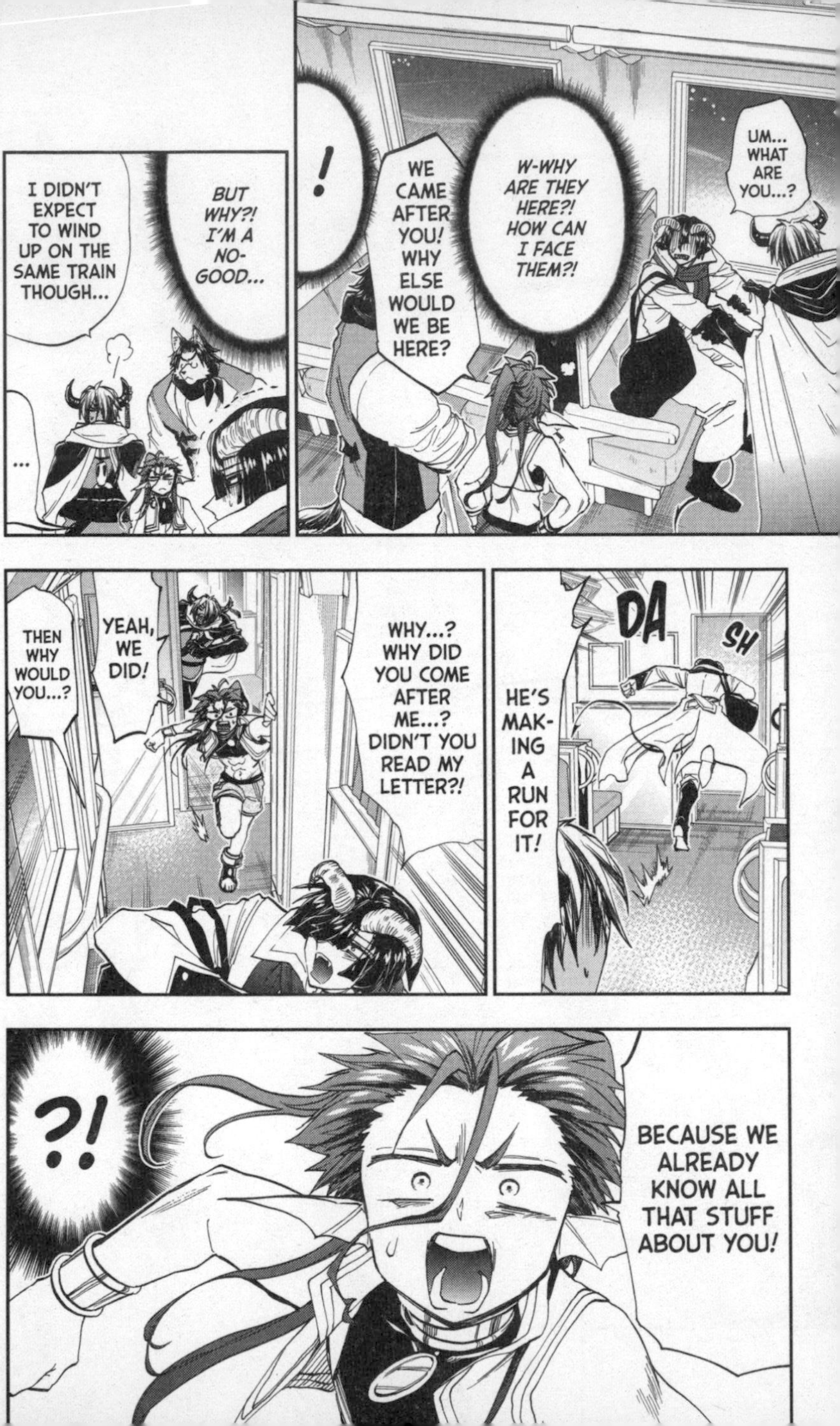
UM... WHAT ARE YOU...?
W-WHY ARE THEY HERE?! HOW CAN I FACE THEM?!
WE CAME AFTER YOU! WHY ELSE WOULD WE BE HERE?
!
BUT WHY?! I'M A NO-GOOD...
I DIDN'T EXPECT TO WIND UP ON THE SAME TRAIN THOUGH...
...
DASH
HE'S MAKING A RUN FOR IT!
WHY...? WHY DID YOU COME AFTER ME...? DIDN'T YOU READ MY LETTER?!
YEAH, WE DID!
THEN WHY WOULD YOU...?
BECAUSE WE ALREADY KNOW ALL THAT STUFF ABOUT YOU!
?!

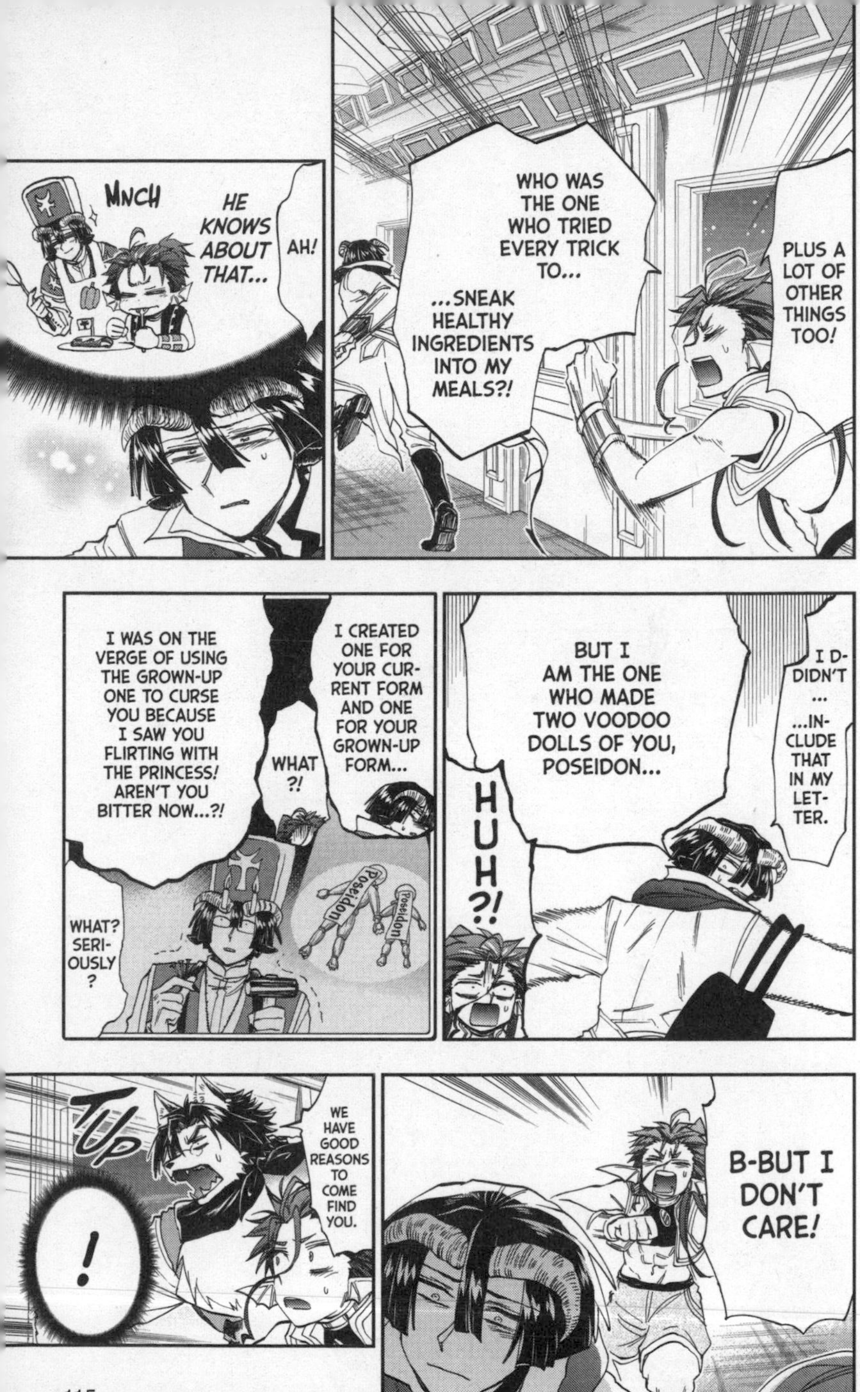
WHO WAS THE ONE WHO TRIED EVERY TRICK TO...
...SNEAK HEALTHY INGREDIENTS INTO MY MEALS?!
PLUS A LOT OF OTHER THINGS TOO!
AH!
HE KNOWS ABOUT THAT...
MNCH
BUT I AM THE ONE WHO MADE TWO VOODOO DOLLS OF YOU, POSEIDON...
HUH?!
I D-DIDN'T ... ...INCLUDE THAT IN MY LETTER.
I CREATED ONE FOR YOUR CURRENT FORM AND ONE FOR YOUR GROWN-UP FORM...
WHAT?!
I WAS ON THE VERGE OF USING THE GROWN-UP ONE TO CURSE YOU BECAUSE I SAW YOU FLIRTING WITH THE PRINCESS! AREN'T YOU BITTER NOW...?!
Poseidon
Poseidon
WHAT? SERIOUSLY?
B-BUT I DON'T CARE!
WE HAVE GOOD REASONS TO COME FIND YOU.
TUP
!

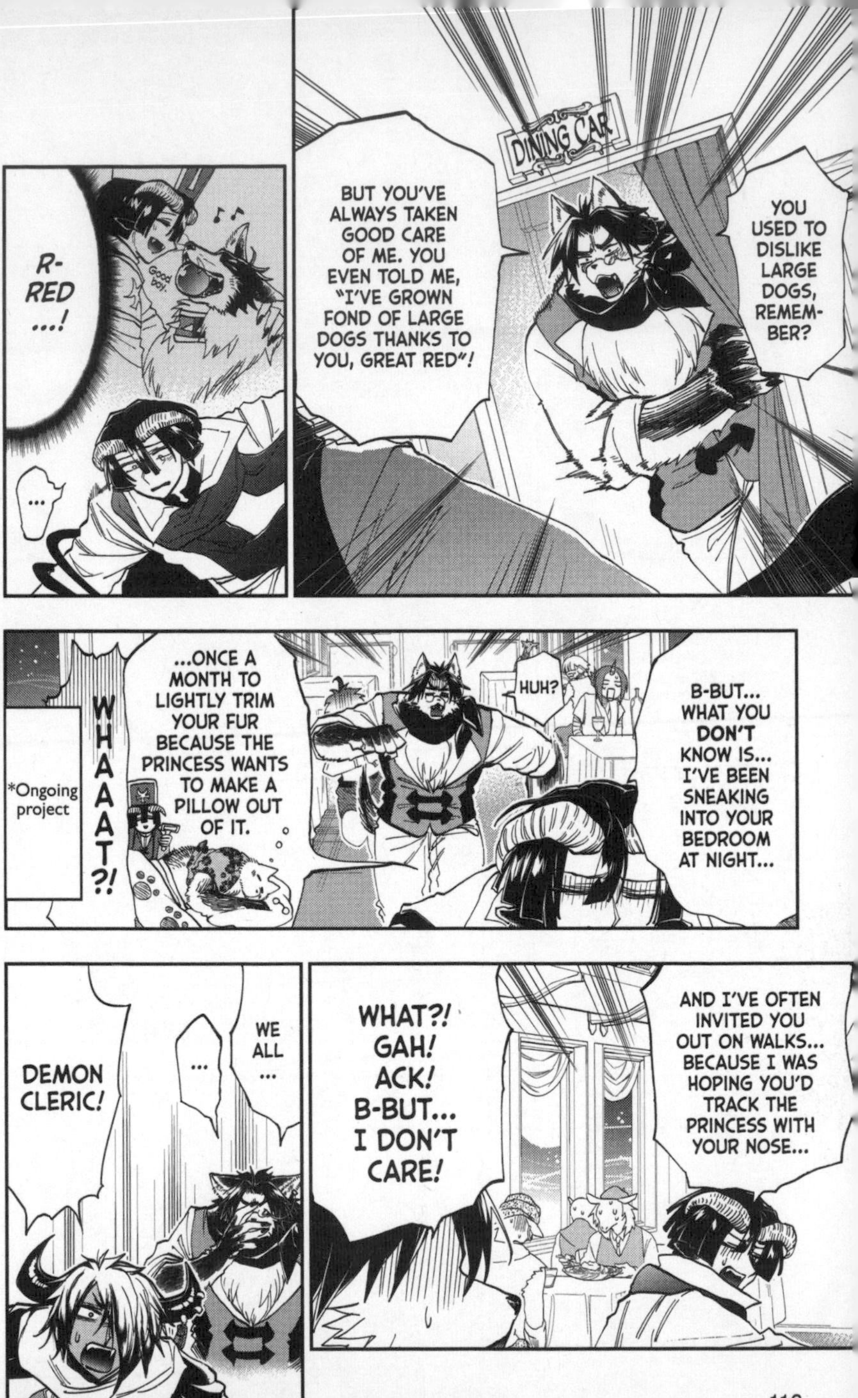
DINING CAR
YOU USED TO DISLIKE LARGE DOGS, REMEMBER?
BUT YOU'VE ALWAYS TAKEN GOOD CARE OF ME. YOU EVEN TOLD ME, "I'VE GROWN FOND OF LARGE DOGS THANKS TO YOU, GREAT RED"!
R-RED ...!
Good boy.
...
B-BUT... WHAT YOU **DON'T** KNOW IS... I'VE BEEN SNEAKING INTO YOUR BEDROOM AT NIGHT...
HUH?
...ONCE A MONTH TO LIGHTLY TRIM YOUR FUR BECAUSE THE PRINCESS WANTS TO MAKE A PILLOW OUT OF IT.
WHAAAAT?!
*Ongoing project
AND I'VE OFTEN INVITED YOU OUT ON WALKS... BECAUSE I WAS HOPING YOU'D TRACK THE PRINCESS WITH YOUR NOSE...
WHAT?! GAH! ACK! B-BUT... I DON'T CARE!
WE ALL ...
...
DEMON CLERIC!

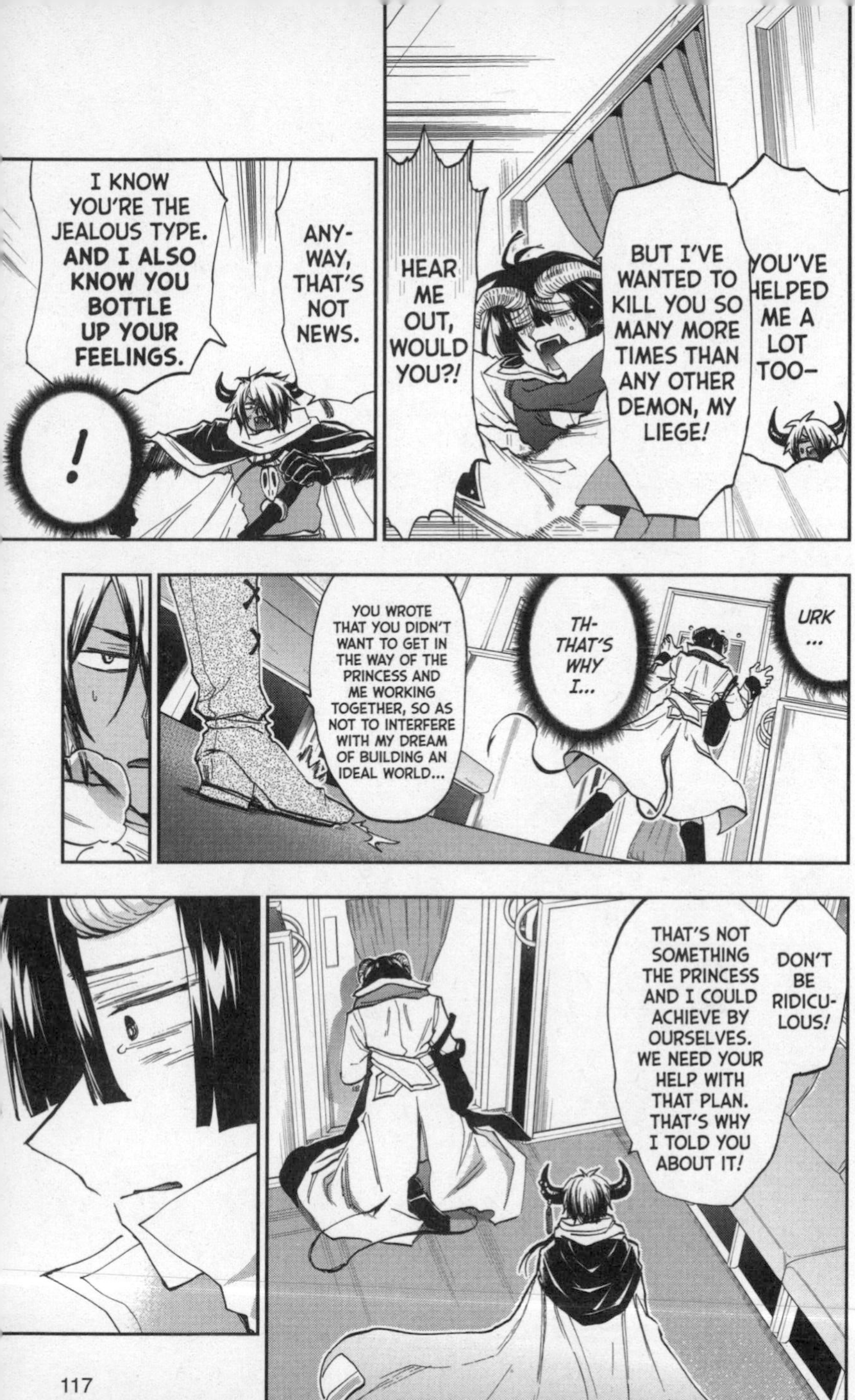
YOU'VE HELPED ME A LOT TOO—
BUT I'VE WANTED TO KILL YOU SO MANY MORE TIMES THAN ANY OTHER DEMON, MY LIEGE!
HEAR ME OUT, WOULD YOU?!
ANY-WAY, THAT'S NOT NEWS.
I KNOW YOU'RE THE JEALOUS TYPE. AND I ALSO KNOW YOU BOTTLE UP YOUR FEELINGS.
!
URK...
TH- THAT'S WHY I...
YOU WROTE THAT YOU DIDN'T WANT TO GET IN THE WAY OF THE PRINCESS AND ME WORKING TOGETHER, SO AS NOT TO INTERFERE WITH MY DREAM OF BUILDING AN IDEAL WORLD...
DON'T BE RIDICULOUS!
THAT'S NOT SOMETHING THE PRINCESS AND I COULD ACHIEVE BY OURSELVES. WE NEED YOUR HELP WITH THAT PLAN. THAT'S WHY I TOLD YOU ABOUT IT!

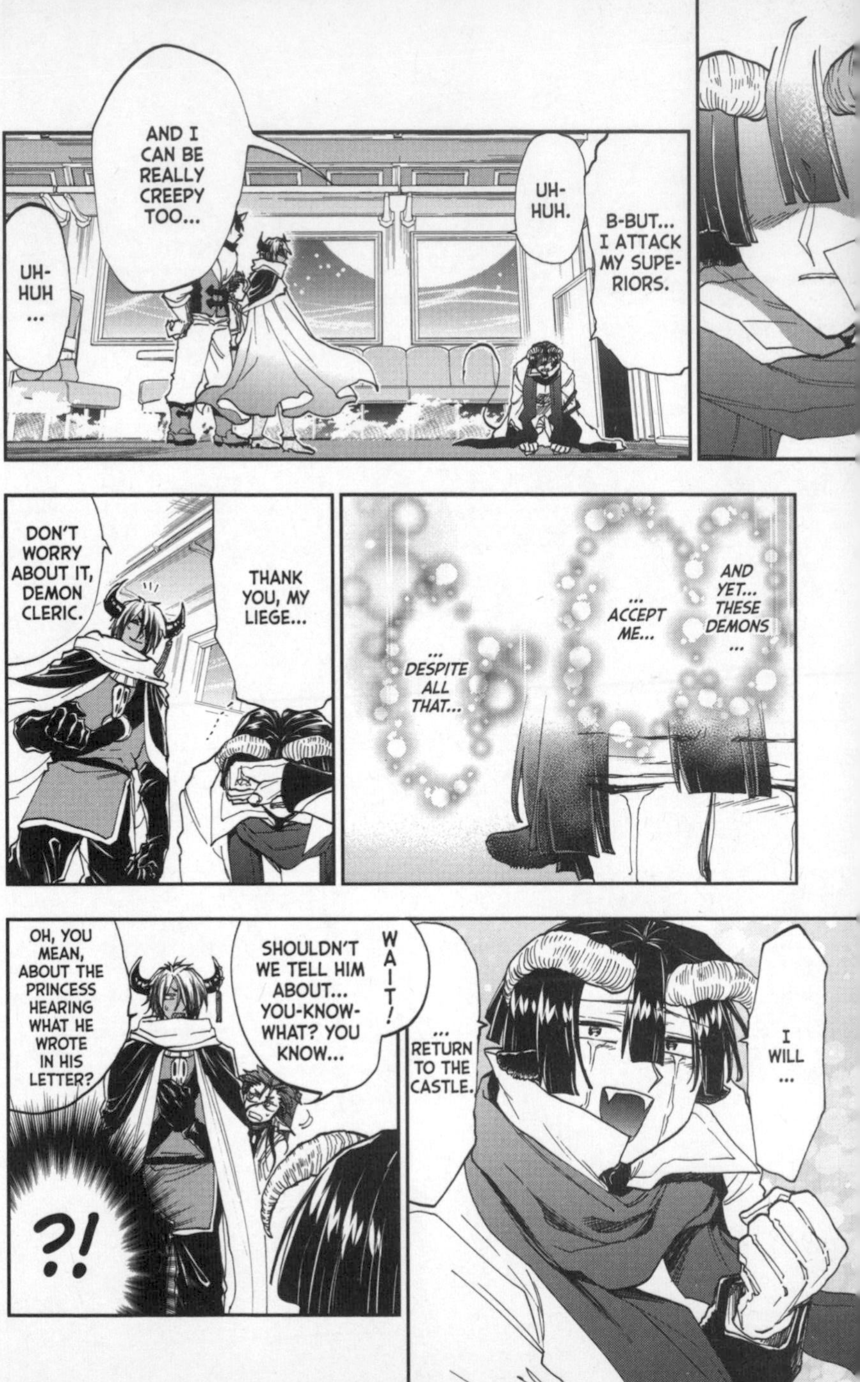
B-BUT... I ATTACK MY SUPERIORS.
UH-HUH.
AND I CAN BE REALLY CREEPY TOO...
UH-HUH ...
AND YET... THESE DEMONS ...
... ACCEPT ME...
... DESPITE ALL THAT...
THANK YOU, MY LIEGE...
DON'T WORRY ABOUT IT, DEMON CLERIC.
I WILL ...
... RETURN TO THE CASTLE.
WAIT!
SHOULDN'T WE TELL HIM ABOUT... YOU-KNOW-WHAT? YOU KNOW...
OH, YOU MEAN, ABOUT THE PRINCESS HEARING WHAT HE WROTE IN HIS LETTER?
?!

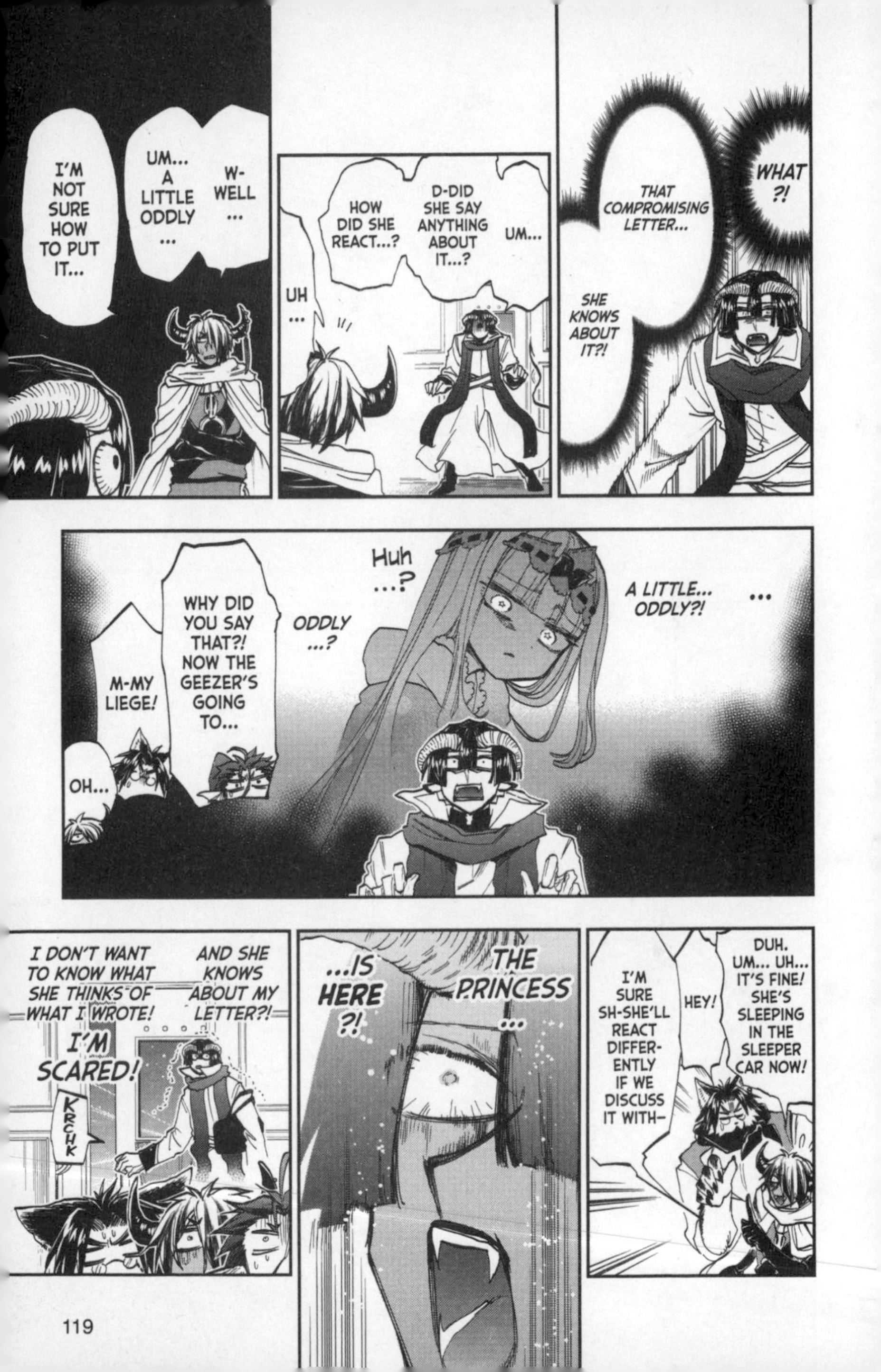
WHAT ?!
THAT COMPROMISING LETTER...
SHE KNOWS ABOUT IT?!
UM...
D-DID SHE SAY ANYTHING ABOUT IT...?
HOW DID SHE REACT...?
UH ...
W- WELL ...
UM... A LITTLE ODDLY ...
I'M NOT SURE HOW TO PUT IT...
...
A LITTLE... ODDLY?!
Huh ...?
ODDLY ...?
WHY DID YOU SAY THAT?! NOW THE GEEZER'S GOING TO...
M-MY LIEGE!
OH...
DUH. UM... UH... IT'S FINE! SHE'S SLEEPING IN THE SLEEPER CAR NOW!
HEY!
I'M SURE SH-SHE'LL REACT DIFFER-ENTLY IF WE DISCUSS IT WITH-
THE PRINCESS ...
...IS HERE ?!
AND SHE KNOWS ABOUT MY LETTER?!
I DON'T WANT TO KNOW WHAT SHE THINKS OF WHAT I WROTE!
I'M SCARED!
KRCHK

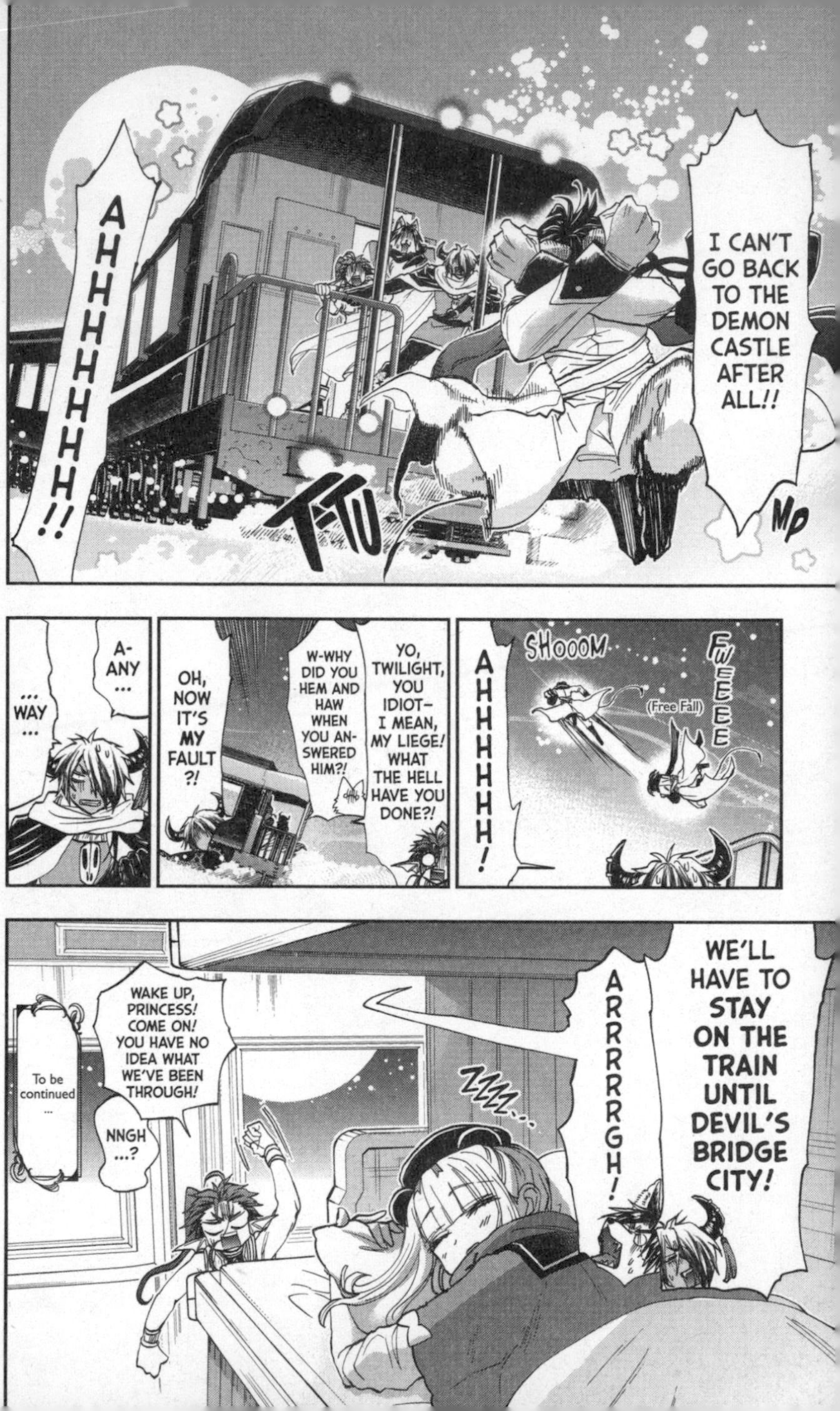
I CAN'T GO BACK TO THE DEMON CASTLE AFTER ALL!!
AHHHHHHHH!!
MP
T-TU
SHOOOM
FWEEEE
(Free Fall)
AHHHHHH!
YO, TWILIGHT, YOU IDIOT— I MEAN, MY LIEGE! WHAT THE HELL HAVE YOU DONE?!
W-WHY DID YOU HEM AND HAW WHEN YOU AN-SWERED HIM?!
OH, NOW IT'S MY FAULT?!
A- ANY...
...WAY...
WE'LL HAVE TO STAY ON THE TRAIN UNTIL DEVIL'S BRIDGE CITY!
ARRRRGH!
ZZZZ...
WAKE UP, PRINCESS! COME ON! YOU HAVE NO IDEA WHAT WE'VE BEEN THROUGH!
NNGH...?
To be continued...

DEMON CASTLE QUESTION CORNER

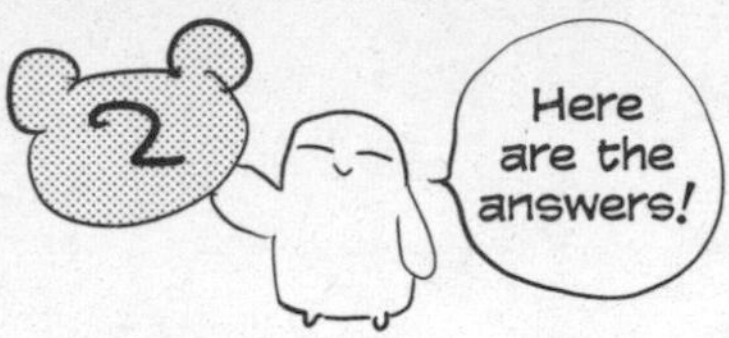
2
Here are the answers!

Are the princess's pom-pom bombs for self-defense? Did she DIY them herself like all the other items she made after becoming a hostage?

A They're for self-defense. Ah, royalty...

I'm really interested in learning about Demonstagram! What kind of posts do the demons at the Demon Castle upload? I'd love to see them.

A A lot of the rookies use it. Dark Elf uses it for sure.

Do the executive members have an official uniform?

A I'm sure they do! That's an exciting idea! I'll design them sooner or later...

Are Princessdrake and Bussy still getting along?

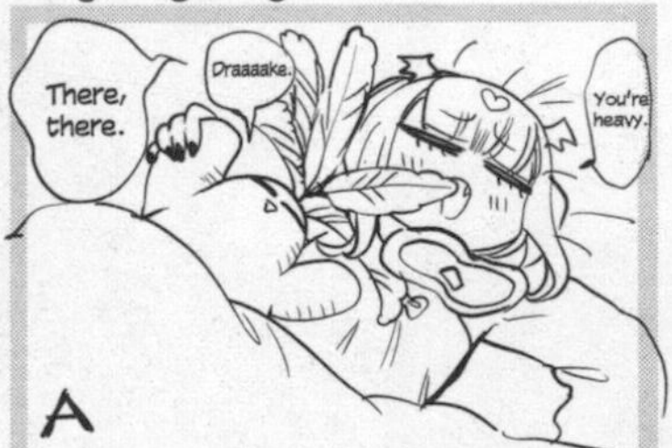
You're heavy.
Draaaake.
There, there.
A

I have a question about the Cursed Musician! Can he fly like his sister?

A He's modeled after this guy, so there's not much hope for him.

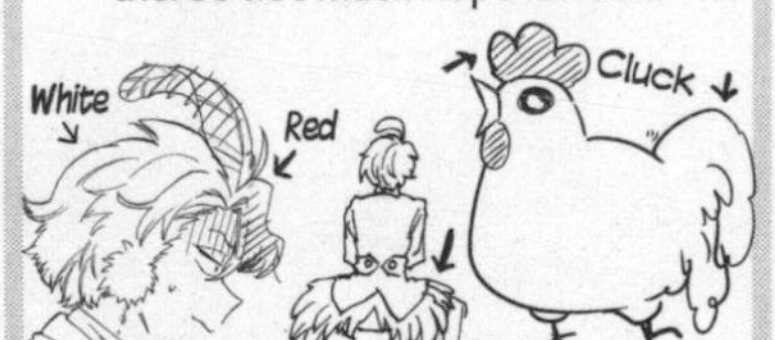
Cluck
Red
White

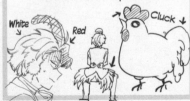

What's the relationship between Dr. Gearbolt and M.O.T.H.E.R.? Collegial? Or familial?

A A very capable employee and his boss. M.O.T.H.E.R. makes his subordinates do all the work.

Teddy Demon is extremely cute. Are there any details you pay extra attention to?

A I see you're a person of sophisticated taste! I'm careful not to make them too slim. And I give them round butts and thick necks.

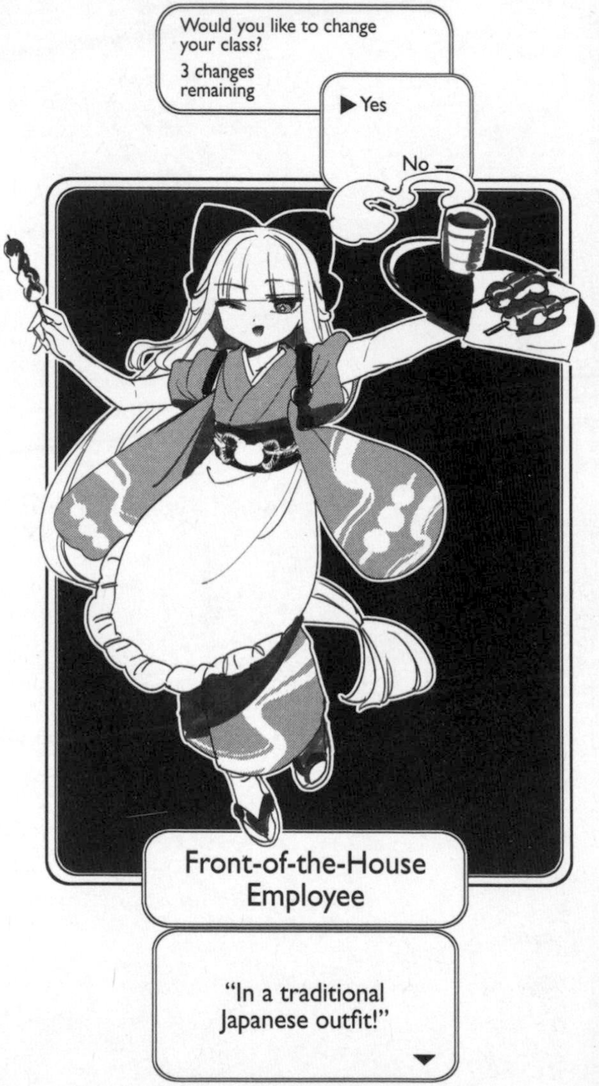
Would you like to change your class?
3 changes remaining
▶Yes
No
Front-of-the-House Employee
"In a traditional Japanese outfit!"

166th Night: The We-Love-Grandpa Fan Club

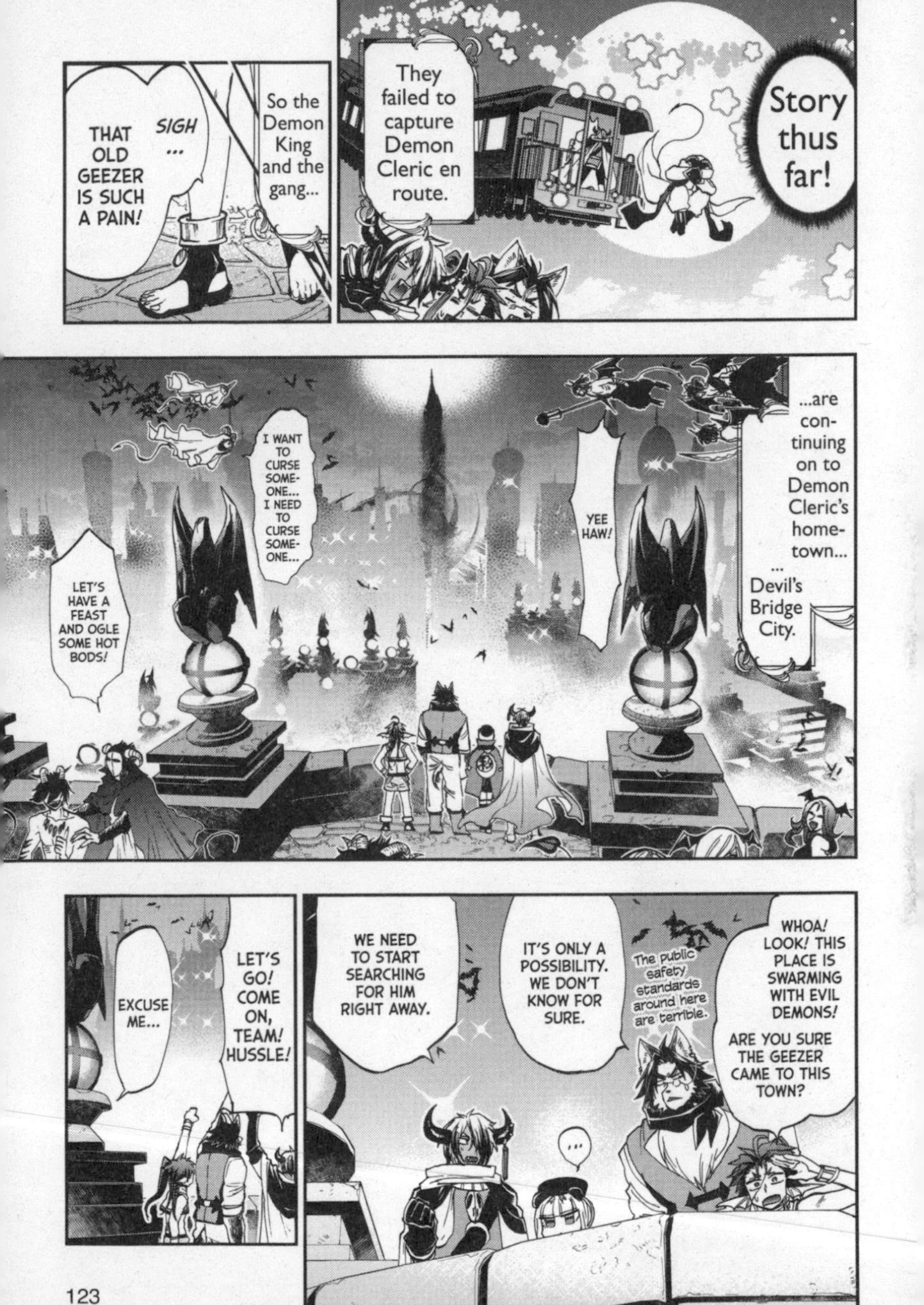
Story thus far!
They failed to capture Demon Cleric en route.
So the Demon King and the gang...
SIGH...
THAT OLD GEEZER IS SUCH A PAIN!
...are continuing on to Demon Cleric's hometown... ...Devil's Bridge City.
YEE HAW!
I WANT TO CURSE SOMEONE... I NEED TO CURSE SOMEONE...
LET'S HAVE A FEAST AND OGLE SOME HOT BODS!
WHOA! LOOK! THIS PLACE IS SWARMING WITH EVIL DEMONS!
ARE YOU SURE THE GEEZER CAME TO THIS TOWN?
The public safety standards around here are terrible.
IT'S ONLY A POSSIBILITY. WE DON'T KNOW FOR SURE.
WE NEED TO START SEARCHING FOR HIM RIGHT AWAY.
...
LET'S GO! COME ON, TEAM! HUSSLE!
EXCUSE ME...

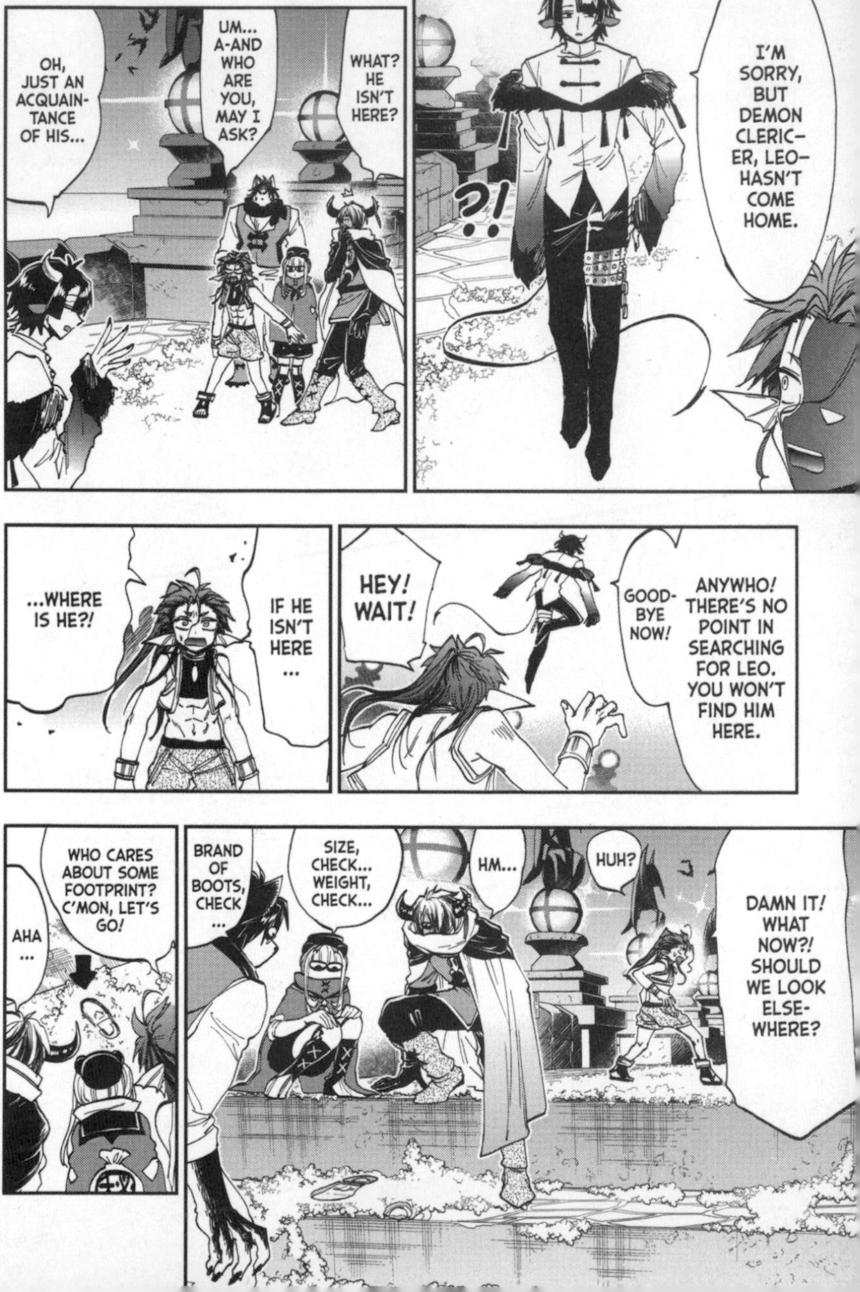
I'M SORRY, BUT DEMON CLERIC-ER, LEO-HASN'T COME HOME.
?!
WHAT? HE ISN'T HERE?
UM... A-AND WHO ARE YOU, MAY I ASK?
OH, JUST AN ACQUAINTANCE OF HIS...
ANYWHO! THERE'S NO POINT IN SEARCHING FOR LEO. YOU WON'T FIND HIM HERE.
GOOD-BYE NOW!
HEY! WAIT!
IF HE ISN'T HERE...
...WHERE IS HE?!
DAMN IT! WHAT NOW?! SHOULD WE LOOK ELSE-WHERE?
HUH?
HM...
SIZE, CHECK... WEIGHT, CHECK...
BRAND OF BOOTS, CHECK...
WHO CARES ABOUT SOME FOOTPRINT? C'MON, LET'S GO!
AHA...

166th Night: The We-Love-Grandpa Fan Club

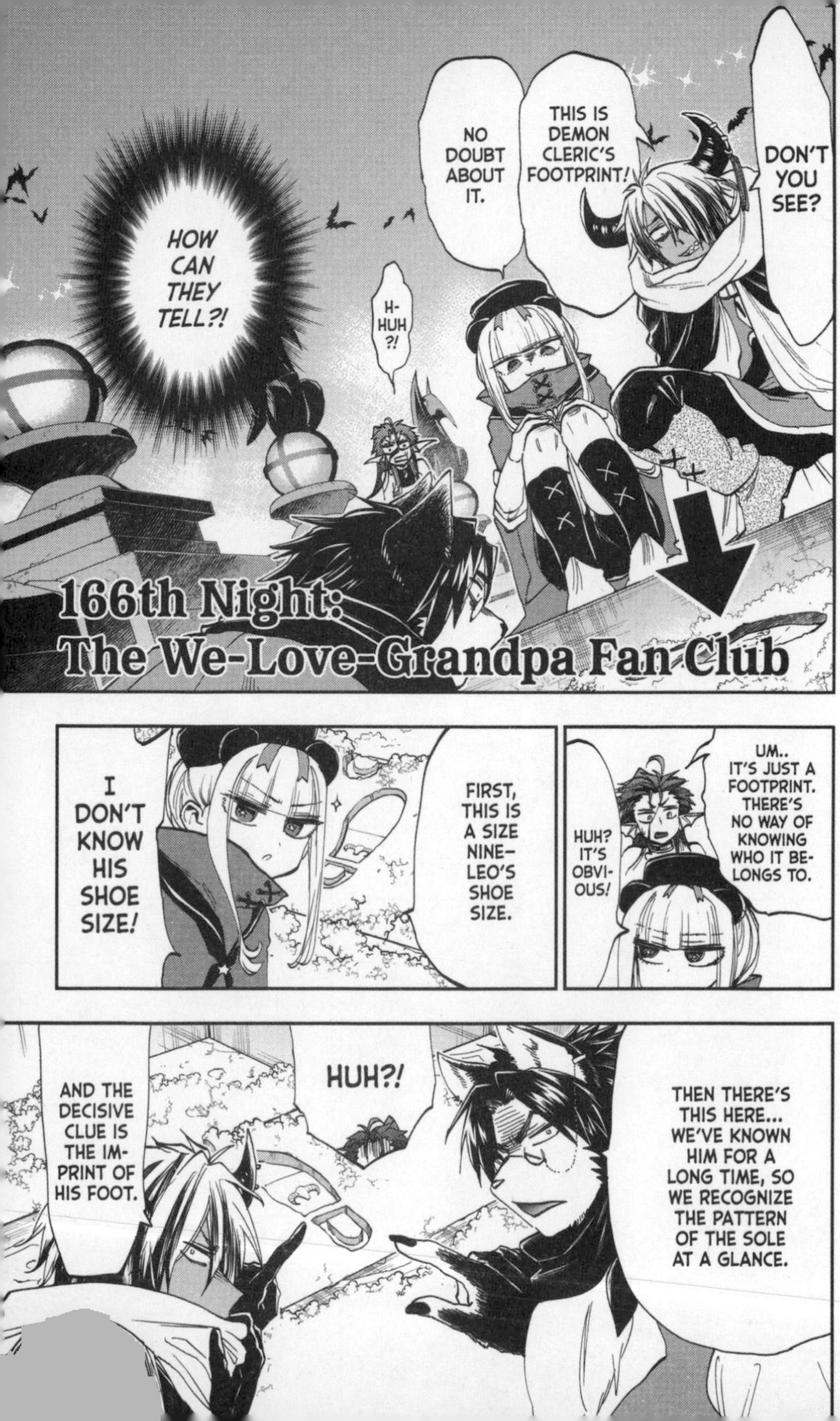
DON'T YOU SEE?
THIS IS DEMON CLERIC'S FOOTPRINT!
NO DOUBT ABOUT IT.
H-HUH?!
HOW CAN THEY TELL?!
166th Night: The We-Love-Grandpa Fan Club
UM.. IT'S JUST A FOOTPRINT. THERE'S NO WAY OF KNOWING WHO IT BELONGS TO.
HUH? IT'S OBVIOUS!
FIRST, THIS IS A SIZE NINE—LEO'S SHOE SIZE.
I DON'T KNOW HIS SHOE SIZE!
THEN THERE'S THIS HERE... WE'VE KNOWN HIM FOR A LONG TIME, SO WE RECOGNIZE THE PATTERN OF THE SOLE AT A GLANCE.
HUH?!
AND THE DECISIVE CLUE IS THE IMPRINT OF HIS FOOT.

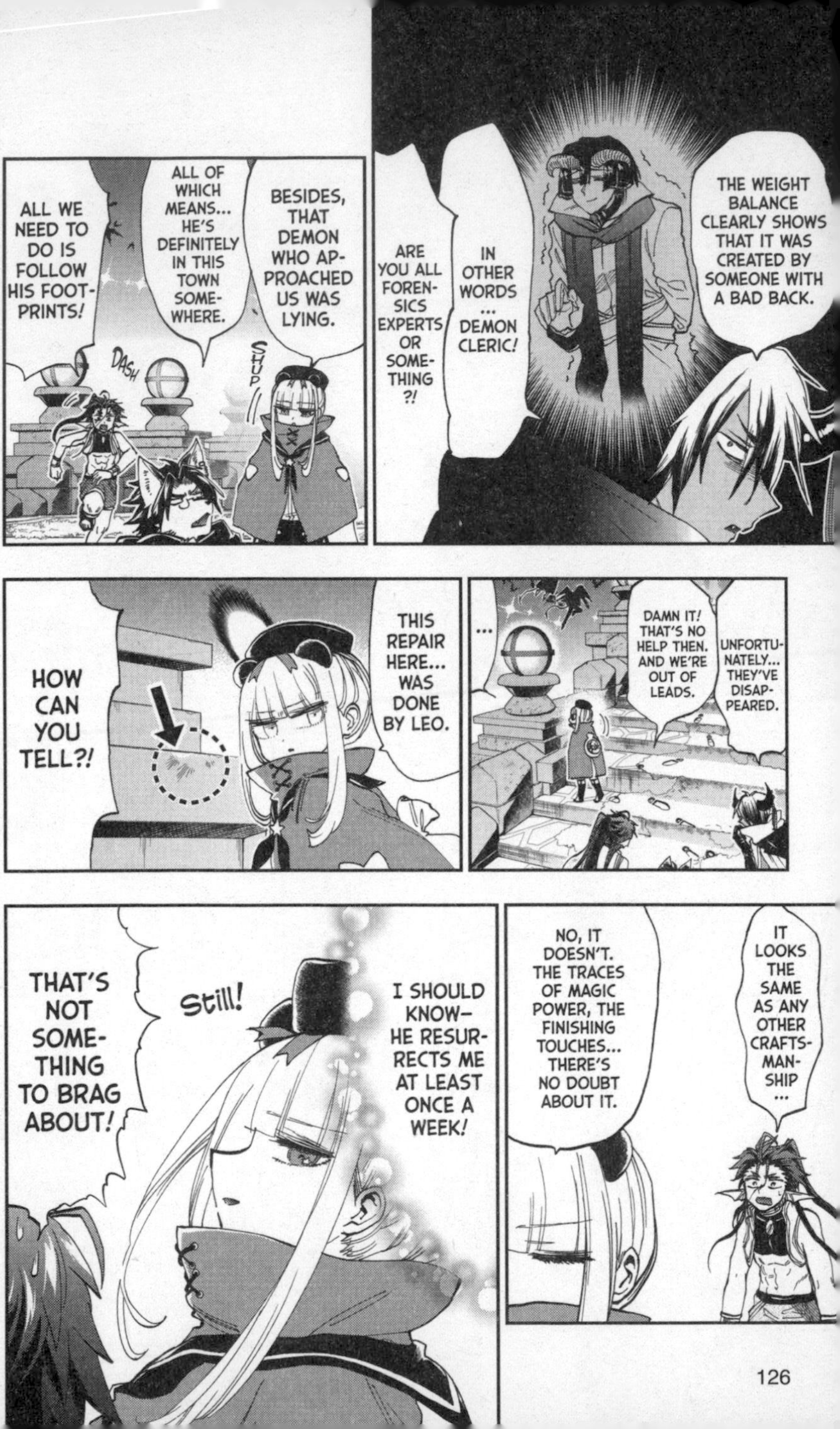
THE WEIGHT BALANCE CLEARLY SHOWS THAT IT WAS CREATED BY SOMEONE WITH A BAD BACK.
IN OTHER WORDS... DEMON CLERIC!
ARE YOU ALL FORENSICS EXPERTS OR SOMETHING?!
BESIDES, THAT DEMON WHO APPROACHED US WAS LYING.
SHUP
ALL OF WHICH MEANS... HE'S DEFINITELY IN THIS TOWN SOMEWHERE.
DASH
ALL WE NEED TO DO IS FOLLOW HIS FOOTPRINTS!
UNFORTUNATELY... THEY'VE DISAPPEARED.
DAMN IT! THAT'S NO HELP THEN. AND WE'RE OUT OF LEADS.
...
THIS REPAIR HERE... WAS DONE BY LEO.
HOW CAN YOU TELL?!
IT LOOKS THE SAME AS ANY OTHER CRAFTSMANSHIP...
NO, IT DOESN'T. THE TRACES OF MAGIC POWER, THE FINISHING TOUCHES... THERE'S NO DOUBT ABOUT IT.
I SHOULD KNOW—HE RESURRECTS ME AT LEAST ONCE A WEEK!
Still!
THAT'S NOT SOMETHING TO BRAG ABOUT!

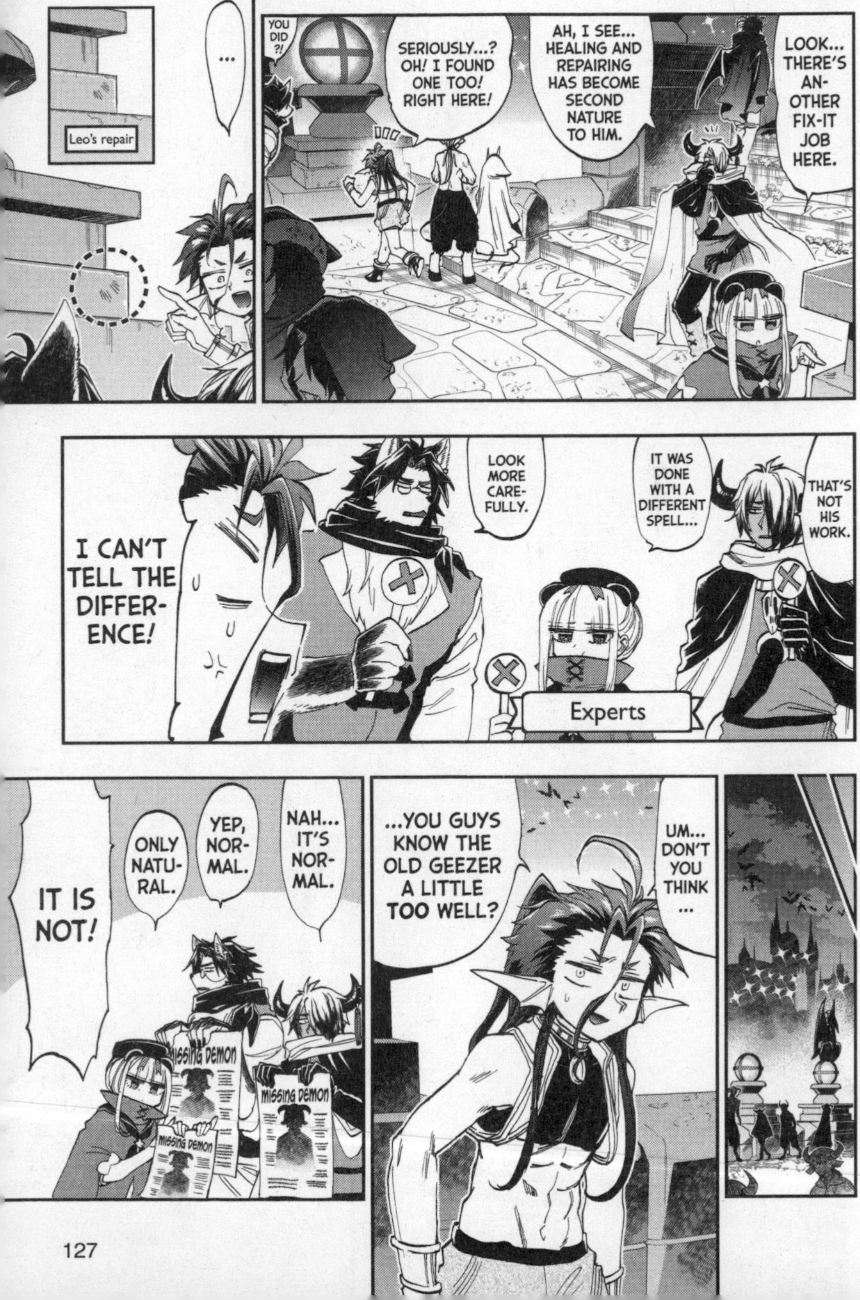
LOOK... THERE'S AN-OTHER FIX-IT JOB HERE.
AH, I SEE... HEALING AND REPAIRING HAS BECOME SECOND NATURE TO HIM.
SERIOUSLY...? OH! I FOUND ONE TOO! RIGHT HERE!
YOU DID?!
...
Leo's repair
THAT'S NOT HIS WORK.
IT WAS DONE WITH A DIFFERENT SPELL...
LOOK MORE CARE-FULLY.
I CAN'T TELL THE DIFFER-ENCE!
Experts
UM... DON'T YOU THINK ...
...YOU GUYS KNOW THE OLD GEEZER A LITTLE TOO WELL?
NAH... IT'S NOR-MAL.
YEP, NOR-MAL.
ONLY NATU-RAL.
IT IS NOT!
MISSING DEMON
MISSING DEMON
MISSING DEMON

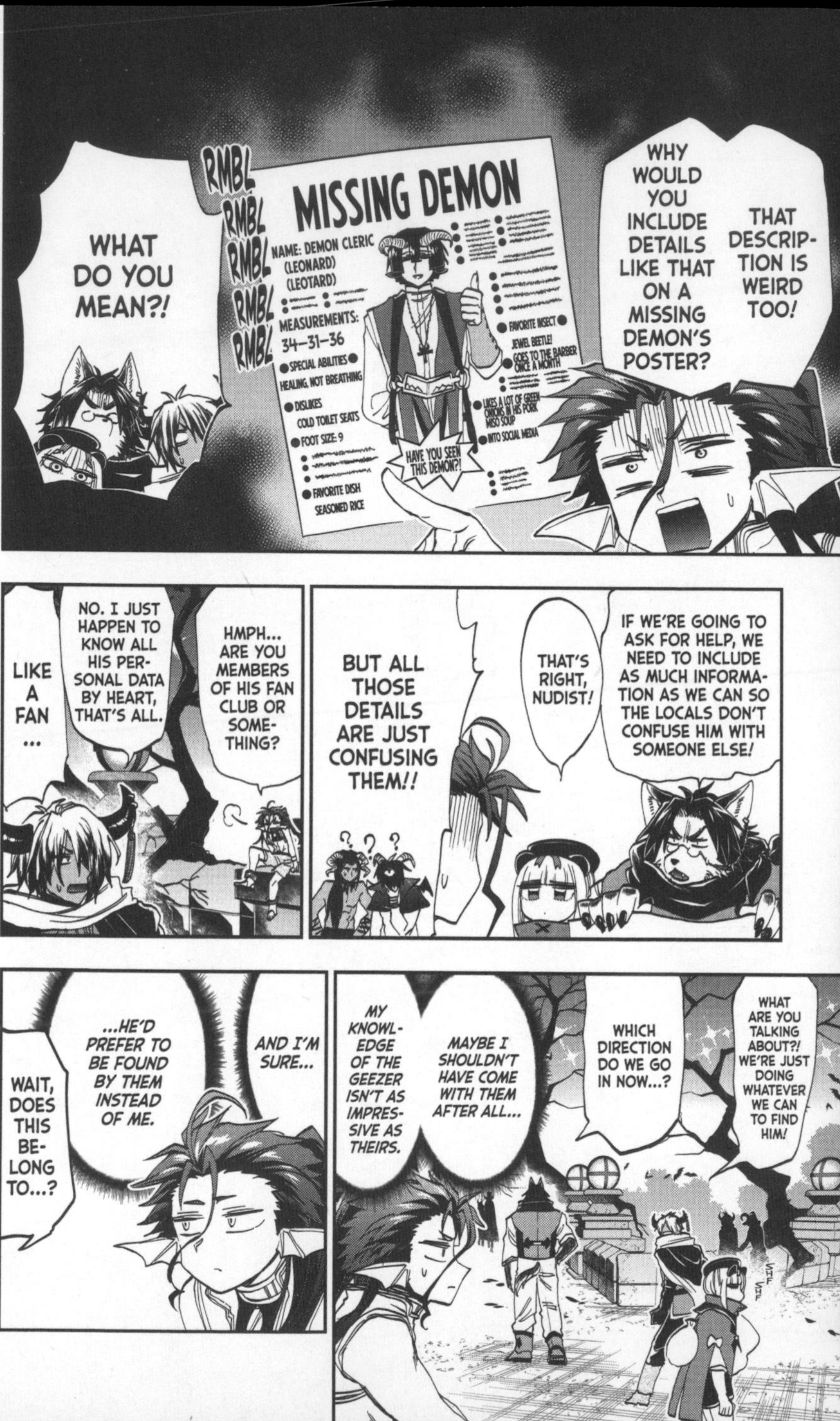
THAT DESCRIPTION IS WEIRD TOO!
WHY WOULD YOU INCLUDE DETAILS LIKE THAT ON A MISSING DEMON'S POSTER?
MISSING DEMON
NAME: DEMON CLERIC (LEONARD) (LEOTARD)
MEASUREMENTS: 34-31-36
SPECIAL ABILITIES HEALING, NOT BREATHING
DISLIKES COLD TOILET SEATS
FOOT SIZE: 9
FAVORITE DISH SEASONED RICE
FAVORITE INSECT JEWEL BEETLE!
GOES TO THE BARBER ONCE A MONTH
LIKES A LOT OF GREEN ONIONS IN HIS PORK MISO SOUP
INTO SOCIAL MEDIA
HAVE YOU SEEN THIS DEMON?!
RMBL RMBL RMBL RMBL RMBL
WHAT DO YOU MEAN?!
IF WE'RE GOING TO ASK FOR HELP, WE NEED TO INCLUDE AS MUCH INFORMATION AS WE CAN SO THE LOCALS DON'T CONFUSE HIM WITH SOMEONE ELSE!
THAT'S RIGHT, NUDIST!
BUT ALL THOSE DETAILS ARE JUST CONFUSING THEM!!
HMPH... ARE YOU MEMBERS OF HIS FAN CLUB OR SOMETHING?
NO. I JUST HAPPEN TO KNOW ALL HIS PERSONAL DATA BY HEART, THAT'S ALL.
LIKE A FAN...
WHAT ARE YOU TALKING ABOUT?! WE'RE JUST DOING WHATEVER WE CAN TO FIND HIM!
WHICH DIRECTION DO WE GO IN NOW...?
SHF SHF
MAYBE I SHOULDN'T HAVE COME WITH THEM AFTER ALL...
MY KNOWLEDGE OF THE GEEZER ISN'T AS IMPRESSIVE AS THEIRS.
AND I'M SURE...
...HE'D PREFER TO BE FOUND BY THEM INSTEAD OF ME.
WAIT, DOES THIS BELONG TO...?

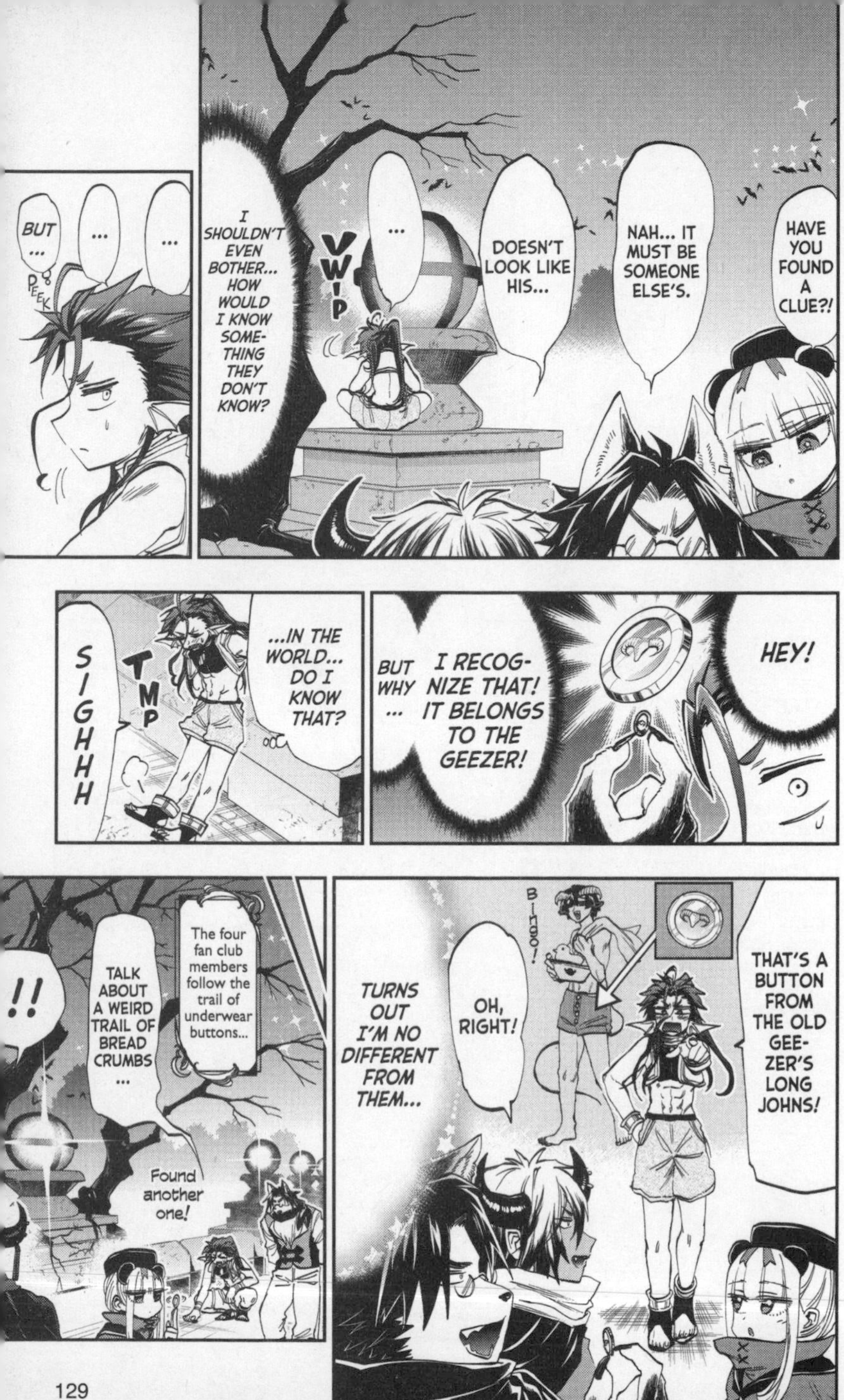
HAVE YOU FOUND A CLUE?!
NAH... IT MUST BE SOMEONE ELSE'S.
DOESN'T LOOK LIKE HIS...
...
VWIP
I SHOULDN'T EVEN BOTHER... HOW WOULD I KNOW SOMETHING THEY DON'T KNOW?
...
...
BUT ...
PEEK
HEY!
I RECOGNIZE THAT! IT BELONGS TO THE GEEZER!
BUT WHY ...
...IN THE WORLD... DO I KNOW THAT?
TMP
SIGHHH
THAT'S A BUTTON FROM THE OLD GEEZER'S LONG JOHNS!
Bingo!
OH, RIGHT!
TURNS OUT I'M NO DIFFERENT FROM THEM...
The four fan club members follow the trail of underwear buttons...
TALK ABOUT A WEIRD TRAIL OF BREAD CRUMBS ...
!!
Found another one!

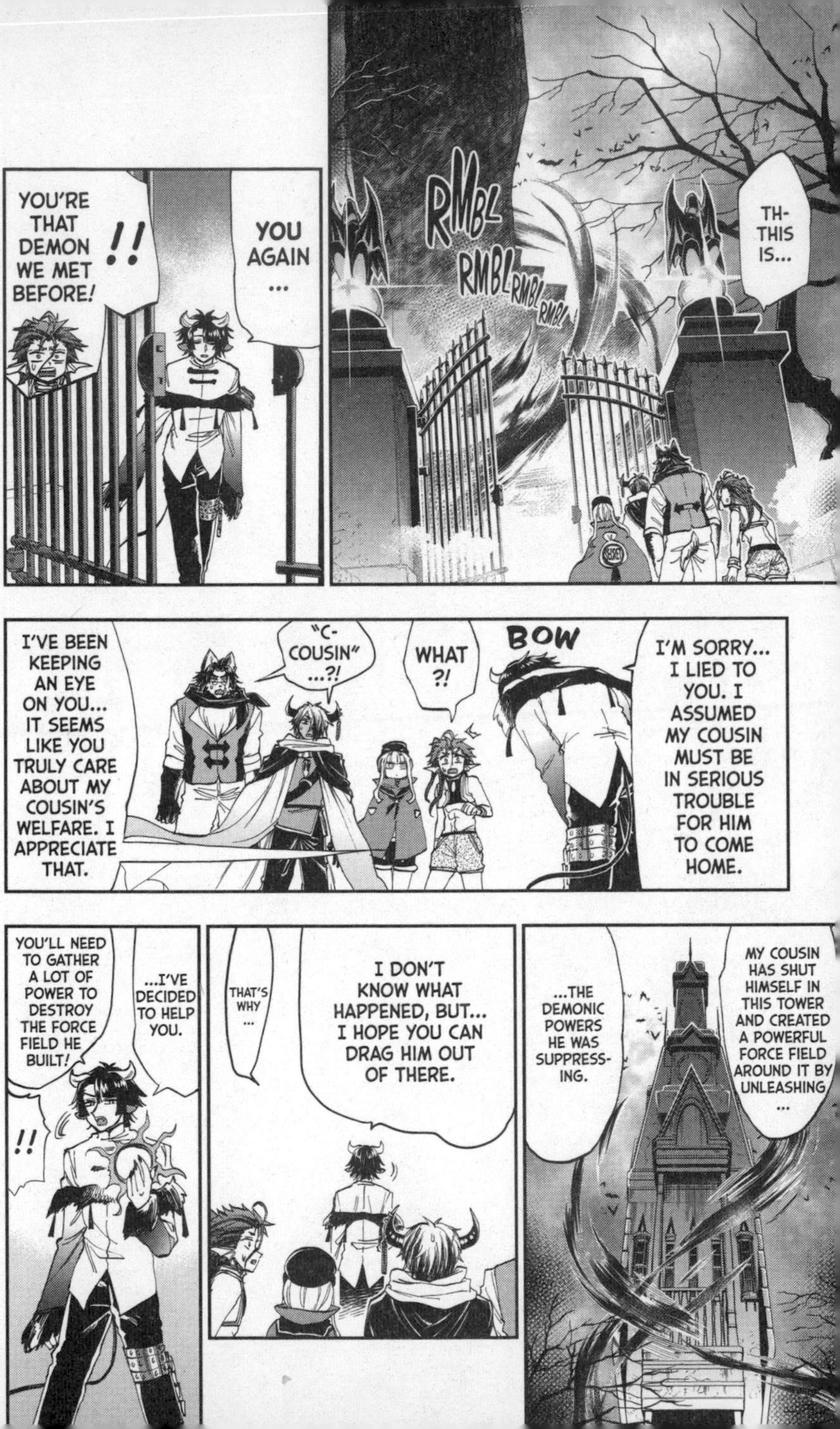
TH- THIS IS...
RMBL RMBL RMBL RMBL
YOU AGAIN ...
YOU'RE THAT DEMON WE MET BEFORE!
!!
I'M SORRY... I LIED TO YOU. I ASSUMED MY COUSIN MUST BE IN SERIOUS TROUBLE FOR HIM TO COME HOME.
BOW
WHAT ?!
"C-COUSIN" ...?!
I'VE BEEN KEEPING AN EYE ON YOU... IT SEEMS LIKE YOU TRULY CARE ABOUT MY COUSIN'S WELFARE. I APPRECIATE THAT.
MY COUSIN HAS SHUT HIMSELF IN THIS TOWER AND CREATED A POWERFUL FORCE FIELD AROUND IT BY UNLEASHING ...
...THE DEMONIC POWERS HE WAS SUPPRESS-ING.
I DON'T KNOW WHAT HAPPENED, BUT... I HOPE YOU CAN DRAG HIM OUT OF THERE.
THAT'S WHY ...
...I'VE DECIDED TO HELP YOU.
YOU'LL NEED TO GATHER A LOT OF POWER TO DESTROY THE FORCE FIELD HE BUILT!
!!

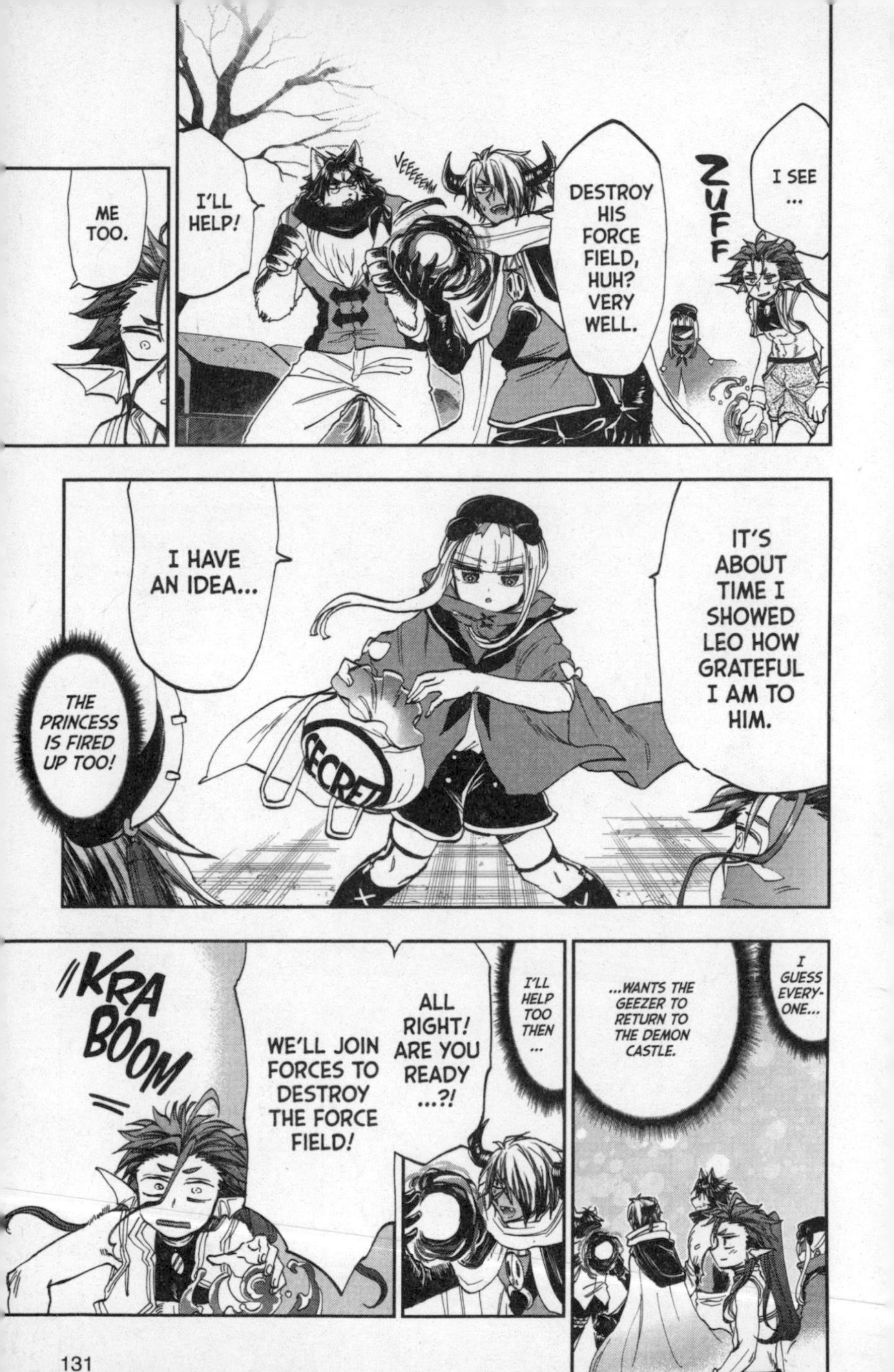
I SEE ...
ZUFF
DESTROY HIS FORCE FIELD, HUH? VERY WELL.
VEEEEEMM
I'LL HELP!
ME TOO.
IT'S ABOUT TIME I SHOWED LEO HOW GRATEFUL I AM TO HIM.
I HAVE AN IDEA...
SECRET
THE PRINCESS IS FIRED UP TOO!
I GUESS EVERY-ONE...
...WANTS THE GEEZER TO RETURN TO THE DEMON CASTLE.
I'LL HELP TOO THEN ...
ALL RIGHT! ARE YOU READY ...?!
WE'LL JOIN FORCES TO DESTROY THE FORCE FIELD!
KRA BOOM

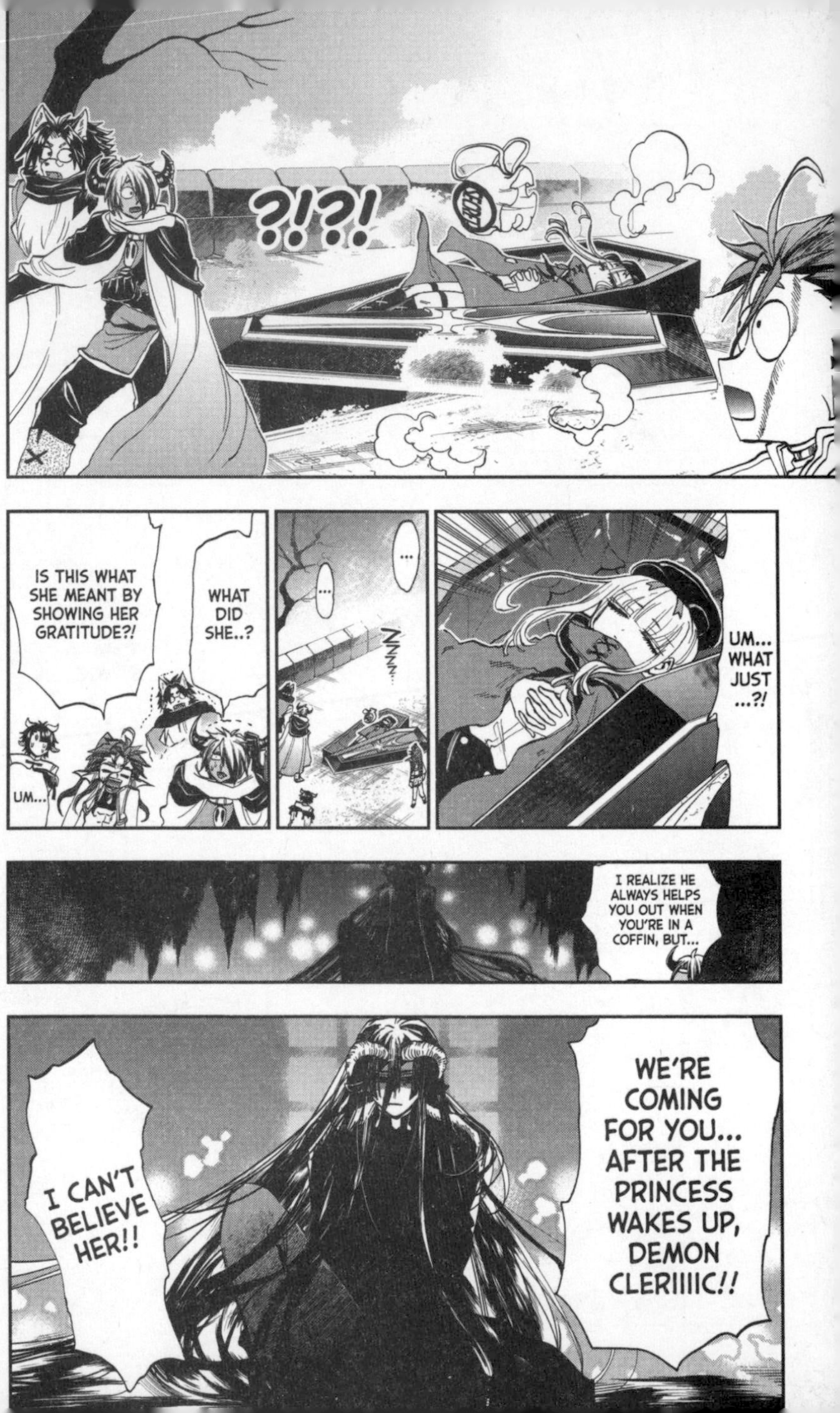
?!?!
UM... WHAT JUST ...?!
...
...
ZZZZ...
WHAT DID SHE..?
IS THIS WHAT SHE MEANT BY SHOWING HER GRATITUDE?!
UM...
I REALIZE HE ALWAYS HELPS YOU OUT WHEN YOU'RE IN A COFFIN, BUT...
WE'RE COMING FOR YOU... AFTER THE PRINCESS WAKES UP, DEMON CLERIIIIC!!
I CAN'T BELIEVE HER!!

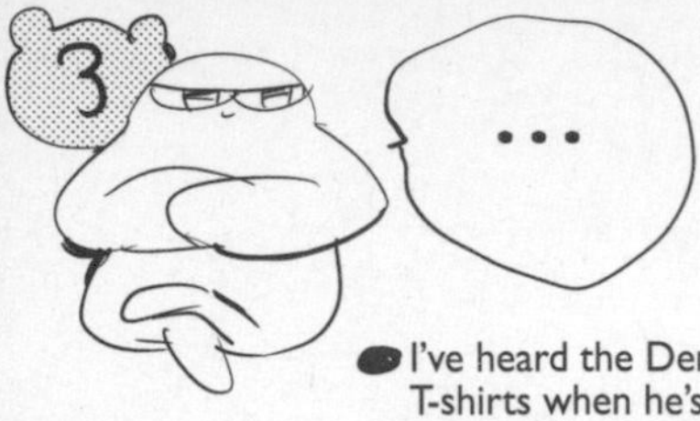

3
...

DEMON CASTLE QUESTION CORNER

● I've heard the Demon King wears tacky T-shirts when he's off duty. Where does he get them?

A At the castle's armor shop.

● Will Great Red Siberian get stomachaches and bald patches from stress? I'm worried about him.

A His master gives him a good rubdown every day, so he'll be fine.

● Please tell me anything you can about the hero Dawner.

A He's been searching for a special someone all his life...

● Who is older, Master Hypnos or Demon Cleric?!

● How does Master Hypnos travel between the current Demon Castle and the Old Demon Castle?

A Two questions from two people. Hypnos is the eldest, and he travels through dreams. He often appears through Baku, the dream-eating demon.

● I want to see what Mr. Oh My's face looks like!

A I actually drew it already and saved it on my computer.

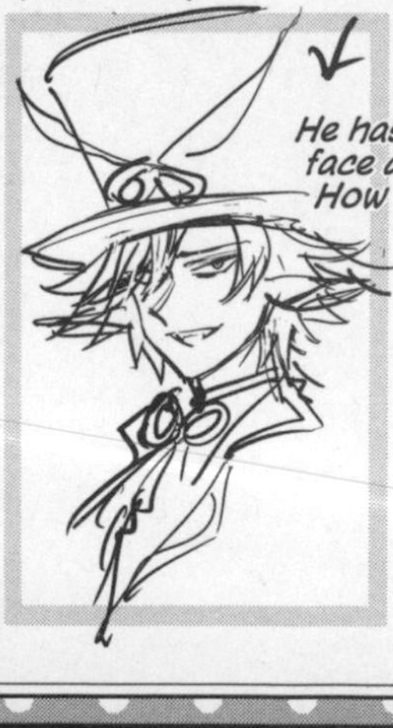

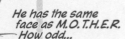

He has the same face as M.O.T.H.E.R. How odd...

● Who's your favorite character?

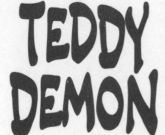

TEDDY DEMON

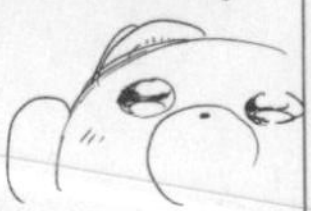

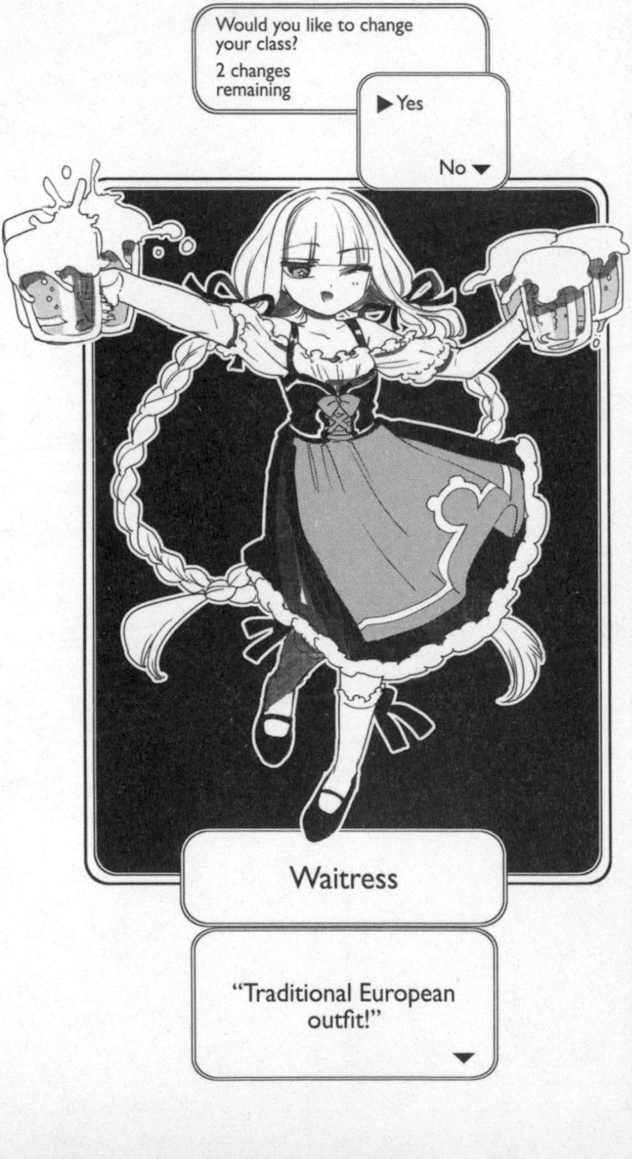
Would you like to change your class?
2 changes remaining
▶Yes
No
Waitress
"Traditional European outfit!"

167th Night: Don't Forget to Write

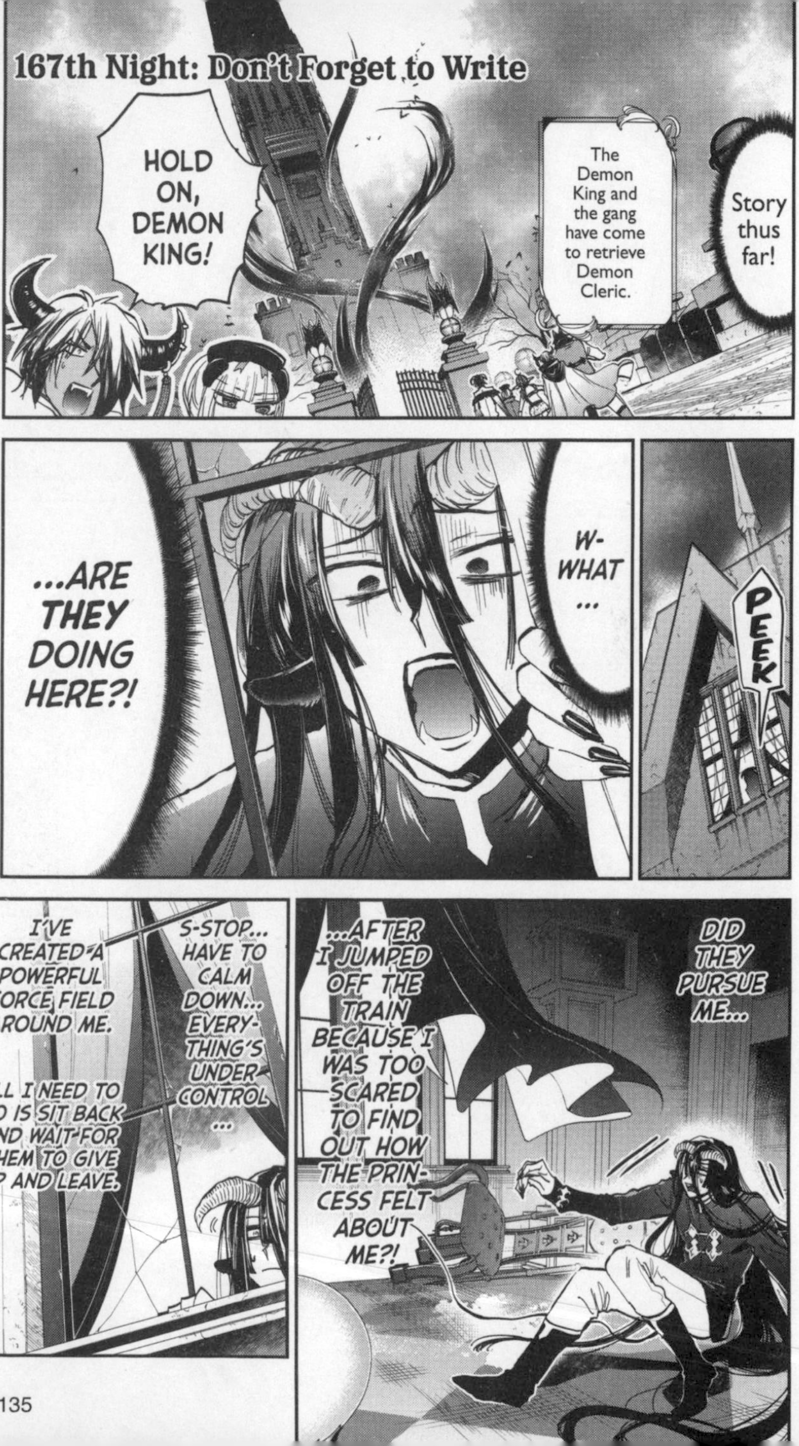
Story thus far!
The Demon King and the gang have come to retrieve Demon Cleric.
HOLD ON, DEMON KING!
PEEK
W-WHAT...
...ARE THEY DOING HERE?!
DID THEY PURSUE ME...
...AFTER I JUMPED OFF THE TRAIN BECAUSE I WAS TOO SCARED TO FIND OUT HOW THE PRINCESS FELT ABOUT ME?!
S-STOP... HAVE TO CALM DOWN... EVERYTHING'S UNDER CONTROL...
I'VE CREATED A POWERFUL FORCE FIELD AROUND ME.
ALL I NEED TO DO IS SIT BACK AND WAIT FOR THEM TO GIVE UP AND LEAVE.

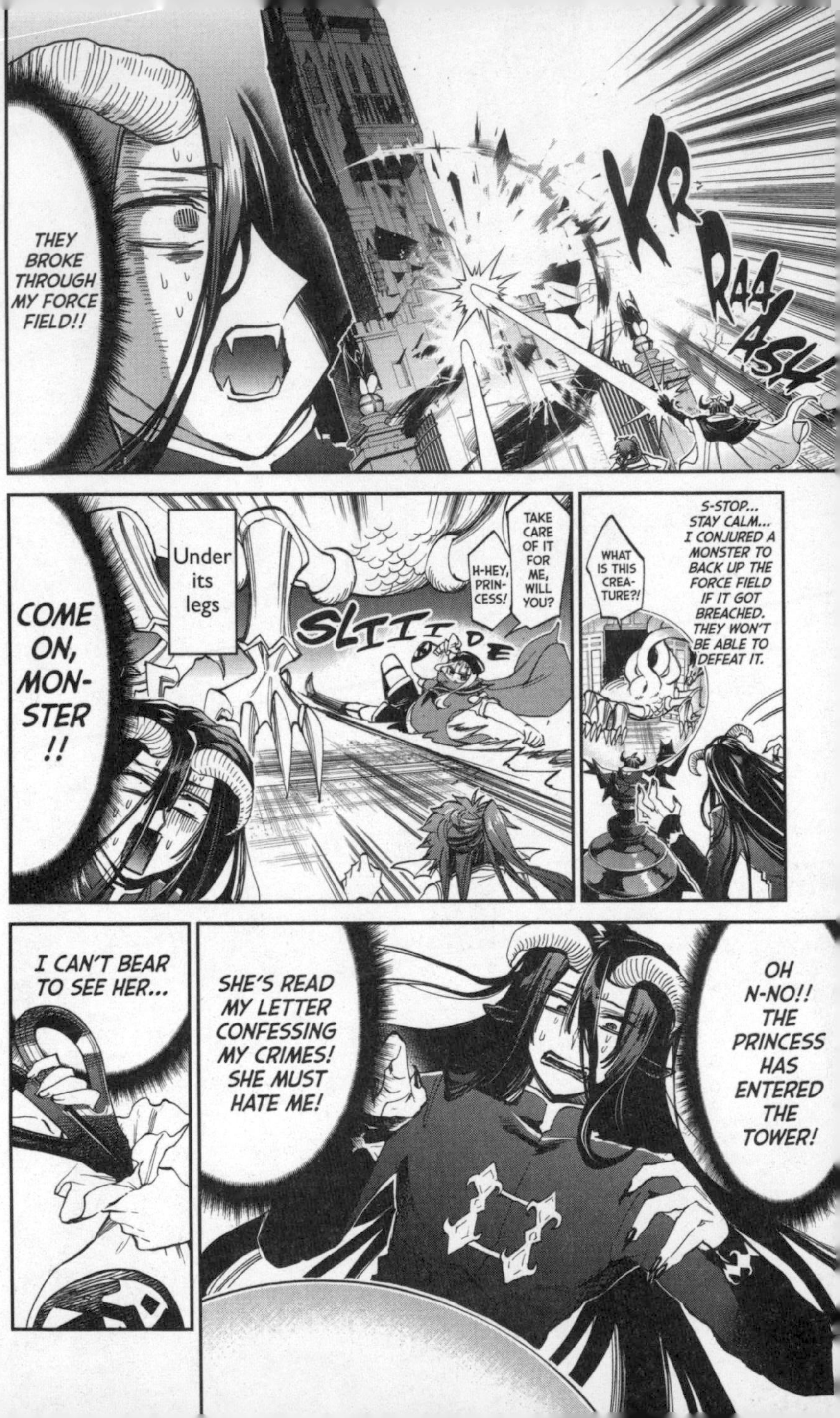
KRRAAASH
THEY BROKE THROUGH MY FORCE FIELD!!
S-STOP... STAY CALM... I CONJURED A MONSTER TO BACK UP THE FORCE FIELD IF IT GOT BREACHED. THEY WON'T BE ABLE TO DEFEAT IT.
WHAT IS THIS CREA-TURE?!
TAKE CARE OF IT FOR ME, WILL YOU?
H-HEY, PRIN-CESS!
Under its legs
SLIIIDE
COME ON, MON-STER!!
OH N-NO!! THE PRINCESS HAS ENTERED THE TOWER!
SHE'S READ MY LETTER CONFESSING MY CRIMES! SHE MUST HATE ME!
I CAN'T BEAR TO SEE HER...

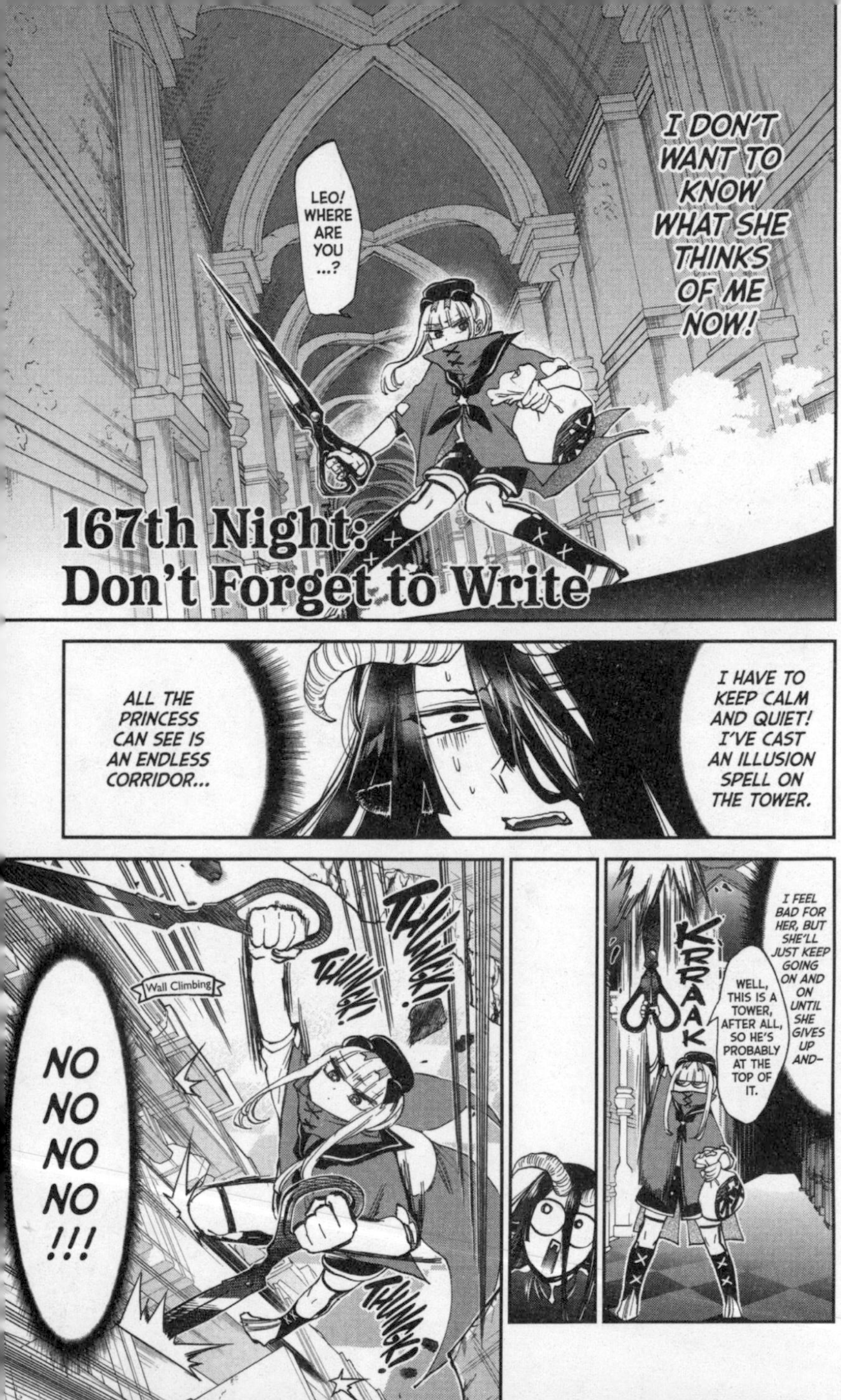
I DON'T WANT TO KNOW WHAT SHE THINKS OF ME NOW!
LEO! WHERE ARE YOU ...?
167th Night: Don't Forget to Write
I HAVE TO KEEP CALM AND QUIET! I'VE CAST AN ILLUSION SPELL ON THE TOWER.
ALL THE PRINCESS CAN SEE IS AN ENDLESS CORRIDOR...
I FEEL BAD FOR HER, BUT SHE'LL JUST KEEP GOING ON AND ON UNTIL SHE GIVES UP AND–
KRRAAK
WELL, THIS IS A TOWER, AFTER ALL, SO HE'S PROBABLY AT THE TOP OF IT.
THUNK!
THUNK!
Wall Climbing
NO NO NO NO NO !!!
THUNK!

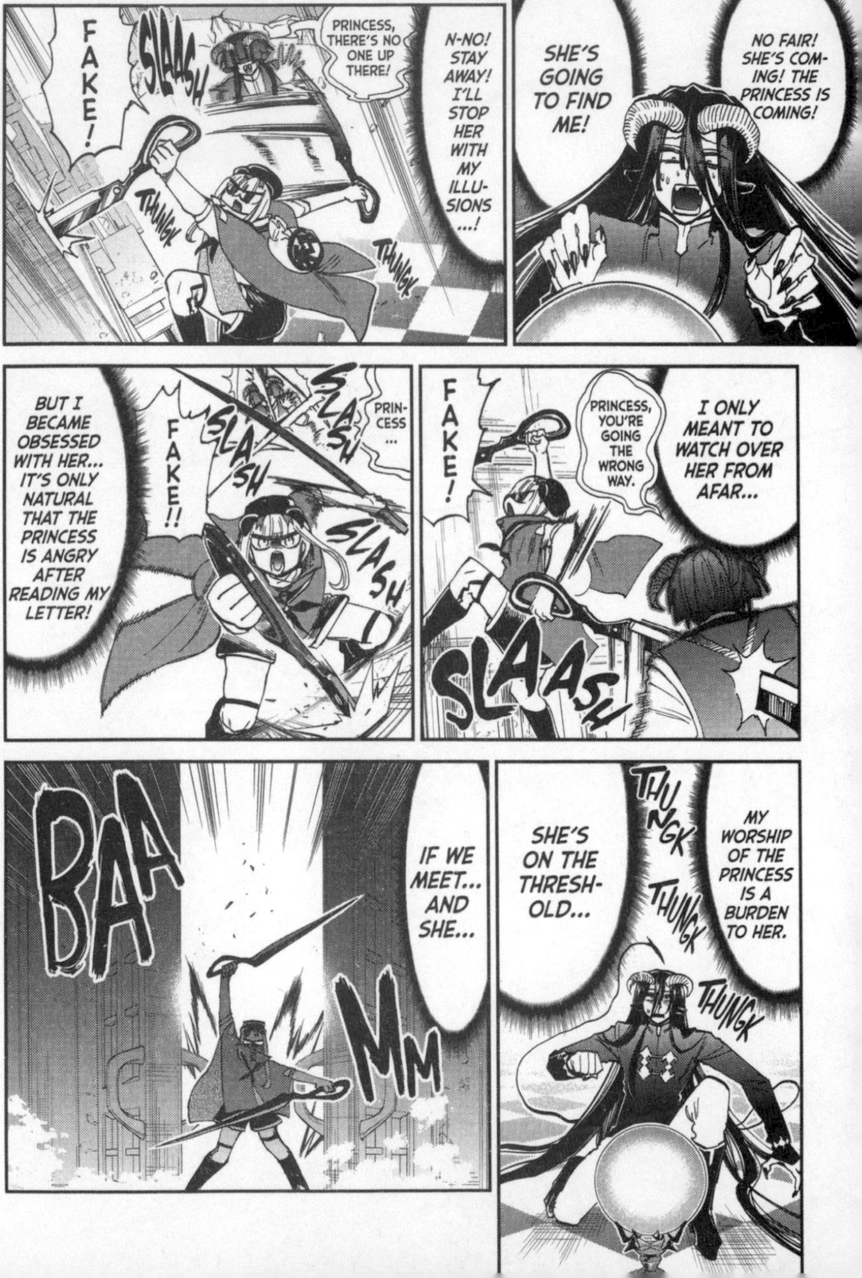
NO FAIR! SHE'S COM-ING! THE PRINCESS IS COMING!
SHE'S GOING TO FIND ME!
N-NO! STAY AWAY! I'LL STOP HER WITH MY ILLU-SIONS ...!
PRINCESS, THERE'S NO ONE UP THERE!
SLAASH
FAKE!
THUNGK
THUNGK
I ONLY MEANT TO WATCH OVER HER FROM AFAR...
PRINCESS, YOU'RE GOING THE WRONG WAY.
FAKE!
SLAASH
PRIN-CESS ...
SLASH
SLASH
FAKE!!
BUT I BECAME OBSESSED WITH HER... IT'S ONLY NATURAL THAT THE PRINCESS IS ANGRY AFTER READING MY LETTER!
SLASH
MY WORSHIP OF THE PRINCESS IS A BURDEN TO HER.
THUNGK
SHE'S ON THE THRESH-OLD...
THUNGK
THUNGK
IF WE MEET... AND SHE...
BAAMM

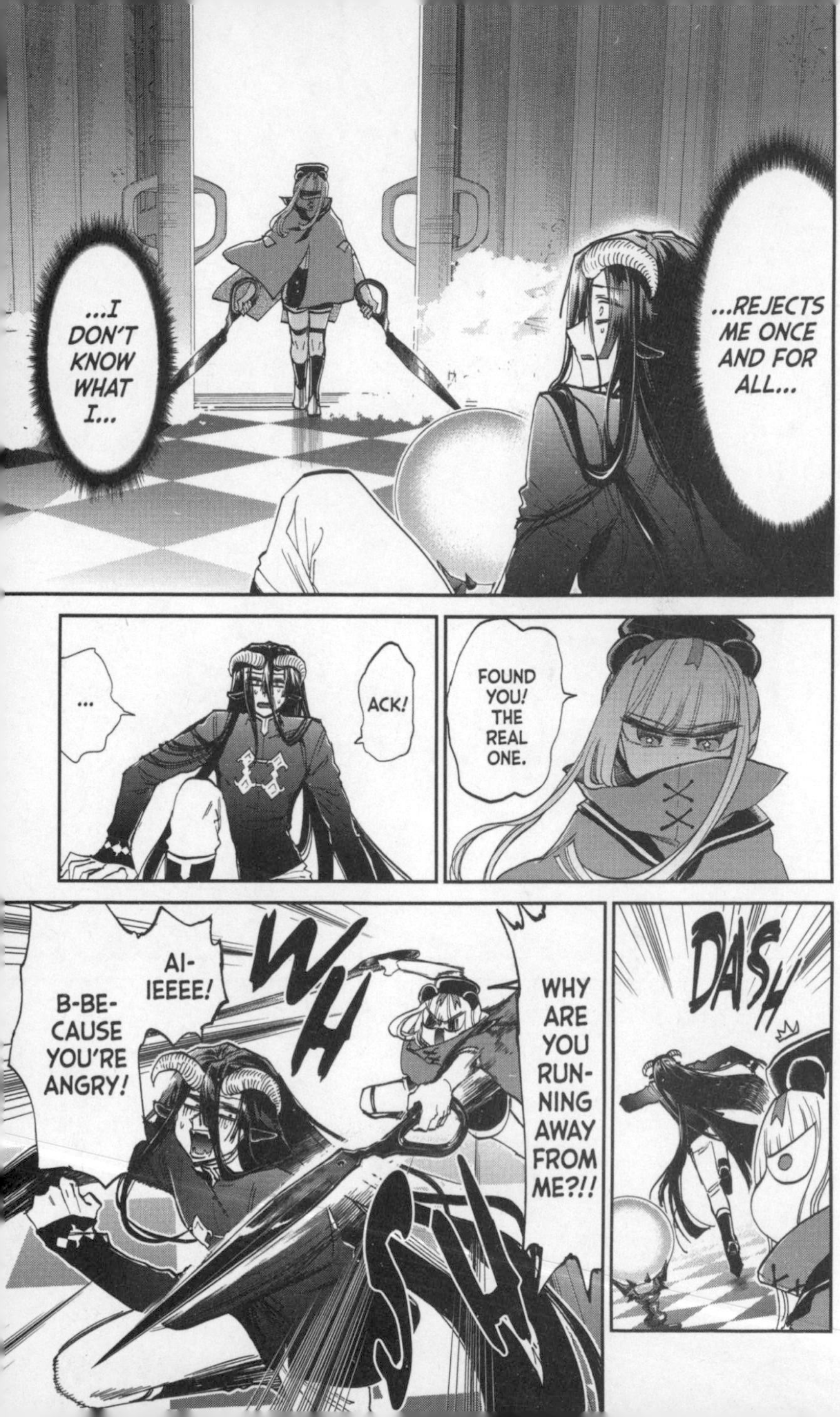
...REJECTS ME ONCE AND FOR ALL...
...I DON'T KNOW WHAT I...
FOUND YOU! THE REAL ONE.
ACK!
...
DASH
WHY ARE YOU RUN-NING AWAY FROM ME?!!
WH
AI-IEEEE!
B-BE-CAUSE YOU'RE ANGRY!
SH

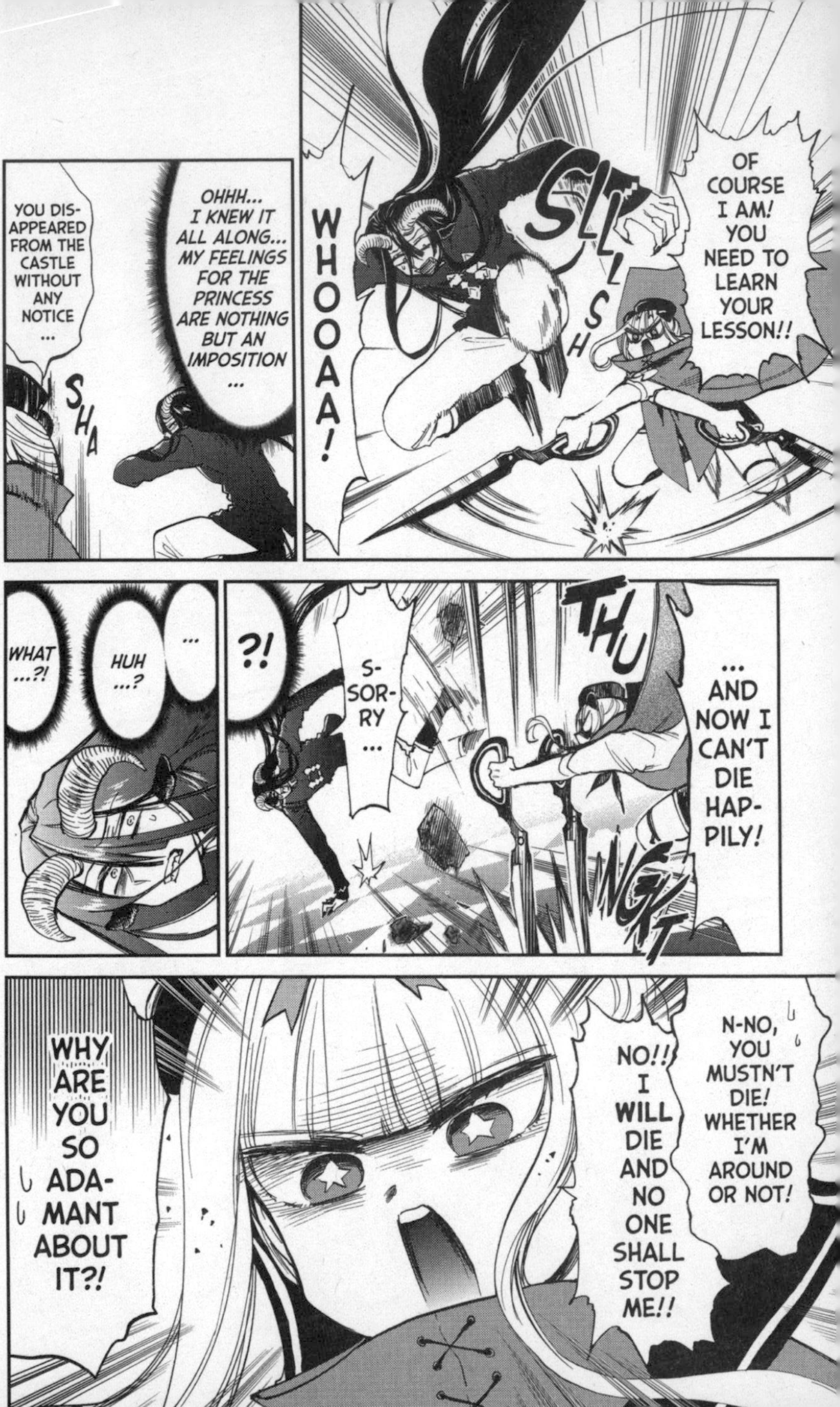
OF COURSE I AM! YOU NEED TO LEARN YOUR LESSON!!
SLLLSH
WHOOAA!
OHHH... I KNEW IT ALL ALONG... MY FEELINGS FOR THE PRINCESS ARE NOTHING BUT AN IMPOSITION ...
YOU DIS-APPEARED FROM THE CASTLE WITHOUT ANY NOTICE ...
SHA
THU
... AND NOW I CAN'T DIE HAP-PILY!
S-SOR-RY ...
?!
WNGKT
...
HUH ...?
WHAT ...?!
N-NO, YOU MUSTN'T DIE! WHETHER I'M AROUND OR NOT!
NO!! I WILL DIE AND NO ONE SHALL STOP ME!!
WHY ARE YOU SO ADA-MANT ABOUT IT?!

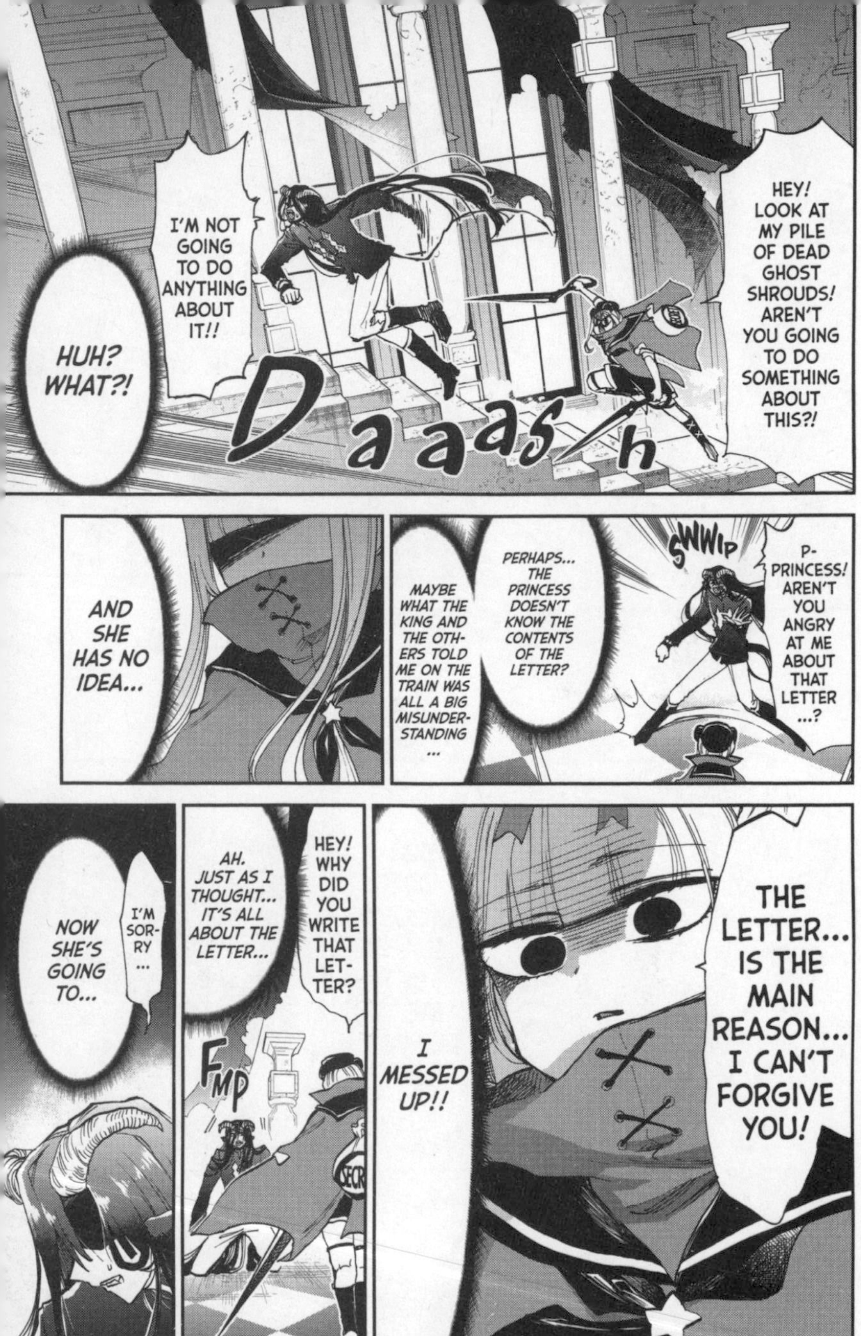
HEY! LOOK AT MY PILE OF DEAD GHOST SHROUDS! AREN'T YOU GOING TO DO SOMETHING ABOUT THIS?!
I'M NOT GOING TO DO ANYTHING ABOUT IT!!
HUH? WHAT?!
Daaash
SWWIP
P-PRINCESS! AREN'T YOU ANGRY AT ME ABOUT THAT LETTER ...?
PERHAPS... THE PRINCESS DOESN'T KNOW THE CONTENTS OF THE LETTER?
MAYBE WHAT THE KING AND THE OTH-ERS TOLD ME ON THE TRAIN WAS ALL A BIG MISUNDER-STANDING ...
AND SHE HAS NO IDEA...
THE LETTER... IS THE MAIN REASON... I CAN'T FORGIVE YOU!
I MESSED UP!!
HEY! WHY DID YOU WRITE THAT LET-TER?
AH. JUST AS I THOUGHT... IT'S ALL ABOUT THE LETTER...
FMP
I'M SOR-RY ...
NOW SHE'S GOING TO...

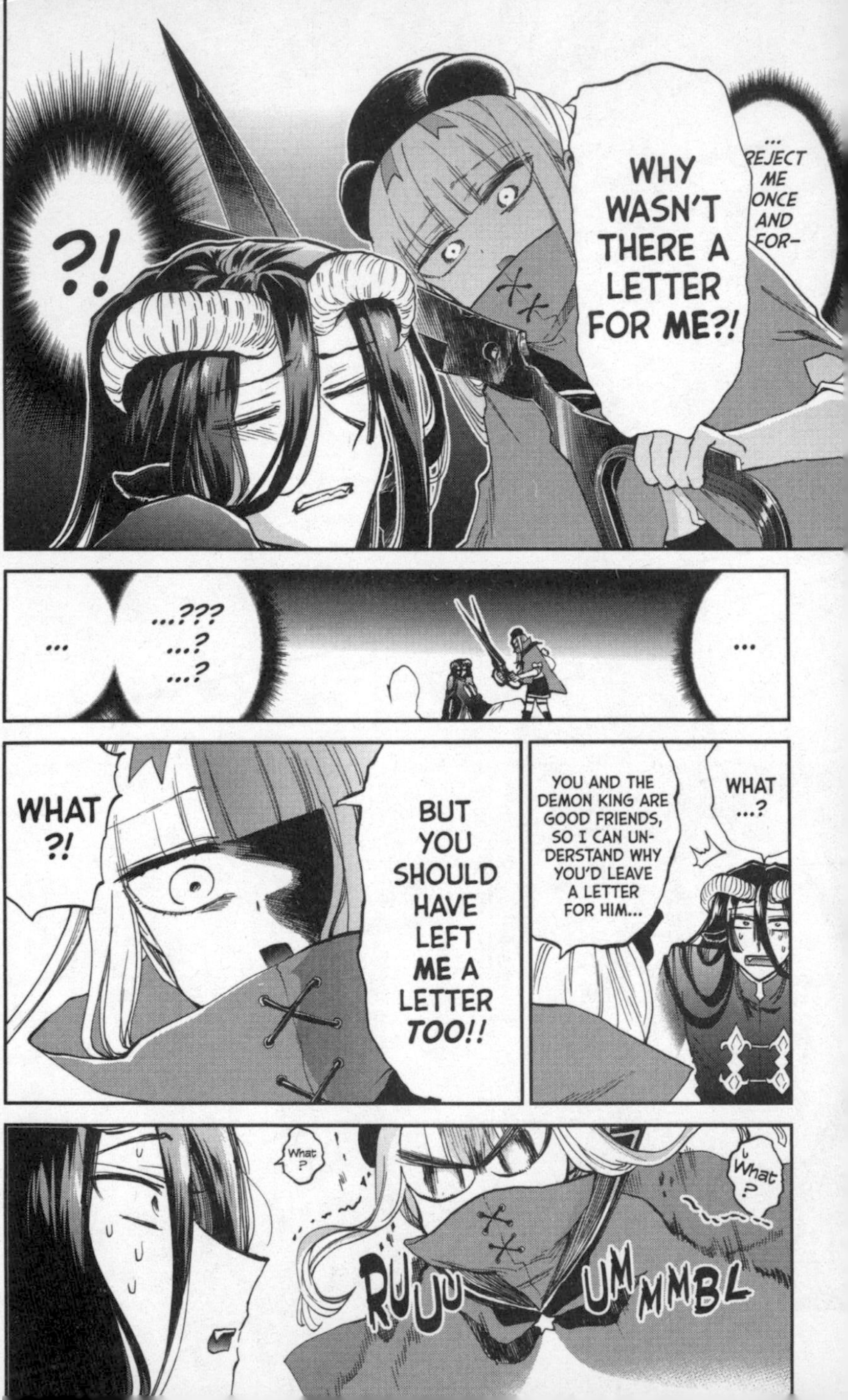
...REJECT ME ONCE AND FOR—
WHY WASN'T THERE A LETTER FOR ME?!
?!
...
...??? ...? ...?
...
WHAT ...?
YOU AND THE DEMON KING ARE GOOD FRIENDS, SO I CAN UNDERSTAND WHY YOU'D LEAVE A LETTER FOR HIM...
BUT YOU SHOULD HAVE LEFT ME A LETTER TOO!!
WHAT ?!
What ?
What ?
RUUU UMMMBL

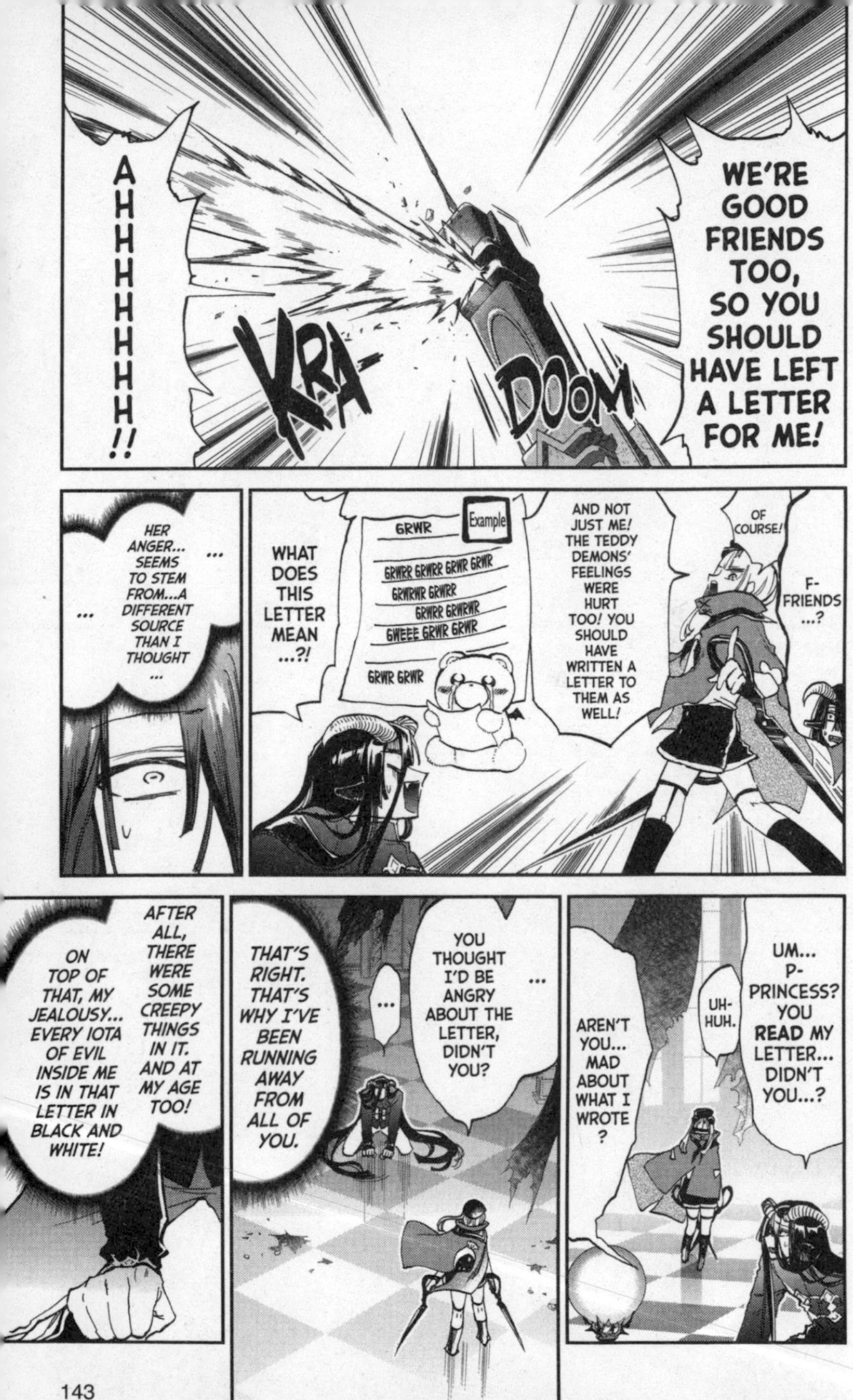
WE'RE GOOD FRIENDS TOO, SO YOU SHOULD HAVE LEFT A LETTER FOR ME!
AHHHHHHHH!!
KRA-
DOOM
OF COURSE!
F- FRIENDS ...?
AND NOT JUST ME! THE TEDDY DEMONS' FEELINGS WERE HURT TOO! YOU SHOULD HAVE WRITTEN A LETTER TO THEM AS WELL!
WHAT DOES THIS LETTER MEAN ...?!
Example
GRWR
GRWRR GRWRR GRWR GRWR
GRWRWR GRWRR
GRWRR GRWRWR
GWEEE GRWR GRWR
GRWR GRWR
...
HER ANGER... SEEMS TO STEM FROM...A DIFFERENT SOURCE THAN I THOUGHT ...
...
UM... P- PRINCESS? YOU READ MY LETTER... DIDN'T YOU...?
UH-HUH.
AREN'T YOU... MAD ABOUT WHAT I WROTE ?
...
YOU THOUGHT I'D BE ANGRY ABOUT THE LETTER, DIDN'T YOU?
THAT'S RIGHT. THAT'S WHY I'VE BEEN RUNNING AWAY FROM ALL OF YOU.
...
AFTER ALL, THERE WERE SOME CREEPY THINGS IN IT. AND AT MY AGE TOO!
ON TOP OF THAT, MY JEALOUSY... EVERY IOTA OF EVIL INSIDE ME IS IN THAT LETTER IN BLACK AND WHITE!

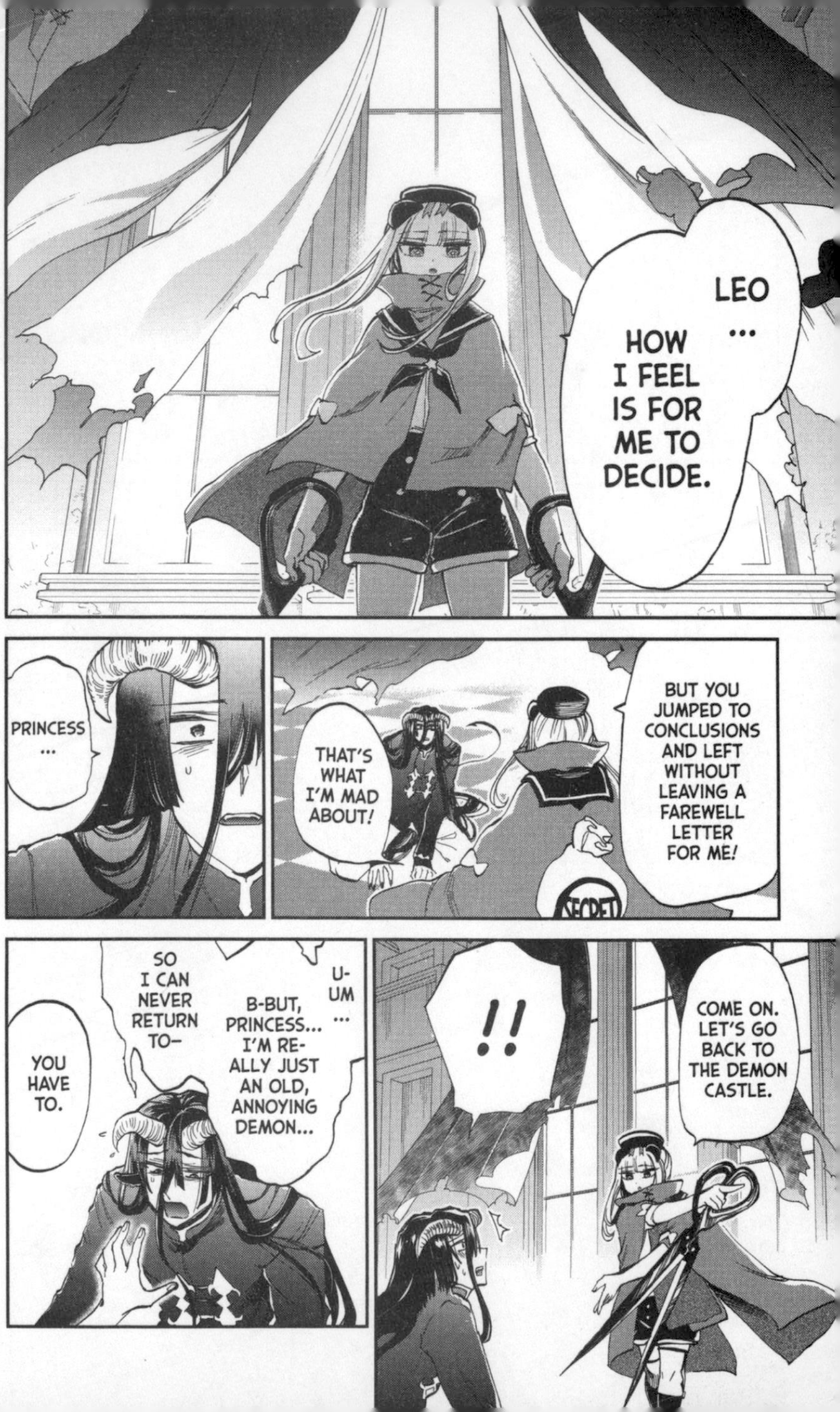
LEO ...
HOW I FEEL IS FOR ME TO DECIDE.
BUT YOU JUMPED TO CONCLUSIONS AND LEFT WITHOUT LEAVING A FAREWELL LETTER FOR ME!
THAT'S WHAT I'M MAD ABOUT!
SECRET
PRINCESS ...
COME ON. LET'S GO BACK TO THE DEMON CASTLE.
!!
U-UM ...
B-BUT, PRINCESS... I'M RE-ALLY JUST AN OLD, ANNOYING DEMON...
SO I CAN NEVER RETURN TO–
YOU HAVE TO.

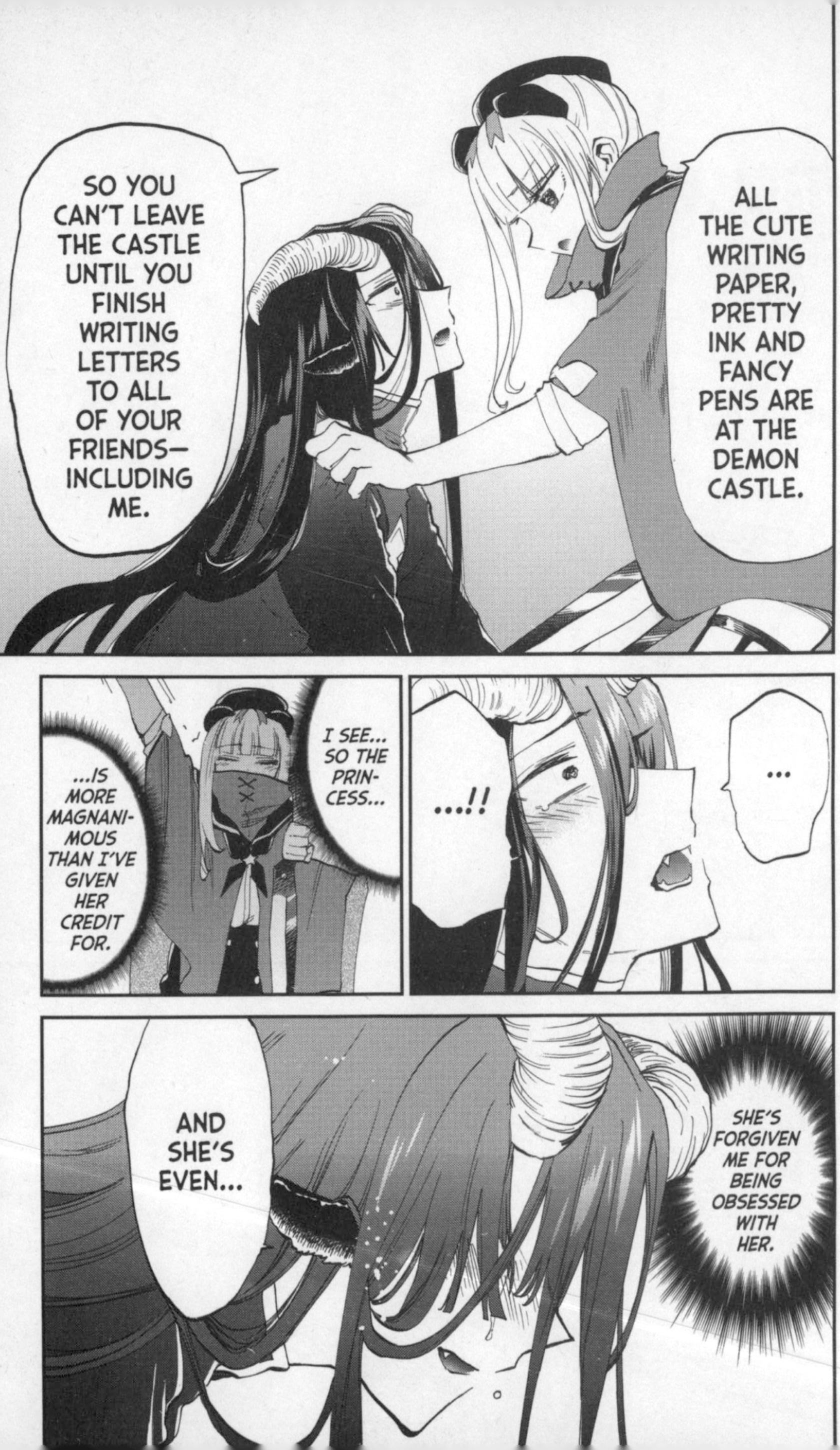
ALL THE CUTE WRITING PAPER, PRETTY INK AND FANCY PENS ARE AT THE DEMON CASTLE.
SO YOU CAN'T LEAVE THE CASTLE UNTIL YOU FINISH WRITING LETTERS TO ALL OF YOUR FRIENDS—INCLUDING ME.
...
...!!
I SEE... SO THE PRIN-CESS...
...IS MORE MAGNANI-MOUS THAN I'VE GIVEN HER CREDIT FOR.
SHE'S FORGIVEN ME FOR BEING OBSESSED WITH HER.
AND SHE'S EVEN...

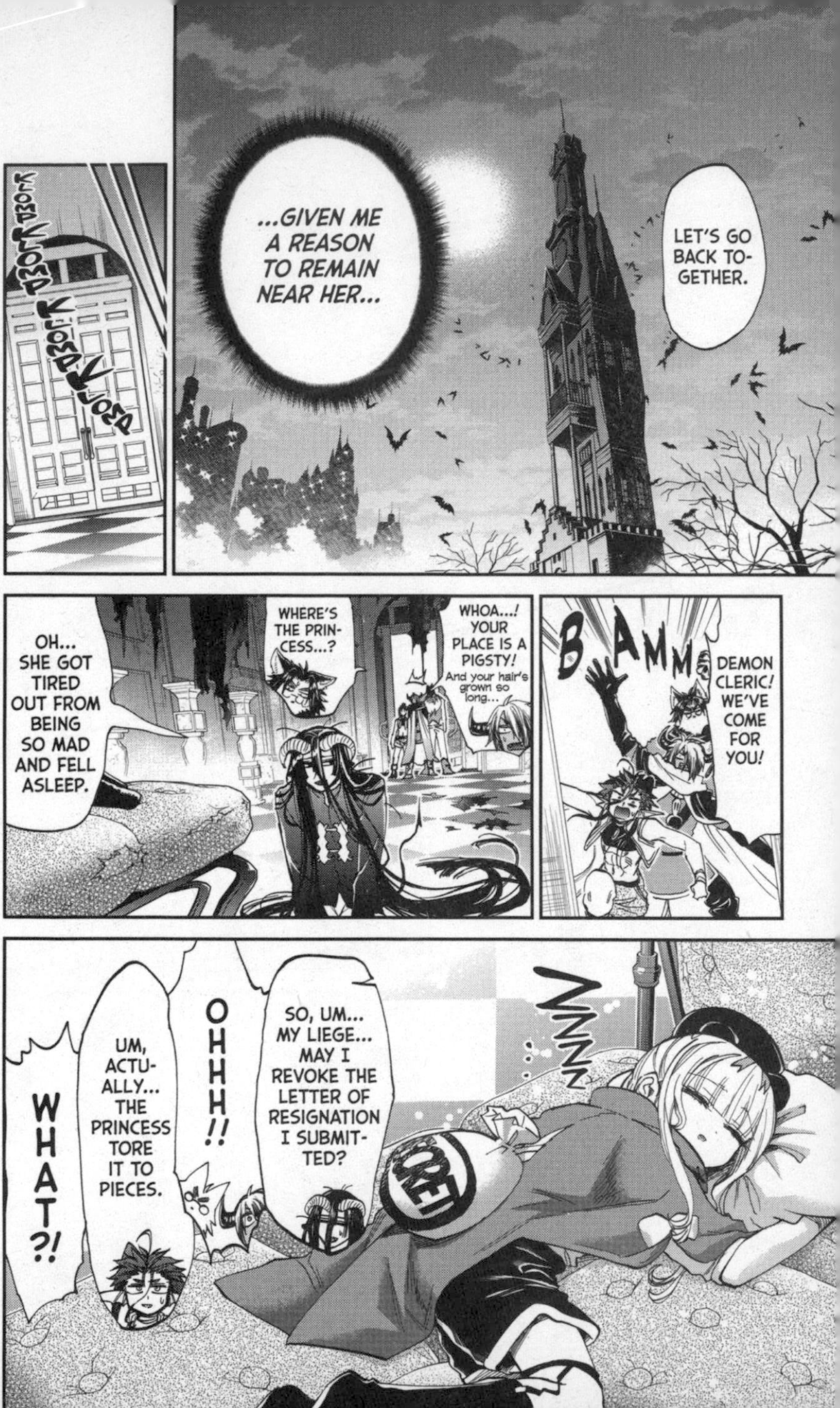
...GIVEN ME A REASON TO REMAIN NEAR HER...
LET'S GO BACK TO-GETHER.
KLOMP KLOMP KLOMP KLOMP
BAMM
DEMON CLERIC! WE'VE COME FOR YOU!
WHOA...! YOUR PLACE IS A PIGSTY!
And your hair's grown so long...
WHERE'S THE PRIN-CESS...?
OH... SHE GOT TIRED OUT FROM BEING SO MAD AND FELL ASLEEP.
ZZZZ
SO, UM... MY LIEGE... MAY I REVOKE THE LETTER OF RESIGNATION I SUBMIT-TED?
OHHHH!!
UM, ACTU-ALLY... THE PRINCESS TORE IT TO PIECES.
WHAT?!

DEMON CASTLE QUESTION CORNER

4

● I'd like to know what Teddy Demon and Eggplant Seal would do if they saw a plushy that looked exactly like them.

A1 Sleep together

A2
SNIFF SNIFF
SNIFF SNIFF
Tuck it into bed

● I want to find out what color the snake on M.O.T.H.E.R.'s tail is.

A I've heard it's roughly midway between the darkest fur on his hand and the darkest hair on his head.

● I want to see the brothers Poseidon and Hades laughing.

A
HYUK
HYUK
HYUK
HEH HEH HEH
HEH
HEH

● What are the names of the previous Demon Kings?

A
Twilight
(Current Demon King)
Midnight
(Previous Demon King)
Zero
(Demon King from two generations ago)
Pre-dawn
(Demon King from three generations ago)

● What is the most important thing you pay attention to when drawing the characters? Any simple detail will do—it would be great if you could teach me how to draw them!

A
- Princess: Her bangs should always be at the level of her eyes.
- Demon King: His hair shouldn't be too pointy.
- Leo: His eyes and eyebrows are parallel to each other.
- Poseidon: If something seems to be missing, just add more hair.
- M.O.T.H.E.R.: His eyes should be an inverted triangle.

Those are the most important points in a nutshell.

● The Demon King seems very attached to his father. What was his mother like?

A The being known as a Demon King in this series is a life-form created out of the previous Demon King's huge store of magic power. In other words, they don't have mothers.

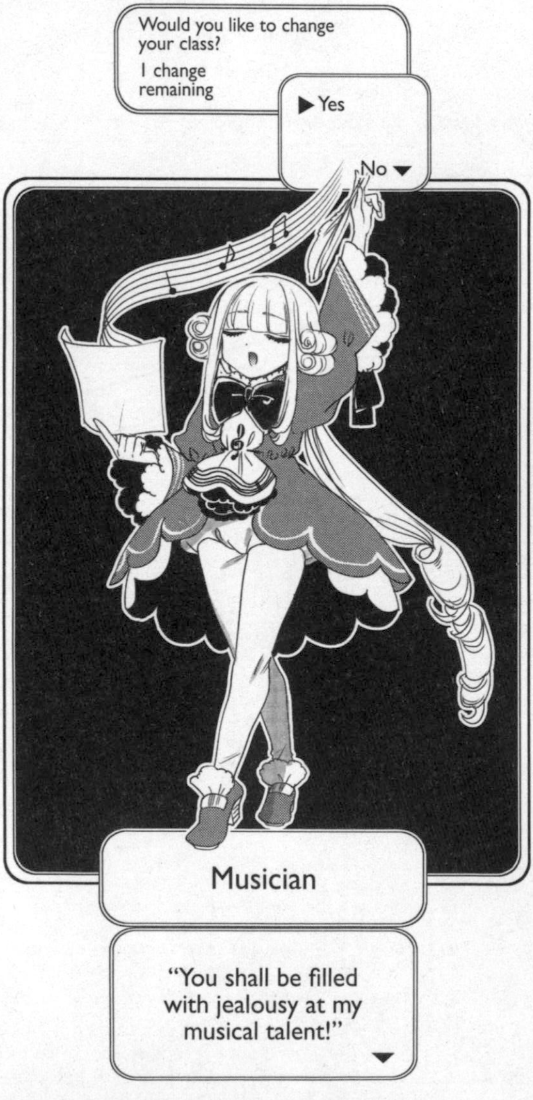
Would you like to change your class?
I change remaining
▶ Yes
No ▼
Musician
"You shall be filled with jealousy at my musical talent!"

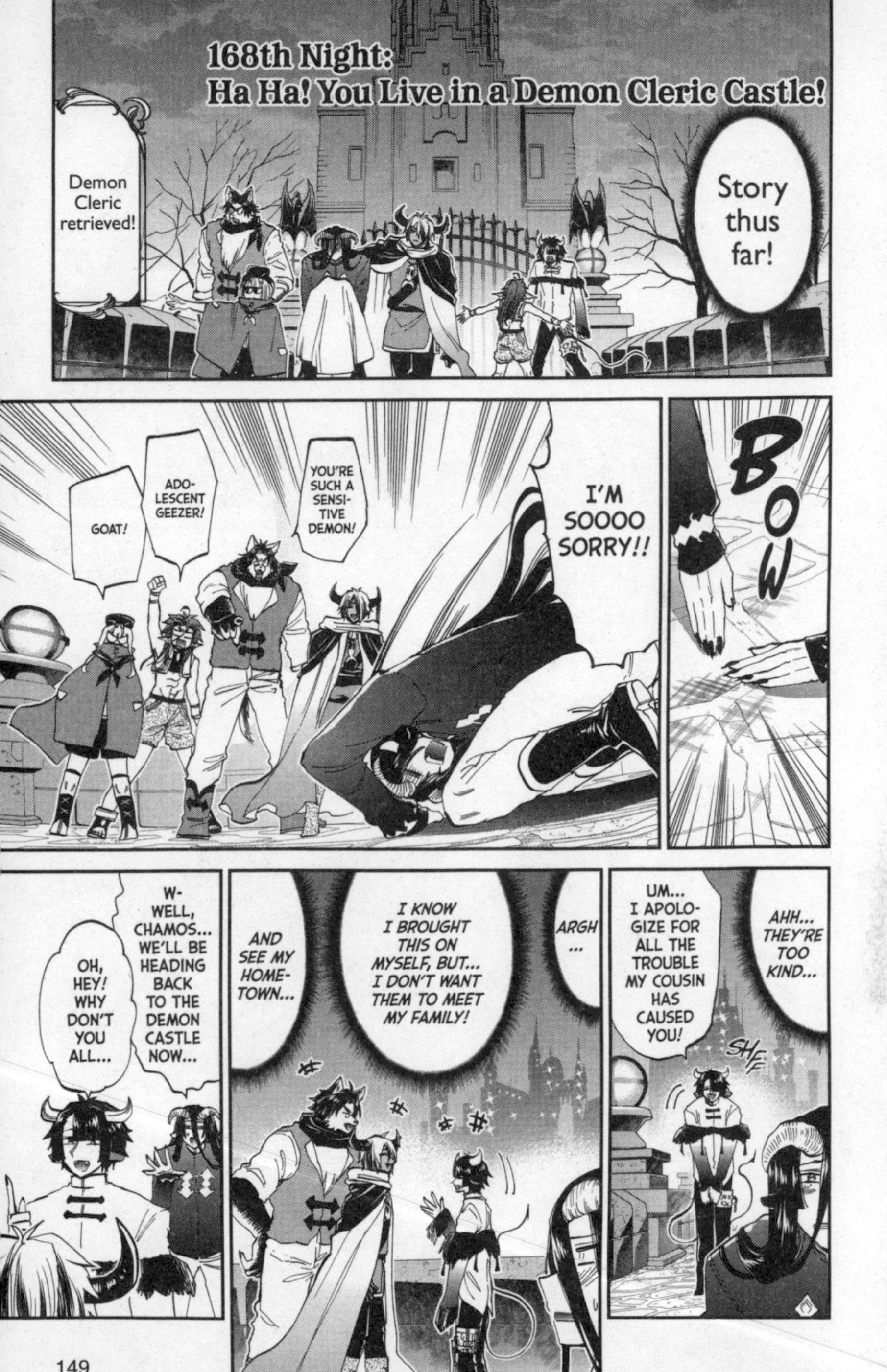
168th Night:
Ha Ha! You Live in a Demon Cleric Castle!
Demon Cleric retrieved!
Story thus far!
GOAT!
ADO-LESCENT GEEZER!
YOU'RE SUCH A SENSI-TIVE DEMON!
I'M SOOOO SORRY!!
BOW
W-WELL, CHAMOS... WE'LL BE HEADING BACK TO THE DEMON CASTLE NOW...
OH, HEY! WHY DON'T YOU ALL...
AND SEE MY HOME-TOWN...
I KNOW I BROUGHT THIS ON MYSELF, BUT... I DON'T WANT THEM TO MEET MY FAMILY!
ARGH...
UM... I APOLO-GIZE FOR ALL THE TROUBLE MY COUSIN HAS CAUSED YOU!
AHH... THEY'RE TOO KIND...
SHF

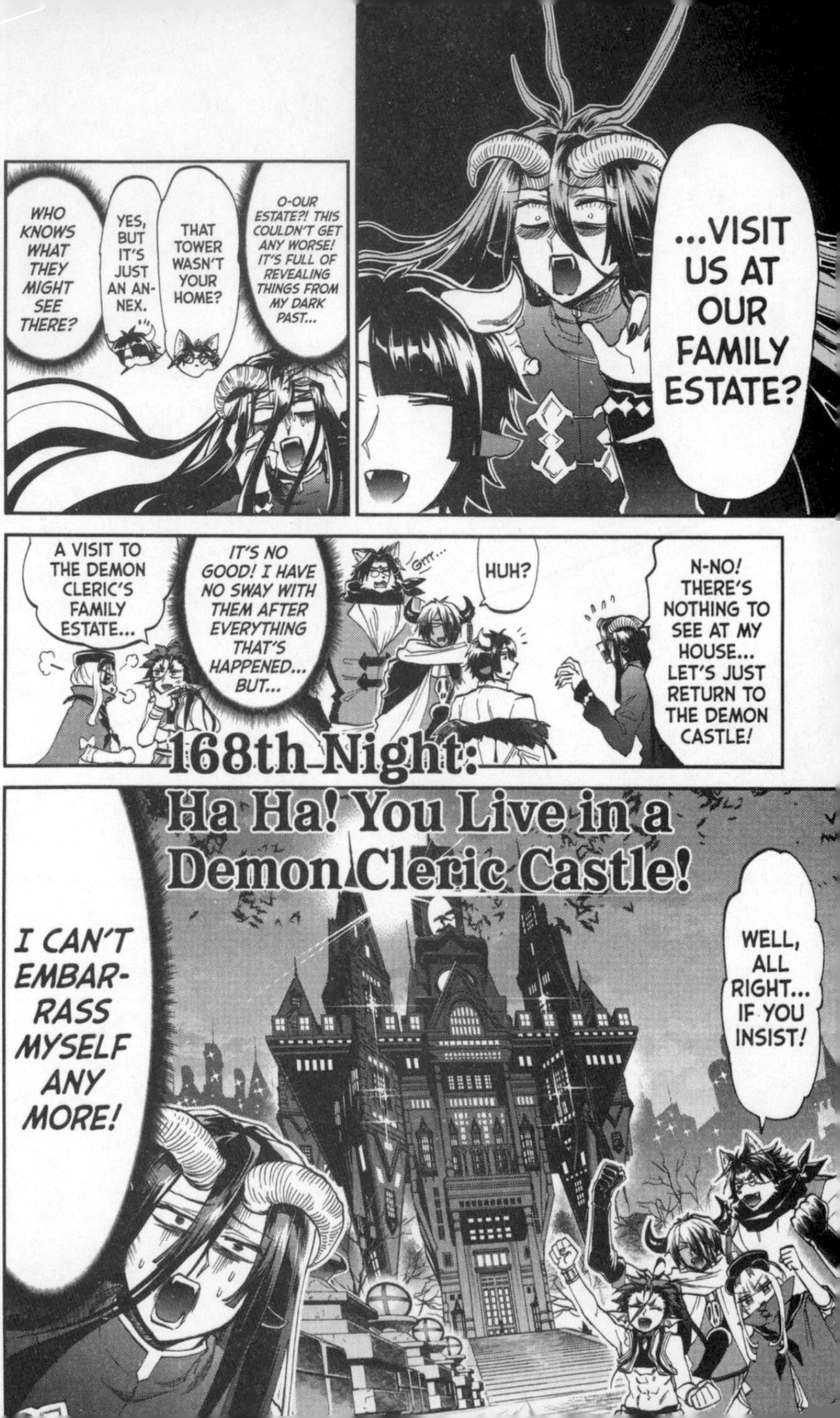
...VISIT US AT OUR FAMILY ESTATE?
O-OUR ESTATE?! THIS COULDN'T GET ANY WORSE! IT'S FULL OF REVEALING THINGS FROM MY DARK PAST...
THAT TOWER WASN'T YOUR HOME?
YES, BUT IT'S JUST AN AN-NEX.
WHO KNOWS WHAT THEY MIGHT SEE THERE?
N-NO! THERE'S NOTHING TO SEE AT MY HOUSE... LET'S JUST RETURN TO THE DEMON CASTLE!
HUH?
Grrr...
IT'S NO GOOD! I HAVE NO SWAY WITH THEM AFTER EVERYTHING THAT'S HAPPENED... BUT...
A VISIT TO THE DEMON CLERIC'S FAMILY ESTATE...
168th Night: Ha Ha! You Live in a Demon Cleric Castle!
WELL, ALL RIGHT... IF YOU INSIST!
I CAN'T EMBAR-RASS MYSELF ANY MORE!

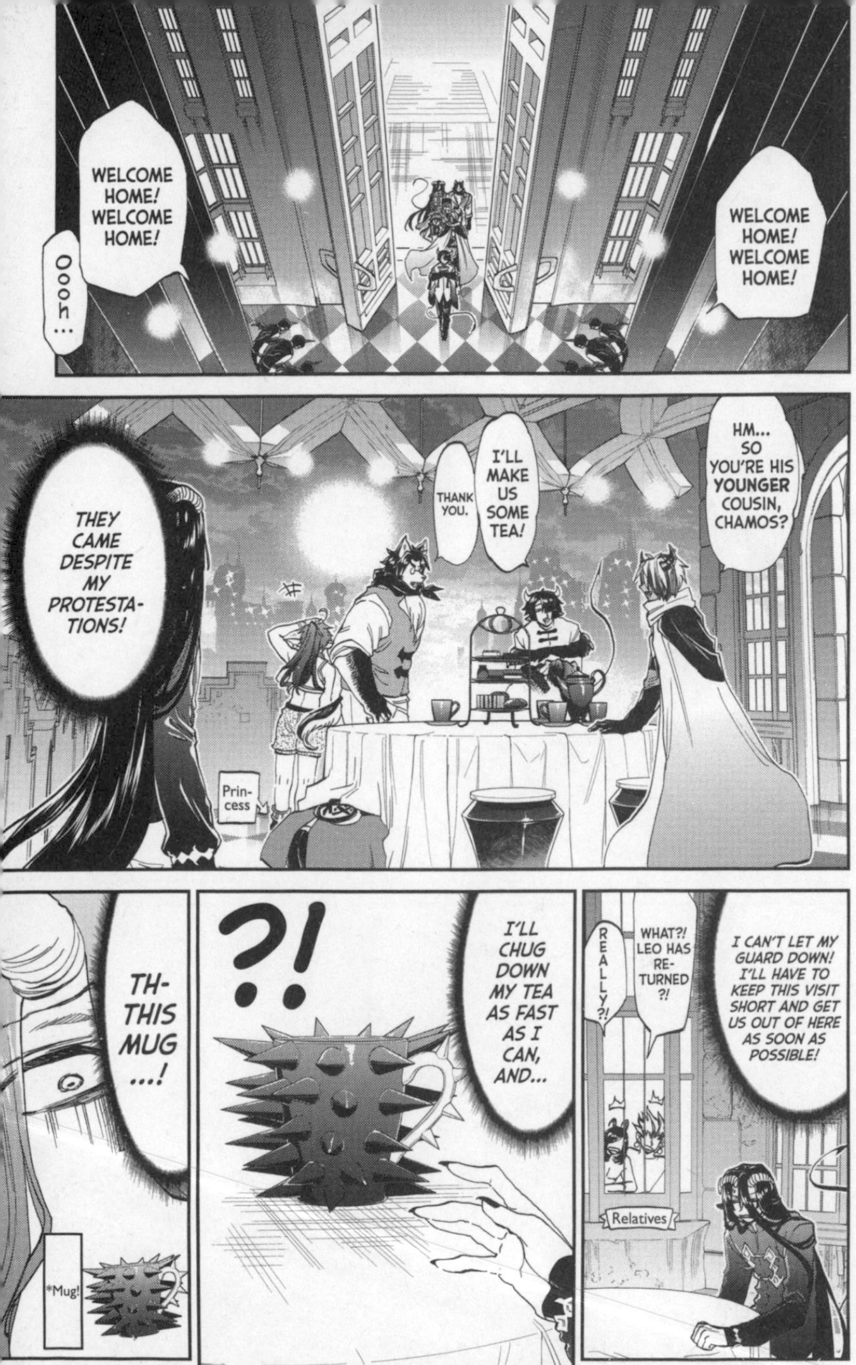
WELCOME HOME! WELCOME HOME!
WELCOME HOME! WELCOME HOME!
Oooh...
HM... SO YOU'RE HIS YOUNGER COUSIN, CHAMOS?
I'LL MAKE US SOME TEA!
THANK YOU.
THEY CAME DESPITE MY PROTESTA-TIONS!
Prin-cess
I CAN'T LET MY GUARD DOWN! I'LL HAVE TO KEEP THIS VISIT SHORT AND GET US OUT OF HERE AS SOON AS POSSIBLE!
WHAT?! LEO HAS RE-TURNED?!
REALLY?!
Relatives
I'LL CHUG DOWN MY TEA AS FAST AS I CAN, AND...
?!
TH-THIS MUG...!
*Mug!

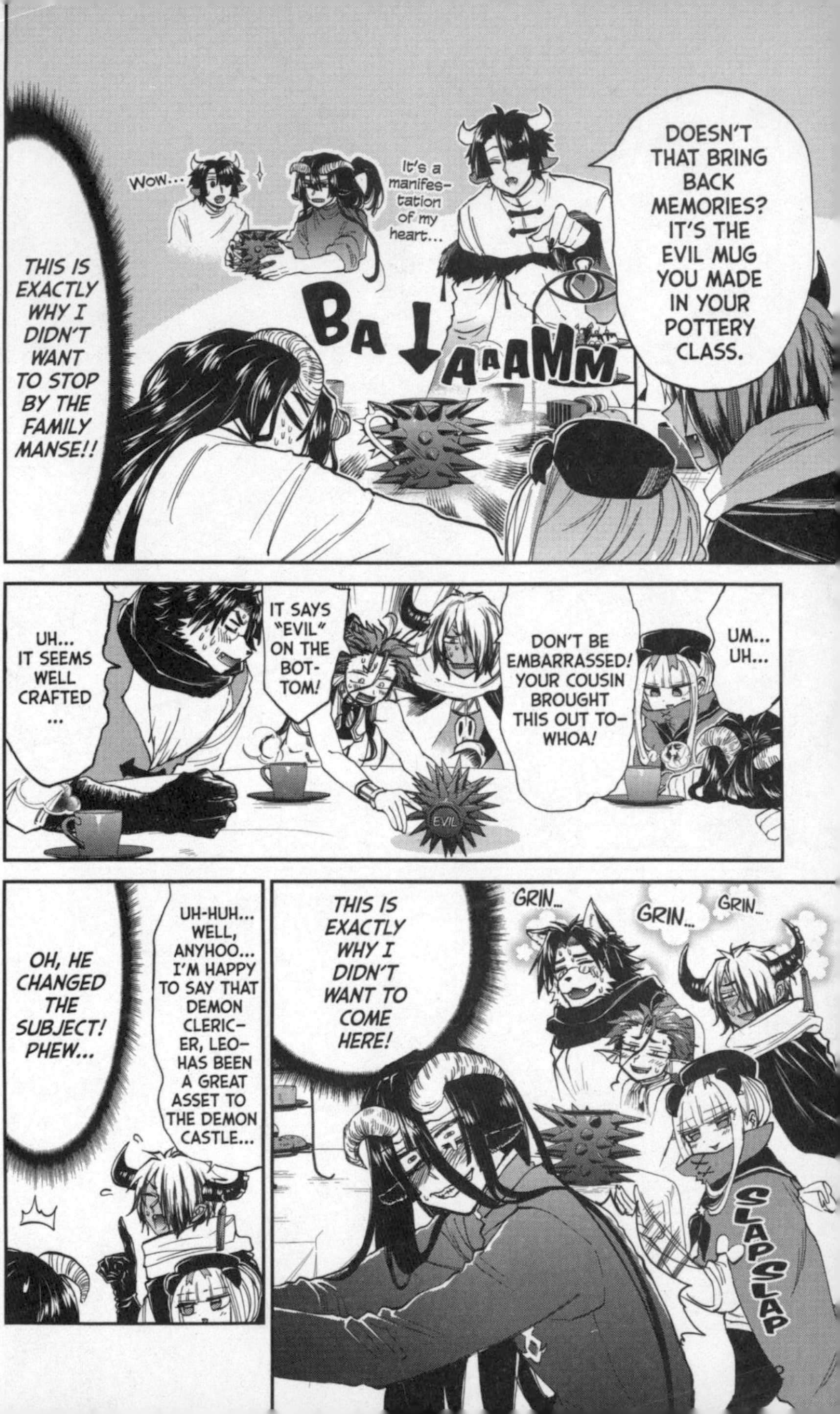
DOESN'T THAT BRING BACK MEMORIES? IT'S THE EVIL MUG YOU MADE IN YOUR POTTERY CLASS.
It's a manifestation of my heart...
Wow...
BA↓AAAMM
THIS IS EXACTLY WHY I DIDN'T WANT TO STOP BY THE FAMILY MANSE!!
UM... UH...
DON'T BE EMBARRASSED! YOUR COUSIN BROUGHT THIS OUT TO— WHOA!
IT SAYS "EVIL" ON THE BOTTOM!
EVIL
UH... IT SEEMS WELL CRAFTED ...
GRIN...
GRIN...
GRIN...
THIS IS EXACTLY WHY I DIDN'T WANT TO COME HERE!
SLAP SLAP
UH-HUH... WELL, ANYHOO... I'M HAPPY TO SAY THAT DEMON CLERIC-ER, LEO-HAS BEEN A GREAT ASSET TO THE DEMON CASTLE...
OH, HE CHANGED THE SUBJECT! PHEW...

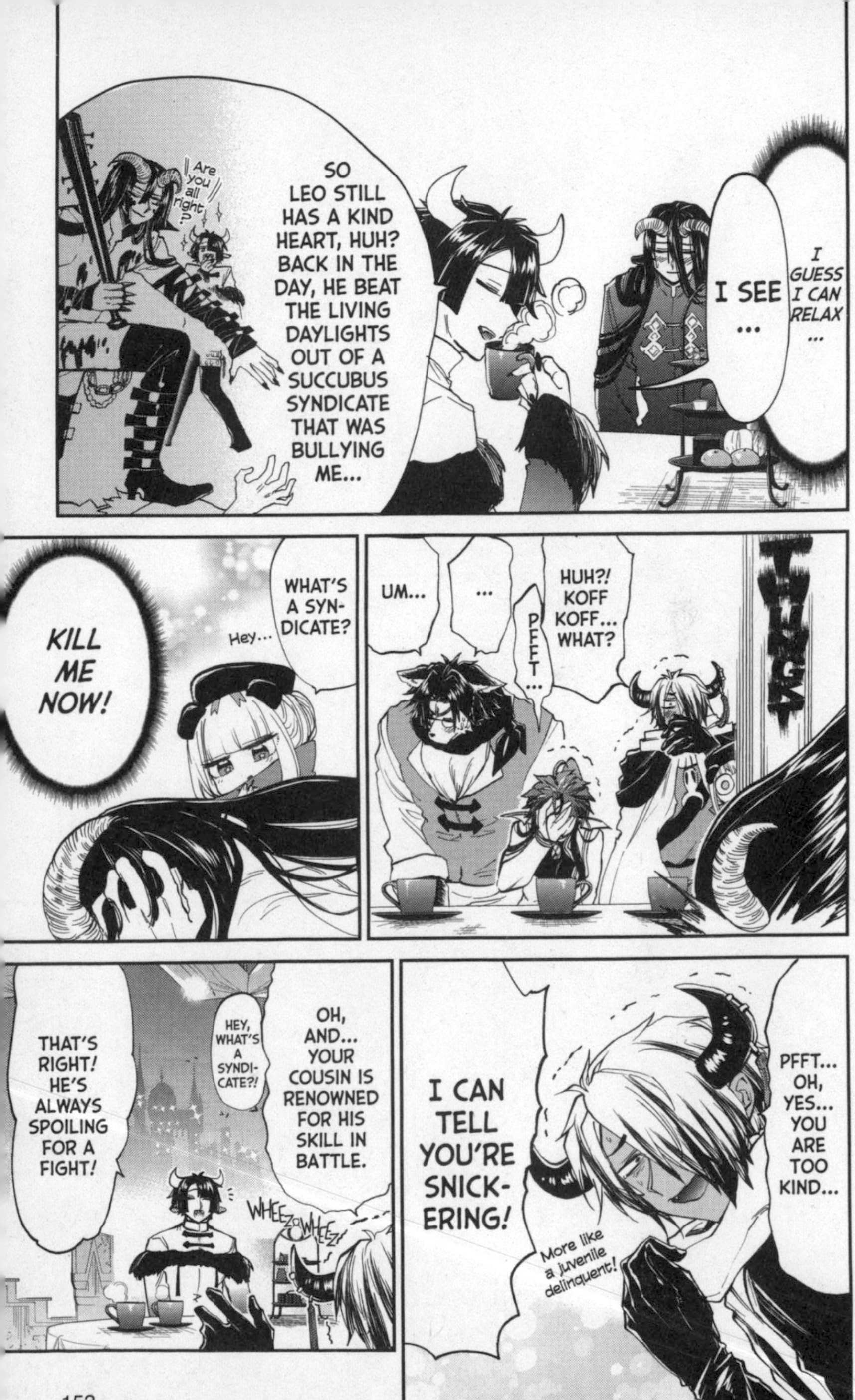
I GUESS I CAN RELAX...
I SEE...
SO LEO STILL HAS A KIND HEART, HUH? BACK IN THE DAY, HE BEAT THE LIVING DAYLIGHTS OUT OF A SUCCUBUS SYNDICATE THAT WAS BULLYING ME...
Are you all right?
HUH?! KOFF KOFF... WHAT?
PFFT...
...
UM...
WHAT'S A SYN-DICATE?
Hey...
KILL ME NOW!
PFFT... OH, YES... YOU ARE TOO KIND...
I CAN TELL YOU'RE SNICK-ERING!
More like a juvenile delinquent!
OH, AND... YOUR COUSIN IS RENOWNED FOR HIS SKILL IN BATTLE.
HEY, WHAT'S A SYNDICATE?!
THAT'S RIGHT! HE'S ALWAYS SPOILING FOR A FIGHT!
WHEEZ WHEEZ

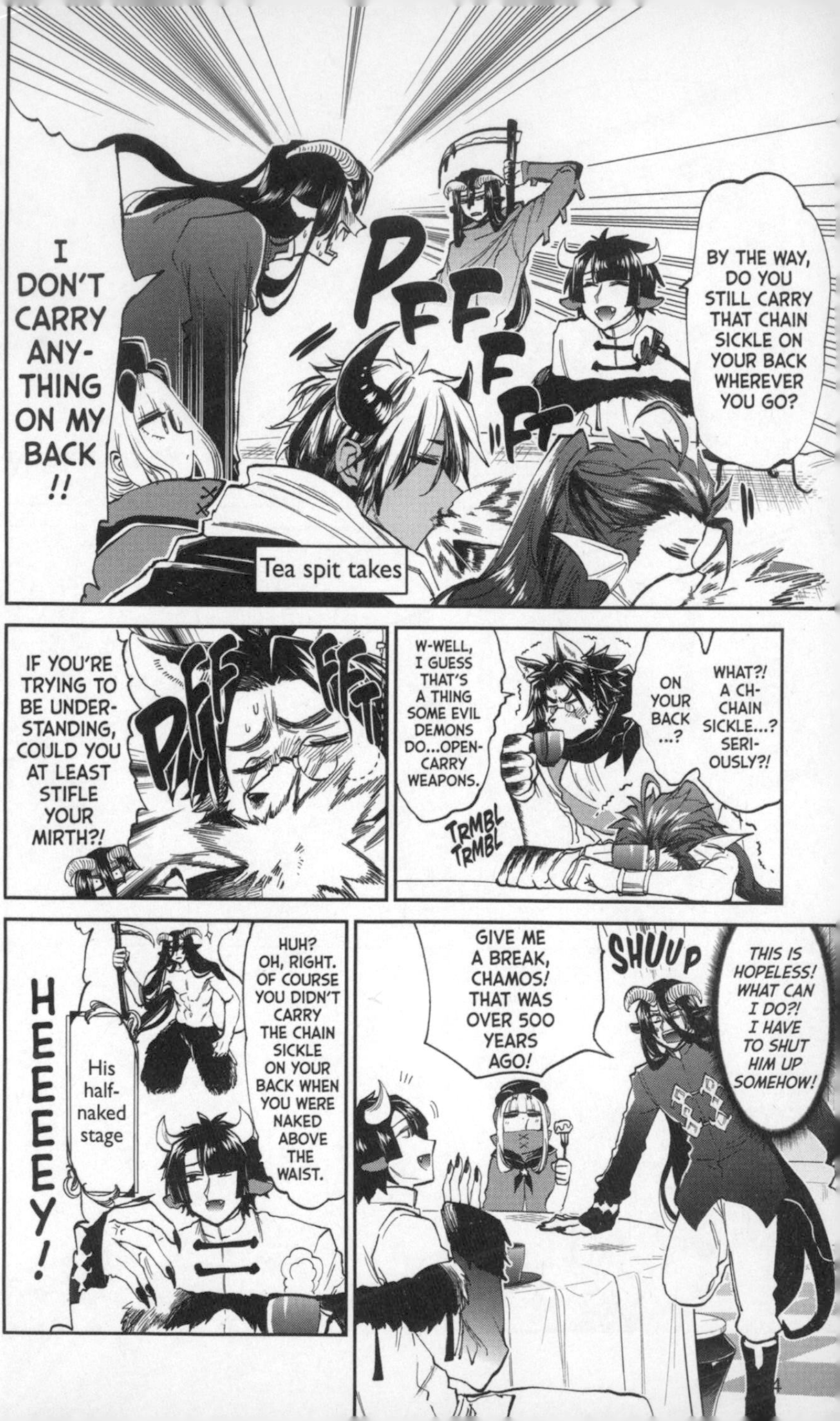
BY THE WAY, DO YOU STILL CARRY THAT CHAIN SICKLE ON YOUR BACK WHEREVER YOU GO?
PFFFFT
I DON'T CARRY ANY-THING ON MY BACK!!
Tea spit takes
WHAT?! A CH-CHAIN SICKLE...? SERI-OUSLY?!
ON YOUR BACK...?
W-WELL, I GUESS THAT'S A THING SOME EVIL DEMONS DO...OPEN-CARRY WEAPONS.
TRMBL TRMBL
PFFFFT
IF YOU'RE TRYING TO BE UNDER-STANDING, COULD YOU AT LEAST STIFLE YOUR MIRTH?!
THIS IS HOPELESS! WHAT CAN I DO?! I HAVE TO SHUT HIM UP SOMEHOW!
SHUUP
GIVE ME A BREAK, CHAMOS! THAT WAS OVER 500 YEARS AGO!
HUH? OH, RIGHT. OF COURSE YOU DIDN'T CARRY THE CHAIN SICKLE ON YOUR BACK WHEN YOU WERE NAKED ABOVE THE WAIST.
His half-naked stage
HEEEEEY!

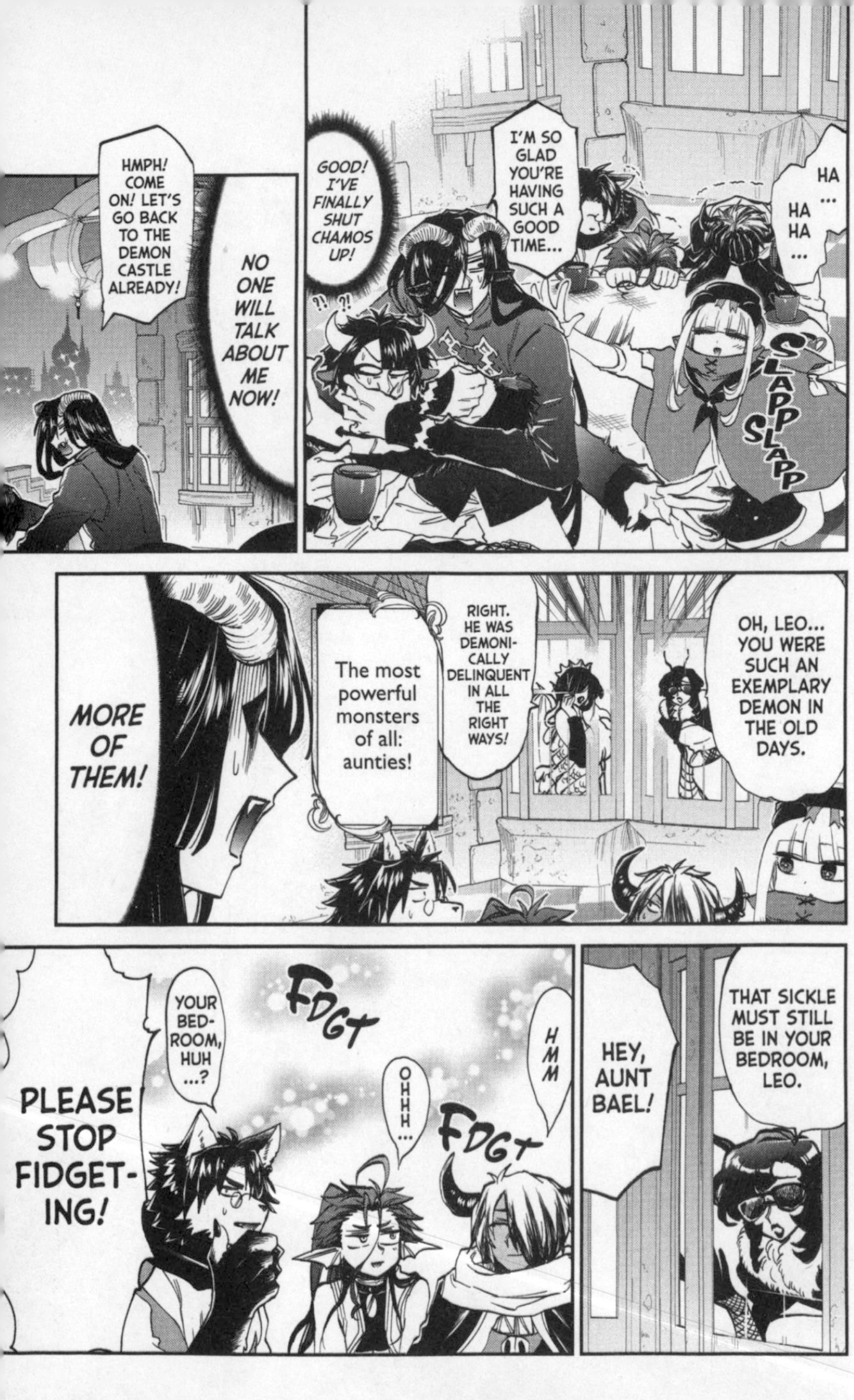
HA... HA HA...
I'M SO GLAD YOU'RE HAVING SUCH A GOOD TIME...
GOOD! I'VE FINALLY SHUT CHAMOS UP!
SLAPP SLAPP
NO ONE WILL TALK ABOUT ME NOW!
HMPH! COME ON! LET'S GO BACK TO THE DEMON CASTLE ALREADY!
OH, LEO... YOU WERE SUCH AN EXEMPLARY DEMON IN THE OLD DAYS.
RIGHT. HE WAS DEMONI-CALLY DELINQUENT IN ALL THE RIGHT WAYS!
The most powerful monsters of all: aunties!
MORE OF THEM!
THAT SICKLE MUST STILL BE IN YOUR BEDROOM, LEO.
HEY, AUNT BAEL!
HMM
FDGT
OHHH...
FDGT
YOUR BED-ROOM, HUH...?
PLEASE STOP FIDGET-ING!

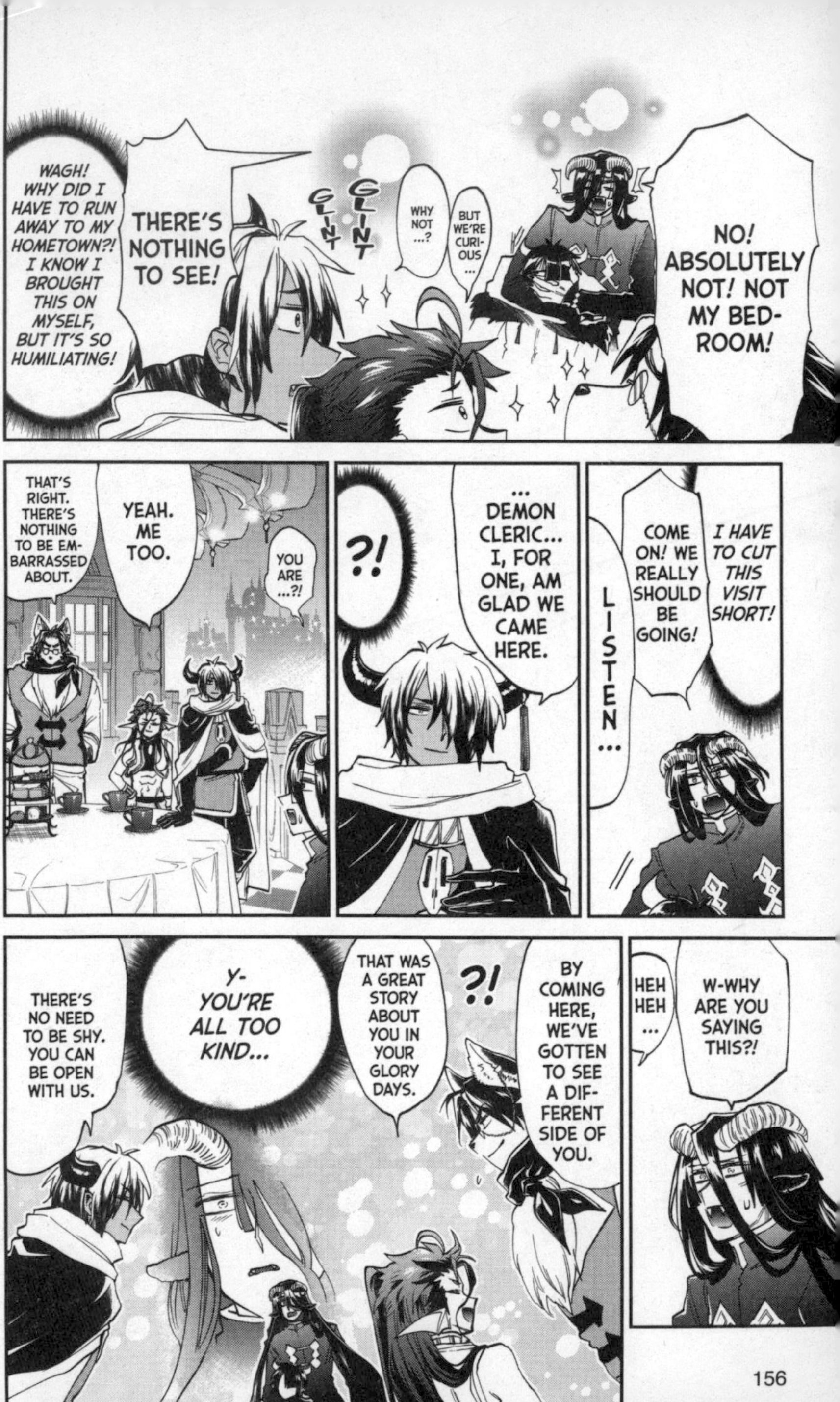
NO! ABSOLUTELY NOT! NOT MY BED-ROOM!
BUT WE'RE CURI-OUS ...
WHY NOT ...?
GLINT GLINT
THERE'S NOTHING TO SEE!
WAGH! WHY DID I HAVE TO RUN AWAY TO MY HOMETOWN?! I KNOW I BROUGHT THIS ON MYSELF, BUT IT'S SO HUMILIATING!
I HAVE TO CUT THIS VISIT SHORT!
COME ON! WE REALLY SHOULD BE GOING!
LISTEN...
... DEMON CLERIC... I, FOR ONE, AM GLAD WE CAME HERE.
?!
YEAH. ME TOO.
YOU ARE ...?!
THAT'S RIGHT. THERE'S NOTHING TO BE EM-BARRASSED ABOUT.
W-WHY ARE YOU SAYING THIS?!
HEH HEH ...
BY COMING HERE, WE'VE GOTTEN TO SEE A DIF-FERENT SIDE OF YOU.
?!
THAT WAS A GREAT STORY ABOUT YOU IN YOUR GLORY DAYS.
Y-YOU'RE ALL TOO KIND...
THERE'S NO NEED TO BE SHY. YOU CAN BE OPEN WITH US.

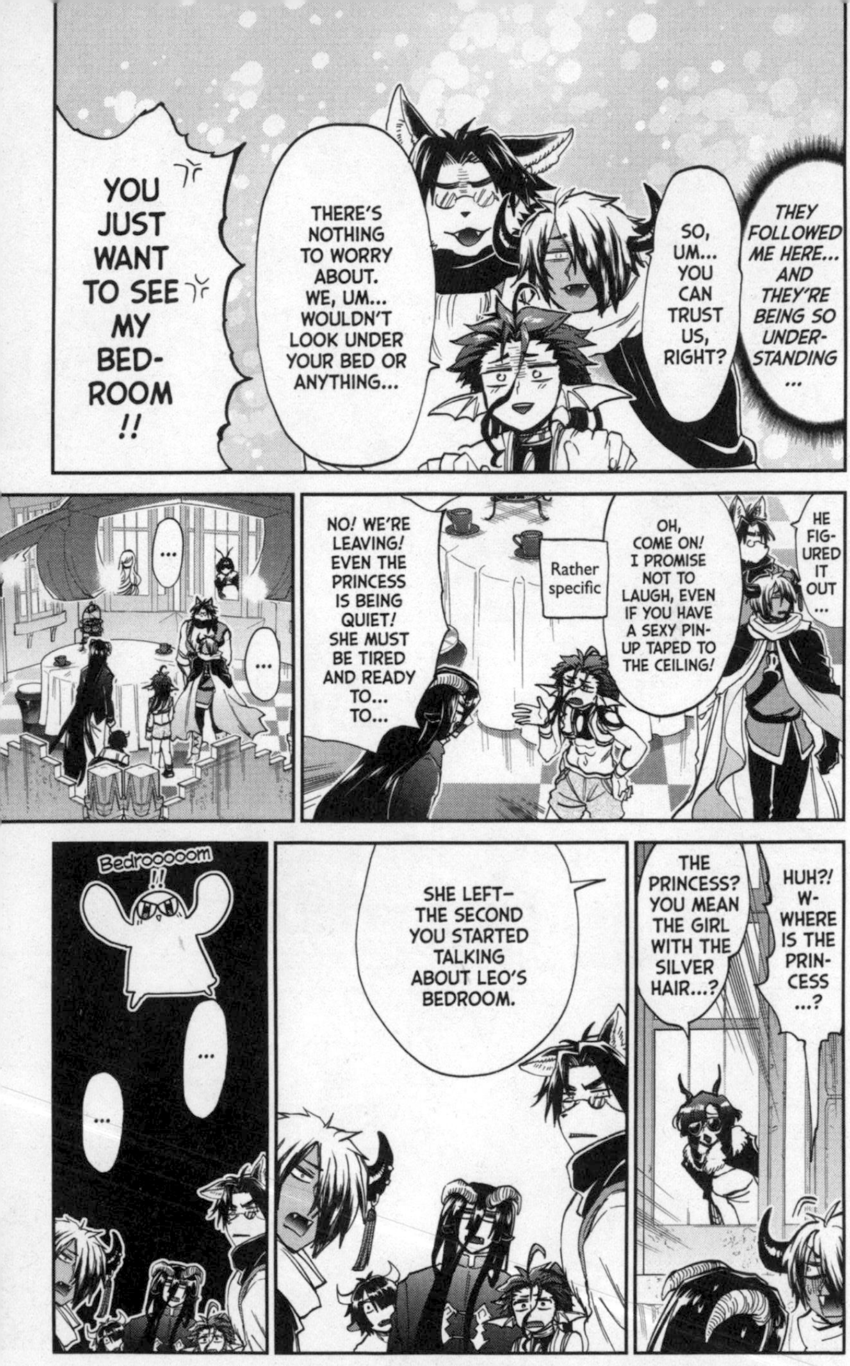
THEY FOLLOWED ME HERE... AND THEY'RE BEING SO UNDER-STANDING...
SO, UM... YOU CAN TRUST US, RIGHT?
THERE'S NOTHING TO WORRY ABOUT. WE, UM... WOULDN'T LOOK UNDER YOUR BED OR ANYTHING...
YOU JUST WANT TO SEE MY BED-ROOM!!
HE FIG-URED IT OUT...
OH, COME ON! I PROMISE NOT TO LAUGH, EVEN IF YOU HAVE A SEXY PIN-UP TAPED TO THE CEILING!
Rather specific
NO! WE'RE LEAVING! EVEN THE PRINCESS IS BEING QUIET! SHE MUST BE TIRED AND READY TO... TO...
...
...
HUH?! W-WHERE IS THE PRIN-CESS...?
THE PRINCESS? YOU MEAN THE GIRL WITH THE SILVER HAIR...?
SHE LEFT—THE SECOND YOU STARTED TALKING ABOUT LEO'S BEDROOM.
Bedroooooom !!
...
...

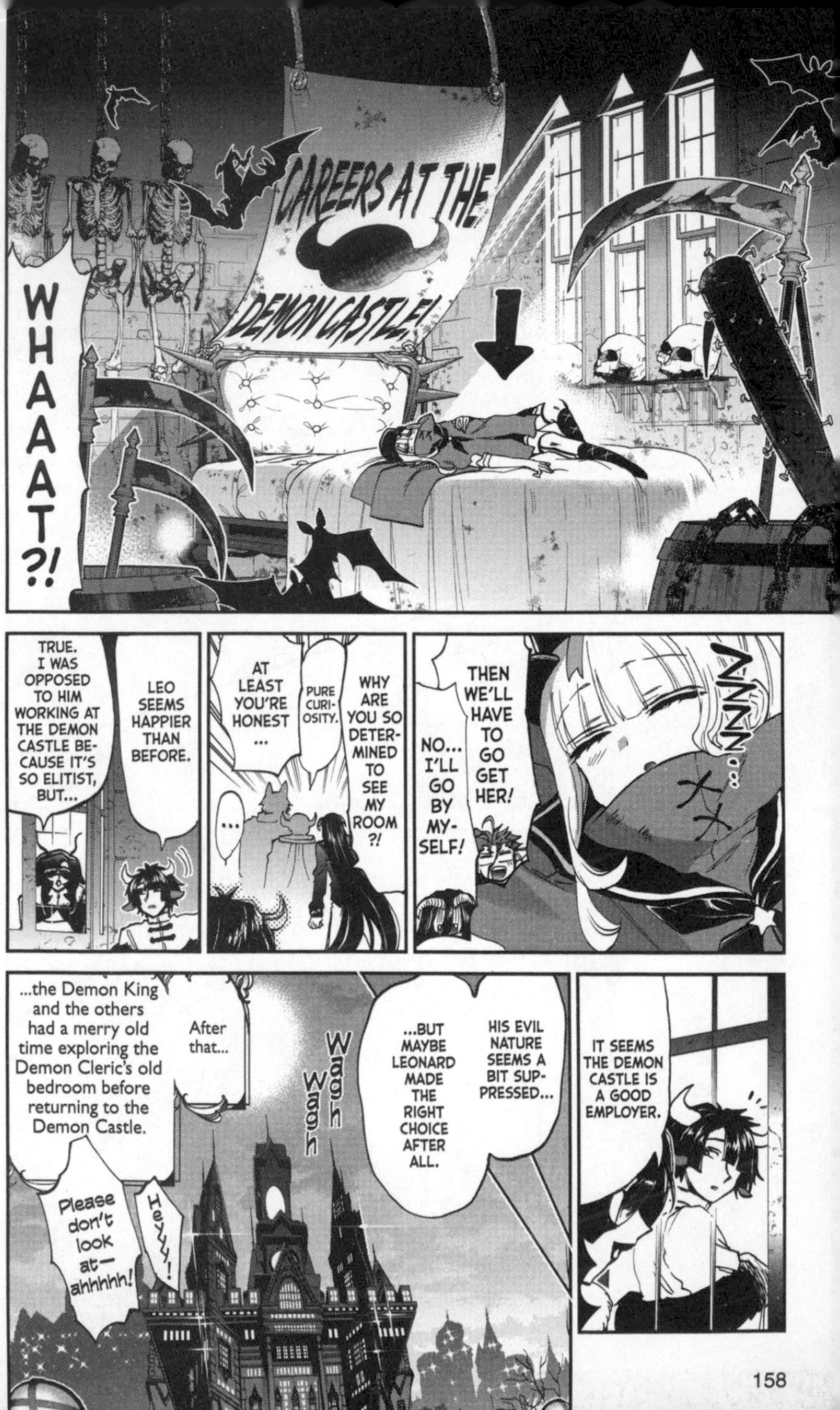
CAREERS AT THE DEMON CASTLE!
WHAAAAT?!
ZZZZ...
THEN WE'LL HAVE TO GO GET HER!
NO... I'LL GO BY MY-SELF!
WHY ARE YOU SO DETER-MINED TO SEE MY ROOM?!
PURE CURI-OSITY.
AT LEAST YOU'RE HONEST...
...
LEO SEEMS HAPPIER THAN BEFORE.
TRUE. I WAS OPPOSED TO HIM WORKING AT THE DEMON CASTLE BE-CAUSE IT'S SO ELITIST, BUT...
IT SEEMS THE DEMON CASTLE IS A GOOD EMPLOYER.
HIS EVIL NATURE SEEMS A BIT SUP-PRESSED...
...BUT MAYBE LEONARD MADE THE RIGHT CHOICE AFTER ALL.
Wagh Wagh
After that...
...the Demon King and the others had a merry old time exploring the Demon Cleric's old bedroom before returning to the Demon Castle.
Heyyy!
Please don't look at—ahhhhh!

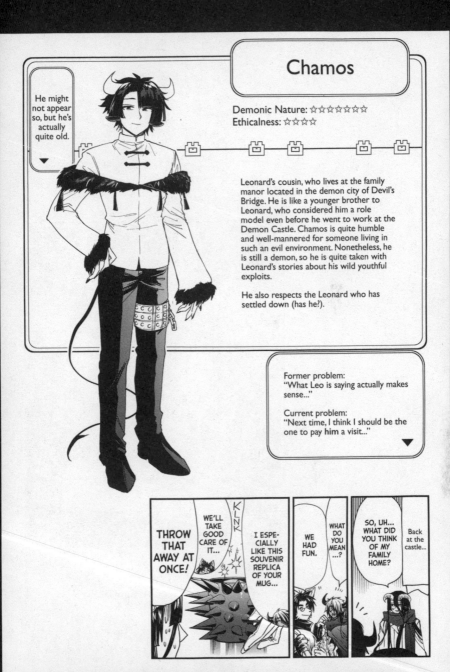

Chamos

He might not appear so, but he's actually quite old.

Demonic Nature: ☆☆☆☆☆☆☆
Ethicalness: ☆☆☆☆

Leonard's cousin, who lives at the family manor located in the demon city of Devil's Bridge. He is like a younger brother to Leonard, who considered him a role model even before he went to work at the Demon Castle. Chamos is quite humble and well-mannered for someone living in such an evil environment. Nonetheless, he is still a demon, so he is quite taken with Leonard's stories about his wild youthful exploits.

He also respects the Leonard who has settled down (has he?).

Former problem:
"What Leo is saying actually makes sense..."

Current problem:
"Next time, I think I should be the one to pay **him** a visit..."

Back at the castle...
SO, UH... WHAT DID YOU THINK OF MY FAMILY HOME?
WHAT DO YOU MEAN ...?
WE HAD FUN.
I ESPE-CIALLY LIKE THIS SOUVENIR REPLICA OF YOUR MUG...
KLNK
WE'LL TAKE GOOD CARE OF IT...
THROW THAT AWAY AT ONCE!

Would you like to change your class?
0 changes remaining

Game Master

"I'll kill you gently..."

169th Night: Princess Syalis Always Smells Nice

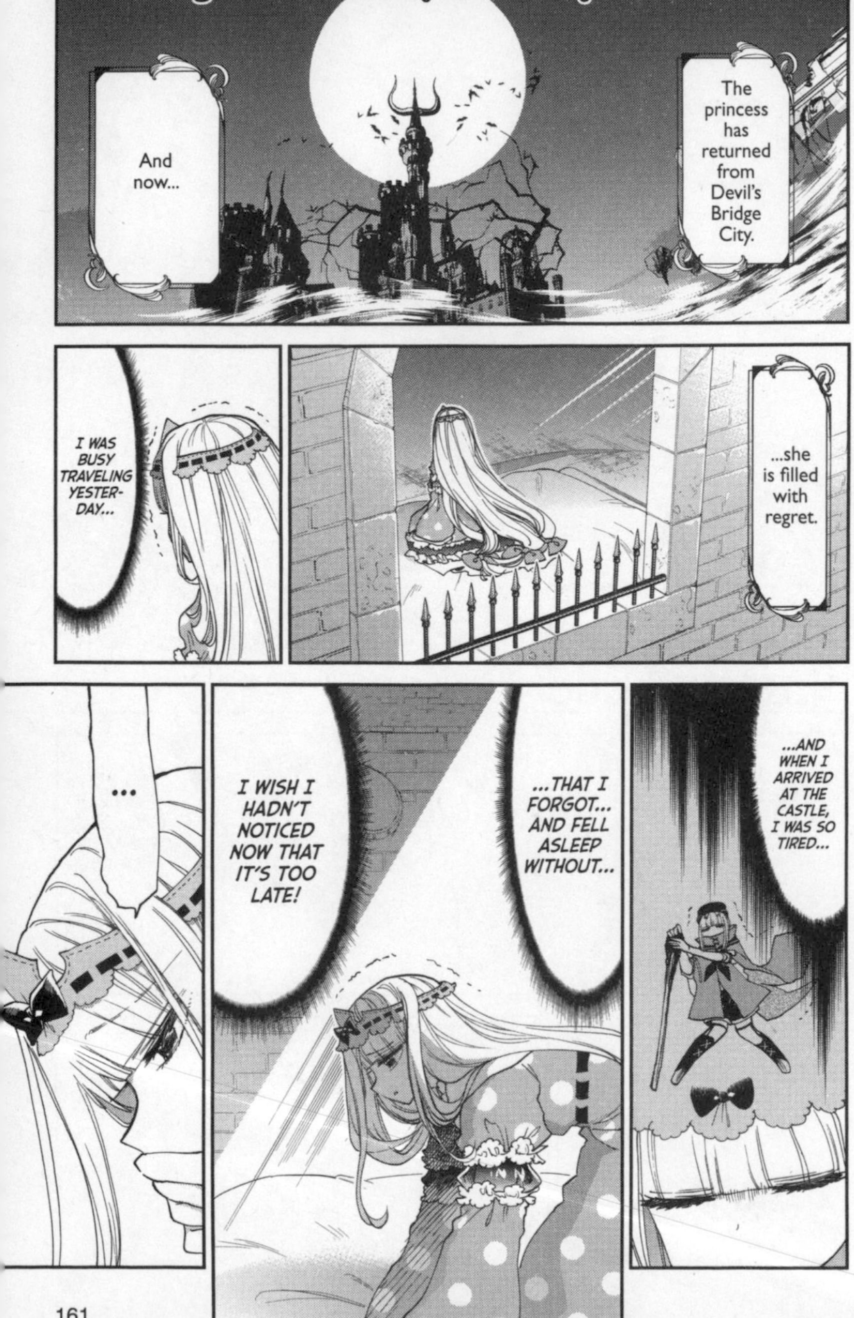

The princess has returned from Devil's Bridge City.
And now...
...she is filled with regret.
I WAS BUSY TRAVELING YESTERDAY...
...AND WHEN I ARRIVED AT THE CASTLE, I WAS SO TIRED...
...THAT I FORGOT... AND FELL ASLEEP WITHOUT...
I WISH I HADN'T NOTICED NOW THAT IT'S TOO LATE!
...

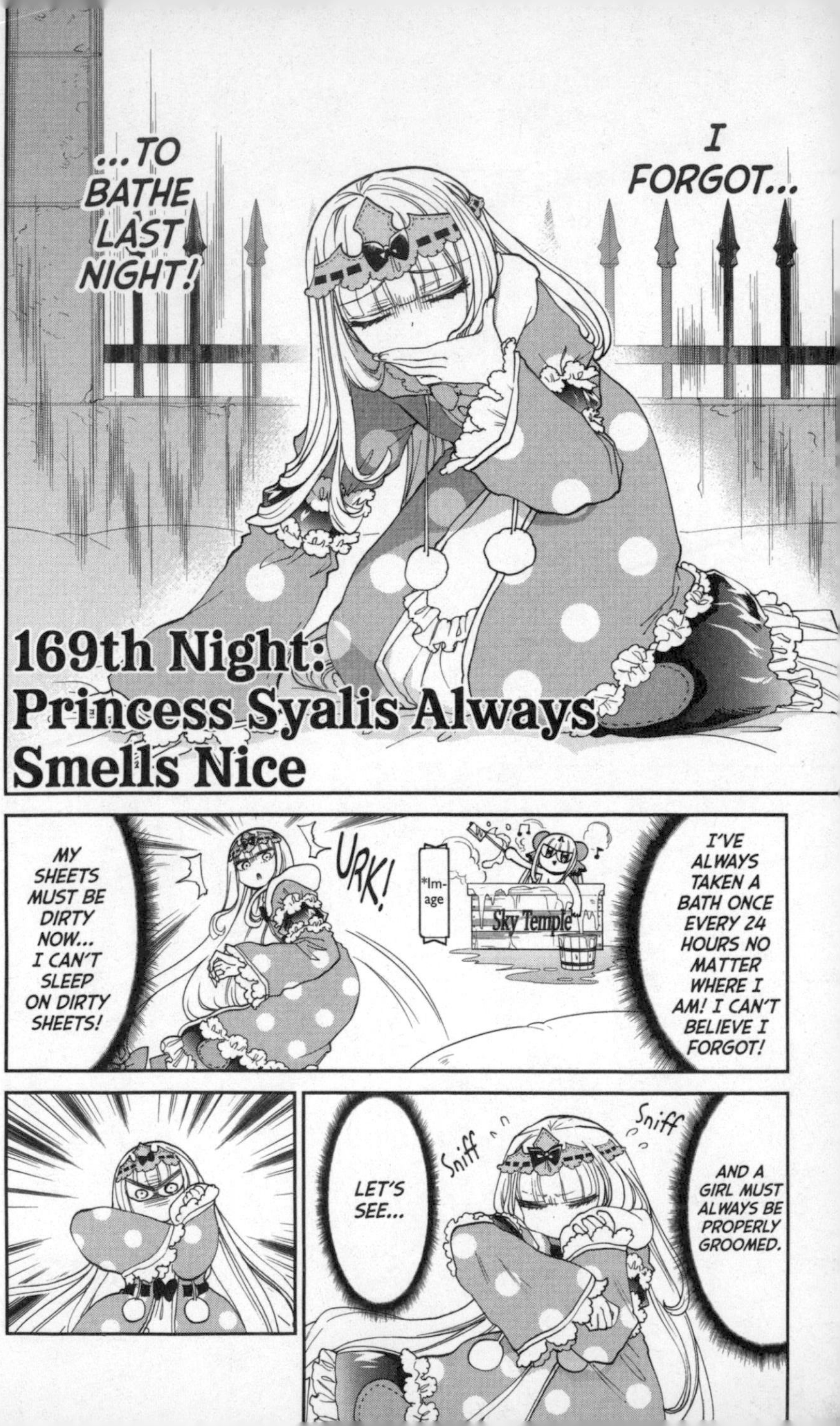
I FORGOT...
...TO BATHE LAST NIGHT!
169th Night: Princess Syalis Always Smells Nice
I'VE ALWAYS TAKEN A BATH ONCE EVERY 24 HOURS NO MATTER WHERE I AM! I CAN'T BELIEVE I FORGOT!
*Image
Sky Temple
URK!
MY SHEETS MUST BE DIRTY NOW... I CAN'T SLEEP ON DIRTY SHEETS!
AND A GIRL MUST ALWAYS BE PROPERLY GROOMED.
Sniff
Sniff
LET'S SEE...

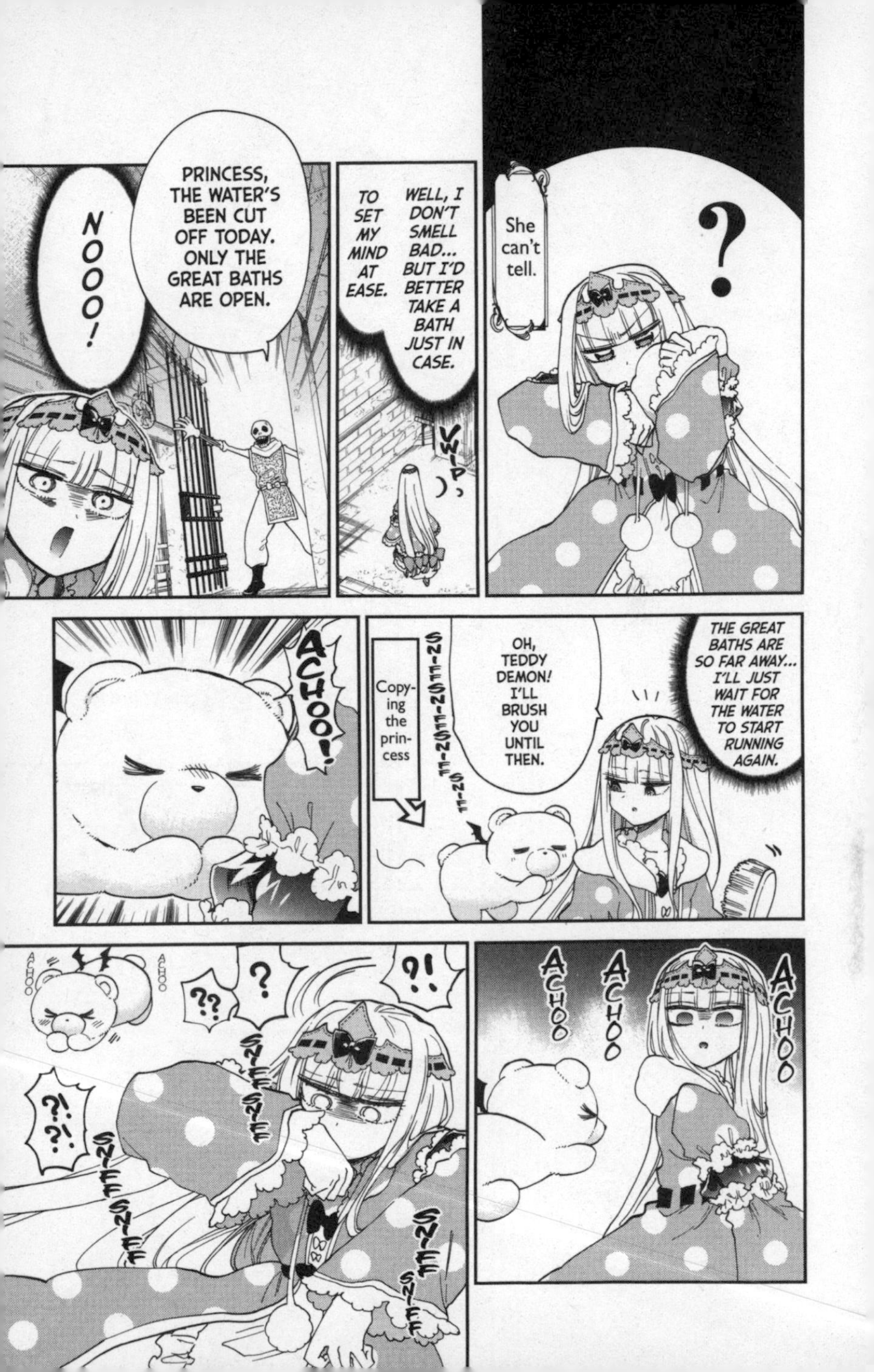
?
She can't tell.
WELL, I DON'T SMELL BAD... BUT I'D BETTER TAKE A BATH JUST IN CASE.
TO SET MY MIND AT EASE.
VWIP
PRINCESS, THE WATER'S BEEN CUT OFF TODAY. ONLY THE GREAT BATHS ARE OPEN.
NOOOO!
THE GREAT BATHS ARE SO FAR AWAY... I'LL JUST WAIT FOR THE WATER TO START RUNNING AGAIN.
OH, TEDDY DEMON! I'LL BRUSH YOU UNTIL THEN.
SNIFFSNIFFSNIFF SNIFF
Copying the princess
ACHOO!
ACHOO
ACHOO
ACHOO
?!
?
??
SNIFF SNIFF
?!?!
SNIFF SNIFF
SNIFF SNIFF
ACHOO
ACHOO

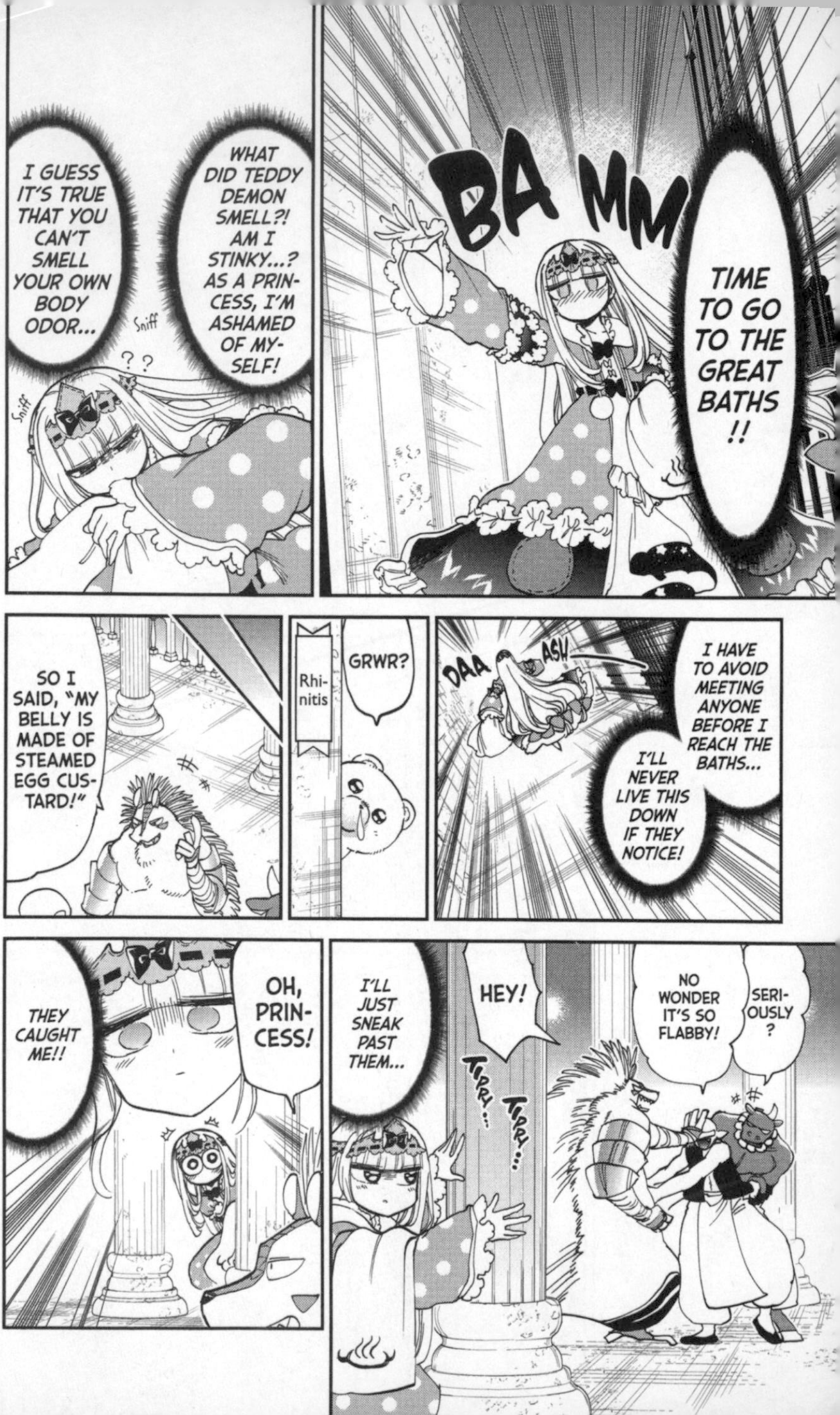

BA MM
TIME TO GO TO THE GREAT BATHS !!
WHAT DID TEDDY DEMON SMELL?! AM I STINKY...? AS A PRINCESS, I'M ASHAMED OF MYSELF!
I GUESS IT'S TRUE THAT YOU CAN'T SMELL YOUR OWN BODY ODOR...
Sniff
? ?
Sniff
DAA ASH
I HAVE TO AVOID MEETING ANYONE BEFORE I REACH THE BATHS...
I'LL NEVER LIVE THIS DOWN IF THEY NOTICE!
GRWR?
Rhinitis
SO I SAID, "MY BELLY IS MADE OF STEAMED EGG CUSTARD!"
SERIOUSLY?
NO WONDER IT'S SO FLABBY!
HEY!
I'LL JUST SNEAK PAST THEM...
TIPPY...
TIPPY...
OH, PRINCESS!
THEY CAUGHT ME!!

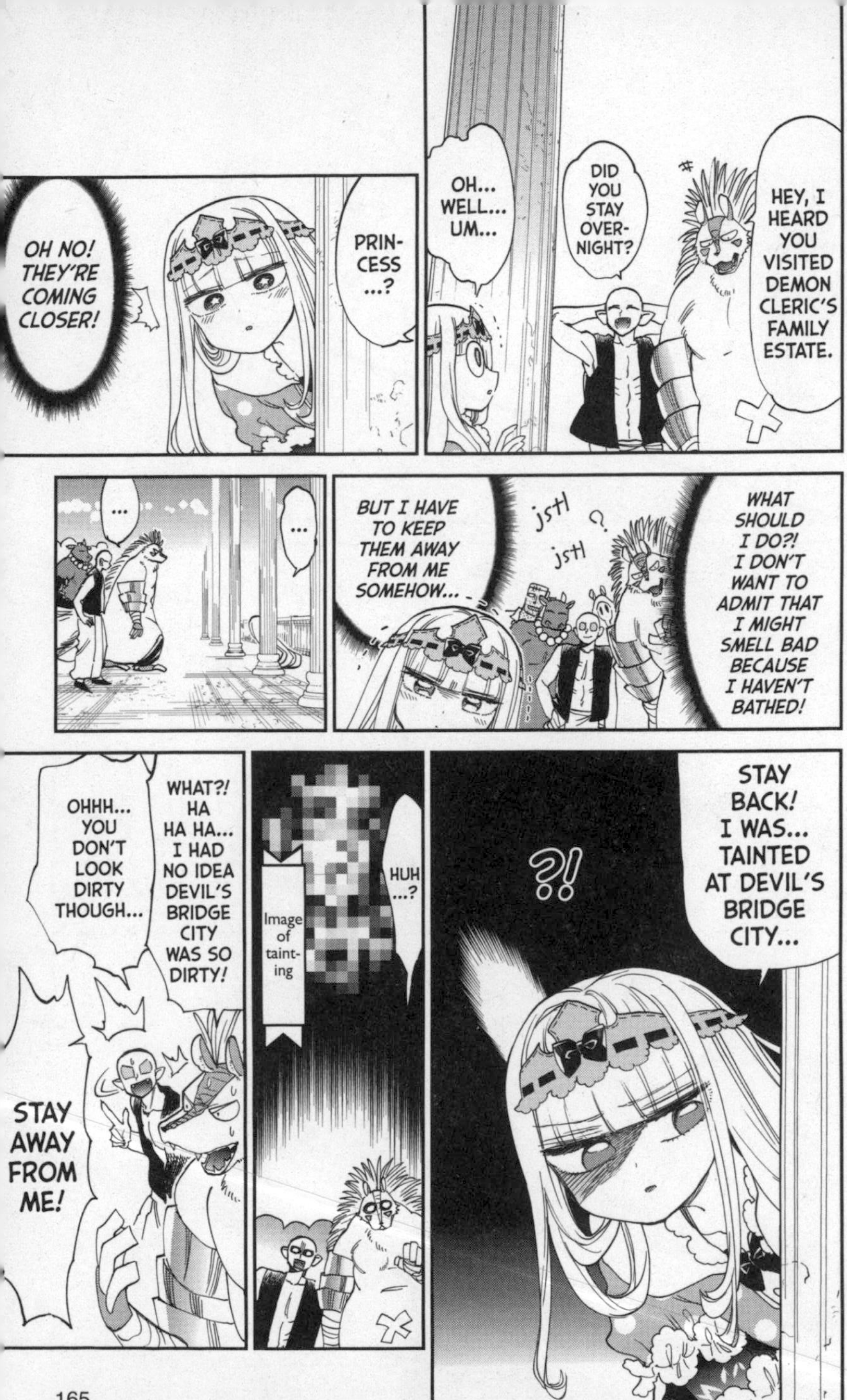
HEY, I HEARD YOU VISITED DEMON CLERIC'S FAMILY ESTATE.
DID YOU STAY OVER-NIGHT?
OH... WELL... UM...
PRIN-CESS ...?
OH NO! THEY'RE COMING CLOSER!
WHAT SHOULD I DO?! I DON'T WANT TO ADMIT THAT I MIGHT SMELL BAD BECAUSE I HAVEN'T BATHED!
jstl
?
jstl
BUT I HAVE TO KEEP THEM AWAY FROM ME SOMEHOW...
...
...
STAY BACK! I WAS... TAINTED AT DEVIL'S BRIDGE CITY...
?!
HUH ...?
Image of taint-ing
WHAT?! HA HA HA... I HAD NO IDEA DEVIL'S BRIDGE CITY WAS SO DIRTY!
OHHH... YOU DON'T LOOK DIRTY THOUGH...
STAY AWAY FROM ME!

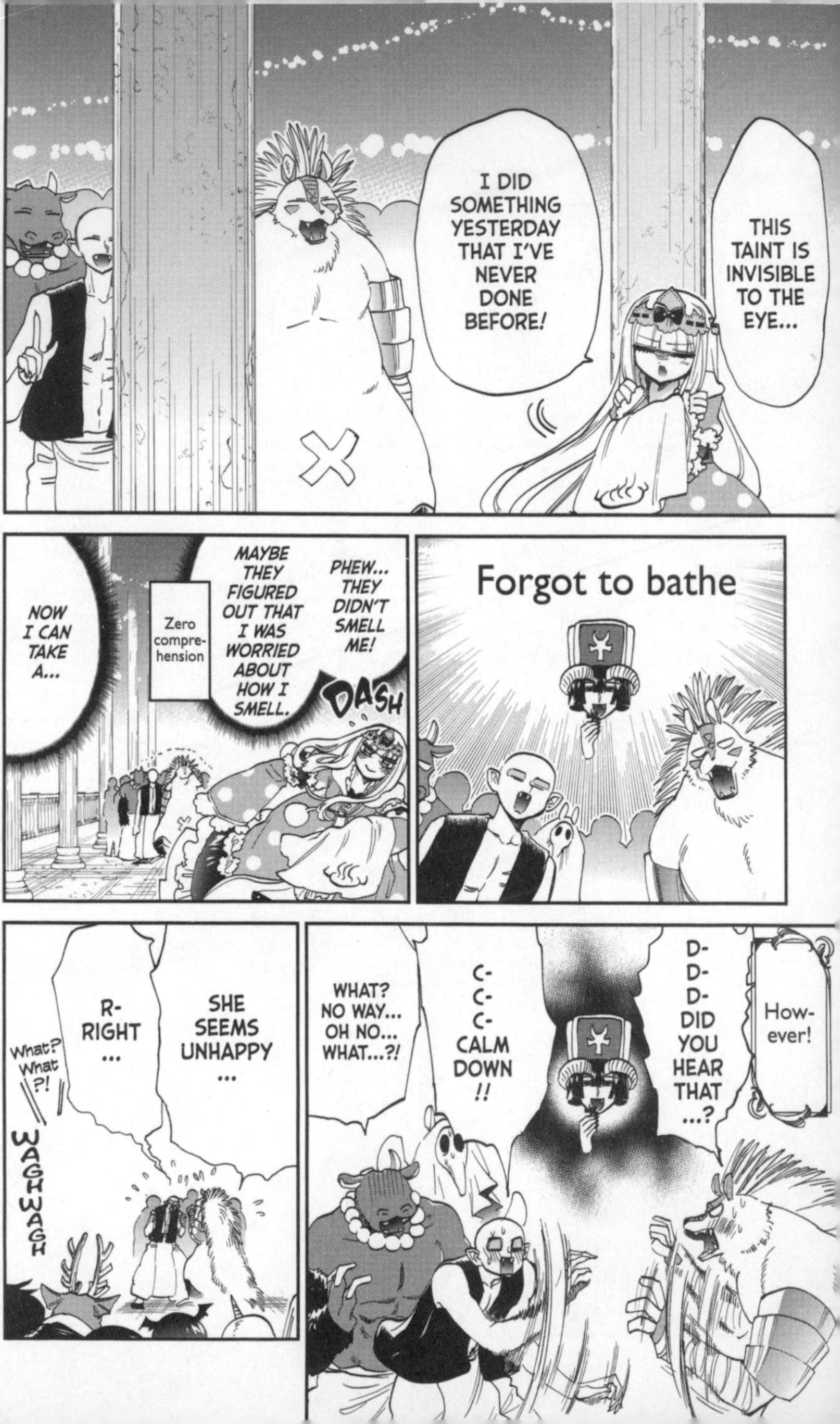
THIS TAINT IS INVISIBLE TO THE EYE...
I DID SOMETHING YESTERDAY THAT I'VE NEVER DONE BEFORE!
Forgot to bathe
PHEW... THEY DIDN'T SMELL ME!
DASH
MAYBE THEY FIGURED OUT THAT I WAS WORRIED ABOUT HOW I SMELL.
Zero compre-hension
NOW I CAN TAKE A...
How-ever!
D-D-D-DID YOU HEAR THAT...?
C-C-C-CALM DOWN!!
WHAT? NO WAY... OH NO... WHAT...?!
SHE SEEMS UNHAPPY...
R-RIGHT...
What? What?!
WAGHWAGH

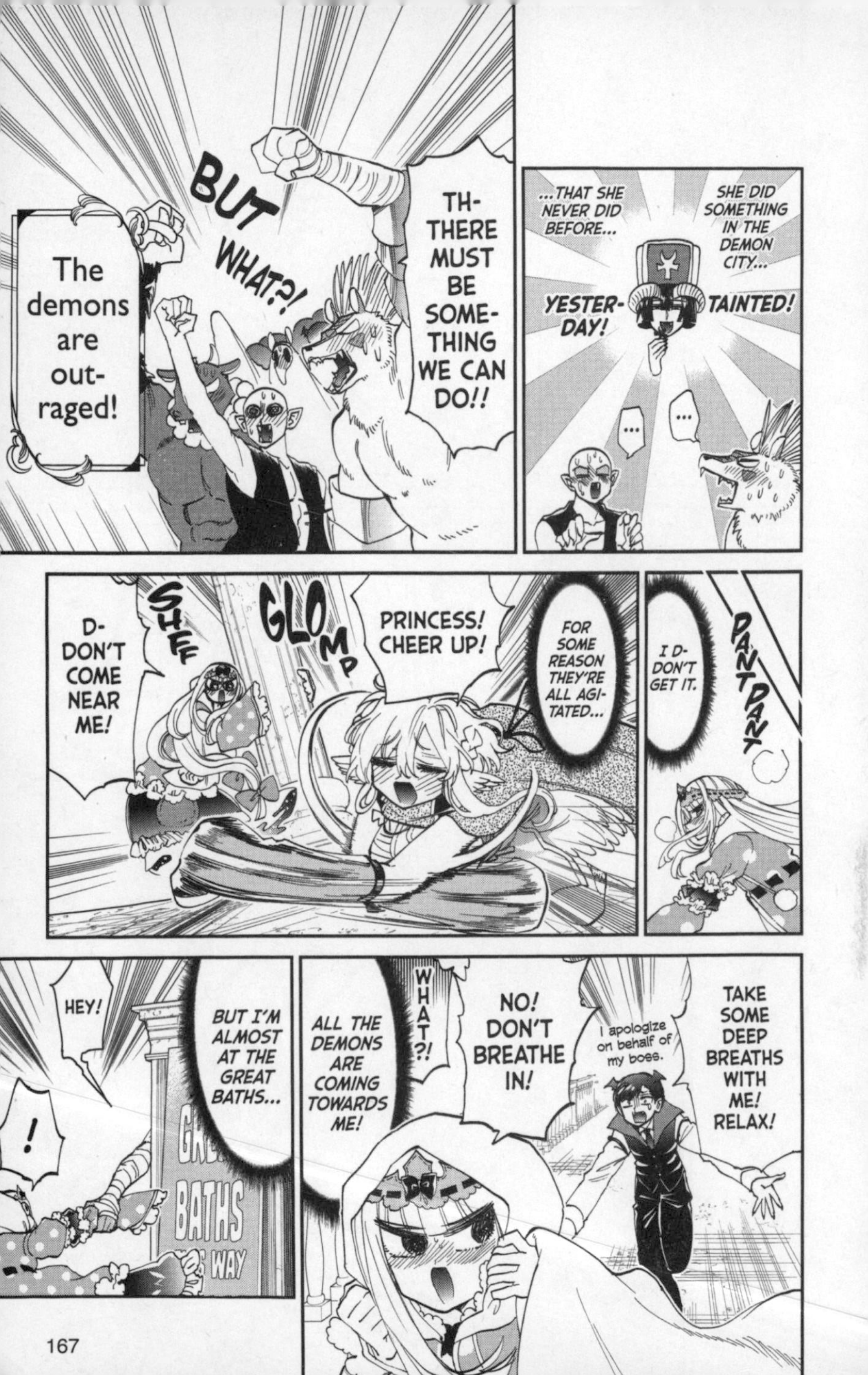
SHE DID SOMETHING IN THE DEMON CITY...
...THAT SHE NEVER DID BEFORE...
TAINTED!
YESTER-DAY!
...
...
TH- THERE MUST BE SOME-THING WE CAN DO!!
BUT WHAT?!
The demons are out-raged!
PANT PANT
I D- DON'T GET IT.
FOR SOME REASON THEY'RE ALL AGI-TATED...
PRINCESS! CHEER UP!
GLOMP
SHFF
D- DON'T COME NEAR ME!
TAKE SOME DEEP BREATHS WITH ME! RELAX!
I apologize on behalf of my boss.
NO! DON'T BREATHE IN!
WHAT?!
ALL THE DEMONS ARE COMING TOWARDS ME!
HEY!
BUT I'M ALMOST AT THE GREAT BATHS...
!
BATHS

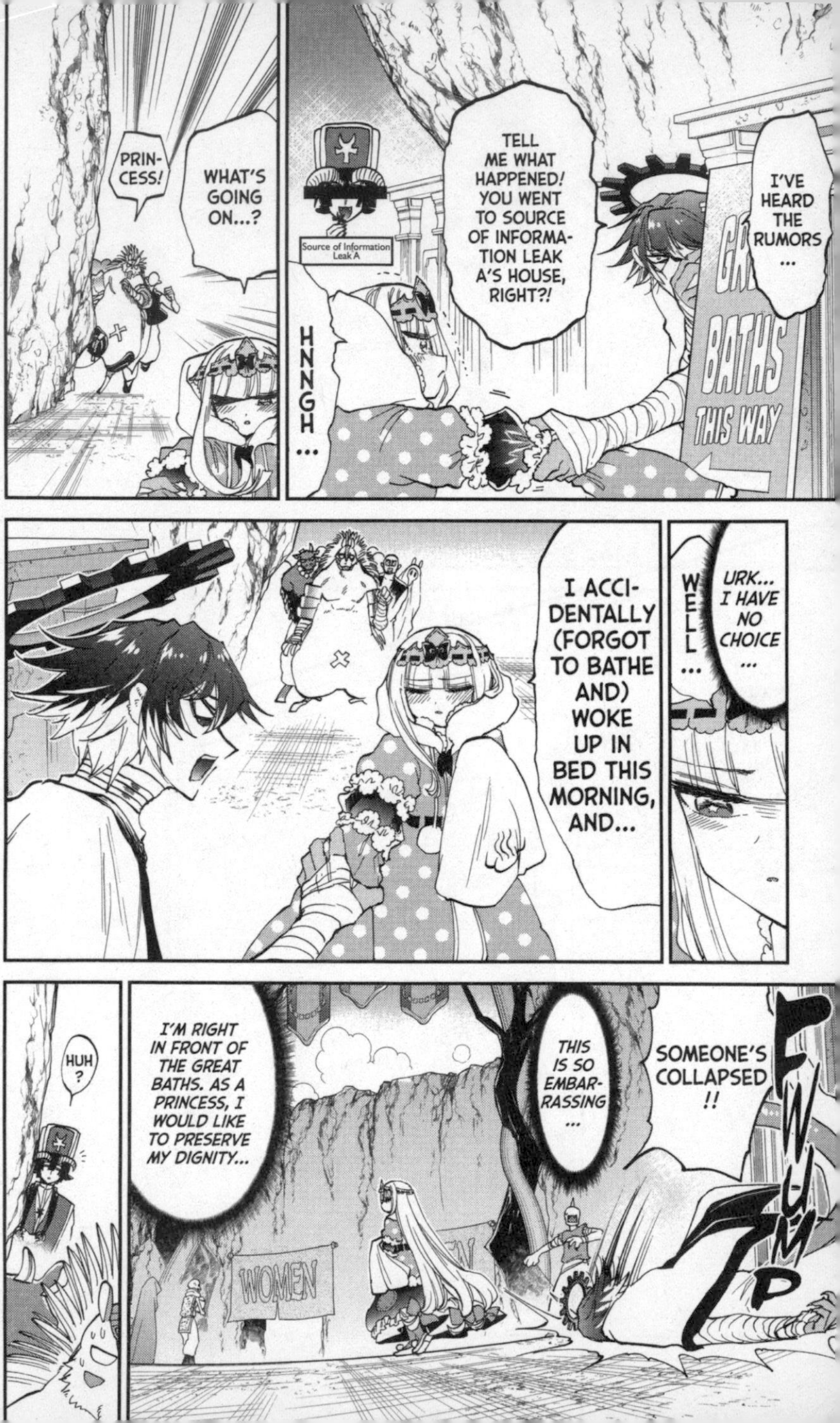
I'VE HEARD THE RUMORS...
TELL ME WHAT HAPPENED! YOU WENT TO SOURCE OF INFORMATION LEAK A'S HOUSE, RIGHT?!
BATHS THIS WAY
Source of Information Leak A
HNNGH...
WHAT'S GOING ON...?
PRIN-CESS!
URK... I HAVE NO CHOICE...
WELL...
I ACCI-DENTALLY (FORGOT TO BATHE AND) WOKE UP IN BED THIS MORNING, AND...
FWUMP
SOMEONE'S COLLAPSED!!
THIS IS SO EMBAR-RASSING...
I'M RIGHT IN FRONT OF THE GREAT BATHS. AS A PRINCESS, I WOULD LIKE TO PRESERVE MY DIGNITY...
WOMEN
HUH?

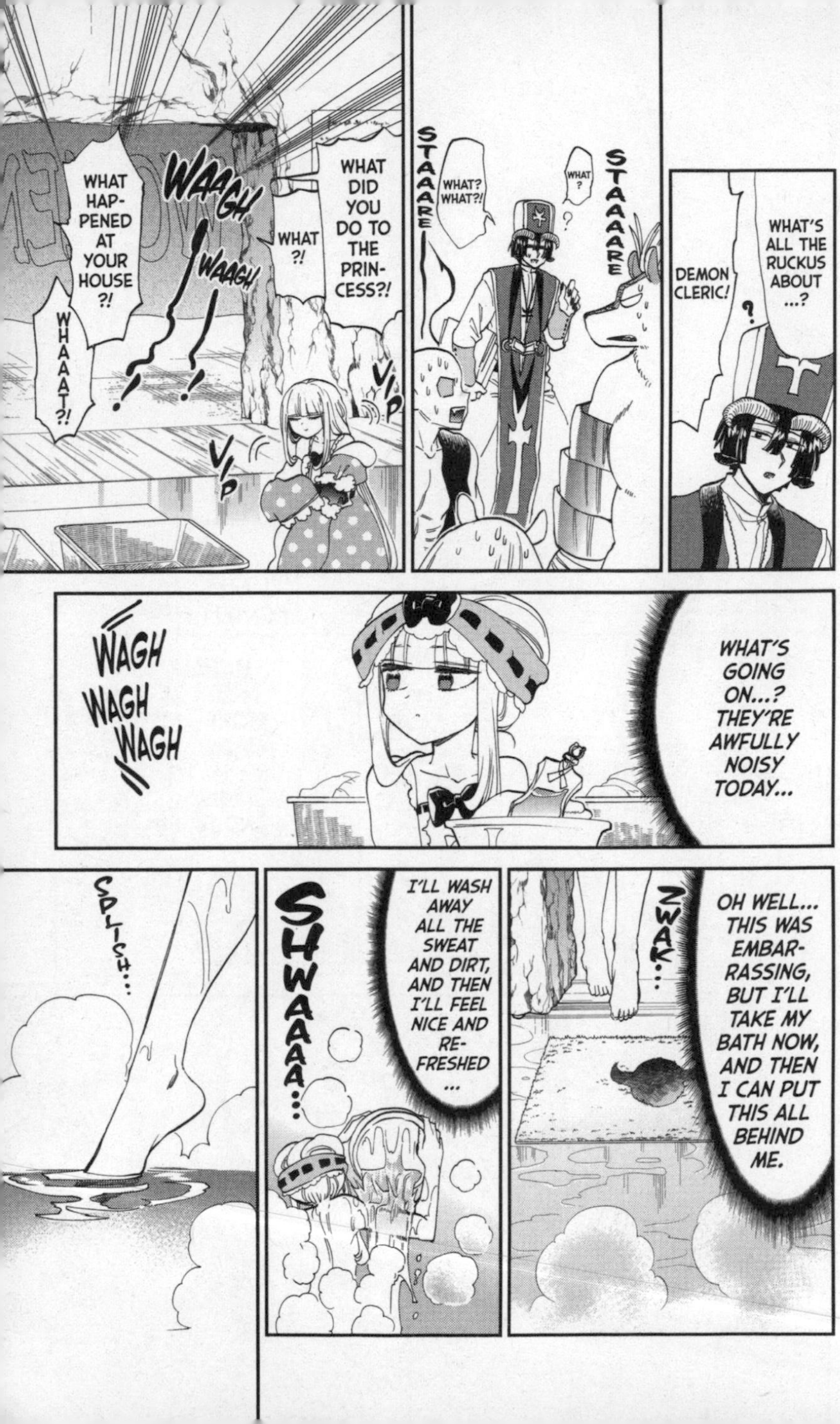
WHAT'S ALL THE RUCKUS ABOUT ...?
DEMON CLERIC!
?
STAAAAARE
WHAT ?
?
WHAT? WHAT?!
STAAAARE
WHAT DID YOU DO TO THE PRIN-CESS?!
WHAT ?!
WAAGH
WAAGH
WHAT HAP-PENED AT YOUR HOUSE ?!
WHAAAT?!
VIP
VIP
WHAT'S GOING ON...? THEY'RE AWFULLY NOISY TODAY...
WAGH WAGH WAGH
OH WELL... THIS WAS EMBAR-RASSING, BUT I'LL TAKE MY BATH NOW, AND THEN I CAN PUT THIS ALL BEHIND ME.
ZWAK...
I'LL WASH AWAY ALL THE SWEAT AND DIRT, AND THEN I'LL FEEL NICE AND RE-FRESHED ...
SHWAAAA...
SPLISH...

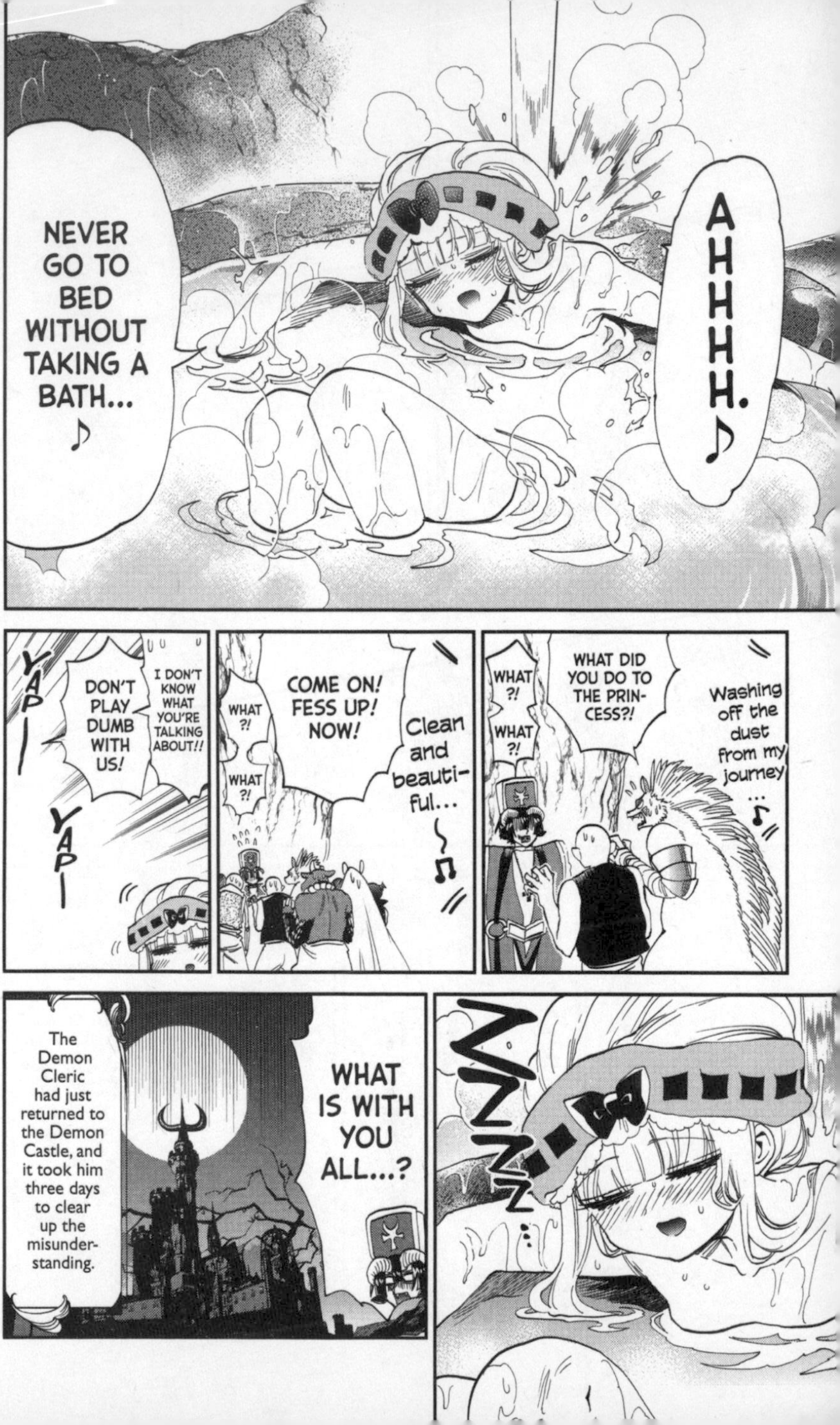
AHHHH. ♪
NEVER GO TO BED WITHOUT TAKING A BATH... ♪
Washing off the dust from my journey... ♪
WHAT DID YOU DO TO THE PRINCESS?!
WHAT?!
WHAT?!
Clean and beautiful... ♫
COME ON! FESS UP! NOW!
WHAT?!
WHAT?!
I DON'T KNOW WHAT YOU'RE TALKING ABOUT!!
DON'T PLAY DUMB WITH US!
YAP
YAP
WHAT IS WITH YOU ALL...?
The Demon Cleric had just returned to the Demon Castle, and it took him three days to clear up the misunderstanding.

Time for a Haircut!

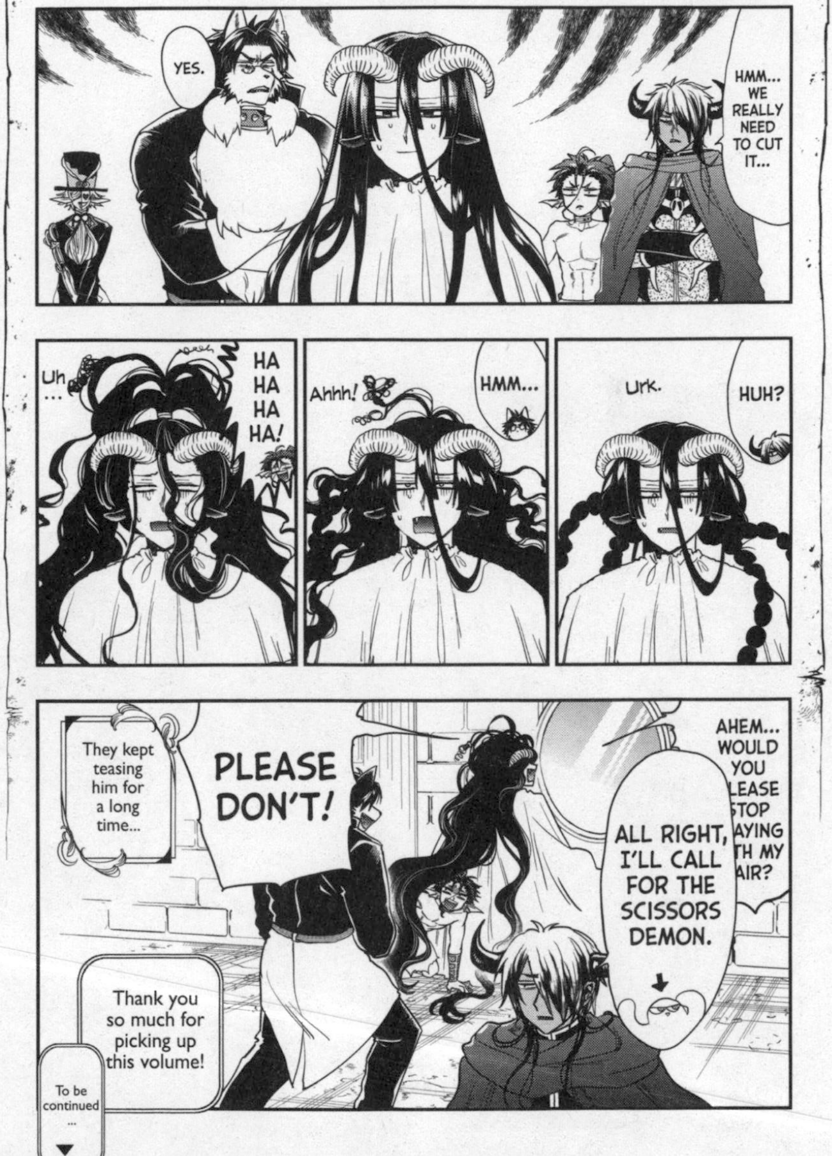
HMM... WE REALLY NEED TO CUT IT...
YES.
HUH?
Urk.
HMM...
Ahhh!
HA HA HA HA!
Uh...
AHEM... WOULD YOU LEASE TOP AYING TH MY AIR?
ALL RIGHT, I'LL CALL FOR THE SCISSORS DEMON.
PLEASE DON'T!
They kept teasing him for a long time...
Thank you so much for picking up this volume!
To be continued...

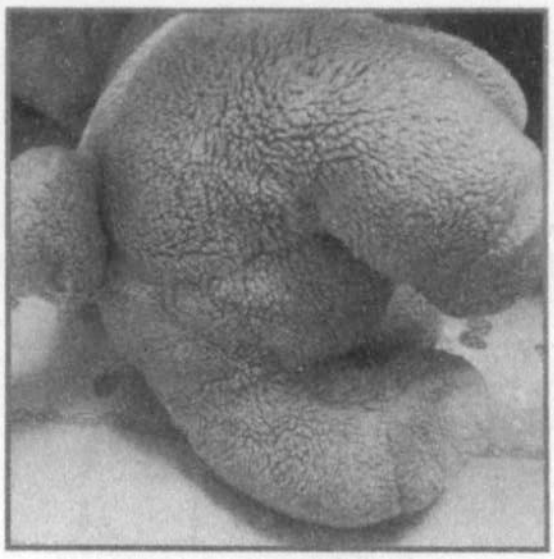

This photo is still cute no matter how many times you look at it, isn't it?

– KAGIJI KUMANOMATA

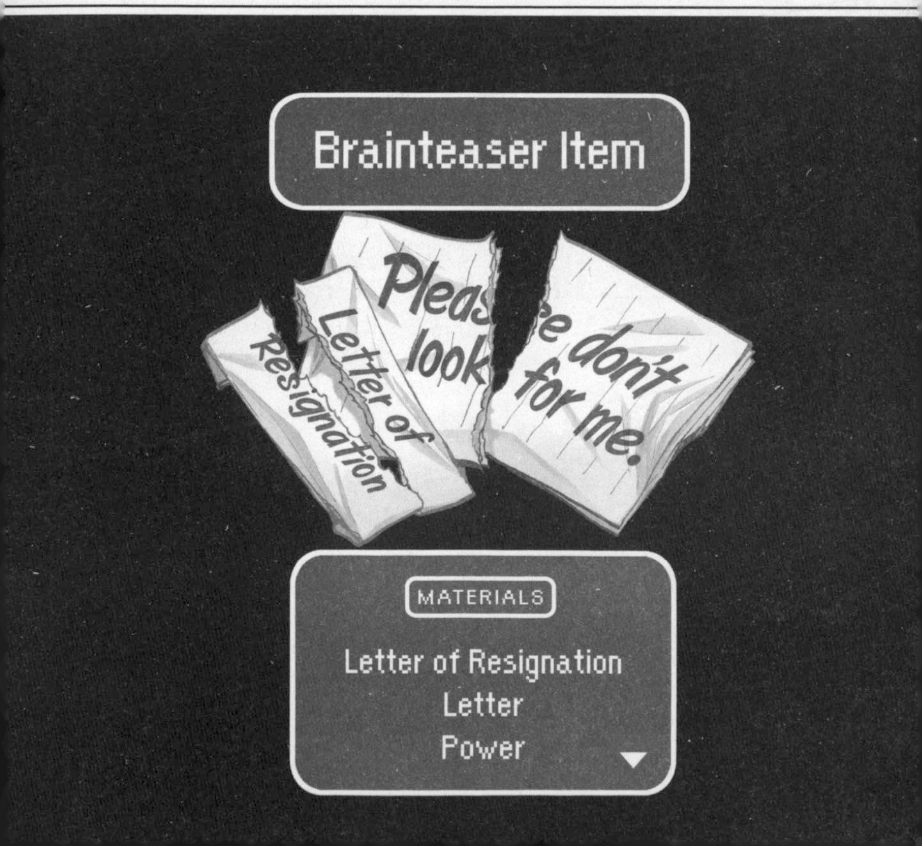

Brainteaser Item
Please don't look for me.
Letter of Resignation
MATERIALS
Letter of Resignation
Letter
Power

Those who lurk beneath the cover...

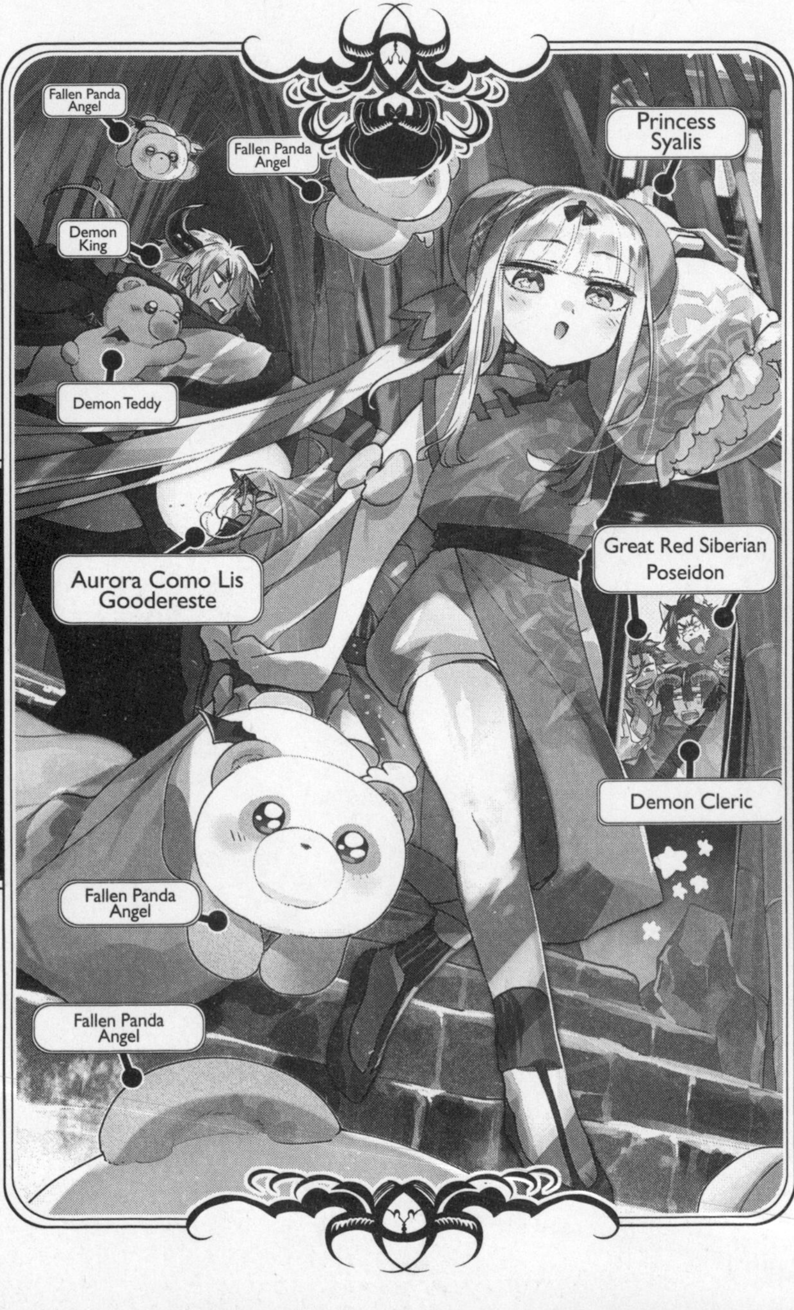

Princess Syalis
Fallen Panda Angel
Fallen Panda Angel
Demon King
Demon Teddy
Great Red Siberian Poseidon
Aurora Como Lis Goodereste
Demon Cleric
Fallen Panda Angel
Fallen Panda Angel

SLEEPY PRINCESS IN THE DEMON CASTLE

13

Shonen Sunday Edition

STORY AND ART BY

KAGIJI KUMANOMATA

MAOUJO DE OYASUMI Vol. 13
by Kagiji KUMANOMATA
© 2016 Kagiji KUMANOMATA
All rights reserved.
Original Japanese edition published by SHOGAKUKAN.
English translation rights in the United States of America, Canada,
the United Kingdom, Ireland, Australia and New Zealand arranged
with SHOGAKUKAN.

TRANSLATION **TETSUICHIRO MIYAKI**

ENGLISH ADAPTATION **ANNETTE ROMAN**

TOUCH-UP ART & LETTERING **JAMES GAUBATZ**

COVER & INTERIOR DESIGN **ALICE LEWIS**

EDITOR **ANNETTE ROMAN**

Printed in the U.S.A.

Published by VIZ Media, LLC
P.O. Box 77010
San Francisco, CA 94107

10 9 8 7 6 5 4 3 2 1
First printing, October 2020

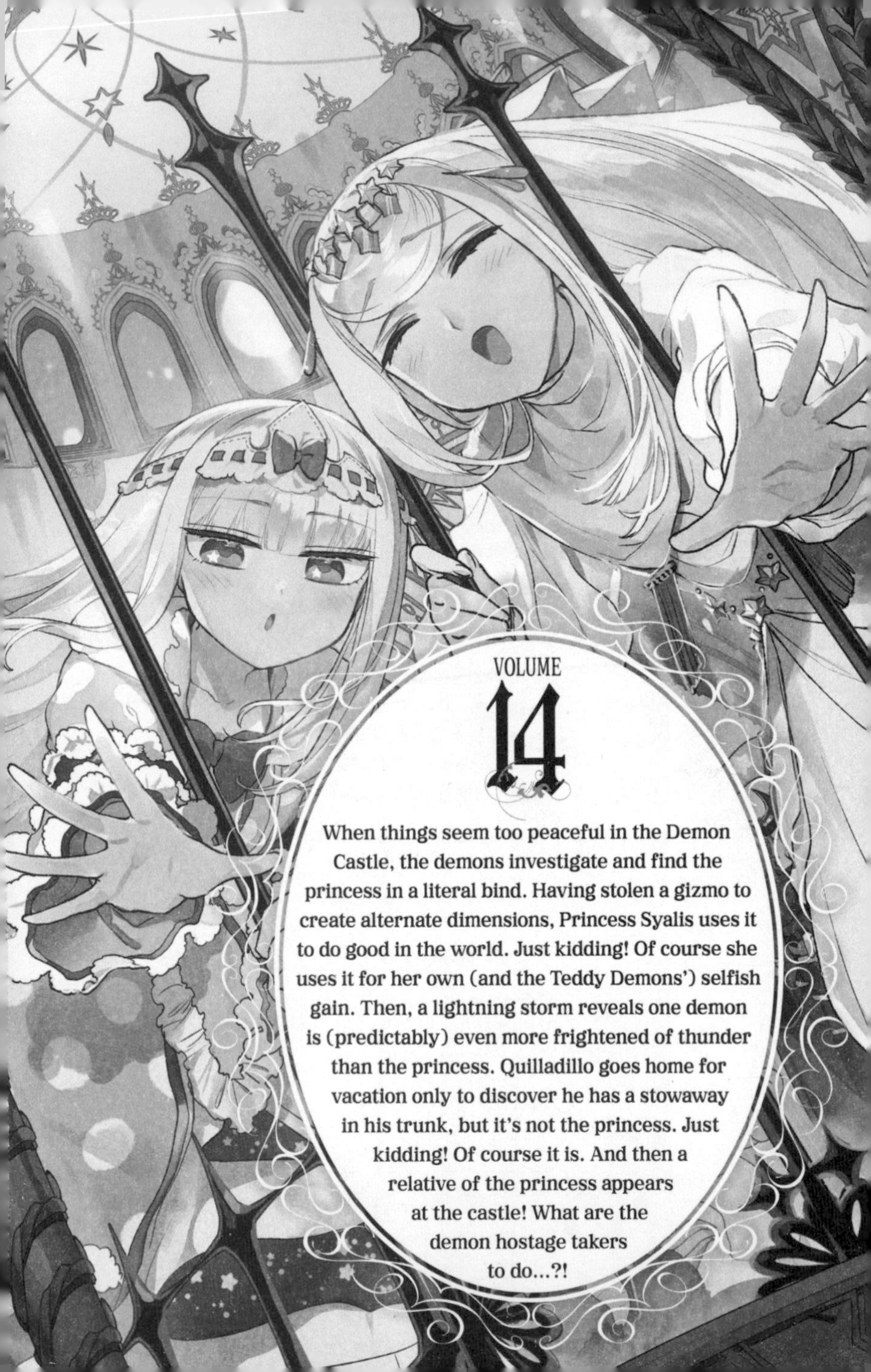

VOLUME

14

When things seem too peaceful in the Demon Castle, the demons investigate and find the princess in a literal bind. Having stolen a gizmo to create alternate dimensions, Princess Syalis uses it to do good in the world. Just kidding! Of course she uses it for her own (and the Teddy Demons') selfish gain. Then, a lightning storm reveals one demon is (predictably) even more frightened of thunder than the princess. Quilladillo goes home for vacation only to discover he has a stowaway in his trunk, but it's not the princess. Just kidding! Of course it is. And then a relative of the princess appears at the castle! What are the demon hostage takers to do...?!